Do You Love Me?

Discover How To Deepen Your Love For God

A Book of 366 Devotionals

Don Schmidt

Do You Love Me?
Discover How To Deepen Your Love For God
Copyright © 2018 by Don Schmidt

Library of Congress Control Number: 2018952111
ISBN-13:   Paperback: 978-1-64398-111-6
                  PDF: 978-1-64398-526-8
                  E-pub: 978-1-64398-525-1
                  Kindle: 978-1-64398-524-4
                  Hardback: 978-1-64398-527-5

Printed in the United States of America

LitFire LLC
1-800-511-9787
www.litfirepublishing.com
order@litfirepublishing.com

FOREWORD

My career as a college professor began in 2003 when I joined the faculty of the Williamson Christian College in Franklin, Tennessee—a four-year liberal arts school. Prior to this I was a pastor for many years. Six years later, Don Schmidt arrived to be the Vice President of Operations and the Director of Student Life. Our friendship grew strong as we became acquainted and served the school together.

Soon after coming to the school, Don began writing a series of daily devotionals which he shared with other staff members, students and friends. This ministry grew as he posted these Bible based writings on a web site. Over the years hundreds of readers have enjoyed his insights for living.

Through these years it has been my privilege to begin each day reading his "Learning to Love God" compositions. Recently, I encouraged Don to put selected devotionals in a book form and make them available to a larger audience. This present volume is the result of his efforts.

The title question, "Do You Love Me?" is an excellent challenge to each of us. In these pages Don helps us to examine ourselves regarding the most important command given by Jesus to His followers. Nothing is as important for us as having a lifestyle that expresses an authentic love for our Lord and Master.

The very interesting and practical guidelines found in this book will help every reader to grow in becoming a true lover of Yahweh. I heartily recommend this volume of Bible based studies for your own personal pilgrimage of faith.

Dr. Jim Harvey

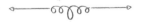

Dean,

Congratulations!

Yeah! Big time!!

60 years - fantastic

A priest — + friend
and lover of God.

Thank you for your
Love of God and
family and
friends.

Lots of Bob +
LOVE Wendy

Our legacy, either good or...

Proverbs 4:18 - The path of the righteous is like the first gleam of dawn, shining ever brighter till the full light of day.

Consider this verse in describing the trail we leave behind us rather than the path in front of us. The life we live. The lives we touch. The love we share. The way we love the Lord and one another. The way we serve. The 'fruit' that we leave behind us, i.e., our testimony in the eyes of those we've encountered and touched - whether good or bad. I think of deer trails that I have seen out in the woods. Some are so faint as to be easily missed. Others are more obvious to the eye. I remember one that looked like a deer Interstate. Anyone could tell that it was a significant trail. The trails were evidence of activity and the presence of deer.

Likewise, the 'trail' or path we leave behind us is a legacy to who we are - and how much we truly love Him. The more we walk in the ways of the Lord the brighter our path becomes. The more we love and serve and bear the fruit of the Spirit - the more we reflect Him. The path we leave is to be about Him. The wonder it is to be His hands extended - for others to see and encounter Him when they interact with us.

Our path is our testimony, but not in our words. It is where we've been and what we've done as described by others and witnessed by those around us both on earth and in the heavenlies. The more we are transformed into the image of Jesus, the brighter it becomes.

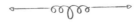

Missing the Lord in the midst of pain and difficulty

Ruth 1:20 "Don't call me Naomi, "she told them." Call me Mara, (bitter) because the Almighty has made my life very bitter. [21] I went away full, but the LORD has brought me back empty. Why call me Naomi? The LORD has afflicted me; the Almighty has brought misfortune upon me."

Can you think of times when your hopeful expectations were met with disappointment and perceived failure? Where everything seems to turn negative and then go from bad to worse? How do we respond in such times? Where is the Lord in the midst of our difficulties? Even if we think everything is 'bitter' as Naomi did, faith leads us to a different conclusion.

The Book of Ruth is also the story of Naomi. Naomi and her family moved from Bethlehem to Moab due to famine. While there her husband died and her two sons married Moabite women. Then her two sons died and Naomi returned to Bethlehem with only her daughter-in-law Ruth, who refused to be separated from her. Although she had Ruth, her focus was on what she lost.

We go though difficulties and misfortunes as well. Losses, hurts, disappointments are part of life. They are not separate from our faith, but God is always in the midst of them. We can respond in faith and trust Him - or be focused on our circumstances and view God negatively. Even when we don't understand, He is faithful and He is with us as we go through the trials.

Sometimes we are able to see the good that comes out of our struggles – sometimes not. But the Lord is always with us and always for us. He is actively at work in us to bring forth His character and to bring about His plan. Remember the marvelous joy we experience when we are tested and come through it faithfully.

Little did Naomi realize that God was using her in a marvelous way – to accomplish His plan of bringing Ruth to Boaz. How different her response at that time might have been if she was aware that her losses and difficulties were essential for God's plan to unfold. Not only was Naomi to be provided for abundantly, but she cared for the child born to Ruth and Boaz who was named Obed. He was the father of Jesse, the father of David.

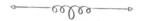

They are new every morning

Lamentations 3:22-23 The steadfast love of the LORD *never ceases, his mercies never come to an end; they are new every morning; great is thy faithfulness.*

These verses make me think of a pastoral picture. Think of a large flower garden with the morning sun upon it. There is a breeze blowing and rain is falling upon the garden from a small cloud above it. Sunshine, rain, a breeze and flowers blooming are all providing both enjoyment and a place to labor. It is a picture of freshness, vitality, beauty and joy. Day by day God's provision is there.

That picture is such a thing of beauty to me, just like the marvelous realities that these verses describe! God's love for us is fixed and unchanging and unending. It never ceases. It doesn't depend upon us thinking it's there. It is there for us to experience – to trust in and to enjoy. It's like the air we breathe; it's there. Think of the times when we feel the wind blowing upon us. The air that we typically don't see or feel manifests itself in a way so we feel it. God does the same thing with His love for us.

Likewise His mercies – they never come to an end and are new every morning. Think of the manna – the bread of Heaven – that came down every day for the Israelites when they were in the wilderness. Each day they could only take what was needed for that day. Tomorrow's manna, came the next day, not today – except on the 6th day when God supplied double because the 7th day was the Sabbath. His mercies are never ending and there for us each day.

Consider that it is impossible for God to be unfaithful. If we think that He is or has been unfaithful, we're simply wrong. Think of situations when you have been faithful to someone or experienced someone being faithful to you. Faithfulness is such a blessing – something so important to be able to count on. In our times of need, God is always there. He's always faithful. The blessings He offers if we but have the eyes to see them and the sense to turn to Him.

Be a blessing to God each morning by recognizing and being thankful for His love, His mercies and most of all, for Him.

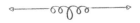

Whose crop? Ours or His?

Proverbs 11:5 The righteousness of the blameless makes a straight way for them.

The Lord wants a man to be a farmer so He gives him a farm. He also provides him all the tools, equipment, seed, fertilizer and instructs him how to do everything. The Lord also provides him with willingness, ability, health, strength, sunlight and rain. He even expresses the desire to assist him in everything. When the man is obedient and he produces a wonderful crop, <u>whose crop is it</u>?

The crop provides food, money, great blessing and more opportunities. The man's actions produced it, so in one sense it is his. Even the Lord considers it the man's as He gave it to him. But without the Lord choosing him and giving him the opportunity, he would have nothing. <u>The man has a choice to make – and he will make a choice</u>.

If the man claims the crop as his own, pride is at work. His primary view is there would be no crop without his hard work and obedience to the Lord; his attitude is one of "it is mine".

On the other hand, the man recognizes the goodness of God and has a heart filled with gratitude for the great blessing from the Lord. Even though he worked hard, he knows he would have nothing without the Lord's generosity and blessing. His view is one of humility - everything that He has belongs to the Lord. He is merely a steward of it. His concern is how to use the blessing in a way that pleases the Lord and is an instrument of blessing to others. It is all His!

The fascinating thing is the Lord considers the crop, the farm, everything to be his – the man's. The Lord gave it to him. The issue is the attitude of the man: pride or humility. Likewise, when we consider the righteousness associated with the obedient and righteous acts that we do, we have a choice to make. Is the righteousness our own? Or is it His?

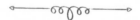

From bad to worse by His design!

Exodus 5:22, 23 Moses returned to the LORD and said, "O Lord, why have you brought trouble upon this people? Is this why you sent me? Ever since I went to Pharaoh to speak in your name, he has brought trouble upon this people, and you have not rescued your people at all."

Moses experienced the miraculous wonder of the burning bush and the encounter with God. He and Aaron came to Egypt and met with the Elders of the Israelites and performed the wonders he was to show them. The people were blessed knowing that God was concerned about them. But then came the meeting with Pharaoh and Pharaoh was not convinced in the slightest. Pharaoh's response was to make everything worse. So much so, the Israelite foremen met with Pharaoh to appeal for relief. Their concern grew when their request was rejected by him. They encountered Moses and Aaron waiting to meet them and declared how they (Moses and Aaron) had made them a stench to Pharaoh. This is not what Moses expected to happen. Things didn't get better – they went from bad to worse. Yet this was God's plan. He just didn't tell Moses that it was going to unfold quite like this. Moses knew that God was going to harden Pharaoh's heart so that he wouldn't let the people go. But Moses didn't expect Pharaoh to make the situation worse. Nor did he expect the Israelites to blame him. God's response to Moses' concern was, "Now you will see what I will do to Pharaoh…"

The principle at work here happens over and over throughout Scripture and in our lives. God calls us to a mission or task and gives us an idea what ultimately will happen. But as we obey, God allows all manner of unexpected difficulties to rise up. He expects us to respond with faith and look to Him. It's through this process that we are changed and God's plan is accomplished. It just doesn't happen the way we thought it would.

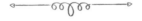

Lord, make this me!

Psalm 130:6 My soul waits for the Lord more than watchmen wait for the morning, more than watchmen wait for the morning.

About twenty years ago, in our Sunday service, a song based on this verse was being sung. The words of the song were describing a passionate longing for the Lord that I didn't have. In the distress of this realization, I went forward in the midst of it being sung and spoke to our rector who was leading worship. I told him, "I can't sing this song because it doesn't describe me." When the song ended, I was so blessed by his words of wisdom. He commented, "When we sing songs that don't describe us, let the song be a prayer that you are asking to become true of you."

God used this experience to create within me the desire to become passionate for Him – with a passion that was palpable. I began searching for verses in the Psalms that communicated passion to me – and I found many of them. Another verse that particularly struck me was Psalm 42:1, *"As the deer pants for streams of water, so my soul pants for you, O God."* I wanted to have my soul pant for the Lord. These verses then became the focus of my "Lord make this me" prayers.

My passion-meter or "passiometer" as I have referred to it, was not budging at all when this began. No passion was being reflected within me as I read and prayed the passion verses that I wanted to become true of me. Week after week; month after month; year after year, I prayed these verses throughout the Psalms.

As time went by, I was thrilled by the realization that the Lord was doing it. He caused passion to grow within me so that I could honestly say that these verses were now describing me. I hadn't "arrived" but my "passiometer" was now registering passion within me as a Geiger counter recognizes radiation.

God in His goodness allowed me to see that I was missing such an important attribute that He wants growing in me. He desires me to become more and more passionate for Him. He gave me a plan and the determination to pursue it so He could bless me by answering it. He will do the same for you.

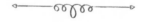

Don Schmidt

What do our responses say about us?

Job 1:22 In all this Job did not sin by charging God with wrongdoing. Job 2:10b
In all this, Job did not sin in what he said.

It's difficult to imagine the impact of all the disasters that happened to Job in chapter one. Scripture describes him as being blameless and upright; one who feared God and shunned evil. But through no fault of his own, loss, destruction and death were involved in each of the 4 messages brought to him, one after another.

Two of the messages described raiding bands of Sabeans and Chaldeans who stole his animals and killed his servants. The last message brought word of the death of his seven sons and three daughters by a mighty wind causing the house they were feasting in to collapse on them. Yet his response to all of this was to fall to the ground in worship.

Seldom will we or anyone we know experience loss of the magnitude that Job did. But we do experience loss, pain and tragedy in many forms. In such times, how wonderful it would be for our immediate response to be one of worshipping the Lord as Job did. Unfortunately many if not most of us would find it difficult to worship freely in such a time of agony. But that is where the verses today are so critically important. How we respond speaks to the Lord AND to those around us.

Job didn't charge God with wrong doing. He didn't say, "God how could you...." He didn't lash out at the Lord or blame Him in any way. It's so important that we understand that such responses are sin. Let's say that again but more pointedly: 'Charging God with wrongdoing is sin.' The importance of all this is further emphasized in Job 2:10b where we learn, **"In all this, Job did not sin in what he said."**

It's not that God won't forgive such responses, but it's what they reveal about us. They reflect an inadequate and inaccurate understanding of who God is and of our relationship with Him. To respond negatively towards God shows us we are weak where we should be strong. When we find ourselves in such difficult situations, think of the difference between these responses: 1) "God how could you..." and 2) Oh Lord, I'm so glad that I have you in the midst of this..." There are times when we are experiencing difficult and painful things that our hearts are not in the place to worship. But hopefully, they are also not in the place to charge our Lord with wrongdoing. In such times let us take the faith position of thanking the Lord for keeping us from sinning and asking Him to work the change in us so that our heart-response is to worship Him in the midst of it all.

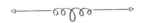

Never did I expect what was going to happen!

Psalm 116:1 I love the Lord, for He heard my voice; He heard my cry for mercy.

My story Part 1: Although I was raised going to church, albeit a liberal one, I never developed faith to speak of. The idea of being born again or meeting Jesus in a personal way was totally foreign to me. When I went to college, what little faith I might have had was lost due to atheistic instructors and discussions with unbelieving students who seemed intent on obliterating any ideas of faith.

I came from a good home. I was close to my mom but my father and I argued when we were together and loved each other while apart. In the fall of 1968, while a junior in college, I agreed to go to a Christian retreat with them. It still amazes me that I went, but nothing was going on that weekend at college and it was important to them - so I went. The retreat center was at an old time camp back in the woods overlooking a small lake in Michigan.

In the first large meeting, a man spoke about the love of Jesus in a way that I had never heard before. In fact he talked as though he knew Him – personally! I was somewhat saddened by it because I thought, "If Jesus were real, that's what He would be like – but what good did it do me?" I couldn't believe – or so I thought. After the meeting, all of the high school and college age went to a separate meeting room. There were about fifteen of us sitting in a circle and I was easily the oldest.

The man came in and asked if there was anyone there who didn't know Jesus as Lord. I was too embarrassed to raise my hand. He then asked if there was anyone with any doubt about it. Something raged within me as I sat there and I struggled with whether or not to raise my hand. In spite of thinking there was no hope for me, I lifted my hand.

I was then startled by one of the young men (age 15) who jumped up from his seat, pushed a chair into the center of the circle of students and enthusiastically said to me, "This is where you meet Jesus!"

To be continued . . .

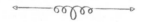

Don Schmidt

My Matterhorn of doubt - leveled in an instant!

Psalm 116:2 Because He turned His ear to me, I will call on Him as long as I live.

My story Part 2: Nothing prepared me for what happened when I raised my hand – acknowledging my doubt about knowing Jesus as Lord. I thought it was hopeless, that I had too many doubts, but what did I have to lose? I was startled to see a young man of about 15 push a chair to the middle of the circle of students and say, "This is where you meet Jesus!"

The evangelist came over to me and said that I could confess my sins and know that I was forgiven - that I would be clean inside; that if I wanted to know Jesus as my personal Savior and Lord – <u>beyond a shadow of a doubt</u> – to walk out to that chair and let them pray for me so I did.

All of the students gathered around me and began praying – and pray they did! There came a point when the evangelist asked me if I knew Jesus as Lord. I replied, "No. But I want to!" At that moment, it happened – I met Him! From the top of my head, through my body to my toes, His power went through me! God gave me a thunderous conversion experience beyond anything I could have ever dreamed of! My Matterhorn of doubt was leveled in an instant. Inside I was utterly changed, cleansed and filled with His presence. <u>Jesus was real and I was His!!!!</u>

I was absolutely overwhelmed. Within me was a tumultuous mass of joy, excitement, freedom, cleanness – there was Jesus, inside of me! And He didn't go away! After praying for others, we walked out of that prayer room into the main area and I so clearly remember looking out the windows at the woods and the lake. I thought, "I'm 20 and life expectancy is about 70. How do I keep this alive and vibrant for 50+ years?" There was nothing in my experience that led me to believe that something this incredibly good could be sustained for any period of time.

It has been 50 years since this remarkable experience and my love relationship with Jesus is more vibrant and more wonderful than ever. It has never grown cold. Words cannot describe the gratitude that I have because God made me His own; the joy of tears streaming down my face because of Jesus. I will love Him forever because He heard my cry. Because He turned His ear to me, I will call on Him as long as I live.

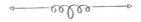

Sophie and Sam: 'doing to give' not 'doing to get'

Proverbs 20:11 Every child is known by his actions,
by whether his conduct is pure and right.

One of my favorite memories is the time years ago when I drove to Ohio where our son Jamie and his family then lived. It was so good to see him, his wife Tiffany and their two children Sophia (age 7) and Sam (age 5). My wife was already there and it had been 16 months since I had seen my grandchildren. I was so blessed by how much Sophia and Sam wanted to see and be with me. I was the recipient of repeated hugs and lovin's. They snuggled next to me just wanting to be near me. They expressed their love verbally and physically. Sometimes it felt like they were applying a tourniquet to my arm or leg they squeezed me so tightly.

The marvelous thing is that they weren't asking for anything. It was clear that they were not "doing to get" but they were "doing to give". They were expressing what was within them. They simply wanted to be with me and they freely expressed their love and affection in wonderful ways.

It's amazing the impact that their expressions of love had on me. I wanted to be with them even more. I wanted to bless them and I found myself looking for new and creative ways to express my love for them. This struck me as a significant aspect of what God wants in us as His sons and daughters.

He desires us to express our love for Jesus, not out of duty or obligation, nor as an attempt to get something from Him. He desires that our lives express the genuine reality that we are thrilled to have Jesus; that we don't take Him for granted. Our actions and attitudes determine the genuineness of our love. The more we walk in His ways and allow the Holy Spirit to transform us, the more we express our love for Him. And He responds to that love in ways that allow us to experience even more aspects of His love for us.

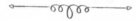

A life-giving gem!

Ephesians 5:10 and find out what pleases the Lord.

There are 7 words in this verse and they present a thought and a command that is important beyond measure. I'm embarrassed by the number of times I've read the book of Ephesians without noticing this verse. I think it tends to get overlooked because the verses surrounding it are so significant.

The verses immediately preceding it deal with being children of light and what that entails. The verses following it instruct us to have nothing to do with fruitless deeds of darkness. These are major ideas of instruction (commands) for us. But between them lies this life-giving gem for anyone with eyes to see or ears to hear.

Who is the focus of our lives as Christians? Why do we do the things that we do? What is the nature of our motivation? What are we trying to accomplish? Who is the love of our life? What is important to Him? What opportunities does He give us that are beyond counting? This verse supplies the key.

We have the incredible opportunity to please Him by what we do – to bring pleasure to our God. This opportunity doesn't occur just once, or once in awhile – but innumerable times every day. His Word and His Spirit will guide us to discover those things that please Him. It's not about earning salvation or earning anything. It's not about us – but about Him, the one we love and belong to. It's not about avoiding punishment or judgment but about blessing Him. It's living for Him.

Think of the pleasure you experience when someone does something important to bless you just because of his or her love for you and not wanting anything in return. By finding out what pleases the Lord – and doing it - we can bring pleasure to our God each and every day of our lives.

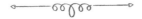

But even if He doesn't...

Daniel 3:16-18 ¹⁶Shadrach, Meshach and Abednego replied to the king, "O Nebuchadnezzar, we do not need to defend ourselves before you in this matter. ¹⁷If we are thrown into the blazing furnace, the God we serve is able to save us from it, and he will rescue us from your hand, O king. ¹⁸But even if he does not, we want you to know, O king, that we will not serve your gods or worship the image of gold you have set up."

BUT EVEN IF HE DOES NOT... These three young men were facing a horrible death for failure to bow to an idol. They were confident that God would rescue them <u>but their faith wasn't dependent upon Him doing it</u>. They were going to remain true to Him even if He didn't. They are in my Hall of Fame for demonstrating how to respond when the going gets tough and threatens to get even worse. Their confidence and proclamation to the king were rooted in God's greatness! No matter what happened, they were going to be true to their God.

While we might not be facing death, many of us are facing all kinds of difficult situations today: loss of job, loss of income, overwhelming bills, uncertainty of the future, threatened layoffs, illness, inability to financially help friends or ministries in need – the list goes on. How are we responding? Are we caught up in the trauma of our need? Or, are we focused on the greatness of our God?

In Habakkuk 3:17-19 the prophet describes barren farms. But even <u>though</u> the farms have no figs, no grapes, no olives, no food, no sheep and no cattle – the response is *"<u>YET</u> I will rejoice in the LORD. I will be joyful in God my Savior. The Sovereign LORD is my strength; he makes my feet like the feet of a deer, he enables me to tread on the heights."*

Let us apply Habakkuk and the example of these three young men to our situations. Fill in the blanks with whatever difficulties you, your family and friends or co-workers might be facing: "The God we serve is able to deliver us from _____, and he will deliver us from _____ – <u>But even if He doesn't</u>..... I will rejoice. I will be joyful in God my Savior. He is my strength. He enables me to walk in precarious places."

This isn't just good theology – this is what Jesus enables our bedrock reality with Him to be. He wants us to have such a relationship with Him that this will just flow out of it. If this doesn't describe where you are, seek Him and He will enable you to get there. Let us remember, Job faced untold calamity but he didn't sin by charging God with wrongdoing, nor did he sin in what he said. He responded with worship and praise. (Job 1:22 & 2:10b).

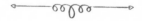

A 'more excellent way'...

Proverbs 3:3-4 Let love and faithfulness never leave you; bind them around your neck, write them on the tablet of your heart. ⁴Then you will win favor and a good name in the sight of God and man.

Love and faithfulness – what marvelous attributes these are! Wouldn't it be wonderful if every Christian was primarily characterized by them?

Consider the contrast by viewing verse 4 in two different ways. On the one hand, verse 4 becomes the question, "What can I do to win favor and a good name in the sight of God and man?" This is an entirely appropriate question and desire. The Lord provides a wonderful answer in verse 3 to accomplish that goal.

But there's another question that can be asked that reflects a subtle yet significant difference in motivation. "Lord, what things are important to You that should characterize my life?" Love and faithfulness (verse 3) is an answer to that question and verse 4 becomes the result of living such a life.

In both scenarios, the obedient Christian will live a life expressing love and faithfulness. This results in favor and a good name. But I think the motivation of the second question expresses a "more excellent way". The distinction is that the goal is not winning favor and having a good name, but living a life that expresses love for God – that will glorify Him.

This all speaks to the issue of "why". Why do we do what we do? What is our motivation? Do we do things to get blessed? Or, do we do things to express our love for Him and one another – and blessings are the fruit?

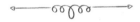

Purifying our motives

James 4:3 When you ask, you do not receive, because you ask with wrong motives, that you may spend what you get on your pleasures.

Why do we do what we do? What is our motivation? Do we do things to get blessed? Do we do things to express our love for Him and one another? Or, does a lot of other stuff become involved creating a mix of motivations? Today's verse highlights that we can have wrong motives. Not much of a surprise there.

Having pure and right motives is wonderful. Hopefully it will be true of us with ever increasing frequency. Unfortunately, there are times when our motives are not what they should be. Disobedience because our motives aren't what they should be is not an option. When we know God wants us to do something, whether through the leading of His Spirit or through His Word, we are to do it.

Think of the times where we encounter problems with co-workers, teachers, friends, clients – people we have to deal with. The Lord says it's easy to love those who love us. It's the unlovely ones that can pose such problems for us.

In such situations I am so grateful for the Holy Spirit and His convicting power. He not only shows us when our motives are wrong, but he provides the grace to recognize it, confess it and deal with it redemptively. By looking to Him in faith, we can find ourselves in a transformative process where He uses our obedience to be the framework to create the right motives within us. When we cry out to Him to do it, it consistently happens – although it might take longer than we would like.

When the Holy Spirit reveals problems with our motives – or anything else for that matter – we see that they are not obstacles but opportunities for Him to transform us more and more into the image of Jesus.

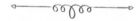

Jesus and the children in Gospel Road by Johnny Cash

Luke 18:16 But Jesus called the children to him and said, "Let the little children come to me, and do not hinder them, for the kingdom of God belongs to such as these."

Back in the 70s, Johnny Cash made a film titled "Gospel Road" about the life of Jesus. I was thrilled a few years ago to discover it had been re-issued. I purchased it and was so blessed to see it was as wonderful as I remembered. It presents aspects of Jesus in a manner that I've never seen in another film. One of my favorite scenes is Jesus with the little children.

Picture a bunch of children playing in the water and on the shore of the Sea of Galilee. They are having a great time splashing and running – just being little kids. Maybe I relate to them so well because I grew up right on Lake Michigan and spent so many hours playing like they were. But then, they see Jesus coming!

The children all run to him and he kneels down on the shore with them and they are thrilled. Can't you just see Jesus sitting on the shore with a little kid in his lap and all the kids playing around them, splashing and carrying on. Then he's digging in the wet sand with them. What a marvelous picture, seeing Jesus and the children grinning and laughing together having just a wonderful time. He even picks one of the kids up and does a "zerrbert" on his chest – laughing all the while.

The children knew Jesus was someone they loved to be around. He was special to them. But they were also special to him. He loved to be with them as well. Can you picture him laughing and grinning? Can you imagine having fun with him? Think of being with him and going home knowing it had been one of the best times of your life – one you wished would never end.

The wonderful news is that we are never too old to experience such joy and delight in Him. We too can experience him smiling and enjoying us. We just need to become more like children.

Think of Jesus smiling & laughing

Nehemiah 8:10c "...for the joy of the Lord is your strength."

Yesterday we wrote of Jesus laughing and playing with little children. A friend emailed me a picture of Jesus laughing and it speaks volumes to me! All too often we think of Jesus as always being serious; always involved in serious things. Maybe our view of Jesus – particularly as it relates to us – is that He is like a parent who is distressed by their child (you or me) who is forever messing up. We don't see the joy and wonder that would have been so evident in Him. We don't see Him smiling, let alone laughing.

Think of Jesus in the boat with the disciples as they rowed the boat and shared their experiences growing up with one another – talking about the fish that got away. Think of Jesus walking on the road with the disciples and they start picking on one of their group and Jesus has to rescue him. I can just see Jesus rolling His eyes at them as He intervenes.

Think of Jesus doing miracles and witnessing the explosion of joy that occurred when the lame walked or the blind saw; or a parent received their dead child back to life.

Think of parents bringing their crippled children to Him and they are made whole. Think of the little kids to whom the miracle occurs! Picture the little kids running around yelling at the top of their lungs that they were healed.

In Acts 3:1-10 there is the story of the crippled beggar who has a miraculous healing. Verse 8 describes his reaction:

> *"He jumped to his feet and began to walk. Then he went with them into the temple courts, walking and jumping, and praising God."*

This man wasn't quietly thankful, soberly contemplating the event that just happened to him. He jumped to his feet and began walking, jumping and praising God. All who saw him were filled with wonder and amazement at what had happened to him. I thank God that He has given me a wonderful understanding of the joy He has in His people. In spite of all my short-comings and frailties, I can see Him smiling at me – while He works with (and on) me. I hope you can see Him smiling at you too.

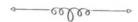

Brown, black and gray...

Proverbs 20:12 Ears that hear and eyes that see— the LORD
has made them both.

Opportunities - they surround us each and every day. How many righteous opportunities do we miss because we don't perceive them? How many unrighteous ones do we walk into because we don't perceive their nature either? Today, let's focus on the righteous opportunities that are there around us.

When our two oldest sons were little we lived in Wheaton, IL. Nearby was Morton Arboretum. We loved to take John & Jamie for hikes there. In the spring of one year something important occurred. We were walking through the woods and I asked them what colors did they see? They answered, "Brown, black, gray." I said to look closer and got the same answer of, "Brown, black, gray." They just saw soil, leaves covering the ground, tree trunks and tree limbs without leaves – all brown, black and gray.

Then I pointed to a tree and said to look beneath it. When they started to answer, "Brown", I said, to look closer – in the leaves to the left of the tree. All of a sudden they shouted, "Oh, there's green!" I pointed to another area and they shouted, "There's pink! Blue! White!"

They began to see the spring flowers in bloom all around us. They just hadn't seen the colorful flowers before because they were distracted by the dominant brown, black and gray. Their eyes were opened, by being trained in what to look for.

We likewise have to train our spiritual eyes and ears to recognize many of the opportunities that the Lord puts in our path. We can miss so much "color" because of the brown, black and gray of life. But with the Holy Spirit's help, we can see and embrace many more of the beautiful and colorful opportunities that are all around us. Ask Him to train your eyes and ears to perceive them, and He will.

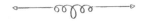

Imagine, God delighting in you!

Psalm 37:23a If Yahweh delights in a man's way,

Our Pekingese, Snuggles, sleeps with us every night. Usually she sleeps through the night but now and then she wakes up having to go to the bathroom. This means I get up, get dressed and take her outside. We haven't lived somewhere with a totally fenced-in yard, so it has meant that I go out with her. From the beginning this struck me as a job for me, not Donna.

Sometimes during the night I don't hear Snuggles when she is making sounds to go outside but Donna does. When that happens, Donna nudges me awake and I take Snuggles out. This is a little "big thing" for me. On my scale of things, it's little, but it sure blesses Donna; to her it's big.

Taking Snuggles out in the middle of the night is an opportunity for me to bless my wife, the girl I love. It's not a chore and it isn't burdensome. Believe it or not, it truly is a source of joy. Standing outside in the cold, snow or rain in the middle of the night for a few minutes isn't a big deal; and invariably, I think of her snuggled in bed and it brings a smile to my face. It's an opportunity for my actions to say "I love you" to her.

What a blessing it is to live our lives together; loving one another. There are so many opportunities for us to communicate that love to each other through our attitudes and actions. While we recognize our responsibilities for tasks needing to be done, pervading it all is the gratitude for the love we share. That love and gratitude bring pleasure to jobs done; bringing delight to each other.

There is delight, in bringing delight to someone – particularly someone we love. This truth is epitomized in our relationship with our Lord Jesus. Given the magnitude and wonder of His love for us, I find it mind-boggling that we have the opportunity to bring Him delight! The realization of this is truly a "Eureka" moment. It's like finding gold!

And bringing delight to God is not just doing things for Him – it's living our lives, doing whatever He tells us to do!! We bring Him delight when we walk in His ways. The more we become like Jesus, the more delight we bring Him. We delight in Him – and He delights in us. WOW!!

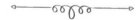

When everything goes wrong...

Habakkuk 3:17-18 Though the fig tree does not bud and there are no grapes on the vines, though the olive crop fails and the fields produce no food, though there are no sheep in the pen and no cattle in the stalls, yet I will rejoice in the LORD, I will be joyful in God my Savior.

These verses are among my very favorite in the entire Bible. They speak of where God wants us to be in our relationship with Him when everything seems to go wrong. They reflect a reality that God wants to work into our lives, thereby making these sentiments genuine. We need to understand that we can be doing everything right and find ourselves in such situations.

In an agrarian society consider the reality of what verse 17 talks about: no buds on the fig trees; no grapes on the vines; a failed olive crop; the fields produce no food; no sheep in the pen and no cattle in the stalls. Nothing is working. Nothing is doing what it is supposed to do. The source of food and income is not there.

Think of this description and apply it to our lives. Some modern counterparts could be; no sales, no income, no results, lost revenue, lost jobs and no success to name a few. Think of everything we attempt to do in terms of work and livelihood being fruitless. But then consider the word YET!

"Yet I will rejoice in the LORD, I will be joyful in God my Savior." In spite of all the negative, I will rejoice in the LORD. In spite of all the losses, I will be joyful in God my Savior. How do we do it? How do we get to a place where this verse genuinely describes the reality in our heart? The good news is God provides a way to get there. I find it to be a practical example of James 4:8, *"Come near to God and He will come near to you."*

It won't happen over night, but it can happen. By His Spirit and by us walking in His ways, He will transform us so that no matter what happens, we will more and more, rejoice in the LORD and be joyful in God our Savior.

To be continued. . .

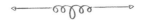

Enabled to go on he heights

Habakkuk 3:19 The Sovereign LORD is my strength; He makes my feet like the feet of a deer, He enables me to go on the heights.

Have you ever watched videos of deer or mountain goats up in the mountains on rocky terrain? How these animals move is amazing. I saw one involving snow leopards. The leopard went after a ram and it was unbelievable how that ram kept its footing and moved at high speed where I couldn't even imagine walking!

They have the ability to walk and run in very precarious places. These precarious places are part of their lives. Walking and running on the heights is normal for them. I never thought that much about the running aspect of it until I saw the video of the leopard chasing the ram. Given that precarious places aren't my thing, I could only imagine moving slowly and deliberately.

But, when we recognize that the Lord is our strength, He does things to us. He gives us abilities that we wouldn't otherwise have. The more we trust Him and walk in His ways, the more we are able to handle whatever comes, whether good or bad, with grace and confidence. This includes anything that life can confront us with even if it be a tsunami, earthquake or terrorism. There are times when decisions need to be made rapidly. He will make our "feet" like the feet of a deer to handle them, even if things are moving faster than we would like.

No matter what happens, our desire is to always respond in a manner that glorifies our Lord. Whether we receive great recognition, or great loss, He is our strength. He is the One we rejoice in. He is the source of our joy. The Lord wants others to see Him in our responses. He wants to use our example to create within them a thirst and hunger for Him.

Isn't it wonderful that we have so many opportunities to bring pleasure to Him, by responding faithfully in every situation we face!

Remembering the special people God used

Philippians 1:3 I thank my God every time I remember you.

While the New Year is a time for making resolutions, let's take some time to remember the very special people that God has used to bless and help us over the years. They may be life-long friends or they may be individuals that God brought into our lives for one moment in time. As I write this I think of a lady who was sitting next to us nearly 40 years ago.

Donna and I were as poor as church mice, and living on faith. An offering was being taken and we had only $5. We prayed and knew the Lord wanted us to put it in the offering, so we did. Then this lady next to Donna turned and gave her a $10 bill. We don't know her name, but we thank God for her.

Think of people who have helped us when we needed it. When Donna and I were going through a difficult time in our marriage in 1992, the Lord provided Ric & Val. What priceless friends they became. He was (and is to this day) a marvelous counselor but they were so much more than that. Their love and friendship provided a safe-harbor for us to address the issues confronting us.

At work back around 1990 the Lord provided Mindy a systems specialist who helped me navigate implementing major accounts on a new claims system. She became a priceless resource for me and helped me innumerable times through the years. I remember being in one meeting where I was representing marketing and the technical discussion was over my head. Then someone made a statement and Mindy spoke up. She said, "Don you need to ask about what he just said because it will negatively affect marketing and your accounts." Thanks to her, something I would have missed was caught and changed. She also was a Christian who has prayed for my family and me for years.

There are so many people that God has used in all our lives. Ask Him to help you to remember them and the situations that someone blessed you in. Sit with a spouse or family member and help each other remember and focus on the positives. It is such a blessing to have our hearts filled with gratitude when we remember those God has put in our lives. Then take one more step and write, email or call and share today's Scripture with them and how they have made a difference in your life.

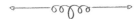

Attributes our God doesn't have!

I Kings 18:27 At noon Elijah began to taunt them. "Shout louder!" he said. "Surely he is a god! Perhaps he is deep in thought, or busy, or traveling. Maybe he is sleeping and must be awakened."

I've wondered why this verse always brings a smile to my face. I'm grinning even as I write this. And now I am laughing. Really! I am sitting here typing and laughing. It's not laughing at the prophets of Baal shouting and dancing trying to get the attention of their god. This verse just taps into such a wellspring of joy within me that comes from Him.

Think of it. This verse paints such a perfect picture of who our God isn't! Our God isn't deaf! He isn't distracted or asleep or busy or traveling. He's never asleep. He doesn't put out a "Do Not Disturb" sign. He never says, come back later I'm too busy now.

Our God never has an "Oops"! He doesn't miss anything. Nothing catches Him by surprise. Nothing catches Him off guard. There is never the need for Him to apologize to us because He was too busy elsewhere or distracted and just missed what happened to us. He'll never say, "Oh, how did that happen?" He'll never ask, "What do we do now?"

This reality must become bedrock in us. Once it does, nothing will shake us. No matter what happens, our first thoughts are of Him. He knows what we're facing. He knows what's coming. If it happens, He allowed it and will get us through it. Our God is always with us! His grace and mercy and strength are there for us. There's nothing He can't redeem. We are never alone, even when we think He is no where around!

The more this wonderful reality of our God dawns on us, the greater is our joy and gratitude. I guess that is the source of my smile – my overwhelming gratitude over who God is (and isn't!) and that He made me His own.

The blessing of repentance

1 Kings 3:5 At Gibeon the LORD appeared to Solomon during the night in a dream, and God said, "Ask for whatever you want me to give you."

Suppose when you went to bed tonight the Lord appeared to you in a dream and said, "Ask for whatever you want me to give you." What would you ask for? Do you know?

Some answers to this question are better than others. Solomon's answer (1 Kings 3:6-9) was pleasing to the Lord and He specifically noted some of the things he didn't ask for. I don't think that Solomon was trying to please Him; he was just answering the question as honestly as he could. The Lord was pleased with his honest answer.

That honesty is what we need to look for within us. What answer truly reflects where we are? What might we learn about ourselves by our answer? We can submit our answer to the Holy Spirit and ask Him to show us anything we need to see.

Years ago when I was a young Christian, I wanted a supernatural ministry, but I was unaware of a problem I had. One night in a dream, Jesus took me to a river nearby and told me to pick up the cloak that was there by my feet (just like Elisha in 2 Kings 2:13). He told me to strike the water with the cloak, so I did. The river immediately parted just like it did for Elisha!

Jesus then asked me if I saw anyone else around or were we alone. I saw no one else; we were alone. He then asked me how much it meant to me. With that question came the painful realization that it didn't mean as much because I wanted people to see me do it. I wanted to be recognized as a man walking with the power of God.

The wonderful thing is that I didn't feel condemned or put down. I was embarrassed but mostly I experienced the loving touch of someone who was for me and wanted me to be free of anything that would hinder me. In my repenting He affirmed me – I was His! Fortunately God is so good and kind at showing us our faults and weaknesses and helping us to repent.

To be continued…

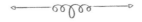

He sets a wonderful 'trap' for us

Psalm 37:4 Delight yourself in the LORD and
He will give you the desires of your heart.

Yesterday we looked at I Kings 3:5 where the Lord appears to Solomon during the night in a dream, and God said, *"Ask for whatever you want me to give you."* As we proceed, it is important to remember that this is not a test – in terms of a right answer means acceptance and a wrong answer rejection. It is the 'quality' of our answer, in the context of our lives and our relationship with the Lord that is important.

Today's verse is remarkably similar to the scenario we have been considering. We simply change the question from, "What do you want me to give you?" to the Lord asking you, "What are the desires of your heart?" If you're like me, that can be a tough question to accurately answer. The difficulty isn't being able to verbalize an answer, but lies in whether the answer I give truly reflects my heart.

But this verse does something wonderful. It tells you how to get the desires of your heart – whether you are aware of what they are or not. The key is to delight yourself in the Lord. Consider it an 'if, then' situation. If we delight in Him, then He will give us the desires of our heart.

This is a wonderful 'trap' He has set for us. When we focus on delighting in Him, He transforms our motivation and our desires. We become caught in the wonder of delighting in Him – that becomes a major desire of our heart! We find ourselves caring less and less about getting anything.

The focus changes from us to Him. We become thrilled with the realization that delighting in Him is something we can grow in. The more we delight in Him, the more we are able to delight in Him. Delighting in Him, and all that entails, can become the desire of our heart!

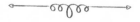

$1 more than we had!

Philippians 4:19 And my God will meet all your needs according to his glorious riches in Christ Jesus.

Donna and I were married in the fall of 1970 right after I graduated from Michigan State. That next January we were involved in a coffee-house street ministry called The Master's House in downtown Lansing, MI. We were open evenings and late into the night. While we had no salary, we were provided with a little 2 bedroom home across from the Oldsmobile forge plant on the west side of town. We got to pray everything else in and were so blessed by God's provision.

We went an extended period where we had no money – not a dime. Groceries, gas, everything was provided - just no money. One evening Judy Potter, a college friend who was helping with the ministry, came up to me and said with a little embarrassment that the Lord had told her to give us $1 – not $5 or $10 – just $1. I grinned and took the dollar and placed it in my shirt pocket and told her is was $1 more than I had.

Later that evening another helper came and asked if we could give him a ride home when we closed. He lived on the south end of Lansing. I was a bit concerned because we were low on gas but I agreed to take him home. Our old Ford had about 8 gallons below empty and we had been on the empty mark for a couple of days.

After dropping him off after midnight, we were near home when we had to stop at a railroad crossing for a train. I no sooner stopped when I ran out of gas. But much to my relief, next to us was a police car! I got out and went over and asked them to call AAA. Fortunately, at Christmas we had been given an AAA membership.

The officers pulled behind us with their lights on and we waited. When the AAA guy arrived, he didn't say a word but he took a 5 gallon gas can, poured it in my car and then walked up to me and his first words were, "That will be $1." (Gas cost 19.9 cents/gallon.) I took the $1 out of my shirt pocket – **the only dollar that we had** - and handed it to him. We rejoiced all the way home!

Our friend didn't give us $5 or $10 but she sensed the Lord said to give just $1 – the exact amount we would need. Here nearly 50 years later I continue to be thrilled by the amazing power of this experience with God.

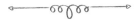

A special prayer for young adults and young at heart

The Scriptures are filled with such wonderful men and women of faith. I trust that you are familiar with all the ones mentioned below. The Lord helped me write this prayer several years ago for a conference. In sharing it, I trust that it will stir within you an increased desire to become everything you can be. Regardless of our age, our focus can be sharpened enabling us to become more of what He wants us to be. God bless you!

Oh Lord Jesus,
    I pray that each of us will become

- like Joseph – that we will stay faithful to You - even when the dreams You give us, seem unlikely to ever come true.
- like Moses – that we will turn aside when You place a burning bush in our path.
- like Joshua and Caleb – that we will be brave and courageous in the face of giants in the land..

I pray that we will be

- like Ruth – that we will live godly lives leading to incredible destinies
- like Isaiah – that in response to hearing Your call, each of us will say, "Here am I. Send me."
- like Esther – that we will recognize the times for which we have been created and face them with faith and courage.
- like Shadrach, Meshach and Abednego – our commitment to You is not based on whether you will save us from a fiery trial or not.

I pray that we will be

- like Peter and Andrew – that we will follow You when you call us to be fishers of men.
- like the 2 disciples on the road to Emmaus – that our hearts will burn within - whenever You speak to us.
- and like Paul – that the day will come, when each of us can say, "I have fought the good fight. I have finished the race. I have kept the faith!"

A verse unlike any other

Question: What did God want when He gave us the gift of Jesus? My answer is probably different than you think. Today's verse is unlike any other and is at the end of the devotional.

A month ago we celebrated the birth of Jesus – the greatest gift that God could ever give. In less than three months we will celebrate His resurrection, which is the most important Christian holy day. Yahweh so loved the world that He gave Jesus, His only Son for us. Through faith in Jesus we are able to be born-again, saved, be born of the Spirit, freed from sin, become children of God, have eternal life, …

The blessings that flow from Yahweh's love for us are beyond measure. But they stem from His desire for something. Can you think of what that might be? Any number of answers might come close: He wanted to undo the results of the fall; He wanted a people for Himself; He wanted to redeem mankind.

A major clue is in the answer Jesus gives to the question, "What is the greatest commandment?" My favorite recording of Jesus being asked this question is Mark 12:28-34. I never cease to be moved by the response of this teacher of the law and then Jesus' response to him.

Over and over again throughout Scripture, Yahweh instructs His people to love Him. He will keep His covenant of love to a thousand generations (Deut 7:9) with those who do love Him and keep His commands. Is there an Old Testament verse that lets us see the impact upon Him of His people from not doing this? The answer is yes.

This verse is Jeremiah 3:19. It reveals Yahweh's heart so clearly. In this chapter, He is calling for unfaithful Israel to repent and return to Him. Yahweh declares, in this verse:

"I myself said, 'How gladly would I treat you like sons and give you a desirable land, the most beautiful inheritance of any nation. I thought you would call me Father and not turn away from following me."

Do we see and feel the pain revealed in that verse??!! He thought they would call Him Father and not turn away from following Him. I know of no other verse where Yahweh so reveals the pain associated with the failure of His people to respond to Him. It's as though His heart is bleeding on the floor in front of us. More than anything else, God wants a people who love Him, and thankfully He tells us very specifically how to do that! How can we do anything less?

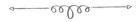

He's made a way for us!

Jeremiah 3:19 "I myself said, 'How gladly would I treat you like sons and give you a desirable land, the most beautiful inheritance of any nation. I thought you would call me Father and not turn away from following me."

Yesterday we looked at this verse that is so revealing of the pain associated with the Israelites going their own way and not responding to God and His love for them. This morning I thought of the parable of the lost son who rebelled and spent his inheritance sinfully and wound up in the pigsty (Luke 15:11-31). What do you think was going on with his father after his son went off?

Imagine his father watching his son walk away from home – not knowing if he would ever return. At meal time he likely noticed his son's empty seat at the table. The stillness of not hearing his voice and not having his presence in the home at times could have been deafening. Can you imagine the heartache whenever his father looked down the road and didn't see his son returning?

I can imagine the pain. He loved his son but was helpless to reach him. Now into this context, think of our God looking at a world with his potential sons and daughters all in pigsties, no matter what their circumstances were; all 'away from home and away from Him'. But our God wasn't and isn't helpless. He made a way for each and everyone of us to 'come back home' to Him.

The way that He made for us is so wonderfully described in John 3:16 *"For God so loved the world that He gave His only Son…"* He didn't and doesn't just write us off – He made a way for us! And His Spirit is wooing every one of us, in the pig sties of life, to come to ourselves and recognize that Jesus can and will 'bring us home'.

When the son came to himself and returned he had no idea the joy that was awaiting him. He recognized just how guilty he was and never expected the response his father gave him. But his father saw him coming even when he was a long way off and ran to him, threw his arms around him and kissed him. The son was stunned by the celebration; so great was his father's joy that he had come home.

Jesus taught that this celebration is what happens in Heaven whenever one sinner repents! And we get to experience it!!! Never in my wildest dreams did I ever expect to experience the overwhelming joy and love that I did when Jesus came into my life. One moment I was lost and in the pigsty, the next I was 'at home' in the embrace of my God, absolutely overwhelmed by His love for me.

Because of the love of God in Jesus, we get to call Him Father and faithfully follow Him all the days of our lives!

The importance of context

Part 1 of a 5 part series: *John 8:31, 32 To the Jews who had believed him, Jesus said, "If you hold to my teaching, you are really my disciples. Then you will know the truth, and the truth will set you free."*

The context in which a Scripture is set is frequently very important to both the understanding of the verse and its application. Unfortunately Christians and people in general have a tendency at times to over look this fact. A good illustration of this point is Psalm 14:1, which contains the statement, "There is no God." But the context makes a world of difference. The entire verse reads, *"The fool says in his heart, 'There is no God.'"*

This importance of context really applies to today's verses. The portion that is so frequently quoted is the 32nd verse, *"...you will know the truth, and the truth will set you free."* It's usually presented as a Biblical promise that one is set free simply by hearing or recognizing the truth. But a closer examination reveals that the context has a very important qualifier in verse 31.

This promise is part of an "If... Then..." situation. If the first condition is true, then the benefit or desired result will follow. If the first condition is NOT true, then it typically won't. The full context presents the two components of what Jesus is saying: 1) IF you hold to my teaching...2) THEN you will know the truth and the truth will set you free.

The context provides a lot of clarity. Jesus is also defining what is required to be a disciple, who then can be the recipient of the promise. It's not just a matter of acknowledging Him as Lord. A disciple is one who holds fast to His teachings and lives in accordance with them. The promise specifically applies to that individual who is a disciple.

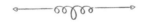

What is your evidence?

Part 2 of a 5 part series: *John 13:35 "By this all men will know that you are my disciples, if you love one another."*

In yesterday's devotional we saw that in order to receive the promise of John 8:32, you had to be a disciple of Jesus. A disciple is one who holds fast to His teachings and lives in accordance with them. Today's verse, gives us a primary answer on how those around us will know if we are His disciples. It is critical to note that the criteria focus on how we actually live our lives.

Back in the Jesus People days of the late 60s, my wife Donna told me of a phrase written as graffiti on a tunnel wall at North Carolina State University. The phrase was, "If you were arrested for being a Christian, would there be enough evidence to convict you?" Think about that for a minute.

Let's take it a step further and place some restrictions on acceptable evidence: 1) Church attendance is only acceptable if it is backed up by other evidence, 2) Your verbal testimony is not admissible as evidence – only the testimony of others reporting what you've said and done is admissible, and 3) Evidence is primarily going to be provided by the testimonies of those who know you, work with you, interact with you or wait on you, i.e., clerks, waitresses, storekeepers, parking lot attendants, etc...

How will others describe you? Simply put, what kind of person are you? What kind of neighbor? Friend? Acquaintance? How do you treat people? Suppose it goes further and they are able to identify everything you watch, read, or view – TV, phones, computers, whatever.

Will the evidence presented confirm that we are loving people? Upon examination, will the testimony confirm that we hold fast to the teachings of Jesus – that we live our lives in accordance with them? Or will the testimony present a picture where our Christian testimony (verbal) is at odds with our lives?

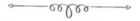

Loving God is not optional

Part 3 of a 5 part series: *John* 14:15 *"If you love Me,
you will obey what I command."*

In our culture we tend to have an allergic reaction to certain words – obey and command are two in particular that Christians tend to react to. Typical responses are to immediately think of such words as part of legalism or to counter with a 'grace not law' type of argument.

Picture yourself in a quiet time and suddenly Jesus is there with you - just you and Jesus – face to face. With a loving yet serious look, eye to eye, he says to you, "If you love Me, you will obey what I command." I imagine that would catch your attention. Afterward those words would likely burn within you.

"If you love Me…" One of the problems we have in English is that there is one word for love. That word love applies to everything around us. We love our sports team. We love fried chicken.. We love beautiful sunsets. We love walks in the woods. It goes on and on. We love potato chips. We love God. What does the word "love" really mean - particularly since we use it so frequently to describe such a wide variety of things.

"If you love Me…" With these words comes the realization that God wants us to love Him. In fact it's more serious than that because there is an implication in this verse that is truly shocking. At face value, the verse says if we love Him, we will obey what He commands. But consider the implication of the reverse: If we don't do what He commands, we don't love Him.

It's imperative that we understand this is not talking about earning our salvation. It is coming to grips with the fact that the God of the Universe – the God of Abraham, Isaac and Jacob – the Father of our Lord Jesus Christ – wants, and expects, His people to love Him.

Let that sink in. Loving God is not optional, nor something to be approached casually. It is at the very heart of our faith. It is what defines us as Christians - the people of God. The wonderful news is that He does not leave us to our own devices to figure out what loving Him means. He gives us the answer!

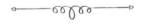

How can I know for sure that I am in fact

loving God?

Part 4 of a 5 part series: *1 John 5:3 This is love for God: to obey his commands. And his commands are not burdensome,*

One evening I was really moved by Jesus' question to Peter: "Do you love me?" The more I thought about it, the question became alive to me - Do I love Him? If so, how do I know for sure that I truly do love Him? What if I'm deceiving myself? The Bible has many examples of His people thinking they loved Him but their lives didn't give any evidence of it – in fact their lives demonstrated that they didn't! Does He leave us to our own devices to determine if we love Him?

As I was crying out to Him about this, a sudden thought shot through my mind, "The answers are in the back of the book." This really spoke to me because I'm good at math. All the math books I used had the answers to the odd problems in the back of the book. Sometimes I had to start with the answers in order to figure out how to work the problems. God was saying the answers to my question were in His book!

Loving God is defined by God as obeying His commands. Scripture is filled with commands on how we should or should not live. Culturally we have the unfortunate tendency to think of them as instructions or suggestions, but they are commands none-the-less - and every day we have nearly unlimited opportunities to obey them.

Every time we obey a command in Scripture, or respond to His Spirit, it is an objective, concrete expression of our love for Him. (Think be kind, be gentle, don't gossip, seek humility not pride, love one another, forgive, etc...) We don't have to wonder if we are really loving Him. We just have to live His word. (Note: As a helpful aid, I have identified 25 different portions of Scripture in the NT that contain such lists and have them written in the back of my Bible under a title of 'Loving God'.)

God also transforms our motivation. Obedience (holding fast to His teachings and living in accordance with them) becomes something we don't "have to" do, but we "get to" do! It becomes a joy to do what Scripture says because His Spirit confirms in our hearts that we are expressing genuine love for Him. The more we obey Scripture and the promptings of His Spirit, the more we love Him. It's like a dream coming true!

Tomorrow – A different perspective on commands

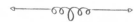

Don Schmidt

A different perspective on commands

Part 5 of a 5 part series: *1 Corinthians 8:3 But the man who loves God is known by God.*

In these past few days we've seen that we love God by obeying His commands. If we want to love Him, He has given us a very precise answer on the way it is done – the only way it is done. And it is something that we can grow in. Our ability to love Him is not static – He intends for it to grow all the days of our lives! When Jesus said to walk in His ways, this is what He meant. Think of the intimacy reflected in today's verse for the ones who do.

I would like to offer a different perspective on commands for your consideration. January 21, 2005 while in Brazil with our son and family, I was struggling with this whole issue of truly loving God. That evening, in a wonderful experience with the Lord and His presence, He brought to mind a movie that has been a favorite of our family. The movie contains something that He just opened to me that night that continues to bless me to this day. (I love to reread my journal entry where this is all recorded)

Have you seen the movie Princess Bride? Peter Falk is a grandpa reading a love story to his grandson – the story of Princess Buttercup and her servant Wesley. Every time she gives Wesley a command to do something he utters the phrase, "As you wish." Her "wish" is his command.

It becomes clear in the movie that "As you wish" means "I love you". They go through all manner of adventures and the movie has a wonderful ending. For the sake of this illustration, don't think of God's commands as commands, but think of them as His wishes. So, we are responding to wishes instead of commands.

Then think of being in love. You want your loved one to share with you their wishes – to which you respond, "As you wish." (Remember the expression 'Your wish is my command!') You then go and do what they wish to bless them and please them and be overwhelmed with joy as you do. God shares His "wishes" with us in His word.

All of His "wishes" become opportunities for you to lovingly say to Him, "As you wish." "As you wish." "As you wish." Each and every time is your opportunity to love Him by what you do, and to say "I love you" to Him. Your heart will be filled with the desire to learn and embrace all of His "wishes" so that you can do more and more of them.

Then, there are the times when we sin, and with painful remorse we come to the Lord and say, "Father - forgive me." To which He replies, "As you wish."

(*Note: A few months later John Ortberg, one of my favorite authors, came out with a book titled, God Is Closer Than You Think. It has a chapter titled "As You Wish")

Together with Him in the morning

Psalm 59:16 But I will sing of your strength, in the morning I will sing of your love; for you are my fortress, my refuge in times of trouble.

What a blessing to have our thoughts preoccupied each morning with the strength and the love of God. Although He loves all mankind, the remarkable thing is His love for you and for me – for each of us individually, not just corporately. If we are going through difficult times, remember He is our fortress and our refuge. We are safe with Him.

King Saul was trying to kill him when David wrote this Psalm. That is likely a bit more difficulty than any of us are encountering now. Yet David's hope and trust and confidence were in the Lord. How much more should the same be true of us.

Most of us have had the privilege of becoming a son or daughter of God, because of His love for us. We have Jesus. We have the Holy Spirit within us. We have God's Word. We have experienced His love in ways that David never did. We have been set free from the power of sin – to live for Him. This Psalm speaks of the wonder of who He is for us. He wants us to have this knowledge firmly rooted in the depths of our being and growing morning by morning. No matter what we experience, He is the same – but our awareness of who He is for us will grow and grow.

We recently sang a song during worship that had this chorus:

> The more I seek you
> The more I find you
> The more I find you
> The more I love you

The words are so true. He loves us to seek Him – and to seek Him regularly. If you don't think of Him in the morning, particularly when you awake and are getting up, create yourself some visual reminders that will help you to do so. He will help you. He wants you to find Him.

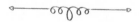

Don Schmidt

My miraculous tornado experience!

Colossians 3:17 And whatever you do, whether in word or deed, do it all in the name of the Lord Jesus, giving thanks to God the Father through him.

In the summer of 1970, I was in my last quarter at Michigan State. I had been a Christian less than 2 years and was going to be married in September after graduation. I had seen and experienced genuine miracles since becoming a Christian, but nothing like what the Lord did one summer day.

Donna was in Lexington, KY working at a Christian ministry. Randy, a college friend offered to drive me down for a weekend to see her. This meant missing a Botany Taxonomy 4 hour lab on Friday. The instructor said that if I helped set up the plots on Thursday afternoon for the field work, I could miss the lab on Friday.

The weather was rainy on Thursday. After helping the instructor and some others set up the plots, Randy picked me up. We were located next to an expressway entrance. We no sooner got on the expressway and cars began honking and pulling off the road! There in front of us in a field to our right was a tornado, touched down and coming right at us – several hundred yards away!!

At that moment, the Spirit of the Lord came down in the car and I came against the tornado in the name of Jesus Christ of Nazareth and commanded it to disintegrate in Jesus' name and it disintegrated – right in front of us! It did not jump up into the sky – it just disintegrated – poof! We praised the Lord all the way to Kentucky and back.

On Monday I was in class waiting for it to begin and telling the other students (college seniors and grad students) about the tornado we'd seen. A little voice in my head said to tell them the rest of the story. So I took a deep breath and told them exactly what happened – as I just described it here. They knew I was a Christian, but when I said how the tornado just disintegrated they all lost it – big time!

Amidst the laughter and uproar, I sat there thinking "Oh Lord...". But then the instructor entered the room and came over to where she lectured. I looked up at her and asked her if she had seen the tornado on Thursday afternoon. Her answer stunned the class and stopped all the laughter and ridicule. She said, "Yes we all did. And it was the strangest thing. As we were standing there watching it, all of a sudden it just disintegrated!"

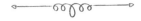

What to do with the miracles...

Romans 1:20 For since the creation of the world God's invisible qualities—his eternal power and divine nature—have been clearly seen, being understood from what has been made, so that men are without excuse.

As I've noted before, I had a thunderous conversion the fall of my junior year in college. The next 22 months saw me at retreats, conferences, prayer meetings, mission trips, Bible studies, witnessing and being discipled. On a side note, I nearly flunked out until I realized that God wasn't glorified if I did - and that He wanted me to graduate. That "revelation" - along with meeting and becoming engaged to Donna - enabled me to focus on my studies my last 4 quarters and graduate.

My last quarter at Michigan State in the summer of 1970 brought another experience that continues to move me to this day. I had opportunities to visit with one of my best professors and talk to him about my becoming a Christian and the many experiences I was having. He was Jewish and an atheist.

In our discussions he expressed a major concern that he had. He believed the most important issue in life was to answer the question, "Is there a God?" Then, if you concluded there was a God, you <u>must</u> discover if that God has any requirements of you. He had seriously pursued this and concluded, "There was no God." But he was very distressed with my peers and so many others that he knew in that they didn't take this issue seriously.

As we talked about my conversion, my experiences and the miracles I'd seen, he felt he could explain away most of my testimony. He seemed settled in his conviction that there was no God, except one thing troubled him – particularly after hearing of my tornado miracle. I can remember him looking at me and saying with a serious thoughtfulness, "I don't know what to do with the miracles."

I was so blessed that he believed that I was truthful and had truly experienced the miraculous. Hopefully, the miracles caused him to reconsider the issue and discover Jesus, his messiah.

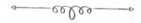

Don Schmidt

A marvelously redemptive continuum!

1 Corinthians 7:19b Keeping God's commands is what counts.

Have you ever noticed how doing the right thing is a whole lot easier when you have a right attitude / good motives? Obedience just seems to flow out of a right attitude, when our motives are good – even when the circumstances are difficult.

Your spouse or kids or parents need help with something and you just got home and have just collapsed into a chair exhausted. All you want to do is relax. But when your heart is to help them, getting yourself up isn't that difficult to do, in spite of how you feel.

But what happens when your attitude isn't right? Doing the right thing can be made a lot more difficult if our wrong or bad attitude prevails. Another trap is to disobey because we wrongly focus on our motives rather than on repentance and obedience.

Picture this:

Godly Motives & Attitudes <---------------Faith---------------- >Obedience

Right motives and attitudes coupled with faith lead to obedience. The great news is that the opposite can happen! Obedience, coupled with faith (honesty with God) can lead to Godly motives and attitudes! This continuum can go either way!

When our attitudes / motives are less than they should be (or are awful), our obedience can become the framework for God to use in shaping and transforming them. Think of cement forms for laying a walkway. The forms are put into the correct shape and the cement is poured in. Once it hardens the forms are removed. Our obedience is like the concrete forms. It, coupled with our acknowledgement of our sin, provides the framework for God to use.

We cannot avoid obeying God because of a bad attitude. When I am in situations like this, I find myself confessing my sinful attitudes / motives to God and asking Him to transform them as I obey and do the right thing. Through my continued obedience and repentance, God transforms my heart moving it to the Godly end of the above continuum.

It is a marvelously redemptive process that we can confidently use whenever our attitudes and motives are less than they should be.

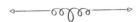

Avoiding being a lemon

Staying with - *I Corinthians 7:19b Keeping God's commands is what counts.*

What really matters in our lives, overall? What are the main convictions/ values that drive us? If one of our answers is our faith, what is it about our faith that is at it's core? How does our faith impact our lives and those around us? Although this verse is in a particular context, it can really stand alone. It is telling us that it isn't enough to talk the talk.

Think of buying a product with a brand name and then having nothing but problems with it. Or maybe it's okay most of the time, but it has a knack of not working when we need it most. If someone asked us if we would recommend it, we'd say NO. Although the product might look good, and it might perform well much of the time – that's not enough. The issue is that it's lacking in quality and reliability. It's subpar. You might even call it a lemon.

In light of this illustration, consider the verse again, *"Keeping God's commands is what counts."* I'm reminded of a major manufacturer whose corporate motto was, "The quality goes in before the name goes on!" We were bought at a great price. We are new creatures in Christ Jesus. We have His Spirit within us. We are freed from the power of sin. God has expectations and requirements of all of us as His sons and daughters. They are not optional.

As believers, the Holy Spirit uses Scripture to teach us how to live. He also convicts us of sin in our lives. He shows us our wrong motivations, our frailties, weaknesses, shortcomings and all manner of things in order to help us to obey – to become more like Jesus. He convicts. We repent. He empowers and transforms us. We co-operate with Him. Our lives become testimonies of keeping His commands.

A portion of this verse is a very important definition and was in the devotional a few days ago (Part 4 of 5 – 1 John 5:3). Keeping God's commands is the Biblical definition of loving God. Why is obeying His commands so important? Paraphrasing today's verse sums it up really well: **"Loving God is what counts."**

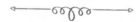

Commands – and our adventure with this word

1 John 2:28 (Children of God) And now, dear children, continue in Him, so that when he appears we may be confident and unashamed before Him at his coming.

Our focus has been upon loving God and Scripture defines that upon as keeping God's commands. We paraphrased 1 Corinthians 7:19b as "Loving God is what counts." But our focus today is to reorient ourselves to the word "commands". The concern is that when the word "commands" is mentioned, we think of Moses, the tablets of stone and the Law. We have a tendency to not think of commands as applying to us.

The Amplified Bible amplifies commands to be His orders, ordinances, precepts, teachings. They are all the instructions in how to live a Christian life. Today's verse is speaking to children of God (Christians) and instructs them to "continue in Him". In simple terms, this is another way of saying obey His commands. But do we recognize the instructions in the New Testament as truly being commands?

I went through the New Testament and identified over two dozen different portions of Scripture where the writer is listing a host of instructions on how we are to live. Romans 12:9-21 is one such list. Doing the things in this list is a way we "continue in Him". They are commands – instructions how to love God. By doing them we may be confident and unashamed before Him at His coming.

Consider this listing of a few of the "instructions" contained in these 13 verses in Romans: Love must be sincere. Hate what is evil. Cling to what is good. Be devoted to one another in brotherly love. Honor one another above yourselves. Be joyful in hope. (Be) patient in affliction. Do not be proud. Do not repay anyone evil for evil. And so on…

These are commands. Doing these things is how we continue in Him. These kinds of verses are all over the New Testament. They are the "answers in the back of the book" to the questions I discussed in my earlier devotional – How can I know for sure that I am in fact loving God? Do you realize the incredible news this is?!!

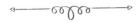

The lessons we learned from gymnastics

1 Timothy 6:11 But you, man of God, flee from all this, and pursue righteousness, godliness, faith, love, endurance and gentleness.

Back in the 80s, two of our sons, Jamie and Andrew, were very interested in gymnastics. Both joined a gymnastics club in NE Ohio. They had a lot of fun and enjoyed their teams very much but there was a significant problem – in competition their respective teams didn't do well because none of the individual gymnasts did well. From year to year, when they passed from one age grouping to another, they still all did poorly. The competing clubs whose gymnasts consistently did great, continued to excel as those gymnasts moved from age bracket to age bracket.

In talking to judges, one comment stood out: When in doubt, form wins out. Unfortunately, the boys' coach was committed to them doing difficult moves in their routines but he didn't emphasize form - therefore their scores were poor. Competitors doing simpler routines with great form were consistently beating them. We listened to the judges and changed clubs.

Their new coach emphasized form. When they did simple things well, they moved to greater difficulty, but the issue was always excellence. Both boys were very talented and motivated – but now their energies and efforts were properly focused and directed. The results were amazing!

They switched to the new club in the summer of 1989. That previous spring Andrew had finished 70th out of 73 in the state meet as an 8 year old. Jamie was middle of the pack as a 15 year old. The following spring in 1990, after one year at the new club, both boys were state champions! The issue wasn't how hard they worked or how much they cared or wanted it. **It was that they were now doing the things "required by" the results they sought after.**

The same truth applies to our pursuit of righteousness, godliness, faith, love, endurance and gentleness. Wanting these things isn't enough. We must do the things required by 'these results' in order to get them. God's Word tells us how we are to live so that - as we pursue these things, we experience excellence, not mediocrity.

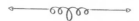

More lessons from gymnastics

Psalms 1:1 Blessed is the man who does not walk in the counsel of the wicked or stand in the way of sinners or sit in the seat of mockers.

In yesterday's devotional, we wrote about the experiences two of our sons, Jamie and Andrew, had in gymnastics. Good intentions and hard work did not bring excellence when they were at the first gymnastics club. Their gymnastics routines had too many things wrong with them that were not dealt with.

When they transferred to the 2nd club where they became champions, it wasn't a matter of just learning what the routines were supposed to look like. The new coach had to work with them to undue all the bad habits that they had developed. This was a challenge all in itself. Bad process leads to bad results. Watching video of themselves, they could see how they were doing things incorrectly. By eliminating the bad habits, he was able to help them develop the good practice habits that would lead to excellence.

Fortunately at the new gymnastics club, there were a bunch of other quality gymnasts. Jamie and Andrew could see others performing their routines correctly. The gymnasts helped one another – pointing out glitches and helping each other to learn to do it right. All of these gymnasts wanted to win, not only as individuals, but as a team. In order to win, their performances had to meet gymnastics' standards.

Many Christians today find themselves with habit patterns consistent with our sons' first gym. Good intentions, fun and participation are the rule. Unfortunately, all manner of bad habits and bad practices (read that sin) abound because their lives are more formed by culture than by God's Word. Worse still is the reality that these bad habits produce a spiritual deafness to the Holy Spirit making it more difficult to hear Him speak: Stop! Don't go there! Don't watch that. Come this way.

The great news is that God doesn't want to leave us there. Once we recognize that our lives must be filled with His excellence, and we choose to truly be His disciple, He will help us undue all the bad "practice habits" and show us how to do everything the right way. After all, He is the best Coach there is!

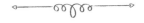

The Lord's 'spiritual spell check'

Romans 12:2 Do not conform any longer to the pattern of this world, but be transformed by the renewing of your mind. Then you will be able to test and approve what God's will is—his good, pleasing and perfect will.

Are we aware that our lives are being conformed to something – it's just a matter of what that something is? What is right? What is wrong? What is appropriate? What is wise? The more we do things or see others around us do them, the more susceptible we become to accepting those behaviors as the norm. Sadly, we can accept some very wrong things as being okay, simply because we have unknowingly been conformed to a worldly standard.

Think of typing a note in email. Typically, we have to hit spell check in order to have errors identified. But then we only do that if spelling and grammar are important to us. Even if we reread the email carefully, we can miss all manner of mistakes – that are only caught by clicking on spell check.

Now, think of typing in word processing software. As we type, misspelled words or duplicates have red lines under them. Grammatical problems have green lines under them - the warnings are there as we type. We then have the option of correcting them or leaving them. The choice is ours.

The Lord wants us to live lives where we become aware of problems, issues, sin, etc… as we encounter them or are making decisions. He provides the warnings if we but have eyes to see and ears to hear. The Holy Spirit is a fully functional 'Spiritual check' that we don't have to click on for him to work. But, the more we are conformed to the pattern of the world, the less we notice the still, small voice speaking within us. Worse, we can lose any awareness of even caring that we are doing what is right or wrong.

Suppose our lives were laid out as documents with all our thoughts, intentions, beliefs, actions put into grammatical form with a fully functioning "Spiritual" spell check in place. What would our 'edited documents' look like? Do we know or have an idea? Would they be filled with red underlines? If so, how would we respond? Would we experience remorse from the recognition that all the red indicates a life that doesn't love our God? Would we have the desire to repent and make the needed changes?

This illustration is far more accurate and applicable than you might imagine.

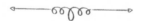

Dealing with our leaks – and we can leak!

*Matthew 13:16 But blessed are your eyes because they see
and your ears because they hear.*

Years ago a friend of ours named Paul bought a home that had been through a fire. He was good at construction and was able to do most of the work himself. The plumbing had to be redone for most of the house so he had a plumber friend come and handle all of that. When the plumber was about finished he came to check out his work. Paul was amazed by what happened.

As they were walking down the stairs into the large basement, the plumber stopped. He asked Paul, "Do you hear that?" They were both quiet and Paul didn't hear anything. The plumber said it's over there and pointed toward a corner of the basement. Paul asked him what was over there. His friend said, "A leak" – as he motioned with his finger the timing of the drips.

Sure enough, when they got to the corner, behind a bunch of stuff, there was the leak. Drops of water were falling to the floor at a frequency just like the plumber had indicated. Paul asked him why he (the plumber) could hear them while Paul couldn't. The plumber responded, "This is my business. I have my ears trained to hear such sounds."

Typically, today's verse is thought of in terms of recognizing or understanding God's truth. But today, let's consider our lives to be the plumbing system of the house and the leak(s) to be the sinful behaviors that we allow to encroach into them. (We can develop 'leaks'!)

In difficult, stressful times it seems our blindness and deafness can increase regarding negative behaviors and responses in our lives. We can get so overwhelmed by our circumstances that we lose sight of the stuff growing in our lives that is incompatible with our faith. We have 'leaks' and don't know it – and those leaks cause real problems for us and those around us.

No matter how overwhelmed we might feel, let's stop to seek the Lord and ask Him to open our eyes and ears and enable us to see and hear the 'leaks' in our lives; and enable us to repent and repair them. In difficult times, we can be 'deaf' to things in our lives that in quieter, less stressful times would not likely occur. Remember, the more difficult the situation we find ourselves in, the greater is our opportunity to glorify Jesus with how we respond.

When the difficult times end, we will look back. Hopefully it will not be with eyes of regret. We have such opportunity to live righteously in the midst of difficulty. I often think of Esther and Mordecai…"for such a time as this."

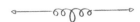

Being grateful for what He has done

Luke 17:15, 16 One of them, when he saw he was healed, came back, praising God in a loud voice. He threw himself at Jesus' feet and thanked him—and he was a Samaritan.

These verses are at the heart of the story of Jesus healing the ten lepers. All ten were cleansed but only this one returned and gave praise to God. Jesus wondered where the other nine were – why they didn't come back too.

But let's focus on the one who responded as they all should have. There's a good possibility that he led a normal life until he became a leper. Maybe he was a farmer or a shepherd. He likely had family and friends. Then came the day when he discovered that he had leprosy.

I cannot imagine the pain of being separated from wife, children, parents, friends, your home – your entire world. This separation is on top of having this dreaded disease. The leprosy forces you to live a life where you are shunned by everyone except those who have the same disease.

Then you hear about Jesus - a Nazarene who is performing all manner of miracles. Think of the discussions among the lepers as they dared to hope that Jesus might heal them. And then He does. All ten are cleansed. But this one, in his incredible joy, returns loudly praising God and finding Jesus to thank Him.

Then, imagine returning to your wife and children – to your parents and brothers and sisters and friends. This man had his life not only returned to him – but it was as though all things became new. Can you see him asking God to help him to never forget what Jesus did for him? Can you see him thanking God every day for all the normal little things that he can now do again?

Spend some time thinking about the wonderful things that Jesus has done in your life. Think of where you might be, if He hadn't responded to your cry for help. Ask the Lord to restore gratitude within you if it is missing. Hopefully, we all will be overwhelmed with gratitude for the loving kindness of our God.

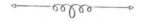

Valentine's Day: The 2 greatest love gifts given to me!

1 John 4:9, 10 ⁹This is how God showed his love among us: He sent his one and only Son into the world that we might live through him.
¹⁰This is love: not that we loved God, but that he loved us and sent his Son as an atoning sacrifice for our sins.

Valentine's Day is a special day to remember those who are especially dear to us. I tend to be the romantic type and I love to give my sweetheart flowers, particularly yellow roses or a gardenia. Today is a special day to say and to be told, "I love you." A special day to remember the love we give and the love we receive.

While the giving of cards, flowers or gifts is special, it's particularly wonderful to be together – to take the time to enjoy one another. In the midst of busy schedules, we need to slow down and be there for each other. I so relate to Thumper in the movie Bambi when Donna smiles at me and I see the twinkle in her eyes. The thrill that goes through me is beyond words. I will thump my chest with my hand just like Thumper 'thumping' the ground with his foot – and we will laugh.

The two greatest gifts in my life are gifts of love and I never dreamed that I would ever receive either of them. Never did I think that a girl would love me the way Donna does! And even more amazing is the fact that our love not only doesn't grow old – it gets better with time. We 'get to' spend every day of our lives loving one another! Our love was a gift to us from our Lord. And as wonderful as this gift of love is, He gave us one even better. He gave us Himself in Jesus.

How do we describe the absolute wonder of His love for us? It is so much more than a theological reality – it is an experiential reality that He perpetually blesses us with. He loves us and enables us to be blessed even more by loving Him in return. I still pinch myself at times because it seems like I have won the Lotto of the Ages. The day He broke through into my life (October 11, 1968) is even more stunning than the day that Donna and I met and were engaged (2 ¼ hours later – August 25, 1969). I went from lost to found; from left out to included in; from being lonely to being chosen; from having a Matterhorn of doubt to seeing it leveled and being swept up in love like I never dreamed existed.

My whole world became new – inside and out! Jesus not only became my Lord, He made me His own. The wonders of being made clean inside and being forgiven still overwhelm me. They never grow old; like His mercies they are new every morning. Please take time today not only to communicate your love to those dear to you, but to focus upon Jesus. After all, His coming for us is the very definition of love.

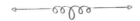

Critically essential to our lives

Exodus 19:18 Mount Sinai was covered with smoke, because the LORD descended on it in fire. The smoke billowed up from it like smoke from a furnace, the whole mountain trembled violently,

Can you imagine the excitement, wonder, awe and fear that we Christians would experience if God manifested his presence like this before us? This is our God, the God of Abraham, Isaac and Jacob, the Holy One of Israel. We have His Spirit within us and we belong to Him.

This verse describes what the Israelites saw and experienced. After spending their lives as slaves in Egypt, God rescued them miraculously. They were witnesses to the supernatural plagues that He sent upon Egypt. They experienced His presence daily in the cloud and pillar of fire by night. They experienced the parting of the Red Sea and walking through it. They knew that God considered them His.

The experience of the Israelites who saw and heard this on Mt. Sinai was dominated by fear. In response, Moses said to the people, *"Do not be afraid. God has come to test you, so that the fear of God will be with you to keep you from sinning."* Ex 20:20.

There is a strong message in this scene for us – as Christians today. This is our God and He hasn't changed. On the one hand He can be frightening beyond imagining. On the other, He tells us not to be afraid. He tests us, far more than we think He does. We experience His incredible love through Jesus yet He offers us the opportunity to fear Him in order to keep us from sinning. I think of the Apostle John falling down as though dead upon seeing Jesus in Revelation 1:17. Jesus then put his hand upon John and said, *"Do not be afraid."*

The fear of the Lord must be a vital part of our lives. It is one of the most important gifts that He has given us. It is not just awe and respect – it involves recognizing God for who He is. It is not in conflict or at odds with the love of God that we have experienced in Christ Jesus. It is the opposite side of the same coin.

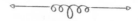

Don Schmidt

Fruit sweet to the taste vs. sour grapes

Isaiah 27:2b-3 "Sing about a fruitful vineyard: [3]I, the LORD, watch over it; I water it continually. I guard it day and night so that no one may harm it.

I grew up in Southwestern Michigan in an area known as the Fruitbelt. Orchards and vineyards were everywhere and the area had renown for its wonderful non-citrus fruit. Strawberries, peaches, apples, grapes, plums, blueberries... – it makes me hungry just writing about them. So many different varieties yet how wonderful they all were.

Every farmer and buyer wanted a fruitful season – as well as anyone who enjoyed fruit. I remember walking through vineyards and seeing the vines loaded with ripening grapes. It was particularly nice to be able to pick a bunch of grapes and eat them as we walked. There is something very special about tasting sweet fruit out in the field; that juicy taste in our mouths that says, "YES! – I want another one!!"

But there is a well known expression that covers an experience that we don't want to have. That expression is 'sour grapes'. Think of walking along, picking a grape and when you bite into it, your mouth is filled with sourness! You spit it out! Think of being in a fruit market where you are able to sample the fruit before purchasing it. Does the fruit pass the taste test?

Today's verse particularly applies to Israel, but I love its application to us, both individually and corporately. I love the picture of being a vineyard that the Lord watches over and is sung about. I want to be a fruitful vineyard and I also want to be part of a fruitful vineyard. Jesus said He is the true vine; we are the branches; and the Father is the gardener (think vine dresser). The goal is bearing much fruit – sweet fruit. If we remain in Jesus we will bear much fruit and the Father will prune us so that we will bear even more.

Think of the people that are in our lives. They can be anything from strangers to close friends or family. Also think of our lives being a vineyard where they sample the fruit that we are bearing. What if we have no fruit or if the fruit we have is sour? That is our testimony no matter what we might say. But think of the joy of having abundant fruit and the fruit is sweet. Our lives glorify our Lord Jesus and He will work with us so that we bear even more.

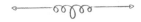

A disciple of Jesus but...

John 15:8 This is to my Father's glory, that you bear much fruit,
showing yourselves to be my disciples.

When I was a new Christian I remember being given some advice by an evangelist friend. He said it was a good idea to identify those around me who were really like Jesus and to go rub up against them in hopes that some of it would rub off. After we quit laughing, I took to heart the importance of identifying the qualities of Jesus in others and learning from them how to make them in my own life.

This led me to realize that I had to learn what the qualities of Jesus were. It was a whole lot more than just someone who is nice or pleasant to be around. Have you ever had a friend who was nice but cheated at games you played? What about friends who would talk about Jesus in a great way, but then they would go out and involve themselves in immorality?

Or being a sales person and stretching the truth regarding their products in order to get the sale? What about not following through on commitments made, leaving it to others to pick up the loose ends? What about someone one who is nice with everyone but has a habit of taking their frustrations out on their spouse? They might be wonderful to their spouse most of the time, but with some degree of frequency they let their anger fly wounding the one they say they love the most.

This was the one that I was so guilty of 25+ years ago. I was so blind to the anger I would let fly at home. I had to come to grips with the reality that in spite of all wonderful things I did for and with my wife, this one "fruit" was undermining it all. I was so embarrassed that my grasp of the obvious in this area was so totally malfunctioning. Fortunately, God dealt with it and me, and our marriage became better and stronger than ever. Using the fruit illustration we've been talking about, it was like seeing a beautiful apple and turning it in our hands and finding it rotten on the back. Thankfully, repentance and forgiveness works!! Jesus can touch that "apple" and make it rich and new.

The simple reality is that we don't become perfect overnight – or in a lifetime. But when we are truly disciples of Jesus, the Holy Spirit enables us to more and more walk in His ways. We are continually being transformed into His image. We learn to recognize our sins much more quickly so that Godliness flourishes in every area of our lives. No matter where we are or what we're doing or who we're doing it with, we want our lives to glorify our Father in Heaven. This comes by bearing the fruit consistent with being full-time disciples of Jesus.

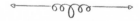

Don Schmidt

The fear of the Lord is wonderful

The fear of the Lord

As we consider the fear of the Lord, take a moment and think of the story of Pinocchio. A wooden puppet becomes a real boy. Something inanimate becomes alive and vibrantly real. For many the fear of the Lord is a static inanimate thing – and not particularly attractive. But that is such a misperception.

The good news is that the Lord will enable us to see and understand how vibrantly wonderful the fear of the Lord is, and how valuable it is for us to possess it. Listed below are a number of verses that speak of the fear of the Lord. It truly is a multi-facetted treasure for us.

- 2 Chronicles 17:10 *The fear of the LORD fell on all the kingdoms of the lands surrounding Judah, so that they did not make war with Jehoshaphat.*

- Proverbs 1:7a *The fear of the LORD is the beginning of knowledge*

- Proverbs 9:10a *The fear of the LORD is the beginning of wisdom*

- Proverbs 14:27 *The fear of the LORD is a fountain of life, turning a man from the snares of death.*

- Proverbs 16:6b *through the fear of the LORD a man avoids evil*

- Proverbs 22:4 *Humility and the fear of the LORD bring wealth and honor and life*

- In the New Testament in Acts 5:11 it talks of great fear seizing the whole church because of events involving Ananias and Sapphira.

- Acts 9:31 *Then the church throughout Judea, Galilee and Samaria enjoyed a time of peace. It was strengthened; and encouraged by the Holy Spirit, it grew in numbers, living in the fear of the Lord.*

Hopefully these verses will produce a desire to learn more about this important subject. One of the more practical applications for me over the years was *"through the fear of the Lord a man avoids evil"* coupled with the verse from Numbers *"your sin will find you out"* At times my motivation wasn't what it should be, but I didn't sin. This is also an example of the fear of the Lord is the beginning of wisdom. Not sinning is always wise.

A Scripture that always moves me is Revelation 1:17 *"When I saw him, I fell at his feet as though dead. Then he placed his right hand on me and said: "Do not be afraid. I am the First and the Last. "*This is John's response to seeing Jesus.

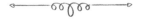

Expressions of love negated by our actions

Proverbs 8:17 I love those who love me, and those who seek me find me.

Donna and I are going to celebrate our 49th anniversary this year. They have truly been wonderful years and my heart is to learn to love her more and more with each passing day.

But in the early 90s we went through a time of difficulty that could have ended our marriage. I loved Donna, or so I thought, except I was doing all kinds of things that were a mass of contradictions. I would tell her of my love, take her on dates and trips, buy her cards and flowers, help around the house, etc…

On the other hand, I would walk away from her when she was talking to me or just ignore her. I would lose my temper with her. My frustrations with work were taken out on her. My anger would flare and she got so she never knew when I was going to vent or even why. There was no infidelity or physical abuse – it was all thoughtlessness, carelessness and blindness on my part. All too often I was a real jerk. This all exploded out as my oldest son John and I were leaving for a few days on the Outer Banks. Fortunately, a Northeaster arrived just as we got there so I got to face this situation instead of fishing.

I have a notebook from that weekend with pages of things I was doing wrong – things that were communicating "I don't love you!" These things were effectively undermining and obliterating all the good things I was doing that were speaking of my love. God in His goodness turned me every way but loose that weekend. He opened my eyes and let me see all the contradictions between my expressions of love and the actions of my life.

The Lord just did a wonder in me at the beach, and I needed it because I came home to a very hurting wife. Fortunately, our commitment to Jesus and to each other trumped everything. The Lord provided a marvelous Christian counselor who was priceless. Although it took months, the Lord brought us through. Our marriage wasn't put back together – it was transformed – from a caterpillar to a butterfly!

This experience with Donna had a profound impact on my relationship with the Lord. It made me aware of how blind I could be – how my expressions of love could be negated by my actions. The good things I do being trumped by my sin – sin I could be blind to see.

Loving God is the most important thing we can ever do. We don't want anything in our lives that undermines that. We want to love Him more and more. The marvelous thing is that the more we genuinely love Him, the more we experience His love for us.

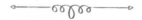

A priceless gift - the most powerful dream I've ever had

Ephesians 5:25 Husbands, love your wives, just as Christ loved the church and gave himself up for her,

This morning I woke up thinking about the pain of couples who quit loving one another. I was reminded of a dream that is unquestionably the most powerful and vivid dream I've ever had. This dream occurred several years after Donna and I went through our marital difficulties (1992) that were due primarily to me – my being unkind and behaving like a jerk. At the time of the dream, our marriage had become the best it had ever been. But in this dream Donna and I had divorced one another and that was the given for what then happened.

In the dream I walked into a small room and there in front of me was a small narrow table with Jesus sitting on one side of the table and a chair opposite Him. I sat down across from Him and looked up into His face. I don't remember what he looked like but I will never forget his eyes and the tones in His voice.

With a smile on his face and joy in His voice He looked at me and said, "Tell me how you loved my daughter who I gave to you to be your wife." I did not say anything as my heart sank. (Remember in the context of the dream we had divorced.) His smile vanished and there was no longer any joy in His voice when He began a series of rhetorical questions. By the rising tone in His voice with each question, He knew the answers.

With great deliberation Jesus asked, "What do you mean you didn't love her?!" "What do you mean you left her?!!" What do you mean you divorced her?!!!!" I cannot begin to describe the shame and distress that I experienced in the dream; hearing my Lord's voice say again and again with growing incredulity and disapproval, "WHAT DO YOU MEAN…." He wasn't yelling, but if you've ever been called on the carpet and confronted by your father or a boss for serious mistakes you've made, you get the idea.

Then, all of a sudden, in the dream, I was Donna and the scene repeated itself. Jesus asked with a smile and joy in His voice, "Tell me how you loved my son who I gave to you to be your husband." When He began the "What do you mean…" questions I immediately woke up. What a mixture of pain and joy – pain at remembering the dream – joy and relief in knowing that Donna and I truly loved one another and had not divorced.

This dream was a priceless gift to me because it allowed me to see and experience the incredible importance that our Lord places upon marriage. It also gave me a gut-wrenching taste of displeasing Him. I cannot begin to describe how excruciatingly painful that was – and still is. I pray that I never forget it.

But importantly, the dream generated a core conviction in the depth of my being that loving my wife is a primary way that I love Jesus. If I don't love her, I don't love Him – and He and His Word describe what love is. Love is a whole lot more than affection. What joy there is in waking up each day able to love our Lord and love our spouse!

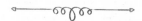

An important lesson from our white and pink dogwood tree

James 1:27 Religion that God our Father accepts as pure and faultless is this: to look after orphans and widows in their distress and to keep oneself from being polluted by the world.

I would like us to focus on the last thought of this verse, "to keep oneself from being polluted by the world." It involves the disparity between the lives many Christians lead and the lives Scriptures call them to.

My parents had a young dogwood tree in their backyard that had pink and white flowers. The flowers were all supposed to be pink and they wondered how this could be happening. We called a family friend who had a nursery and he had the answer. He told us if we examined the trunk of the tree, we would likely see two intertwined trunks growing out of the ground. In the grafting process, somehow the natural growth (white) was able to take hold and grow along side the grafted (pink).

Sure enough, it was just as he said. We had to carefully identify which trunk was which and cut off the trunk with white flowers at the ground. If we didn't, the natural, wild dogwood would eventually eliminate the grafted in – the pink would disappear and the tree would be entirely white. When we cut off the trunk with the white flowers, we had to be careful as we separated them and removed the white. The two "trees" were totally intertwined with each other.

This is a frighteningly wonderful illustration of our lives in Christ. He intends for our lives to show forth the "pink attributes" – the grafted in desirable ones that come from walking in His ways. If we don't live as He directs us, we produce the old nature "white attributes" – that come from being polluted by the world. If we try to have it both ways, the result is an intertwining of pink and white – righteous and unrighteous – and the unfortunate message that sends to those around us. Left undealt with, the unrighteous white will slowly replace the righteous pink.

May we live lives that only produce the righteous attributes of Him.

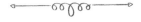

The life we 'get to' live

Matthew 5:16 Let your light so shine before men that they may see your moral excellence and your praiseworthy, noble, and good deeds and recognize and honor and praise and glorify your Father Who is in heaven. Amplified

Think of it! We have the opportunity to live our lives in such way as to bring praise and honor to God. We get to live lives of righteousness and do good works that bless others and honor Him. We get to be extensions of Him. We don't do it out of obligation – but out of love and gratitude for the amazing life that He has given us in Jesus.

Think of the attributes of people you interact with in normal situations. Those attributes that you like – patience, kindness, goodness, love, truthfulness, helpfulness, honesty, humility, gratitude to name a few. Isn't it refreshing to interact with people whose lives are characterized by such qualities? Whether you're at work, or in a store or wherever – how noticeable it is when those around us demonstrate such positive traits.

Unfortunately, all too often, we experience the negative attributes of people, particularly in difficult situations, or when they are rushed or simply preoccupied. More difficult still is when the ones acting negatively are Christians – or claiming to be. The question then becomes how are we going to respond? Will it be as they are treating us? Or will we treat them the way we wished they were treating us – in the way Scripture instructs us to?

It's amazing what kindness can do when it's offered in response to unkindness; – or patience to impatience – helpfulness to selfishness – honesty to dishonesty – courtesy to rudeness. Sometimes the only affect will be within the conscience of the ill-mannered person as they walk away thinking about your positive behavior. Other times, it can produce an immediate change where they respond positively.

But the issue isn't really them and their behavior. The issue is us and the attributes we demonstrate to those around us – day in and day out. What kind of co-worker, friend, relative, spouse, parent, neighbor, teammate, classmate, lab partner are we? The more our lives are characterized by Godly attributes, the greater the positive impact on those around us will be.

These Godly attributes are the praiseworthy, noble, and good deeds we all can do. They are vital components of the light we are to shine forth. They bring honor and glory to our God and blessing to all those around us.

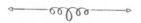

Is our witness a glow or a glare?

Matthew 5:14 You are the light of the world. A city on a hill cannot be hidden.

Years ago a wonderful Christian friend of ours named Hal was hired to manage a type of music store by a major corporation. They informed him that they were giving him a young salesman who had all kinds of potential but it wasn't being realized.

This was due to a problem he had - he was forever witnessing to employees and customers about his Christian faith. He was more interested in witnessing than he was in doing his job. Hal was informed that this was the young man's last chance. If he didn't turn it around, he would be fired.

Hal called the young man into his office. After talking a bit, he asked the young man to take the lampshade off the lamp that was on an end table next to them and to turn the lamp on high so that the light was at its brightest. He then had the young man look directly at the light and Hal asked him to describe what he was experiencing. The young man complained that the glare of the light was uncomfortable to look at.

Hal then put the lampshade on the lamp and asked him to now describe his experience. He said that the light was attractive and pleasant to look at. Hal explained that with the lampshade, he was seeing a glow. Without the lampshade, he was seeing a glare. A glow attracts and a glare repels.

The same was true of his Christian witness. God wanted his witness done wisely, so that it was a glow – not a glare. It was also critical that his manner of working not compromise or undermine the testimony of his faith. By witnessing the way he had been doing and by not doing his job, he was coming on with a glare.

Fortunately, the young man was teachable and embraced the wisdom from Hal. He became the star salesman that everyone knew he could be, and importantly, he eliminated the compulsiveness of his witnessing. He was still able to share his faith, but with Hal's help he did so in a manner that drew people to him and to the Lord rather than pushing them away.

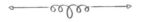

God's grace is never missing

2 Corinthians 12:9a But he said to me, "My grace is sufficient for you, for my power is made perfect in weakness."

Have you ever had the experience of trying to put something together only to discover a key part is missing? Or getting a group together to address an issue at work and someone vital to solving the problem is unable to attend?

I know there have been numerous times when my wife is making something in the kitchen and she calls me to run to the store to get a missing ingredient. Sometimes you can get by with what's missing or substitute something similar. But often times there is no getting around the problem posed by a key item being missing.

Fortunately the missing 'key part' problem never applies to God's grace. It's always in sufficient supply for every situation we encounter. Can you imagine the uncertainty and trauma we would go through if God routinely withheld His grace from us? Think of the nightmare if He allowed temptations to come our way that were more than we could bear. Our faith would be radically impacted – and undermined.

Faith and grace are there for us to apply to everything we do. We need them for the problems we face AND how we respond to the problems. Suppose we are asked to do something and we do it in a negative manner. In God's scheme of things, it's possible that the only reason we were asked to help was for Him to reveal our attitude problem to us; that we were not walking in His provision for us.

One of the most helpful paraphrases I've been taught applies to the Lord's Prayer and to the *"Lead us not into temptation"* phrase. The teacher paraphrased this, "Lord let there not be anything in my heart that would cause you to put me to the test." God never tempts anyone (with evil) (James 1:13, 14) but He will allow us to encounter situations that reveal problems we have that we might be unaware of – like spiritual termites.

What a privilege we have in God enabling us to respond in a way that glorifies Him no matter what we encounter. The key is for our faith to focus more and more on Him throughout each day recognizing that He and His grace are there for us to respond righteously.

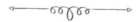

Do we know what the 'right thing' is?

Joshua 23:11 So be very careful to love the LORD your God.

I once was able to attend a meeting in which the author Stephen Covey spoke (7 Habits of Highly Effective People). There was a large crowd and the hall that he spoke in was in the round. He was in the center and the crowd surrounded him. He asked everyone to raise their arm and point in the direction that they thought was north. There were people pointing in all manner of directions.

He proceeded to place a compass on an overhead and was able to identify which way was north. He made a comment that has always stuck with me. He noted that, **"Which direction is north is not subject to public opinion!"** It is what it is and we cannot change it. Life is filled with principles that are true.

Some time ago a newspaper, The Tennessean, had an article on cheating with cell phones in high schools and colleges. The writer (Jennifer Brooks) noted "In one recent study, more than a third of teens with cell phones admit to using them to cheat, at least once. Half of them admit to cheating with the help of the Internet. Worse, the survey released by Common Sense Media two years earlier found that many of the students saw nothing wrong with their actions."

Think about that last sentence – students cheating and seeing nothing wrong with their actions. Even more distressing is the whole-hearted embrace of sexual impurity and immorality by society. Compounding the problem are decisions from courts and legislatures that call evil good and good evil. From God's perspective, sin is sin. Our opinion doesn't change the fact. We are surrounded by a culture that okays all manner of behavior that is incompatible with loving God.

Becoming passionate about loving God makes dealing with the reality of the world around us much more viable. We recognize our utter dependence upon His Spirit and Scripture to instruct us how to do it. We want our lives filled with righteous thoughts, attitudes and actions. We want our eyes open to see things in our lives that shouldn't be there – some of which we might think are okay, but in God's sight they're not. He gives us the grace to repent and change. Loving Him is to be our passion and goal.

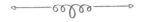

It was God's plan for Joseph

Part 1 in a series on Joseph: *Genesis 42:21 They said to one another,
"Surely we are being punished because of our brother. We saw how distressed he
was when he pleaded with us for his life, but we would not listen; that's
why this distress has come upon us."*

Today's verse is from the remarkable story of Joseph. His brothers have come to Egypt for grain and find themselves being treated as spies by the Governor of Egypt who is Joseph. He had recognized them and when they bowed down to him, he remembered his dreams about them. But they did not recognize him.

Joseph spoke harshly to them and held them in custody for 3 days. When told that they would be allowed to return home by leaving one of the brothers in custody in Egypt, the brothers spoke today's verse to one another. In spite of his pleadings, they remembered their cruelty to him.

Picture the scene 21 years earlier when Joseph found his brothers near Dothan. A young man of about 17, he was simply obeying his father in finding his brothers, to see how they were doing. He had no idea what lay in store for him – what God had in store for him. When he got to them, they stripped him of his richly ornamented robe and threw him into a dry cistern.

Can you imagine what Joseph was experiencing? He faced the anger of ten older brothers who wanted to kill him. It's possible that he heard them debating over whether to kill him or not and how they would cover it up if they did. At this time, the caravan of Midianite merchants passed by. Joseph finds himself being pulled up out of the cistern, not to be set free or killed, but to be sold as a slave and taken to Egypt.

Think of Joseph as the caravan moved on to Egypt. Did he have any hope of seeing his father again or his brother Benjamin? Did he have any thoughts of the dreams that he'd had? Was he grateful for simply being alive - that they hadn't killed him? Did he cry out to God?

Did he have any idea that being sold into slavery by his brothers was God's plan for his life?

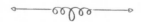

Don Schmidt

Things happen…how will we respond?

Part 2 in a series on Joseph: *Genesis 37:36 Meanwhile, the Midianites sold Joseph in Egypt to Potiphar, one of Pharaoh's officials, the captain of the guard.*

Life is filled with all kinds of experiences – many good, some not-so-good, and some downright awful. I think at this point, Joseph probably viewed his situation in the downright awful category. How do you adjust from being free and part of a family – deeply loved by your father, and suddenly find yourself as a slave – sold by your brothers no less – in a foreign land?

Joseph had a short time to come to a decision on how he was going to respond to his situation. He might have viewed escape as impossible and viewed slavery as his lot for the rest of his life. His attitudes and demeanor could have played an important role in who he was purchased by. Did he realize or have a clue that the events of his life were being orchestrated by the God of his fathers?

He was purchased by Potiphar, one of Pharaoh's officials, the captain of the guard. At this point, the Scriptures note that, *"The Lord was with Joseph and he prospered…"* – so much so, that Potiphar saw that the Lord was with Joseph and was giving him success in whatever he did.

Remember, this is occurring long before Moses and the law. Joseph's knowledge of God would have been from the stories passed on by Abraham, Isaac and his father Jacob. Yet Joseph responded rightly to what was occurring in his life.

While it is difficult for us to relate to being sold into slavery, there are those in the world right now that are having this happen to them. Famine, plague, war, bombings, slavery, natural disasters – they are occurring now, all around us. In our lives it might be loss of jobs, or loved ones – disappointments, accidents, bankruptcy, acts of violence. These things happen - things that we don't want – wouldn't choose – wouldn't want to happen even to people we don't like. But they happen to us or people we care about. God expects us to respond consistently with our faith – not like the world responds.

As Christians, our Lord has promised to never leave us or forsake us. In the midst of every situation, no matter what happens, He is there. There is nothing He cannot redeem. Pray that this knowledge of the Lord being with you - ALWAYS - becomes a rock-solid reality in your heart. It will transform you – and those around you.

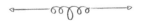

When temptation comes...

Part 3 in a series on Joseph: *Genesis 39:9 "No one is greater in this house than I am. My master has withheld nothing from me except you, because you are his wife. How then could I do such a wicked thing and sin against God?"*

The story of Joseph has such amazing twists and turns. He's a young man of 17 loved by his father Jacob, who gave him a richly ornamented robe as a sign of his love. This provoked hatred in his brothers because they saw that Jacob loved Joseph more than he loved them. Then Joseph received the two dreams in which it appeared that his family was bowing before him. This made his brothers hate him even more.

Shortly thereafter, the brothers sold him into slavery, instead of killing him. Once in Egypt he was purchased by Potiphar, captain of the guard for Pharaoh. God proceeded to bless Joseph in everything he did and Potiphar recognized it. So Potiphar put Joseph in charge of his household and everything he owned. Everything Joseph did was being blessed.

Into this success came serious temptation in the form Potiphar's wife, who was attracted to this handsome young man. Day after day, she repeatedly tried to get Joseph to sleep with her. Joseph recognized the temptation for what it was and is – a wicked thing; a betrayal of Potiphar's trust; and a sin against God. When she finally grabbed his cloak to get him to come to bed with her, he fled and ran out of the house. He refused to yield to sin.

What an example for us. In Christ, we have the opportunity to be a blessing to all around us. But in the midst of it, temptations will come. Pray that we have the eyes to see them, as Joseph did – and also the firm resolve to resist them, no matter what. Sin is sin. The enemy of our souls wants us to sin against God – who allows the temptations to come. God wants to see us stand firm against them - and flee if need be, in order to affirm who we are in Him – to demonstrate the quality of His workmanship in us.

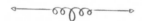

How to respond to unjust suffering...

Part 4 in a series on Joseph: *1 Peter 2:19 For it is commendable if a man bears up under the pain of unjust suffering because he is conscious of God.*

We have a tendency to expect positive results when we do the right thing. Nothing wrong with that, but we must be aware that often that isn't the case. Peter is talking about us bearing up under the pain of unjust suffering because we are conscious of God – just like Joseph did.

Joseph refused to yield to the temptation presented by Potiphar's wife. Day after day she talked to him and he repeatedly refused to go to bed with her or even be with her. When she caught him by his cloak one day, they were the only ones in the house and Joseph fled. She proceeded to lie to Potiphar accusing Joseph of being the one wanting her.

It appears that Potiphar believed his wife for Scripture says, "he burned with anger." I've often wondered if he ever asked for Joseph's side of the story – and would he have believed him if he did. Potiphar then took Joseph and put him in prison. Joseph did what was right and wound up in jail. In spite of doing right, because he was conscious of God, he experienced even more pain of unjust suffering.

"But while Joseph was there in the prison, the Lord was with him; He showed him kindness and granted him favor in the eyes of the prison warden." Gen 39:20b, 21 In the midst of it all, Joseph could see that God was there with him.

Do we understand the importance of maintaining a godly attitude and godly behavior when in trying situations? We too can be falsely accused. We can be fired or receive unfavorable treatment because we refuse to go along with illegal or unethical demands. We can lose sales or clients because we are unwilling to lie or deceive. We can face the loss of "friends" because we refuse to participate in activities that are sinful. If our focus is Jesus, we will make the right decisions and do it with grace – not self-righteousness. Our goal is to do it right. Wherever we wind up, the Lord will be there with us.

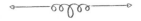

The lesson of shackles and chains for us

Part 5 in a series on Joseph: *Psalm 105:17-19 ...and He sent a man before them— Joseph, sold as a slave. They bruised his feet with shackles, his neck was put in irons, till what he foretold came to pass, till the word of the LORD proved him true.*

Prior to being sold into slavery, Joseph was given two dreams by the Lord. In the first, Joseph and his brothers each had a sheaf of grain. His sheaf stood upright, and the sheaves of his brothers gathered around it and bowed down to it. Upon telling his brothers this dream, they hated Joseph all the more.

In the second dream, the sun, the moon and eleven stars were bowing down to him. He shared this dream with his father, Jacob, as well as with his brothers. Jacob rebuked him asking about the dream, *"Shall your mother and I and your brothers indeed come to bow down to the earth before you?"*

Twenty years before the famine would arrive, God gave Joseph these dreams. I wonder what he thought about them. Did he think they would come true sometime soon? Joseph had no idea what coming. Instead of a life of blessing, growth and prosperity with his family – he experienced the opposite: betrayal by his brothers, sold as a slave, taken to Egypt, harsh treatment, blessed as a slave for an Egyptian master, and then imprisoned because he wouldn't sin.

<u>We tend to overlook the shackles and bruises on his feet, and the irons around his neck. He wasn't politely taken to Egypt – he was forcibly and painfully taken. All of this was done because of God's plan.</u> Joseph's dreams were going to come true – his family was going to bow before him. But first would come this path of preparation that God had for Joseph.

It's so important that we recognize that God has plans for each of us – plans that require preparation. While we probably won't encounter anything like Joseph did, God will do whatever it takes to prepare us and enable us to do what He wants us to do. Many things might be hard, but we must learn to embrace them – looking to the Lord to accomplish His plan and purpose within us. Hopefully we will emulate Joseph and walk faithfully through all we encounter, being conscious of God's presence with us – leading us on.

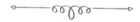

Being a slave and a prisoner was irrelevant!

Part 6 in a series on Joseph: *Genesis 40:6-7 When Joseph came to them the next morning, he saw that they were dejected. So he asked Pharaoh's officials who were in custody with him in his master's house, "Why are your faces so sad today?"*

Have you noticed how nice it is to work with thoughtful people who do their jobs well? They are good examples to emulate in terms of their work habits, but their thoughtfulness is something special. They are the ones, who notice things; who go out of their way to help or cheer people up. They care about their jobs but they care about those around them.

This verse today has always blessed me because it speaks of such quality in Joseph. The Lord was blessing Joseph in prison just as He had in Potiphar's house, giving him success. The warden had put Joseph in charge of all those held in the prison, and he was made responsible for all that was done there (Gen 39:22).

Joseph was in charge – basically running the place, but he wasn't bitter about all that had happened to him. He wasn't inwardly focused so that he was blind to what was going on around him. He noticed that two of the prisoners were dejected and asked them why. He cared – and he didn't keep it hidden.

Earlier when he refused to go to bed with Potiphar's wife, it wasn't just because it was a sin against God. Joseph saw it as wickedness because it was also a betrayal of the trust that his master had in him. Joseph had honor and integrity. The fact that he was a slave and a prisoner was irrelevant. The quality in Joseph just continued to shine.

The Lord gives us opportunities every day to let His light shine through us to bless others. What a privilege that is. Giving someone an encouraging word, being kind or helpful is like giving a thirsty person a drink of water. Remember Joseph, that he did it in the context of doing his responsibilities well. Integrity and thoughtfulness – may our lives have them in abundance.

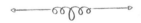

Why was Joseph there?

Part 7 in a series on Joseph: *Genesis 40:8 "We both had dreams," they answered,*
"but there is no one to interpret them." Then Joseph said to them,
"Do not interpretations belong to God? Tell me your dreams."

Joseph asked these two men, *"Why are your faces so sad today?"* They responded by telling him that they each had a dream and they didn't know what the dreams meant and they thought there wasn't anyone to interpret them. Because Joseph asked the question, he was in a position to address their concern.

This event of Joseph interpreting their dreams would later play a crucial role in Joseph becoming Governor of Egypt. But let's take a moment to reflect on the sequence of events that were responsible for Joseph being there.

Joseph encountered these two prisoners because they had been assigned to his care. He was able to ask them his question, because he was in prison with them. He was in prison because Potiphar's wife lied. She lied because Joseph refused to sin with her. He was in her house because he was a slave purchased by Potiphar, her husband. He was purchased by Potiphar because his brothers sold him into slavery. He was sold into slavery because God sent him ahead. Joseph was God's man to deal with the coming famine.

God chose the path that Joseph needed to take – with all its pain and difficulty. God was with him, blessing him – helping him. Each step of the way, Joseph was exactly where God wanted him to be – and was faithful in allowing God to make him the man he was destined to be.

We have the same opportunity, just much different circumstances. There are all manner of challenging and difficult things that God will take us through in accomplishing His purposes and transforming us into the image of Jesus. Our focus must be on Him and not on ourselves or our difficulties. By responding to the Spirit working in us, our lives increasingly speak of the love and wonder of our God. We are able to joyfully follow Him, wherever He leads, and endure any difficulties in order to become the men and women He wants us to be – and to be His hands extended to those we encounter.

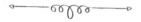

Without anger or a desire for revenge

Part 8 in a series on Joseph: *Genesis 40:14-15* *[14]"But when all goes well with you, remember me and show me kindness; mention me to Pharaoh and get me out of this prison. [15]For I was forcibly carried off from the land of the Hebrews, and even here I have done nothing to deserve being put in a dungeon."*

When the chief cupbearer and the baker told Joseph they both had dreams and there was no one to interpret them, Joseph's response was, *"Do not interpretations belong to God? Tell me your dreams."* So they did.

The chief cupbearer told him his dream of a vine with three branches; of grapes forming and him squeezing them into Pharaoh's cup and putting the cup in Pharaoh's hand. Joseph then told him that within three days, Pharaoh would restore him to his position as his personal cupbearer.

The baker heard the favorable interpretation so he shared his dream with Joseph. Unfortunately for him, Joseph informed him that Pharaoh was going to execute him by hanging him in a tree within three days. On the third day, things happened exactly as Joseph foretold.

In the middle of this narrative is a real gem that most don't notice. The verses for today are where Joseph shares his situation with the cupbearer in a truly righteous appeal for help. Read the verse again and note the tenor of the words. The appeal Joseph makes is done without the anger or a desire for revenge that we would typically expect. Even though Joseph has endured 13 years of slavery and prison, he is simply stating things that are true—and doing it in a way that is acceptable! On top of that he was betrayed by family. All these years he has been able to righteously carry the wrongs that have been done to him.

What an example for us! We all have had wrongs done to us. Joseph demonstrates that it is possible to righteously carry the knowledge of wrongs done in a way that is pleasing to God.

His trust was in God

Part 9 in a series on Joseph: *Genesis 40:23 The chief cupbearer, however, did not remember Joseph; he forgot him.*

Today's devotional is special to me because it describes an insight that became clear to me the evening while writing it, regarding Joseph's response to his experience with the cupbearer. Even though I've read this story many times, my thoughts had been more on how disappointed and distressed Joseph might have been. Even though Scripture is silent on this issue, his overall life suggests that this different perspective could be a more accurate understanding of Joseph's response to this event. The principle involved is one that has proved priceless to me in its impact on my life over the years.

As I was writing, I began wondering about what Joseph's response was in the days following the chief cupbearer being restored. I imagine that he had real hope that his situation was about to change – that he would be set free. Maybe he thought about returning to his father Jacob; or getting married and having a family. Maybe he thought he might have to stay in Egypt, but at least he would be out of prison. As the days passed and became weeks, he realized that no one was coming to free him.

Today's verse explains why – the cupbearer forgot him! What a disappointment to live with each day – and it would be, if it was his focus. But I don't think it was. Instead of looking at the failure of the cupbearer to do anything or even to communicate that Pharaoh refused to act, I believe Joseph had his focus elsewhere. His focus was on God!

Yes there would have been disappointment to deal with, but I believe Joseph was encouraged by the reality that God had intervened into his situation by giving him the interpretation of the dreams. He saw the interpretations come true. He knew that he could not have interpreted them without God. The depth of his pain and disappointment was overshadowed by his see seeing God manifest Himself in his life. The fact that Joseph didn't understand the 'Why' of it was irrelevant. He knew he didn't have to understand. God was with him and he would trust his God.

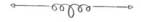

God's plan required Joseph to be in prison

Part 10 in a series on Joseph: *Genesis 41:1 When two full years
had passed, Pharaoh had a dream.*

"Did Joseph spend two more years in prison due to a cupbearer's faulty memory?" Isn't that a great question? A companion question to it is, "Did God intend for Joseph to be in the dungeon for those two additional years?"

None of the magicians or wise men of Egypt could interpret Pharaoh's dreams. It was then that the cupbearer remembered Joseph and recounted his experience with Joseph while in prison. Pharaoh sent for Joseph. Why did the cupbearer forget?

One of the important things for us to recognize in this situation is that God was working both in Joseph and in the bigger situation that he found himself in. 'Stuff' was going on that he knew nothing about. The timetable that God was working on involved Joseph, but it also involved a much bigger picture of people and events. When things were in place, pharaoh had a dream. Isn't it interesting that one of the individuals who had been in prison with Joseph was the cupbearer – who just happened to be with Pharaoh when this dream happened?! Isn't it interesting that the cupbearer too had experienced a dream with Joseph and had been witness to his interpretation being fulfilled?!

Isn't it interesting that none of Pharaoh's wise men or magicians could interpret the dream – thus setting the stage for the cupbearer's memory of Joseph to be turned back on. In the meantime, Joseph was just faithfully performing the duties assigned to him in prison. He probably had no idea how God was involved in the orchestration of events until after events unfolded and he looked back in amazement!

This is such an important principle for us to recognize and embrace. God is at work in our lives and in the circumstances around us to bring about His plan and purposes. We are not alone. We are not left to ourselves. Many times the issue of timing is vital. Things don't happen because they are dependent upon other things – possibly beyond our control – happening first.

It seems clear to me that Joseph spent two more years in prison because that is where God wanted him to be. <u>He was **not** subject to a cupbearer's faulty memory.</u> If anything, I think God caused the cupbearer to forget. God was working in Joseph and until the time of Pharaoh's dream, the Lord wanted him there – in the dungeon. Of course God could have given Pharaoh the dreams two years earlier. But that wasn't His plan.

It is critical that we recognize that God is intimately involved in our lives – particularly in the difficult seasons that we go through. If our prayers don't bring relief, it could be that God wants us to be exactly where we are, and is going to keep us there – just like He did with Joseph in prison. Hopefully, we will respond as faithfully as Joseph.

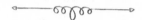

Called from a dungeon

Part 11 in a series on Joseph: *Genesis 41:14 So Pharaoh sent for Joseph, and he was quickly brought from the dungeon. When he had shaved and changed his clothes, he came before Pharaoh.*

It's clear from Scripture that Joseph had favor and responsibility while in prison, but I find the word dungeon to be noteworthy. Prison is bad enough, but dungeon sounds even worse. It had been two years since he interpreted the cupbearer's dream. It had been thirteen years since he was sold into slavery by his brothers. Had Joseph resigned himself to being a prisoner for the rest of his life?

I wonder what Joseph was doing when word came that he was to be 'quickly' brought before Pharaoh. Think of the impact in our lives if the Secret Service showed up at our door and told us to quickly change because they were taking us immediately to see the President! Had Joseph given up any hope of the cupbearer remembering to speak to Pharaoh about him? Had word spread about Pharaoh's dreams? What was going through Joseph's mind as he was brought to Pharaoh?

The important thing is that Joseph had lived righteously during all these years. The Lord was with him and he prospered. He wasn't a complainer. He didn't allow his circumstances to negatively alter his attitudes and how he behaved. In spite of such negative and underserved surroundings, Joseph honored the Lord in how he lived.

When Pharaoh told Joseph that he had heard it said of him that he could hear a dream and interpret it, Joseph responded in humility and confidence. *"I cannot do it,"* Joseph replied to Pharaoh, *"but God will give Pharaoh the answer he desires."* Gen 41:16. What a wonderful combination! I picture a strong, young man, with a good spirit about him, acknowledging that while he cannot do it, God can and would do it. He wasn't fearful. Joseph behaved the same whether he was in the dungeon or in the throne room of Pharaoh. What an example for us.

Being ready to walk through the door
of opportunity

Part 12 in a series on Joseph: *Genesis 41:38 So Pharaoh asked them, "Can we find anyone like this man, one in whom is the spirit of God?"*

Joseph has just interpreted Pharaoh's dreams. But he's done more than that. He has given instructions on what needs to be done to prepare for this famine that God is sending upon Egypt. Key to this will be Pharaoh finding a wise and discerning man to put in charge of the land of Egypt. Pharaoh chooses Joseph.

This moment in Joseph's life speaks to me of a number of wonderful principles in Scripture. I think of Matthew 5:16 first of all: *"In the same way, let your light shine before men, that they may see your good deeds and praise your Father in heaven."* Joseph didn't know what was coming. He was simply called to appear and given an opportunity. He didn't try to negotiate for himself his release from prison. He spoke the truth. Pharaoh recognized that the divine was present – that there was more going on here than simply a man giving an answer.

I think of Luke 12:11, 12 *"When you are brought before synagogues, rulers and authorities, do not worry about how you will defend yourselves or what you will say, 12for the Holy Spirit will teach you at that time what you should say."* Although the context of this verse deals with the defense of believers, the principle of the Holy Spirit being with us, giving us the words to say is something we are to rely on. It is no excuse for lack of preparation, but it instructs us where our faith and trust are to be. It's not us, it's Him. Joseph's confidence was in God. His faith assured him that God would give him what was needed.

Another powerful element of our faith is expressed in Psalm 57:2 *"I cry out to God Most High, to God, who fulfills {his purpose} for me."* Joseph walked faithfully where God had put him. I'm sure he cried out to God trying to understand what had happened to him. But in the end, God's purpose was fulfilled. Joseph was prepared and ready to walk through the door of opportunity that God opened. Let us renew our commitment to our Lord and His dealings in our lives so that the same will be true of us.

Don Schmidt

Why not Benjamin?

Part 13 in a series on Joseph: *Genesis 42:3, 4 Then ten of Joseph's brothers went down to buy grain from Egypt. ⁴But Jacob did not send Benjamin, Joseph's brother, with the others, because he was afraid that harm might come to him.*

It has been about 8 years since Joseph entered the service of Pharaoh to prepare for the famine that has now arrived. It is about 21 years since he was sold into slavery by his brothers. The famine is everywhere, not just Egypt, and word has spread that there is grain available in Egypt for purchase. So Jacob instructed his sons to go to Egypt and purchase grain to save their lives. But he did not send Benjamin.

Why was Jacob afraid that harm might come to Benjamin if he sent him with his brothers? He didn't just have a suspicion – he was afraid. Twenty-one years earlier, Joseph had disappeared leaving a bloody robe – apparently killed by a wild animal. That had a devastating impact on Jacob. He mourned for Joseph many days and refused to be comforted.

One suspects that the idea of foul play by Joseph's brothers had occurred to Jacob. The brother's hatred of Joseph was as visible as was Jacob's love for him. It had been apparent to the entire family that Jacob loved Joseph and Rachel, his mother, so much more than any of the rest of them including his other wife Leah. All these years Jacob lived with the horrible suspicion that his sons had killed Joseph.

One of the sobering things in all this is that Jacob experienced 21 years of pain as part of God's plan. He not only lived with the thought that Joseph had met a cruel death, but he was also deprived of all those years of having Joseph with him. Would God do such a thing? Yes he would!

We need to come to grips with the fact that God will allow or cause all manner of things to happen that will accomplish His will - many of which are things that we would view as highly negative – yet they are part of God's plan. Often our viewpoints are far more influenced by our culture than by our understanding of God. We must learn and understand His ways and come to know Him more intimately. If we do, we can better respond with faith no matter what happens to us.

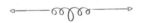

Responding rightly to offense

Part 14 in a series on Joseph: Genesis 42:6 Now Joseph was the governor of the land, the one who sold grain to all its people. So when Joseph's brothers arrived, they bowed down to him with their faces to the ground. Proverbs 18:19a An offended brother is more unyielding than a fortified city…

If anyone in Scripture had occasion to be offended and respond in kind it was Joseph. His brothers' actions resulted in him being in slavery and prison for 13 years. When he recognized his brothers when they came for wheat, he could have exercised extreme vengeance upon them. He could have made them pay for what they did to him. But he didn't.

Upon recognizing them and seeing them bow in front of him, Joseph remembered his dreams. Fortunately for them, Joseph had responded righteously to their actions and was not a man to take revenge. He did cause them a bit of grief – but nothing like he could have done. He was not ready to reveal himself to them but his actions enabled him to sustain the encounter with them. He wanted to see Benjamin and Jacob. Imagine all the thoughts that must have been running through his mind.

The example of his Godly response to their actions is so important. Taking offense and then allowing that condition to fester are to be avoided like the plague! They are a hotbed for unrighteousness. As Proverbs 18:a describes, allowing ourselves to become offended, and not dealing with it, will result in us becoming as unyielding as a fortified city. We become unresponsive to reasonable overtures from others. Unfortunately that isn't the worst of it. We become unresponsive to the Spirit of God working in us to promote righteousness. We will tend to stonewall Him just like we do everyone else.

Yes offenses can hurt and deeply wound, but we have a Savior who has made a way for us to respond with grace and forgiveness. We must be on our guard to recognize when offense happens and respond in Christlike fashion – versus yielding to the temptation to sin that it is. We begin with forgiveness and then look to Him to help us deal with all the attendant feelings we typically have. It might take some time, but it is a pathway of righteousness leading to life.

It's difficult to imagine anything happening to us to compare with what happened to Joseph. Yet he dealt with it righteously – and he did not have the new nature, freed from the power of sin that we Christians have. His focus was upon God. He is a stellar example of God's way to respond to the negative actions of others. Today, ask the Lord to show us if there is anywhere in our lives where we need to deal with this.

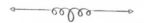

Don Schmidt

Joseph reveals himself to his brothers

Part 15 in a series on Joseph: Genesis 42:21-24a ²¹ *They said to one another, "Surely we are being punished because of our brother. We saw how distressed he was when he pleaded with us for his life, but we would not listen; that's why this distress has come on us." ²²Reuben replied, "Didn't I tell you not to sin against the boy? But you wouldn't listen! Now we must give an accounting for his blood." ²³ They did not realize that Joseph could understand them, since he was using an interpreter. ²⁴ He turned away from them and began to weep,...*

Today's verses describe one of the most poignant scenes in the whole story of Joseph. His brothers have come to Egypt to purchase grain. They encounter Joseph; he recognizes them but they do not recognize him. He then remembered his dreams about them and accuses them of being spies. In challenging them they reveal that there is another brother – the youngest – and he is with their father back in the land of Canaan. He then asserts again that they are spies and holds them in custody for 3 days.

After 3 days, he informed them what they must do to live. One of them will be held hostage and the others will return to Canaan with grain and then bring back the youngest brother to confirm they are telling the truth. It was at this point that the above exchange takes place. Here it is over 20 years later and they express their belief that they are being punished (by God) because of what they did to Joseph. Because Joseph was using a translator, the brothers had no idea he could understand what they were saying.

For the first time, Joseph heard them acknowledge that they know what they did was wrong. He also learned that Reuben, the oldest brother, was opposed to mistreating Joseph and had spoken in his behalf but they wouldn't listen to him. His father and younger brother were still alive. The dreams that he had so long ago had come true! Here he was the 2ⁿᵈ most powerful man in Egypt and his brothers who had wronged him were before him – under his control and at his mercy. What would he do?

Can you imagine all that Joseph was experiencing as he listened and participated in this exchange? His remembrance of the dreams had to be of major significance to him as he dealt with them. I wonder if it really hit home then that he was able to be there in Egypt – where God wanted him to be, in the position God wanted him to be in – only because God used his brothers to get him there. I am so grateful that Joseph is such a wonderful example of walking righteously with God in the most difficult and trying circumstances. His life has so many wonderful lessons for us to learn.

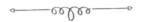

Joseph revealing God's plan

Part 16 in a series on Joseph: *Genesis 45:3 Joseph said to his brothers, "I am Joseph! Is my father still living?" But his brothers were not able to answer him, because they were terrified at his presence.*

What an amazing moment this is! Joseph's brothers didn't have a clue that they were dealing with their brother – the one they had sold into slavery over 20 years earlier! Events leading up to this moment had surely brought Joseph to mind because they were struggling with the idea that all the difficulties they had been encountering in Egypt were due to their mistreatment of Joseph.

If pressed, they probably would have thought he was dead. But regardless what his fate had been, they were likely convinced they would never see him again. Then, in the midst of this latest distressing turn of events with the cup found in Benjamin's sack, they were beside themselves with grief because Benjamin would have to remain in Egypt as a slave. Their distress was so great that it finally became more than Joseph could stand.

Joseph ordered all of his attendants out of the room and revealed himself to his brothers. All of a sudden, the brothers' distress turned into their worst nightmare! The one they describe as the 'ruler of all of Egypt' is not only the brother they sold into slavery, he is now in a position to wreck vengeance upon them. They had no idea how God had worked in Joseph's heart. Consider Joseph's next comments: Genesis 45:5-8

> *⁵And now, do not be distressed and do not be angry with yourselves for selling me here, because it was to save lives that <u>God sent me ahead of you.</u> ⁶For two years now there has been famine in the land, and for the next five years there will be no plowing and reaping. ⁷<u>But God sent me ahead of you</u> to preserve for you a remnant on earth and to save your lives by a great deliverance. ⁸"<u>So then, it was not you who sent me here, but God.</u> He made me father to Pharaoh, lord of his entire household and ruler of all Egypt.*

Think of it! Joseph had God's perspective on all that had happened to him. He recognized that his brothers were simply the tools that God had used to get him there so he could fulfill the destiny God had for him. He bore them no ill will. He wasn't just keeping himself from repaying them in kind for what they had done. God was using him to preserve for them a remnant and to save their lives. He was overjoyed!

Don Schmidt

Jacob and Joseph together at last!

Part 17 in a series on Joseph: *Genesis 45:25-26 So they went up out of Egypt and came to their father Jacob in the land of Canaan. They told him, "Joseph is still alive! In fact he is ruler of all Egypt." Jacob was stunned; he did not believe them. But when they told him everything Joseph had said to them, and when he saw the carts Joseph had sent to carry him back, the spirit of their father Jacob revived.*

The emotions associated with the realization that Joseph was still alive must have been overwhelming to Jacob. On top of that, he was ruler over all Egypt. Can you imagine the questions that went through Jacob's mind – particularly after they loaded up and were on their journey back to Egypt – the hours of travel, thinking about seeing his son again? Did he ask his sons, "How did Joseph wind up in Egypt?" "What happened?"

If he did, I wonder what they said. Would they have spoken the truth to their father? Sometime in the coming days, Jacob likely learned the truth – whether from his older sons or from Joseph. That would have been something for him to deal with. But overshadowing it all would have been the intervention of God.

There were the dreams when Joseph was a teenager. There was the reality of the dreams coming true – he was now the ruler over Egypt! How could that happen without God? Then there was the vision at Beersheba that Jacob – now called Israel by God – received after offering sacrifices to the God of his father, Isaac. God reassured him about going to Egypt.

And God spoke to Israel in a vision at night and said, *"Jacob! Jacob!" "Here I am," he replied. "I am God, the God of your father," he said. "Do not be afraid to go down to Egypt, for I will make you into a great nation there. I will go down to Egypt with you, and I will surely bring you back again. And Joseph's own hand will close your eyes."* Genesis 46:2-4.

Think of the joy and excitement that Jacob and Joseph were both experiencing – knowing that they would get to see each other again! Then the day came when Jacob arrived and Joseph saw him. Joseph threw his arms around him and wept for a long time. They had been apart for about 22 years.

The pain, the years of separation, the difficulties, the slavery, the prison, the loneliness, the sacrifices – all were part of God's plan. We need to understand that if God's plans and purposes require them, He will cause us to experience similar things. This is why it is so critical to have our faith and trust rooted firmly Him. When hard times come – and they will – He is our rock, our confidence and our hope. Our trust will be securely in Him no matter how much we don't understand. We too can be – and must be - like Joseph and walk faithfully through whatever trials may come.

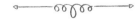

The Old Testament is such a gift to us!

Part 18 in a series on Joseph: *1 Corinthians 10:6,11 Now these things occurred as examples to keep us from setting our hearts on evil things as they did. These things happened to them as examples and were written down as warnings for us, on whom the fulfillment of the ages has come.*

We have been looking at Joseph who experienced one negative situation after another. Yet he responded faithfully and God blessed him. Those circumstances, that none of us would choose, were God's plan for him. A lesson there is that God will do the same with us. The circumstances of our lives are our testing ground. Will we respond faithfully when we find ourselves in unpleasant, difficult or very negative situations? Will our focus be upon the Lord rather than upon ourselves or our 'problems'?

The Old Testament is such a gift to us. It provides so much more than history or prophecy. It teaches us God's ways. It shows us how much God has wanted – and wants - a people to be His own and live accordingly. He wants a people that recognize His great love for them and then love Him in return.

The Lord wants a people that walk in His ways – who demonstrate from their lives that they belong to Him. It has everything to do with how we live. Do our hearts belong to Him? Disobedience, complaining, anger, revenge, idolatry, rebellion, etc… have such negative consequences and such actions and attitudes communicate the very opposite message that should come from our faith in Christ. Joseph is such an example of rightly responding in the good times and the bad.

Today's verses focus our attention on His people in the Old Testament and what happened to them. We are to look at their lives and see how they responded to God and to the situations they encountered. Their situations repeatedly gave them opportunities to affirm that they were His. We are seriously warned that they are examples for us to learn from. We are not to make the same mistakes they did.

Will we recognize and reject the sinful responses that can work their way into our lives without us even being aware of them? Will we respond like Joseph – no matter what we encounter? We have seen Joseph time and again respond righteously to what life brought him. Let us be inspired by his example to live our lives in faithfulness and righteousness thereby reflecting the love of our God to all.

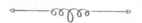

Why we can be so different

Luke 10:33 But a Samaritan, as he traveled, came where the man was;
and when he saw him, he took pity on him.

Jesus told the story of the Good Samaritan in answer to the question, "Who is my neighbor?" The story was used by Jesus to help his questioner identify who his neighbor was, since we are commanded to love our neighbors as ourselves. When Jesus finished, the questioner rightly concluded that of the three travelers, the Samaritan was the neighbor of the man who fell into the hands of the robbers, because the Samaritan had mercy on him.

Our focus today is on the Samaritan – not the other two who failed to respond. Note that when the Samaritan saw the man in need, he took pity on him. It wasn't a matter of the Samaritan having an internal argument within himself on what was the right thing to do in this situation. Hi kindness and generosity were expressions of his life. The Samaritan was a loving man.

We Christians want to be the same kind of loving people that he was. We want our love to be genuine – a love that moves us to respond with right hearts. This is something that we grow in. By responding to the situations we see, He opens our eyes to see more. God is working within each of us so that kindness and generosity will be natural responses that we make to situations we encounter. This is how we love those around us - how we love our neighbors.

Do you realize that we can be the answer that God sends in response to the prayers of those in need around us? That's want He wants! Maybe they don't pray or think about God, but because of the kindness through us, they will take note of our love and wonder where it comes from. Think of the joy and honor of being asked by someone, "Why are you so different? Why are you so thoughtful and kind?" To which we can answer, "Let me tell you about Jesus."

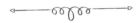

Imagine her testimony of meeting Jesus!

*John 8:3, 4 The teachers of the law and the Pharisees brought in a woman caught
in adultery. They made her stand before the group ⁴and said to Jesus,
"Teacher, this woman was caught in the act of adultery.*

In another time and another place this woman would have been stoned to death. In the
midst of her sin, she was caught and had the good fortune to be brought to Jesus by these
leaders. They weren't concerned about her well being, but were interested in using her
and her adultery to set a trap for Jesus.

There she was, in the temple courts, standing with the leaders and Jesus but also
surrounded by *"all the people who had gathered around (Jesus)"* to be taught by Him. As
she stood there, this possibly could have qualified as the worst moment of her life.

I wonder what was going through her mind. Did she know who Jesus was? Maybe
she had heard of Him or heard Him teach. Maybe she had been amazed by the miracles
He'd done. If she had known of Him, this would not have qualified as the way she would
have liked to meet Him. That is until this experience unfolded.

Jesus dealt with the leaders and with her. His comments to them forced the leaders
to recognize their own sin. Imagine her amazement as all of the religious leaders slowly
began to go away one at a time, the older ones first, until only Jesus was left, with the
woman still standing there.

*Jesus straightened up and asked her, "Woman, where are they? Has no one condemned
you?" "No one, sir," she said. "Then neither do I condemn you," Jesus declared. "Go now and
leave your life of sin." John 8:10-11*

Jesus not only freed her from condemnation, better still, He offered her the opportunity
of leaving her life of sin; no, make that He commanded her to leave her life of sin – just
as He does with us. When Jesus saves our lives and instructs us on the way to go, do we
really think or behave as though His words are just suggestions?

I can see her eyes irresistibly drawn to His and her heart filled with the overwhelming
desire to follow Him. She might not have had any idea what the future held, but following
Jesus would change everything. Can't you see her in the days ahead tearfully sharing her
testimony of how Jesus saved her life – both physically and spiritually – and recounting
this event, moment by moment, that led to her becoming a follower of Him?!

Don Schmidt

A lesson from the movie Frequency

Mark 10:21 Jesus looked at him and loved him. "One thing you lack," he said. "Go, sell everything you have and give to the poor, and you will have treasure in heaven. Then come, follow me." ²²At this the man's face fell. He went away sad, because he had great wealth.

Yesterday, when I was pondering about the woman caught in adultery who was set free by the Lord with the command to *"leave your life of sin"*, I thought of the rich young ruler and a favorite movie. The movie is *Frequency*, a 2000 science-fiction film that contains elements of time travel, thriller and alternate history, starring Dennis Quaid and James Caviezel as father and son.

In the movie, the father, Dennis Quaid is a fireman killed in a warehouse fire in 1969. His son, Jim Caviezel is in 1999, and even though it's 30 years later, he is still hurting from the death of his father. He has his father's ham radio and due to unusual aurora borealis (northern lights) activity, they are stunned to be talking to each other on the radio, although separated by 30 years.

For the father, the conversation occurs the day before the warehouse fire that kills him. For the son it is the day before the 30ᵗʰ anniversary of that fire. Though the father doesn't believe that it's his son that he's talking to on the radio, the son is able to shout out a warning about the fire that took his life the next day.

Sure enough a day later as he tries to escape the burning warehouse he remembers his son's warning to not go the way his instincts and training tell him to. He goes the opposite direction that at the time looks like the worse alternative and escapes safely. His original direction led to death; the alternate way led to life. This time he made the right choice!

"Go, sell everything you have and give to the poor, and you will have treasure in heaven. Then come, follow me." For the rich young ruler, this was the alternate way out of the "burning warehouse". This was the way for him that led to life. Unfortunately, due to his wealth he went away sad. Jesus communicated a precise way to life that specifically addressed his situation. Hopefully, he later repented and obeyed.

Jesus told the woman caught in adultery, *"Go now and leave your life of sin."* She too was in a 'burning warehouse" and the way she was going would result in death. But Jesus gave her a way out that led to life. Jesus does the very same with all of us. By His Spirit we are warned to turn, to repent, to follow Him in a new direction that leads to life. He has redemptive, life giving paths for us to take no matter where we find ourselves.

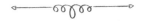

The blindness that comes with calloused hearts

Mark 3:1-6 ¹Another time he went into the synagogue, and a man with a shriveled hand was there. ²Some of them were looking for a reason to accuse Jesus, so they watched him closely to see if he would heal him on the Sabbath. ³Jesus said to the man with the shriveled hand, "Stand up in front of everyone." ⁴Then Jesus asked them, "Which is lawful on the Sabbath: to do good or to do evil, to save life or to kill?" But they remained silent. ⁵He looked around at them in anger and, deeply distressed at their stubborn hearts, said to the man, "Stretch out your hand." He stretched it out, and his hand was completely restored. ⁶Then the Pharisees went out and began to plot with the Herodians how they might kill Jesus.

It is difficult to find words to describe everything contained in these few verses. So many big things happen. Jesus had compassion on a crippled man and does a wonderful miracle. Jesus not only discerned the stubborn hearts of the Pharisees, he was angry with them. The Pharisees were unable to see their own stubbornness and unbelief. In the face of the miraculous, they were blind and deceived. I think this is one of the most frightening things in the Scriptures. They saw Jesus and wanted to kill Him.

How could anyone see such a wonderful miracle and not be moved and humbled by it? These religious leaders believed in God, yet the condition of their hearts made them blind to God right in front of them. They were witnessing a demonstration of the power of God unlike any seen in the history of mankind. Yet they failed to see Immanuel, (God with us) in their midst.

Surely they too had family or friends who were sick, crippled or in bondage. Jesus was doing miracles everywhere. Why didn't they go and get them and bring them to Jesus? Instead, the Pharisees become so angry that they wanted to kill Jesus – because He did the miracle on the Sabbath. How could these men not recognize the wonder they were beholding? They clung to arguments rather than recognizing the Son of God – right in front of them.

I think of Isaiah 6:9, 10 *⁹He said, "Go and tell this people: "'Be ever hearing, but never understanding; be ever seeing, but never perceiving.' ¹⁰Make the heart of this people calloused; make their ears dull and close their eyes. Otherwise they might see with their eyes, hear with their ears, understand with their hearts, and turn and be healed."*

We must recognize that the same spiritual deafness and blindness can happen to us. We can miss God working in our lives and right in front of us through the 'callousing' of our hearts.

What should we desire?

*Psalm 20:4 May He give you the desire of your heart
and make all your plans succeed.*

I remember reading this verse and not having a clue what the desire of my heart was. On top of that, I didn't know what my specific plans were either. A close friend asked me if I could do anything I wanted, what would it be? I couldn't answer him either - other than saying to be prosperous or successful.

This began a search for me. I just hadn't thought that much about what my desires were. It seemed there were things I could say that sounded good, but they really didn't reflect a deep-seated desire. It was a given that I wanted to provide for my family and do well at my job, but it seemed that this verse was talking about something deeper than that.

This search became a part of my relationship with God. I was seeking to become more passionate in my love for Him. I wanted my life to better demonstrate my love for Him by doing the things His word says to do and to refrain from doing those things it says to avoid. It became clear that in order to love God more, my life had to become more conformed to His word. The more it did, the more I loved Him and pleased Him.

Through this search it became delightfully clear to me, that the Lord was giving me understanding about what He wanted our primary desires to be – that He in turn would grant. More than anything else, He wants us to love Him and please Him in everything.

He also opened my eyes to see that loving my wife, Donna, was inextricably interwoven with loving Him. Loving Him more, meant loving her more. (Think of 1 John 4:20b *For anyone who does not love his brother, whom he has seen, cannot love God, whom he has not seen.*) Having warm, wonderful emotional feelings for your spouse and for God is great, but loving someone is so much more than that. We must recognize the reality that our feelings can be communicating one thing, but our attitudes and actions can be sending a very different message. The reality of life has a way of revealing where we are weak and in need of change. Who better for the Lord to use than those closest to us to reveal such things? If we could neither speak nor write – our love must be evident by the life we live. The desire of our heart must be such a life.

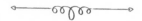

A rock to stand on

Psalm 25:12 Who, then, is the man that fears the LORD?
He will instruct him in the way chosen for him.

I went to Brazil in August 2006 to visit our John & Fabi and their young girls. It was a marvelous time with them. One of the blessings of the trips there is the wonderful times that I have with the Lord. Their apartment was on the ocean and there is just something special about having quiet times in the hammock on the balcony overlooking the ocean, hearing the waves and feeling the breeze. It's as wonderful as it sounds. (I think their record cold is 68 degrees)

The Lord really spoke to me about today's and yesterday's verses on that trip. As I noted yesterday, when it talked about making my plans succeed, I couldn't identify what my specific plans were. I wanted His plans for me – for my plans to truly be his plans. It is a faith issue. He has plans for all our lives, and by faith we follow Him. We trust Him to guide us.

On that trip, I was really wrestling with the whole issue of His specific plan for me. Then I read this verse and saw the incredible promise that it contained. God will instruct the man or woman who fears the Lord in the way chosen for them. We don't have to know the specific details. Our confidence is in Him – that He will instruct each of us in the way He has chosen for us. We simply have to fear the Lord and look to Him in faith.

So many of the characters in the Bible have such twists and turns in their walk with God. So many things happen that are unexpected or seemingly negative – yet they are part of God's plan for them. The same is true for us. In this verse, He has given us a rock to stand on. As we fear the Lord, our God will guide us in the way He has chosen for us. This is something for us to claim with faith and thankfulness.

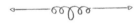

An outrigger for those in need around you

*Psalm 34:18 The LORD is close to the brokenhearted
and saves those who are crushed in spirit.*

In church we sang a song that had a verse that really touched me. It spoke of the tired and weary, the lost and lonely, and the brokenhearted. All of us have probably experienced all these things at one time or another. Hopefully in those times, we have experienced the closeness of the Lord and been blessed by His love and presence. But each of these can be formidable things to deal with.

The thing that I was particularly struck by was the thought of all those around us, who may or may not know Jesus, who are experiencing one or more of these things. Take a moment to think of those in your circle of relationships. Are there any who are tired and weary? I don't think this is talking about physical tiredness that comes from working hard or doing something physically demanding. It seems that it is referring to a weariness of spirit, which would be similar to one being lost or lonely, or brokenhearted. Typically, these conditions come with discouragement.

An illustration that has really been helpful to me is that of an outrigger on a canoe. It is there to stabilize the canoe in turbulent water. I've found that there are times when we are able to come along side of a friend or coworker who's going through difficulties and the Lord enables us to function like an outrigger on their canoe as they go through "whitewater" in their life. We're there to encourage; pray with them; listen to them; give help and advice if asked; possibly share our faith. The Lord gives us the opportunity to help them keep their "canoe" from tipping over. We're there to help them get through the difficulties. It's all about loving them.

It's not about evangelizing – it's about being the fragrance of Christ. It's about being salt and light. It's about loving those around us – being able to touch them with the love of God. The Lord is close to the brokenhearted – and sometimes He wants us to be the ones, through whom, they experience Him.

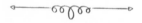

Expressing the fragrance of Jesus

*2 Corinthians 2:15 For we are to God the aroma of Christ among
those who are being saved and those who are perishing.*

I would like us to consider aroma and fragrance. These words have to do with the sense of smell, and in a positive sense, things like food cooking, perfumes, the scent of flowers. The things that we do – our very lives when centered in Christ – emanate the richness of our God. And this richness is noticed by those we interact with.

Think of all the positive things that impact us – that we notice – that are helpful or make our lives richer: an encouraging word, a helpful hand, the thoughtful presence of a friend, acts of kindness. All of these things can communicate the love of our Lord. This opportunity we have is expressed wonderfully by Paul: *"But thanks be to God, who always leads us in triumphal procession in Christ and through us spreads everywhere the fragrance of the knowledge of him."* 2 Corinthians 2:14

The day by day journey of our lives is as important as the ultimate destination. Day by day others can experience Jesus as revealed in our attitudes, words and actions. The more our lives reflect His ways, the more they will emanate the wondrous fragrance of our God.

Think of it! In a world of darkness and despair He has chosen to spread His fragrance through us. Some will recoil because they are not interested in Him. But others will be attracted because they are responding to the work of His Spirit, drawing them to redemption. We get to share His fragrance with all who surround us, knowing and trusting that there are those who will respond to Him.

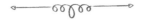

Becoming lovers of God

Mark 12: 28–31 ²⁸One of the teachers of the law came and heard them debating. Noticing that Jesus had given them a good answer, he asked him, "Of all the commandments, which is the most important?" ²⁹"The most important one," answered Jesus, "is this: 'Hear, O Israel, the Lord our God, the Lord is one. ³⁰Love the Lord your God with all your heart and with all your soul and with all your mind and with all your strength.' ³¹The second is this: 'Love your neighbor as yourself.' There is no commandment greater than these."

This portion of Mark describes a wonderful interaction between Jesus and a teacher of the law. It is one of my favorites because this teacher recognized the truth. This teacher is one of the very few leaders who interacted wisely with Jesus. Jesus is asked to identify the most important commandment – which He does in quoting Deuteronomy 6: 4, 5

Note how Jesus describes loving God. Jesus describes it as loving Him with all your heart and with all your soul and with all your mind and with all your strength. This is something that you work at in accomplishing – not something that just happens. It requires intentionality and is all consuming. Also remember that this is the greatest commandment. Nothing is greater.

Let's look at it from a different perspective. Consider loving God as an acquired skill. It is defined by a whole set of beliefs, attitudes, motives and actions. It has standards all its own, and Scripture details what they are. It involves learning the specific required skills in order to become good at it. In order to develop excellence, a great deal of practice is required. We might think of it as being lifelong apprentices – we never stop learning how to do it better.

When we were born again we became new in Christ. We were freed from the power of sin in order to become the people that God wants us to be. Jesus' answer describes the people we are to become – lovers of God. But loving God goes beyond skill sets we acquire because it involves who we are as a person. Praise God, the Holy Spirit is the master craftsman, our personal trainer, coach, enabler and so much more. He is God's gift to us so that this might all come about.

We may start out doing many of these things because we are supposed to, but as we embrace the process, the Spirit will transform us so that it all becomes a genuine expression of a life committed to Jesus. We more and more become that which we are doing. Loving God becomes the passion of our lives.

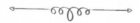

Don Schmidt

An important insight from golfing with Jay

Mark 12:32 –33 "Well said, teacher," the man replied. "You are right in saying that God is one and there is no other but him. ³³ To love him with all your heart, with all your understanding and with all your strength, and to love your neighbor as yourself is more important than all burnt offerings and sacrifices."

Years ago, I had a friend who was a marvelous golfer. Better still, whenever friends played golf with Jay, he made it into a golfing lesson to help us. I really appreciated the fact that throughout the round he would give me tips and help me become a better golfer. One day another friend of mine joined us for a round of golf. I had told him that Jay would help him with his game. As we started playing it became apparent that his golf game was really hurting.

We played the first few holes and Jay hadn't said anything to him yet in terms of helping his golf game. As we were walking down the 4th fairway, Jay came over to me and said, "I will help him, but he's doing so many things wrong, I haven't figured out where to start."

Loving God and loving one another have some interesting similarities to playing golf. They all take practice and it's wonderful to have friends around who will help us do it better. We have to be around them and be willing to listen. If we want to become better at golf, we work at it. Maybe we take lessons. We watch better golfers to learn what we can from them. We find time to play more golf. We have to be intentional about it. The same principles apply to our faith.

How good it is when we have individuals in our lives who exemplify what Scriptures teach. But we need to know what Scripture teaches in order to really recognize genuine Godliness. In golf, we have par. In life, we have all kinds of different things claiming to be right.

That is where Scripture and the Holy Spirit are so important, along with being a part of a vibrant life giving church. We have a lot to learn and God wants us to learn from one another. One advantage of our faith is that we get to live and "practice" it everywhere: at work, at play, at home or out with friends. No matter where we are, or what we are doing, loving God and loving one another applies. We need to learn to do it well.

What is the flavor of our fruit?

*Galatians 5:22-23 But the fruit of the Spirit is love, joy, peace,
patience, kindness, goodness, faithfulness, 23gentleness
and self-control. Against such things there is no law.*

I grew up in southwestern Michigan which is an area that has been known as the Fruit Belt since the 1800s. In the spring there are strawberries, followed in the summer and fall by cherries, blueberries, peaches, plums, pears, apples, and grapes. The trees that produced much of the fruit all bore blossoms in the spring. It was so wonderful to drive through the countryside and see fruit trees in bloom everywhere.

The blossoms, although beautiful in their own right, are a promise of something to come. Whether the bearer of the fruit is a tree, a bush or a vine, the fruit is the natural result of the plant – and typically the fruit is supposed to be sweet and flavorful.

Have you ever been in an orchard where you could pick and eat the ripe fruit as you walked along? Regardless where you find it, how pleasant it is to bite into sweet fruit and savor its taste. Unfortunately, we've all probably tasted fruit that is anything but sweet and flavorful! The typical result is wanting to spit it out.

The Scriptures are clear that Christians produce fruit. The question then isn't, are you producing blueberries or grapes, but rather what does your fruit "taste" like? The fruit of the Spirit listed above is sweet and flavorful. The "fruit of the flesh" if you will, would be the antonyms of the fruit of the Spirit and characterized as sour and bitter. Which fruit do we want to taste in others? Which fruit do we want in our own lives? We have choices to make because good fruit doesn't happen by accident.

Think of the blessing that others receive from tasting love; from savoring faithfulness; from encountering kindness – from experiencing any of the fruit of the Spirit. God wants those who encounter us – His people - to be able to walk through the orchard of our lives and taste the sweet and flavorful fruit of His Spirit. Once they do, they'll be back for more.

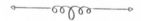

Our primary weapon is love

1 Corinthians 16:14 Do everything in love.

This verse today is particularly interesting because of something we will get to in a moment. It instructs us to do everything in love. Think about that. What is excluded from everything? And how do we do everything in love? What exactly does it mean?

But something else struck me about this verse. Do we men have a tendency to view a statement like this as being more feminine? Is it more "manly" to talk about the armor of God - shield and sword and breastplate? Think of Mel Gibson as William Wallace in Brave Heart when he was riding back and forth challenging the men to fight. "I am William Wallace! And I see a whole army of my countrymen, here in defiance of tyranny. You've come to fight as free men... and free men you are. What will you do with that freedom? Will you fight? "

Or how about Aragorn, who in Return of the King, challenges the men just before the last battle in front of the gates of Mordor? Aragorn begins by saying, "Hold your ground, hold your ground! Sons of Gondor, of Rohan, my brothers! I see in your eyes the same fear that would take the heart of me. A day may come when the courage of men fails, when we forsake our friends and break all bonds of fellowship, but it is not this day."

There's no question that we have been strongly impacted by our culture. We've also been affected by a lack of understanding of what love really is. The interesting thing that I referred to about this verse, is it's context - specifically, verse 13 in front of it. Today's verse is the last item in a list of five specific commands given by Paul. Picture yourself in a group of believers being challenged with these five commands:

- Be on your guard
- Stand firm in the faith
- Be men of courage
- Be strong
- Do everything in love

Wallace and Aragorn were talking to men about to fight with swords and spears. We must recognize that we too are in a battle – a spiritual one - and that a primary weapon that we are to live with and fight with, is love.

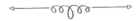

A spectrum such as sour to sweet

Scripture to follow...

One of the realities that we live with is that we are all works in progress. We have strong points and weak points. There are areas where we have really grown in God, and then there are those areas where our growth is stunted or nonexistent. We can become callous to the reality of who we are; the 'who we are' that others encounter.

In looking at our lives, there are many attributes of our character. I would like us to look at each of the following and prayerfully ask the Lord to help us to have eyes to see where we are in the continuum that exists for each. This assumes that we know what each of the attributes is. Do we know what being polite looks like? What about the nuances of being rude? Do we readily recognize inappropriate pride in our lives? How does it differ from humility?

Where do you see yourself on each of the following spectrums?

- Rude   to   Polite
- Proud   to   Humble
- Boastful   to   Not boastful
- Unkind   to   Kind
- Easily angered   to   Not easily angered
- Remember wrongs   to   Overlook wrongs
- Impatient   to   Patient
- Envious   to   Not envious
- Self-seeking   to   Not self-seeking
- Delight in evil   to   Rejoice with truth
- Unprotective   to   Protective
- Untrusting   to   Trusting
- Skeptical   to   Hopeful
- Gives up easily   to   Perseveres
- Fails   to   Never fails

We must recognize that the ingredients on the right are those of God's Kingdom. Those on the left speak of another kingdom in this world. (It's a place we aren't even supposed to visit let alone live there!)

You have probably surmised that this listing has to do with the attributes of love from 1 Corinthians 13. The more our lives fall to the right side of each of the above continuums, the more they are demonstrating love of Christ. Think of them as identifying '**whose**' we are! (Children of Light or children of darkness) Here is the way Paul puts it:

1 Corinthians 13:4-8a *⁴Love is patient, love is kind. It does not envy, it does not boast, it is not proud. ⁵It is not rude, it is not self-seeking, it is not easily angered, it keeps no record of wrongs. ⁶Love does not delight in evil but rejoices with the truth. ⁷It always protects, always trusts, always hopes, always perseveres. ⁸Love never fails.*

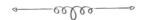

Blessed by a stranger named Jeff

2 Corinthians 9:8 And God is able to make all grace abound to you, so that in all things at all times, having all that you need, you will abound in every good work.

I experienced a kindness shown to me by a stranger that really moved me. We were having family over for dinner that night and needed a couple items from the store. So in the afternoon I went to Aldi's to get those items plus some fruit and vegetables.

The total came to $16.27 and I used my debit card only to have it declined. That was unexpected and I thought it was just a computer glitch so we tried the card again only to have it declined again. I was mystified because I thought I had sufficient funds in the checking account to cover a small purchase. The cashier suggested I call the bank. So the transaction was suspended while I went to make my call.

I walked over to the counter area where customers pack their groceries after paying for them and called Donna to have her check the account online. Just then another customer came over to me. He had just purchased his groceries and had witnessed my little adventure. He got my attention and said, "I'll pay for your groceries for you."

What an unexpected kindness! I thanked him and said that my wife was checking our account right then. He said he would wait to find out. I was embarrassed to discover that I had let our checking account balance get down to $14. So Donna transferred money online from savings into the account. All the while this gentleman was standing patiently next to me with cash in hand to pay for the groceries.

It's difficult to describe what was going on within me once he made his offer. Although I was on the phone with Donna while she accessed our account, I was so aware of the kindness that was being extended to me by this stranger. Further, I was blessed by the fact that he didn't leave me when I informed him we were transferring the money. He just stood there patiently waiting to see if the card would be approved.

Once Donna completed the transfer, I went back to the cashier; we reran the card and it was approved. He was still standing there, waiting. I turned and thanked him again for his generosity and kindness, and asked his name – it was Jeff.

As we walked to our cars I was so grateful for the kindness the Lord had shown me through Jeff. On the one hand, it's something that I don't want to happen again. But on the other, I was grateful that I had inadvertently allowed the account to have such a low balance so that I could experience the Lord's kindness to me through a stranger named Jeff.

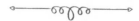

A different and better perception of the word 'shallow'

Hebrews 13:1 Keep on loving each other as brothers.

I grew up in a little town right on Lake Michigan across from Chicago. Going to the beach was a favorite pastime in the summer. There was a particular beach that we loved to go to. It had sand dunes to climb on and big sandbars in the water that were wonderful to play on. Typically, when we entered the water it would get a little deep but as you kept going out the water became shallow. The water there was less than knee deep. When there were waves, the sandbar was a great place to body surf. Out beyond the sandbar it got much deeper going way over our heads.

Today, the word <u>shallow</u> often refers to something that is superficial or not really desirable. It is not a word typically used in a positive way. I would like to change our reference point with the word shallow because it is a very helpful and descriptive word that can really shed some light in our lives. Think of the word shallow as it applies to the water level on a sandbar or in a swimming pool. It simply means the water isn't very deep. <u>Amplifying a bit further, the water is real, just not very deep.</u>

Now think about the friendships and relationships we have. Doesn't the word <u>shallow</u> constructively describe many of them? They are real – just not very deep. Many of these people would be there for us in a time of need, but there just isn't much time spent together. Our lives are just so busy and we are often spread too thin for it to happen.

Depth in relationship takes effort – it takes learning to love one another. It involves intentionality because such relationships typically don't happen by accident. Seeing needs and helping out; caring for one another; being in small groups together; spending time together are all ways that we can develop depth in our relationships. Another way is sharing meals together and simply making time for each other.

We can't do this with everyone, but there are those in our lives that God wants the relationships to deepen. It involves reordering our priorities and pursuing activities that make it happen – and God will guide us. Developing true community in our churches means that we must pursue the opportunities we have to develop deep, strong relationships. They are a missing reality in so many lives today and God wants that to change.

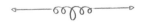

When in dark and difficult places

2 Corinthians 4:18 So we fix our eyes not on what is seen, but on what is unseen. For what is seen is temporary, but what is unseen is eternal.

Have you noticed how birds will sing in the morning as the dawn approaches but it still appears to be totally dark? The other morning I was up very early and the birds were really singing. Somehow they sense dawn coming or maybe they see something we don't see.

A few years ago as we drove through Eastern Tennessee on our way to North Carolina, I was able to view the entire spectrum from darkness to dawn to the rising of the sun. I was thinking of the birds singing while it was still dark and I wanted to detect the very first, faintest hints of dawn. It is such a blessing to watch the dawn unfold in all its glory.

I knew to look east, but importantly, I knew which direction was east. I was also confident; as we all are that the sun will come up. This all speaks to me of faith. When we are in spiritually dark places – even when it is at its blackest, it's important that we know that the spiritual 'dawn' is coming and by faith we know where to look. Faith will sing and rejoice in the coming dawn when others might be wondering if there is anything to sing about. Faith sees what others don't.

I think of Lucy in the Narnia Tales. She is always the first to see Aslan. She sees him when the others don't. It has to do with faith and relationship with our Lord and having eyes that see the unseen. We have a God and Savior who is with us always. In those dark and difficult places we can sense and see the evidences of Him. In fact we can be confident He's there whether we see Him or not. We are not alone. Nor are we at the mercy of anyone but Him.

The next time you feel down or alone, think of it as the early morning before the dawn. Faith enables us to have confidence the spiritual 'dawn' is coming. The Lord is with us and it is to Him that we must look. As we do, faith enables us to experience His blessing and reassurance just as our physical eyes enjoy the dawn.

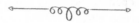

The trial of my weed whacker

*James 1:2 Consider it pure joy, my brothers, whenever
you face trials of many kinds,*

Trials come in many forms. If they were dogs they would be every type of dog you can imagine – and our lives would be full of them! No matter what we're doing or where we are, if a puppy came up to us we'd recognize it as a dog.

One of the problems we have is that we often don't recognize that we are encountering a trial when it happens. Each is an opportunity to respond appropriately in faith. Would you believe that one of my trials today involved my weed whacker? It works fine once it is running. The problem is getting it started.

I put fuel in it; turn the switch to the on position; push the primer bubble 6 times like it says to do; adjust the choke and pull the cord. The instructions say to pull it no more than 6 times in a sequence. Well, this delightful little machine of mine has a gift of resistance to starting. Between pulling the cord, playing with the choke and pushing the bubble some more, I probably pull the starter cord about 100 times to get it started.

The funny thing is kneeling next to it and realizing that it is a trial. I find myself smiling and laughing at this little machine and the difficulty I have getting it going. I pray for it – I pray for the Lord to guide me in how to adjust things and pull things and push things.

Once it kicks in for only a second or two, I know victory is coming. It still might take me a couple more minutes, but I sense victory is at hand. I am going to persevere! I confess I am not exactly mechanically gifted, but I do have a knack for seeing the Lord's gifts to me in difficulties. Such a silly little thing as a hard to start weed whacker, gives me an opportunity to respond in faith and righteousness.

The Lord wants us to recognize situations as trials, whether they be big or small – and look to Him. We then inwardly smile and acknowledge that He is going to help us get through it with faith, joy and righteousness. It is so nice not to get mad at a hard to start weed whacker.

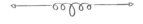

Lesson of the Pamper Pole

*Proverbs 3:5 Trust in the LORD with all your heart and
lean not on your own understanding;*

Our 3rd son Andrew was part of a mission intern program in Colorado from August 1999 – June 2001. The program included an extensive amount of physical training along with the spiritual. During his first year we got to watch the interns working out on the "Ropes Course" that was similar to the one used by the USAFA Cadets.

One event called the Pamper Pole really amazed me. It was a telephone pole about 30 feet high that the interns would climb – wearing a harness and blindfolded. Once an intern got to the top of the pole, he had to somehow get himself up on it so he was standing on the flat top of the pole that was about 15" in diameter. Being blindfolded meant they had to trust the leader who was directing them. He would tell the intern to turn so that he was facing a trapeze bar that was suspended out away from the pole. Then the intern had to leap out from the pole and grab the trapeze bar that he couldn't see.

We saw some interns fall off the pole; while others, who made it to the top, we saw leap out and miss. All of these interns were swinging, high off the ground, in their protective harness. Then there were those who caught the bar, did pull-ups, and were then lowered to the ground by means of the harness.

The interns were doing something that was frightening and difficult. They knew if they made a mistake, the worst that could happen was a little embarrassment and they would be swinging in the air before being lowered to the ground so they could try again. Sounds a lot like life, doesn't it.

The security and safety provided by the harness form a wonderful illustration of how our faith in the Lord is intended to do the very same thing. Faith in Him protects us and enables us to perform adventures that we otherwise wouldn't do. We need to recognize that our faith is every bit as real and protective as the harness the interns wore. We might fall or stumble. We might miss the bar, but faith enables us to overcome fear and pursue the adventures the Lord calls us to.

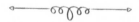

An inspiring lesson from our son Michael's life

2 Corinthians 2:14 But thanks be to God, who always leads us in triumphal procession in Christ and through us spreads everywhere the fragrance of the knowledge of him.

Our youngest son Michael was born with an artistic gift. Even when he was little he could draw beautifully. I describe him as having the eye of an artist. After serving in the army, he joined the National Guard so that he could be trained in Broadcast Journalism. He wanted to become a videographer – one who makes videos. That was his job in the Guard.

Good videography requires technical competence. It's not just taking videos and splicing them together. It is producing a product that accomplishes its intended purpose. The quality and attractiveness of the video produced depends upon the skill and technical excellence of the one producing it. But here is where Michael had a real advantage. He brought the eye of an artist to his trade.

This artistic gift affected everything that he did in the process: camera angles, shots taken, lighting, what to include or exclude, music, editing, how things are put together. This enabled him to produce videos that stood out and received recognition. They have an inherent attractiveness because they combined art and technical skill. The resulting product has an attractive 'fragrance', if you will that art or technical skill by themselves couldn't produce. Michael's officers and others noted the excellence of his work.

This illustration of the importance of artistic gift + technical competence has a wonderful parallel in our Christian life. The gift is the life of Christ within us. It affects everything about us and particularly how we view everything. The technical skill component is walking in His ways. We have the Holy Spirit within us motivating and enabling us to learn from God's Word how to do it. The more we walk in His ways, the greater this component becomes – the more Christlike we become. Without this, excellence is not produced.

Whereas Michael produced excellent videos; we are to produce lives of excellence. People watch us just like they do videos. What are they going to notice and remember? If we truly and seriously commit ourselves to Christ and His transforming work in our lives, we will spread the wonderful fragrance of the knowledge of Jesus wherever we go.

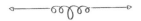

Mary and Joseph – "Tell me again..."

Luke 2:19 But Mary treasured up all these things and pondered them in her heart.

It's difficult for me to imagine what Mary went through as she experienced events leading up to Easter. Fortunately the Lord laid a remarkable foundation that enabled Mary (and Joseph as long as he was alive) to be rock solid in Him. Consider the power of these events in their lives. And let us remember them as well as we walk with Jesus in these days leading to Easter.

Prior to appearing to Mary, the angel Gabriel first appeared to Zechariah, the husband of Elizabeth, Mary's relative. Zechariah lost the ability to speak because he didn't believe what Gabriel told him. But true to the angel's word, despite their old age, Elizabeth became pregnant. After the birth of their baby, Zechariah regained his ability to speak once he acknowledged the baby's name was John.

Joseph had an angel appear to him in dreams multiple times, giving him instructions on what to do. The angel(s) also explained both to Mary and then later to Joseph, exactly who this child was going to be. Elizabeth, filled with the Holy Spirit, proclaimed Mary to be "the mother of my Lord" upon Mary's visit.

The angel of the Lord appeared to the shepherds announcing the birth of a Savior, Christ the Lord. A great company of heavenly host suddenly appeared with the angel praising God. Then there was the star and the Magi from the east bowing down and worshipping the baby Jesus, *"the King of the Jews"*.

In Jerusalem they met Simeon and a prophetess named Anna. The Lord had revealed to Simeon that he would not die before he had seen the Lord's Christ. They both prophetically acknowledged who the baby was.

Mary and Joseph were a young couple, newly married and now new parents. I believe that whatever difficulties they faced then or in the coming years were pale in comparison to the wonder of all that God had given them. One can only imagine their joy as they shared their stories with one another: Gabriel, angels, babies, prophesies, dreams, stars, Magi and heavenly hosts. I can see them sitting alone together looking at the sleeping Jesus and saying, "Tell me again..."

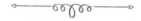

The problem is we have 'wooden edges'

Romans 12:2 Do not conform any longer to the pattern of this world, but be transformed by the renewing of your mind. Then you will be able to test and approve what God's will is—his good, pleasing and perfect will.

The movie Pinocchio is truly a classic and a wonderful story. I find myself fascinated by the transformation that this puppet goes through. In the story Geppetto is a wood carver who creates a magnificent wooden puppet that he names Pinocchio. He then wishes upon a star that Pinocchio would become a real boy. His wish is partly granted in that Pinocchio becomes alive but has to prove himself honest, fair and true in order to become a real boy.

This living puppet goes through adventures with Jiminy, his little cricket friend who is his conscience. He faces and succumbs to temptation but in the end he is transformed into the real boy that Geppetto wanted. Pinocchio is no longer a living wooden boy, but a real boy with flesh and blood.

On a simple level yet profound level, this story presents a helpful perspective of our walk in Christ. Before we come to Christ, we are like the wooden puppet. Then when we are born again, we become living sons and daughters but we have much to learn. For the sake of illustration, we become like Pinocchio, the living, wooden puppet. There is still much change that must occur in us.

We are…and we get to become. Make that, we must become. While we are truly sons and daughters of God when we are born again, there is a life-long transformation process that we must embrace in order to be transformed into the men and women God wants us to be. Our lives – behavior, thoughts, attitudes, words, relationships – all have a lot of wooden edges that He wants us to be free of.

This process involves us no longer conforming to the pattern of the world, but conforming to God's Word and ways. We must make the choices that enable us to become like Jesus. Through this process the life-long transformation is accomplished. The wooden edges are replaced by the real

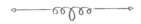

The blessing of saying the right thing

Proverbs 25:11 A word aptly spoken is like apples of gold in settings of silver.

Suppose someone gave you a handful of $10 bills that you were to give out during the day to people that you interacted with. It's safe to say that the people who received the money would notice and be pleased. They'd probably look forward to seeing you again on the chance you had more money to hand out.

Now suppose the Lord let you know that there would be included in your day, several people that you met that had a specific need for $10, that they were praying about. Or possibly they would have a need for the $10 shortly after receiving it. In both cases, their blessing would be far greater than just receiving a $10 gift. They would have the opportunity to recognize that it was a specific provision for a specific need – an answer to prayer. If they did see that, they would likely glorify God for His provision in addition to being grateful for your kindness.

The words that we speak can have a similar impact. They can bring blessing and provision to those around us. Think of the people we work or interact with. Do we recognize the kindnesses they do and do we say thank you? Do we ever acknowledge the good work that people do? When we are in conversations that start going in an unrighteous direction, do we gracefully speak words that redirect the conversation?

Think of the opportunities we have to show interest in others – in helping them with their problems or tasks. The insight we offer might be the missing ingredient they're looking for. Proverbs 15:23 adds this insight, *"Everyone enjoys a fitting reply; it is wonderful to say the right thing at the right time!"* If we are in the middle of a chore, think of the blessing of someone seeing us and saying, "Let me help you with that."

Maybe our words trigger something in their memory enabling them to recall what they need. Sometimes people are just in need of an encouraging word. Remember, it's not just us. We are God's hands extended. He wants to minister life through us that blesses others and draws them to Him. We need to pray that the Lord will open our eyes and ears to see the many opportunities that surround us where we can bring blessing through the words we speak and the kindness we show.

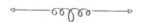

Speak this prayer for yourself

2 Corinthians 9:15 Thanks be to God for His indescribable gift!

Today – a prayer: For the past couple of days I've just been so aware of the wonder we have being loved by our God. This isn't just a general Biblical truth but a faith-filled experiential reality. This is one of those precious times when God heightens our awareness and appreciation of Him.

All my thoughts just keep coming back to how fortunate and blessed I am. I am just overwhelmed with God and His love for me. What follows is written a bit differently. I've written it in first person so that you can read it and pray it and speak it for yourself. I pray that it will bless you as much as it is blessing me.

How can I ever thank you Lord for making me your own? You, the God who created the universe know my name. That is almost beyond imagining. I am in awe of the fact that you care about me; that you would want me to be your child – to be part of your family for eternity. It's beyond words that you have made me your son and you are my father.

How can I ever thank you Lord that you let me experience your presence; that you give my life purpose and meaning? How can I ever thank you for allowing me to be your hands extended; that you give me the opportunity to touch others with your love.

How can I ever thank you for Jesus? Without Jesus, I have nothing. With Him, I have everything. How can I ever thank you for your Spirit who lives within me? I am never alone. You are always with me; loving me, encouraging me, comforting me, convicting me and helping me to repent whenever I need to.

How can I ever thank you for your Scriptures? They teach me all about you – but even more wonderfully, they teach me how to love you! Oh Lord, I do love you! It is just so amazing that you give me the opportunity to be a blessing to you. I don't begin to understand it but I rejoice that I can give you pleasure.

How can I ever thank you for the passion you have put in my heart to live my life for you? - That I can gather with your people and sing to you and worship you and experience you. Thank you Lord for my heart - that is bursting with gratitude for your kindness and love for me.

Forevermore your child, Don

The choice is ours in how we respond

Numbers 13:1-2 The LORD said to Moses, "Send some men to explore the land of Canaan, which I am giving to the Israelites. From each ancestral tribe send one of its leaders."

The twelve spies were given an opportunity by the Lord to see if they would be faithful or not. What kind of report would they bring back? Would they simply describe what they found – or would they do something else?

It's important to remember the history that these 12 men had. They all were leaders who had experienced God's incredible deliverance from Egypt. They saw the miracles. They walked through the parted Red Sea. They saw the pillar of fire by night and pillar of cloud by day. They knew the God of Abraham, Isaac and Jacob was with them. They knew that they were exploring the land promised to Abraham and his descendents.

The 13th and 14th chapters of Numbers tell us what happened. We don't remember the names of ten of the spies but we honor the names of Joshua and Caleb. The ten didn't simply report that there were giants in the land along with all the positive things there. They allowed the giants in the land to provoke fear and unbelief; giving the people a bad report.

Joshua and Caleb focused on the fact that the Lord was with them. He would enable them to take the land. The fact that there were giants and enemies there paled in comparison to the Lord being with them. Unfortunately, the people chose to believe the ten and rebelled against the Lord.

This story illustrates a principle that God uses repeatedly in our lives. He gives us opportunities to follow Him and accomplish things that He has purposed us to do. But in the midst of those things, He allows all manner of problems, difficulties and obstacles to arise. They can be fearful or overwhelming. How are we going to respond? Will fear or faith dominate our responses?

We have a choice to make just like the twelve spies and the children of Israel did. We can be fearful and complain – or we can seek and trust the Lord, lifting all of those problems to Him. We can focus on the problems or we can focus on our God – unbelief versus faith. Each problem is an opportunity for the Lord in His greatness to enable us to overcome. The choice is ours. How will we respond?

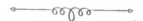

Questions to ask ourselves

1 John 3:1a How great is the love the Father has lavished on us, that we should be called children of God! And that is what we are!

What would we say to someone who asked us to tell them what Jesus has meant to us – and means to us? In practical ways, how has He changed our lives and what difference does He make day to day?

These are questions that each of us should ponder and answer for ourselves. The answers we give will be very revealing because they will reflect how genuine our enthusiasm and joy are for Him. Are we truly excited to be Christians? Do our eyes light up when we talk about Jesus? Do we smile at the thought of Him? Do we find ourselves overcome with gratitude?

As we think about what our honest answer would be, suppose God spoke out for all to hear and said that eternal life is no more – that once we die, it's over. But, that as long as we are alive, all of His promises and provisions in the Bible are still true. What would our response be? Would we walk away from Him?

Or – is our life in Christ so rich and wonderful that we would never leave it even if the promise of eternity with God was gone? This is the point that the earlier questions want to focus on. What is the reality that we have with Him here and now? God has lavished His love upon us – that is something He wants us to richly experience and for our lives to reflect.

If your Christian life – your personal relationship with God – was a garden, what would it be like? Would it be in bloom? Would it be a tiny corner of the yard or would it be expansive? Would people love to visit it because of the beauty there?

As we go about our day, please take note of the flowers and blossoms you see. Let each of them be a reminder of God's lavish love for us and the rich relationship that He wants each of us to experience daily with Him.

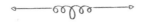

Thirsting and longing for Him

Psalm 63:1 O God, you are my God, earnestly I seek you; my soul thirsts for you, my body longs for you, in a dry and weary land where there is no water.

Think of the contrast between longing for something we are deprived of; versus longing for something where we are filled with wonder and anticipation that it's coming. On the one hand, we can be dominated by our lack - on the other we are dominated by hope and expectancy.

This is one of those verses in the Bible that has gone from being a mystery to me to being a source of unspeakable joy. This was a Psalm of David when he was in the desert of Judah. Since encountering God when I became a Christian in 1968, I could relate to him writing and saying, "O God, you are my God". I could also relate to seeking after God.

The thing I had difficulty with was, 'my soul thirsts for you. My body longs for you'. I didn't understand how that could come about. I wondered how you could get to a place where you could know and feel that your soul was thirsting for Him – that your body was longing for Him. On the one hand, as Christians we have his Spirit within us. Jesus has also promised to never leave us. But on the other hand, I perceived that this verse spoke of something of great value worth pursuing.

I identified the thirsting and longing as passion for the Lord and made it the focus of prayer for weeks, months and years. These were things that I didn't have but wanted. They spoke to me of aspects of relationship with God that were there for those who would pursue them - and Him.

The thing that I discovered in my prayerful pursuit was that these are things that we can experience today. We can thirst for Him and long for Him. He provides us with living water to satisfy the thirst. He provides us with His presence to satisfy the longing for Him.

No matter where we are or what we are doing, we can experience Him. The thirsting and the longing are gifts that He gives that help motivate us to long for Him, to pursue Him, to see Him and to find Him. He wants to be found.

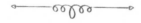

Miraculous healing of club feet

John 12:37 Even after Jesus had done all these miraculous signs in their presence, they still would not believe in him.

Years ago I met a pastor who had a most amazing story. He had been born with club feet – which he no longer had. When he was born, his parents were leaders in a non-Christian sect but they had a Bible. They read in James 5 where it talks about elders anointing the sick with oil in the name of the Lord and their prayer of faith will make the sick person well.

Well they were leaders and they had a baby with club feet. Even though they didn't believe miracles could happen then, they were desperate and acted on what the Bible said. So they got a jug of oil and poured it all on the baby's feet in the name of the Lord and prayed that God would do what the Bible said and heal him. To their utter amazement, then and there, the miracle happened! They watched both feet twist and became normal. One moment their baby son had club feet – the next he was miraculously healed. They were beside themselves with joy and excitement.

Just then there was a knock on the door and the main leader of their sect happened to stop by. They excitedly brought him in to see the baby and witness the miracle that God had done. The leader took one look and angrily declared how it wasn't done by God and he walked out. They were stunned!

Fortunately, they refused to believe him. They recognized that they needed to find the truth and that meant leaving that sect. Their search led them to Jesus and they became Christians – active in a local church. This miracle baby grew up to become a pastor in that denomination and was standing with us telling us his own story.

Thank God that this man's parents chose to follow the miracle – rather than the blindness of the leader. The miracle led them to Jesus and they were set free. That leader had much in common with many of the religious leaders of Jesus' day who refused to believe their eyes.

For me, the most difficult thing to believe in the Bible is not the miraculous; but it's how the religious leaders could see the thousands of miracles Jesus did and NOT believe. Worse still, was their anger at seeing Jesus performing miracles, particularly those done on the Sabbath. They were determined to kill Jesus!

About this time 2,000 years ago, Jesus was headed for Jerusalem with his disciples, telling them it was about to happen. Luke records that the disciples didn't understand what Jesus was saying about His death because the meaning of what He was saying was hidden from them (by God). But we know what happened. Let us make this journey with them as we approach the events of Passion Week.

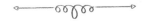

Imagine His entry into Jerusalem

John 12:17-19 The crowd that had been with him when he called Lazarus from the tomb, raising him from the dead, was there giving eyewitness accounts. It was because they had spread the word of this latest God-sign that the crowd swelled to a welcoming parade. The Pharisees took one look and threw up their hands: "It's out of control. The world's in a stampede after him." The Message

Have you ever imagined what it would have been like to be one of Jesus' disciples and been there with Him for His entry into Jerusalem? It would have been so exhilarating to see and hear the huge crowd cheering Him and spreading their cloaks and palm branches on the road before Him; listening to them cry Hosanna to the Lord.

Using an expression common today, I can see the twelve disciples looking at each other and exclaiming "YES!!" The atmosphere would have been electric. It would have been so easy to get caught up in all this and to join in with all the disciples joyfully praising God for all the miracles they'd seen – particularly Lazarus being raised from the dead. The crowd was even proclaiming Jesus, King of Israel!!

Although in the midst of all this celebration and cheering, somewhere in the back of their minds they might have been struggling, unable to understand how this incredible welcome fit with what Jesus had told them. Jesus had said that He would be handed over to the Gentiles and be mocked, spit upon, flogged and killed – here in Jerusalem– on this trip!! How could that happen with a welcome like this? It's like trying to fit a square peg in a round hole.

Even though Jesus told them that He would be raised from the dead in three days, they didn't understand any of this because it's meaning was hidden from them and they didn't know what He was talking about! (Luke 18:34). Only after Jesus was glorified were the disciples able to understand.

Each day, when we read the Scriptures and their description of the events of this week, try to view them through the eyes of the disciples who didn't know nor understand what was about to happen. Think of the incredible pain they experienced seeing Jesus tortured and killed – with no idea that there was a "Rest of the story…" beyond anything they could imagine about to happen.

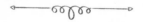

Trials that come

Mark 14:27-31 ²⁷*"You will all fall away," Jesus told them, "for it is written: 'I will strike the shepherd, and the sheep will be scattered.'* ²⁸*But after I have risen, I will go ahead of you into Galilee."* ²⁹*Peter declared, "Even if all fall away, I will not."* ³⁰*"I tell you the truth," Jesus answered, "today—yes, tonight—before the rooster crows twice you yourself will disown me three times."* ³¹*But Peter insisted emphatically, "Even if I have to die with you, I will never disown you." And all the others said the same.*

Think of the impact of seeing the miracles that Jesus did and listening to all he said – getting to be with him three years and being one of the twelve. Peter saw men and women and children beside themselves with joy after being healed or set free from demons or raised from the dead. He even experienced walking on water with Jesus. Then there was the triumphant entry into Jerusalem just a few days ago.

Now he's not only hearing that Jesus will die but that they all will fall away. So now Peter asserts his faithfulness and hears Jesus say how he will disown him three times. Peter can't believe that he could possibly deny his Lord.

A wonderful piece of this exchange at the Last Supper is included in Luke's gospel (22:32) where Jesus says to Peter: *"But I have prayed for you, Simon, that your faith may not fail. <u>And when you have turned back, strengthen your brothers.</u>"*

Later in the pain of having denied Jesus, Peter could have committed suicide like Judas did or totally abandoned the other disciples due to his shame. But in his pain, these prophetic words would have come back to him and been a source of hope, *"And when you have turned back…"*

Just like He did with Peter, God puts us all into circumstances where things in our hearts will be revealed to us. They might be things we aren't aware of, or maybe we just have no idea how significant a problem something within us is. Such experiences can be painful, as this was to Peter. But we, like Peter, can and must respond to His Spirit and the hope we have in Him. We must choose not to give up, but to respond to His grace and change. He doesn't show us these things to reject us, but to give us the opportunity to repent and become free.

Peter's pain and God's encouragement

Luke 22:61-62 The Lord turned and looked straight at Peter. Then Peter remembered the word the Lord had spoken to him: "Before the rooster crows today, you will disown me three times." [62] And he went outside and wept bitterly.

I cannot imagine the pain that Peter experienced after he denied Jesus the third time and the rooster crowed - and he saw Jesus look right at him. Their eyes met! Peter knew - that Jesus knew that it had happened just as Jesus had said it would. Then Peter went outside and wept bitterly. It was bad enough that Jesus had told him a few hours earlier that it would happen; but to have Jesus witness it and to look right at him at that very moment is pain and a sense of failure beyond imagining.

Peter had some other difficult moments. When he walked on water he sank. When he rebuked Jesus for talking about his coming suffering and death, Jesus turned and said to Peter, *"Get behind me, Satan!"* In the garden when Jesus was being arrested, Peter drew his sword and cut off Malchus' ear, earning a rebuke from Jesus.

I find it so encouraging that in spite of these events, Jesus didn't reject Peter and send him packing! Jesus chose him because he believed in him. When Jesus spoke to him of the denials, he also said, *"And when you have turned back, strengthen your brothers."* After Jesus' resurrection, the angel told the women who had come to the tomb, *"But go, tell his disciples and Peter."* Then Jesus appeared separately to Peter. Think of what each of these would have meant to Peter as he struggled with his actions of denying his beloved Lord.

Peter was a mixture, just like you and me - lots of potential and lots of things to work on. In spite of difficulties noted above, Peter was the one who did walk on water. He was the disciple who first acknowledged that Jesus was the Christ, the Son of the living God. He spoke for all the disciples to the crowd in Jerusalem on the day of Pentecost. He was rescued from prison by an angel. He was also the one who received the vision from God regarding the gentiles who then received the gospel at Cornelius' house. He was one of God's chosen servants who never gave up and God used him mightily. What an example he is for us!

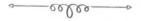

In the midst of despair

Luke 24:25-27 ²⁵He said to them, "How foolish you are, and how slow of heart to believe all that the prophets have spoken! ²⁶Did not the Christ have to suffer these things and then enter his glory?" ²⁷And beginning with Moses and all the Prophets, he explained to them what was said in all the Scriptures concerning himself.

Today's Scripture is Jesus' response to the 2 disciples traveling to Emmaus on Sunday, the day of Jesus' resurrection. They were downcast - even though they were aware that some of the women had been to the tomb and had a vision of angels telling them that Jesus was alive. They didn't understand what had happened or why. They had such hope in Jesus and it was snatched away from them in such an incredibly vicious way.

The Scriptures are clear that understanding of the unfolding events of Jesus' suffering and death were hidden from the disciples whenever Jesus spoke about it prior to his death. It was only afterward that Jesus opened their minds so they could understand the Scriptures.

I find it very difficult to imagine the despair and hopelessness that they experienced at His arrest, crucifixion and death. Our view is so dominated by the knowledge and joy that Jesus rose from the dead. Something that might help us relate better are the scenes of Aslan's death from 'The Lion, The Witch and The Wardrobe'.

Lucy and Susan watched as the hundreds of horrible creatures tortured and then killed Aslan. In their heartbreak they witnessed the jubilation of the Witch and the wicked host. They believed they had won and that nothing could now stop them. Aslan was now gone forever. The girls' tears and misery lasted throughout the night. In the morning they experienced more pain as they tried to untie Aslan's body. They had no idea what was about to happen.

Two thousand years ago, the first disciples spent today in such pain. Wicked men had killed Jesus of Nazareth, the man so used by God and they were helpless to stop it. Many experienced the shame of running and hiding. They deserted Jesus – just as he said they would. They didn't understand what was about to happen.

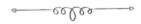

Prevented by God from recognizing Jesus

Luke 24:30-32 ⁰When he was at the table with them, he took bread, gave thanks,
broke it and began to give it to them. ³¹Then their eyes were opened and they
recognized him, and he disappeared from their sight. ³²They asked each other,
"Were not our hearts burning within us while he talked with us on the road and
opened the Scriptures to us?"

This incident of the two disciples on the road to Emmaus encountering Jesus is one of the more wonderful ones in the Bible. These two men were walking along, downcast and discussing everything that had recently occurred, when something unusual happened to them. Jesus himself came along and walked with them, but they were **kept** from recognizing him.

This was the day of his resurrection and they had no understanding of what had happened. The Scriptures are clear that understanding of the unfolding events of Jesus' suffering and death were hidden from the disciples whenever Jesus spoke about it prior to his death. It was only afterward that Jesus opened their minds so they could understand the Scriptures.

So Jesus joined them and as they walked along, *"he explained to them all that was said in the Scriptures concerning himself."* Luke 24:28b. Then, since it was nearly evening, they stopped for the night and strongly urged this man walking with them to stop and stay with them. It's apparent that they were deeply moved by what he had said to them, even though they didn't know who he was.

Moses encountered God when he responded to the burning bush and didn't pass it by. Likewise, these men responded to what God was doing in their hearts and did not let this man pass them by. Because they insisted that he stay with them, they experienced the wonder of God in having their eyes opened to see this man was Jesus - raised from the dead.

Isn't it fascinating that God would have Jesus appear to these two men but prevent them from recognizing him? It was important for them to listen to the message of this stranger and understand the "why" of what happened to Jesus. The events that happened to him were foretold in Scripture and they needed to understand it – rather than simply see Jesus and get excited. When God opened their eyes to recognize Jesus, they understood! The life, death and resurrection of Jesus were fulfillment of God's purpose.

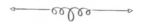

Don Schmidt

How amazing to encounter Jesus

Luke 24:45 Then he opened their minds so they could understand the Scriptures.

Have you ever been frightened to the point that it could be described as being terrified? We use the term 'scared to death' rather casually, but taken literally it describes serious fear. And we're not talking just being startled or frightened by the unexpected. We're talking about a fear provoking reality that is also startling and unexpected.

These words describe the reality experienced by the disciples when Jesus first appeared to the group of them together. The disciples were excited because the evidence was mounting that Jesus had risen. He had appeared to Simon! But their excitement was tempered by that fact that their fear of the Jews caused them to have the doors locked. I assume they were fearful that those who killed Jesus could be hunting for them.

Then the two men returning from Emmaus shared their wonderful story about Jesus being with them and their eyes being opened when He broke the bread! Can't you just feel the electric atmosphere that would have been in that room as they talked about all this? Their Lord was alive! Then "lightning" struck! One minute they're talking excitedly about how Jesus has risen – and the next minute Jesus appears in their midst and they were terrified!

Think about that. They were terrified at seeing Jesus appear suddenly in the room. He didn't knock on the door – and they didn't unlock it to let him in – He just appeared! They thought they were looking at a ghost. He asked them, *"Why are you troubled, and why do doubts rise in your minds?"* Luke 24:38. Then Jesus showed them His hands, feet and side, and told them to touch Him. A ghost doesn't have flesh and bones as He did.

They still were having difficulty believing because of their joy and amazement. Then He asked them for something to eat. After eating He explained again what had happened and why and, *"Then he opened their minds so they could understand the Scriptures."* Think how powerful it was for them to all of a sudden have everything make sense. Praise God that He does the same for us!

Why was it important for them not to understand what was going to happen to Jesus prior to this? I don't know – but I do know that it was! God has His reasons. It is so exhilarating to see how this group of frightened men and women were so utterly transformed by an encounter with the risen Christ! Isn't it amazing that He transforms us as well when we encounter Him!!

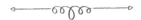

Think of carpentry and splinters

Hebrews 6:1a Therefore let us leave the elementary teachings about Christ and go on to maturity…

When we are born again, God does an amazing work in us. We become new creatures in Christ Jesus. Old things pass away and all things become new. Many of us experience remarkable transformations in our lives that impact behavior, thinking and speaking. The Lord becomes the most important thing in our lives. We are His, but in terms of living our lives here on earth, we have not arrived – we are merely beginning.

Have you ever considered the perspective that Christianity involves a skill set to be learned and lived? Foremost it is a relationship with our Lord, but that relationship with Him and with others has requirements of us. Some we find easier than others to meet. Some we really struggle with because of the ongoing work that the Lord must do in our lives. Although we are new in Christ, it's amazing the lifetime supply of 'stuff' we have in our lives that God will bring to our attention and help us deal with.

Our Christian walk is to become more and more like Jesus. We need to know what that looks like. All too often we think we know but we don't. Think a moment about it in terms of carpentry. It is a learned skill. Items must be smooth to the touch – no splinters! How often in our lives are we prickly or ripe with splinters in our interactions with others – and we might even be totally unaware of it. Some areas of our lives are in need of reconstruction by the Master Carpenter – while others He is putting His finishing touch on.

Change doesn't all happen overnight in terms of our behavior; it's a life-long transformative process with the Holy Spirit working with us. When the Scripture says that they will know we are disciples of Jesus by our love for one another, it's talking about how we live – how we act and talk. What attitudes do we demonstrate? Do we have a servant's heart?

We rejoice both in conforming to His word, and in His dealing with us where we have far to go. Jesus is our focus. I remember the slogan of the Zenith Corporation, 'The quality goes in before the name goes on.' The same is true of us but with a twist. We receive the quality within us in Christ. It's how we live that reflects our name – whether we are truly followers of Jesus.

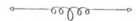

Delighting in Him

Isaiah 61:10a I delight greatly in the LORD; my soul rejoices in my God.

What do you think of when asked to name something you delight in? Is the word 'delight' even a word in your normal vocabulary? By definition, the word 'delight' means a high degree of gratification; joy; *also* extreme satisfaction, something that gives great pleasure. To me, delight has always had a sense of superlative to it. It's more than just being pleased with something, or liking something.

I remember so vividly the time when Becca, our oldest granddaughter, was about 19 months old. She walked up to me, grinned and said, "HI GRANDPA!" Oh my! What I experienced in that moment. If I could have melted I would have been a puddle on the floor.

What do you experience when someone you love calls simply to hear your voice – to see how you're doing? Or how about when the Lord puts someone on your heart and when you call them and give them a word of encouragement, you discover it was exactly what they needed to hear? The Lord used you to bless them. Think of how special that feels!

This sense of delight and rejoicing are not to be occasional things. I think of what I experience whenever my Donna looks into my eyes and smiles at me. Words simply cannot describe what goes on inside of me. I never dreamed that I would be loved as she loves me. I am overwhelmed with the reality that I GET TO love her and be loved by her all the days of my life. I GET TO be with her – every day. It never gets old!

Now think about our Lord. He wants our experience with Him to result in this kind of joy and excitement and pleasure and extreme satisfaction. He really does! He has this for us but we have to respond to Him and pursue Him to find it. If Moses hadn't turned aside to explore the burning bush, he would have missed what God had for him. .

If this is missing in your relationship with the Lord, don't be disheartened. Recognize the GREAT NEWS that He has this 'treasure' there for you – you simply have to pursue it. He wants you to want it and turn to Him for help to find it. The amazing thing is that as you pursue this, you find Him in ways that will thrill you beyond words!

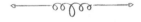

Outcomes are important

John 15:8 This is to my Father's glory, that you bear much fruit,
showing yourselves to be my disciples.

There are organizations that periodically go through a process to have their accreditation re-affirmed and extended. It is a significant process that primarily focuses on outcomes – what is being produced. It is key to being held accountable.

Apparently, years ago, the focus used to be more on resources – what was put into it. While that is still very important, it's the results, referred to as outcomes that are key. Another way of putting it is quality fruit being produced?

The process has those involved addressing lots of questions: What have we done? Where are we? What do we want to accomplish? Where are we weak? What strategies must we implement to become stronger? Are we producing good fruit? Are we producing fruit commensurate with the opportunities and resources given us? It's not enough to have good intentions and lots of effort.

I am struck by how this process and these questions apply to our lives as Christians. Think about them in relationship to yourself, your family, your church, your small group, your ministry or your relationships. Outcomes are important. God's Word lets us know what they should be. God wants us to be fruitful. But remember the issue isn't focused so much on the quantities but on the qualities reflected by who we are and what we do.

John 15 talks about Jesus being the vine; we are the branches; and the Father is the Gardener. He will do what it takes for the branches to bear fruit. He helps us discover weaknesses in our lives, goals we are to achieve – all manner of things. These are daily occurrences in His 'School of the Spirit'. He wants us to respond to Him and respond appropriately. This is how we bear fruit. He is after 'sweet fruit' not 'sour grapes'. We must understand the blessing it is that He is holding us accountable; after all, the goal is for people to see Jesus when they interact with us.

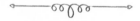

Weeding the garden of our life

*Mark 4:7 Some fell in the weeds; as it came up, it was strangled
among the weeds and nothing came of it.*

It's amazing how many weeds have flowers. I'm not talking about the ones that you see along roads or out in fields. I'm talking about the ones that come up in your gardens along with the flowers that have been planted. How often do we see that our gardens are loaded with both? My problem is telling which is which.

Some flowers are easy to identify: roses, iris, tulips and daffodils. Likewise dandelions are weeds. Even though a field of blooming dandelions might be pretty, that beauty ceases to exist when they are in our yards and gardens. The problem is all the other stuff that is coming up in the garden.

I have never been a gardener so when I look at the garden my thoughts are to get someone who knows this stuff and have them identify the flowers and the weeds. When I look closely though, it's apparent that some of the flower-bearing 'growth' is rapidly filling the garden and choking other plants out. It's almost like this 'growth' wants me to be distracted by its pretty little flowers while it takes over and chokes out the 'opposition' – the true flowers that are intended to grow.

Welcome to the spiritual garden of our lives where we have growing 'cultural' weeds and kingdom flowers – and each of us is responsible for what is found there. The problem is that far too many who call themselves Christian have their spiritual gardens (read lives) filled with pretty little 'flowers' that are all weeds; and these weeds are choking out and obliterating the kingdom life that belongs there.

Jesus warned us about this in the Parable of the Sower from which today's verse comes. We must not underestimate the power of these 'weeds' in our lives when we allow them to become established instead of pulling them out. Here is Jesus' warning as given in The Message:

"The seed cast in the weeds represents the ones who hear the kingdom news but are overwhelmed with worries about all the things they have to do and all the things they want to get. The stress strangles what they heard, and nothing comes of it."
Mark 4:17-18

Pray that the Lord will help us identify the 'weeds' in our lives; and that He will enable us to see where we have allowed ourselves to become deceived into thinking they are genuine flowers that belong there. The Holy Spirit will then enable us to effectively weed the garden of our life.

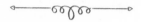

Keeping 'weeds' our of our lives

1 Corinthians 15:33 Do not be misled: "Bad company corrupts good character."

When we look out the kitchen window we see the garden I wrote of yesterday. The roses and iris are in full bloom and they are so beautiful. The pink, red and yellow colors are vibrant and abundant. One thing that really helps is that these plants are a lot taller than the weeds – at least now they are.

The smaller plants around them though are another matter. That is where the war with the weeds is really taking place. But this week I am going to enter the fray and get rid of the weeds. In my love of the dramatic I think of the battle of Helm's Deep in the Lord of the Rings. The good guys (the flowers) are on the verge of being overwhelmed by the bad guys (the weeds) and at the crack of dawn Gandalf and reinforcements (me) arrive and the bad guys are defeated.

We wrote yesterday of our spiritual gardens that the flowers and weeds represent referencing the Parable of the Sower. Jesus taught how the weeds could choke out the life of the good seed (flowers). Today's verse raises another serious threat that presents itself. Using our illustration, it warns that the association with the 'weeds' will corrupt good 'flowers'.

We must recognize the reality that who we are in Christ Jesus can become corrupted by those we associate with. This speaks to those we enjoy being with or hang out with. Unfortunately, we can be blind to this corruption that's taking place. Consider today's verse as it appears in the Amplified Bible:

Do not be so deceived and misled! Evil companionships (communion, associations) corrupt and deprave good manners and morals and character.

We must understand that a culture war is raging and the Gospel of Jesus Christ is the 'bull's eye' for the enemy's attacks. The war is to eliminate or corrupt all those who claim to be Christians. Sadly the evidence of the success of these attacks surrounds us.

When our love for God is what it should be, we resist accommodating the ways of the world – we embrace His ways. We recognize right and wrong. We reject the 'weeds' and keep them out of our lives. Our lives are not judgmental, but filled with love, grace and mercy. We become those who come to the aid of others to help them rid their 'gardens' of 'weeds'.

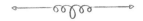

Being wise with humor

Psalm 141:3 Set a guard over my mouth, O LORD;
keep watch over the door of my lips.

Years ago, I'm told that a then famous comedian was asked if there would be comedians in heaven. He answered, "No – because comedy is always at someone else's expense." Some comedy is just funny. But the wrong kind of humor can really be a problem in the context of relationships.

My wife Donna and I have always referred to this kind of problem humor as negative humor. A friend is kidding you and you look at them and say, "You've got a great personality – for an ape!" Everybody laughs but the friend might be wondering what you really think of him. It might not bother him - or it might pierce his soul and wound him significantly. Haven't we all heard spouses, siblings or friends make cutting comments to each other while laughing? How often have we seen someone wince at the pain?

We are so grateful for the teaching we had nearly 50 years ago that led us to recognize negative humor for its destructive nature. Far too often it wounds – and the wound festers, leading to other destructive comments and interactions. Fortunately, we made a decision before we were married to never allow negative humor or sarcasm (a very close cousin) into our family, our relationships or our home.

It is simply too easy to hurt one another. While trying to be funny, we can unintentionally hurt those dear to us. We can develop a blind spot, not even recognizing when we do it or the damage it does. The Lord wants our speech to be wholesome and affirming. Humor is important and it's wonderful to laugh with one another. We simply need to be wise and discerning to avoid the negative.

We have such wonderful memories of times with our sons and now with their families where we would laugh and laugh and laugh. We were once at a restaurant and we all got the silly giggles with each other. Soon all the people at the neighboring tables around us were laughing too. What a marvelous and memorable evening that was and a great heritage to have such wonderful memories.

The choices we make that result in a Godly life

Psalm 1:1-3 [1]Blessed is the man who does not walk in the counsel of the wicked or stand in the way of sinners or sit in the seat of mockers. [2]But his delight is in the law of the LORD, and on his law he meditates day and night.
[3]He is like a tree planted by streams of water, which yields its fruit in season and whose leaf does not wither. Whatever he does prospers.

The beginning of Psalm 1 has always been special to me. It describes the journey to a Godly life. It's a simple summary or overview of what not to do; what to do; and the results of a life so lived. It's like a father talking with a son or daughter and giving them counsel that will help them in all they do. The counsel appears to be general in nature yet presents a clear picture of the types of actions required to have a blessed life.

The principles are really common to us because they exist in all areas of life. No matter what goal we're seeking, there are things and distractions to avoid, an attitude of heart to have, things to embrace, and the results consistent with such actions. Sports, music, school, marriage, child-raising, work, life – it makes no difference, the counsel applies.

Years ago, I was teaching in a private school and in the summer following my third year there, the school without warning closed. With a family to support, I wound up in sales – not somewhere I thought I would ever be. Lots of people fail at sales or only marginally succeed. Many of those around me failed because they wouldn't discipline themselves. They did not avoid the distractions, actions and associations with others that undermined what they were trying to learn. They did not approach the job whole-heartedly.

If we're supposed to be on the phone, making prospect calls, we can't be daydreaming, reading other stuff or talking with others who are in the process of failing as well. If we're supposed to be studying, there's TV, talking, messaging or tweeting. There are things and people and 'stuff' that call us – distract us – keep us, from attaining the goal we set. But we must recognize the issue is us!

Great are the rewards of avoiding the pitfalls, and whole-heartedly pursing the actions that enable us to attain a worthy goal. We must recognize that this reality applies to our relationship with the Lord. The result we achieve will be commensurate to what we do and how we do it.

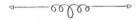

Becoming 'out of tune' and being deaf to that reality

Psalm 1:1-3 ¹Blessed is the man who does not walk in the counsel of the wicked or stand in the way of sinners or sit in the seat of mockers. ²But his delight is in the law of the LORD, and on his law he meditates day and night. ³He is like a tree planted by streams of water, which yields its fruit in season and whose leaf does not wither. Whatever he does prospers.

Years ago I had a good friend in college named Keith. His father who was a piano tuner, trained him in this trade when he was a child. Keith started tuning professionally at age 9 and was very good at it. He was raised near a nationally famous music camp and one summer he tuned for Van Cliburn who was performing at the camp.

There is one thing that I particularly remember about how Keith did his tuning. Although he did it by ear, he disciplined himself to tune periodically with a machine. He found this to be an excellent and necessary way to keep his own ear tuned appropriately. Otherwise, with the passing of time, his ear would go slightly off.

This is such an important lesson for us to consider as we look at our own lives. We have habits, associations, friends, idiosyncrasies, patterns of behavior, thoughts and attitudes – all of which need to be 'in tune' to the standard that God has for us. Without diligence, these practices can become 'off key' just as much as an out of tune piano. We might think everything is fine because we become deaf (and blind) to the disharmony we're producing. What appears normal can become strident without us being aware of it. I trust we understand that I am not talking about music here.

What is sexual impurity? What is gossip? Dishonesty? Immodesty? Immorality? What is stealing (in terms of habits and practices done at work)? How about jealousy or gossip? Where do you hang out on Friday or Saturday nights? Where do we draw the lines on these things? What is our standard for right and wrong? Acceptable and unacceptable?

These are all items, along with many others where we must be in tune with God's Word. We must care enough to submit everything about our lives to Him. Prayerfully read His word and allow the Holy Spirit to touch anything in our lives. If we're really listening, He will show us where we are 'out of tune'.

Each life is a symphony

Ephesians 5:19 Speak to one another with psalms, hymns and spiritual songs. Sing and make music in your heart to the Lord,

Take My Life And Let It Be – Frances Havergal, 1874

Take my life and let it be,
Consecrated, Lord, to Thee,
Take my moments and my days,
Let them flow in ceaseless praise.
Let them flow in ceaseless praise.

Above, I have the first verse of this wonderful hymn that many of us have sung in our worship services. In the midst of this verse I believe the Lord allowed me to see a picture of something in a way I hadn't seen it before. It came in an instant and I saw and understood it.

This verse talks about our lives - <u>our moments and our days</u>. Our prayer is to let them flow in ceaseless praise. Think of that ceaseless praise as a symphony – performed by an entire orchestra – not an individual. Drums, strings, woodwinds and brass – All the musicians, with their many different instruments, have their appropriate parts to play. The symphony is to be a harmonious blend of them all. They are all to be in-tune with each other! – And must follow the conductor's lead in order to blend together.

In this picture, I saw that our lives, consisting of thoughts, attitudes, actions, words, intents, motives and everything about us – are continually doing two things. First, our lives are creating a musical score. Second, our lives are playing as a symphony, <u>the score as we create it</u>. Each and every one of these aspects of our lives is an instrument and plays a part. Nothing is left out. Nothing is too small or insignificant. Nothing is silent.

The question becomes, 'How do we sound?' Is the 'music' pleasing or discordant? A pleasing sound is dependent upon the transforming work of the Holy Spirit and our obedience to walk in His ways. Nothing escapes His care and attention. We are to become increasingly responsive to His touch. When we co-operate with Him, He will bring everything in our lives into submission to His will. He will create within us the harmony and the wonder of a symphony of life that will glorify our Lord.

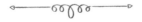

The wonder of kindness

1 Corinthians 13:4a Love is patient, love is kind.

Have you ever thought about how wonderful kindness is? There is really nothing like it. Unfortunately, we are not accustomed to encountering kindness or to being kind ourselves. Think of all the times we encounter crabby, curt people. Think of all the times when **we** are the crabby, curt people!

Being kind is such a wonderful weapon in our arsenal. People don't expect it. It disarms them and leaves a wonderful aroma in its wake. It is particularly powerful when experienced in our families, close friendships and with our co-workers.

The reality is that we can be the most unkind to the people we are closest to; parents to kids; kids to parents; spouses to each other; siblings to each other. We don't mean to be, it just works out that way. Some of the worst difficulties families encounter are the best opportunities for kindness to do its wonderful work.

Instead of taking offense at a spouse's crabbiness, respond with kindness. It is so disarming. Instead of reacting to your child's rebellion with anger, learn the power of kindness rooted in righteousness. We can communicate the standards God requires of us while still being kind to our sons or daughters and their friends. Kindness isn't defense – it is offense. It isn't expected and can have such a powerful impact.

I was re-reading an email from one of my sons in which he recounted incidents years earlier where Donna and I had profoundly impacted him by such simple things as taking groceries to him when he was in college. I took McDonald's to him and his friends at 6 AM when they camped out overnight for concert tickets. I guess they were stunned. His friends were welcome in our home. He said they loved me because I was polite and nice to them.

Kindness brings results, but those are in God's hands. People don't always respond the way we would like, even when we are kind. (We still remain kind in spite of how they act.) But our confidence is in our Lord. We don't know the hidden impact our kindness is having. We simply get to experience the joy of being kind and knowing that we are expressing God's love to those around us.

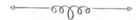

Are commands really suggestions?

John 14:15 "If you love me, you will obey what I command."

When I was a student at Wheaton Grad School I was blessed to be able to take a course taught by Dr. Merrill Tenney, a great Bible scholar. In one class we were talking about the importance of words – their meaning and the context in which they occur. He mentioned that the two words 'sight' and 'vision' were perceived by most people to have the same meaning. But then he noted that if he described someone's wife as a sight and his wife as a vision, the meanings are very different!

I would like to pose something that is just the opposite of Dr. Tenney's illustration. It is where two words are considered as having distinctly different meanings, yet a certain context can cause them to be viewed as having the same meaning.

The two words are 'suggestion' and 'command'. There is a similarity to these words in that they are at opposite ends of a spectrum. In a college environment we might simply think of one as an elective course and the other as a required course. Electives are optional, required courses are – well, required!

A suggestion may or may not be a good idea, but we have the freedom to choose to follow it or not. A command is decidedly different. We typically think of a military context when considering commands. Commands are to be obeyed.

What is the context that causes these two words to potentially have the same meaning? Unfortunately, that context for Christians is the context of our lives. How we <u>live</u> defines how we view the word 'command'. All too often, Christians in day to day life, treat Jesus' commands as suggestions. They aren't approached as requirements, but as options or electives. But Scripture doesn't give us that option.

If someone told us that if we follow their suggestions he would give us $1,000,000 – we would promptly ask, "What are your suggestions?" The Lord offers us far more, if we obey His commands. Our response should be an eagerness to learn what they are and pursue doing them. This is not an issue of legalism or earning salvation - it is a requirement of our faith. But more than that, it is an issue of love. It is the only way God has given us to show we truly love Him!

Lord, may our lives be living demonstrations that Jesus' commands are not suggestions.

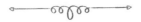

Not optional nor suggestive

Luke 9:23 Then he said to them all: "If anyone would come after me, he must deny himself and take up his cross daily and follow me.

If you're like me, you take advantage of the resources available on line to seek answers to the 'How To' questions we have. There's stuff we need to do, and by going to Google we can type in our issue and find sources that tell us how to do it. Today's verse offers us a prime example of a 'How To' issue. We might ask, "Please tell me 'How To' 1) deny myself, 2) take up my cross, and 3) follow Jesus. We want to do these things, but how?

Some of the themes we've been writing about are walking in His ways; obeying His commands; loving God; and continuing in His word. We have contrasted suggestions versus commands. We've talked about the problem some of us have when we hear the word 'commands'. It's like we have an allergic reaction to the word. But we must get past that to recognize they are the answers to the great 'How To' questions of our faith.

Our goal is to help us come to grips with the fact that the New Testament is filled with such 'answers' that we as Christians are to 'do'. Today let's look at some of the 'answers' that are spread throughout the New Testament that describe denying ourselves, taking up our cross and following Jesus:

- Do everything in love.

- Do nothing out of selfish ambition or vain conceit

- In humility consider others better than yourselves

- Your attitude should be that of Christ Jesus

- Continue to work out your salvation with fear and trembling

- Do everything without complaining or arguing

- Rejoice in the Lord always

- Let your gentleness be evident to all

- Do not be anxious about anything

- Put to death whatever belongs to your earthly nature: sexual immorality, impurity, lust, evil desires and greed, which is idolatry

- Clothe yourselves with compassion, kindness, humility, gentleness and patience

- Bear with each other

- Forgive whatever grievances you may have against one another

- Let the peace of Christ rule in your hearts

- Be thankful

- Let the word of Christ dwell in you richly

- Whatever you do, work at it with all your heart, as working for the Lord, not for men

Do we understand that these are not suggestions! And they are just a handful of what the Bible contains for us. They are not elective or optional. By embracing these things and allowing the Holy Spirit to do His work in us, we deny ourselves and take up our cross to follow Jesus. This is the way – and the only way – to express our love to God.

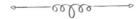

Belonging to Him

*Psalm 85:5 You are forgiving and good, O Lord, abounding
in love to all who call to you.*

I have kept journals for years. I love to look back five or ten years ago to see what was happening in my life. Sometimes I rediscover experiences that bring back great memories of family or trips or things at work. Other times I read about struggles and difficulties we've gone through.

One of the cool things that I've done with some of my journals over the years is to highlight with a marker special times with the Lord. I get blessed again reading about the times when He has really blessed me by showing me things in my life or by manifesting His presence while I'm in prayer. There are times when He just overwhelms me with joy – where I simply weep because I am so overcome with gratitude for His goodness to me.

It is so wonderful to be forgiven – and more than that – to be chosen; to belong; to be loved. Years ago, when we were just married, we were about to become involved in a ministry to street people. I prayed and asked the Lord how I could relate to them since I had basically been a good kid. I never did drugs and I had a good home. The Lord spoke so clearly to me. He said, "You know what it's like to be lonely." And I did. Only half-jokingly did I talk about myself being left out, un-chosen and left behind.

But when Jesus made me His own – all that changed. For over 50 years, God's forgiveness, His goodness and His abounding love have been life to me. And the great news is that He has this for all of us. He wants us all to be so caught up in the wonder of Him and His love that we want to live for Him more than anything.

He is not distant. He is not aloof. He does not leave us alone. He never forsakes us. He paid the greatest price imaginable for us to become His family. The more we say 'yes' to Him, the richer our relationship with Him becomes. These realities become bedrock within us – able to withstand any 'storm' that we go through. What a thrill to be passionately in love with Him!

Don Schmidt

Friends

John 15:14 You are my friends if you do what I command.

Friends. Have you ever considered what a broad spectrum that word covers? People we see and speak to at church, at school or at work. People we hang around with. Our neighbors or the people in a small group we're a part of. From people we enjoy seeing and being with – to those who are important in our lives – to those we absolutely treasure.

Hopefully, we all have some friendships that are in the 'treasured' category. Typically, we don't have many and to have even one is beyond a blessing. Some friendships move into this treasured category because of shared hardship. One of you, or a couple, was going through a very hard time and you were there with them – or they were there with you. Praying together, crying together, hurting together; friend letting friend know they are important and loved! It's a refining process that brings forth a quality and depth of friendship that wouldn't be there without it.

I never cease to be blessed by the treasured friends Donna and I have who enjoy us as much as we enjoy them. They love to bless us as much as we love blessing them. They enjoy being with us as much as we enjoy being with them. The joy and pleasure we experience when we see that a call or text or email is from them. They brighten our lives.

This is the nature of the friendship that Jesus offers us. It's not just being one of the group. It is an opportunity – an open door to a relationship that He wants to have with us. It is not just a theological truth. **It is real** – something that **He wants** to manifest in our lives. It is the stuff that dreams are made of – dreams that can come true!

Treasured friendships are priceless and Jesus offers each of us the best one we can ever have – a friendship beyond imagining. All we have to do is love Him. Thankfully He has given us His commands so that we can know that we do love Him.

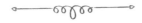

Life is filled with 'soufflés'

Psalm 119:105 Your word is a lamp to my feet and a light for my path.

This morning I would like us to consider a cooking illustration. Do we view God's Word like recipe cards? They sit on a shelf or in a drawer until we want to cook a dish where we need the specific recipe. Even then, we might think we are familiar enough with the recipe so we go ahead without looking for it. I did this with one of my favorite casseroles lately – twice – and both times I forgot something.

We've all grown up around kitchens, so we have a familiarity with cooking. We can fry eggs; make sandwiches; use the microwave to warm up a dish; etc... Typically, the ladies who have raised families are much more knowledgeable about cooking because they've had to learn. They answer our questions like, 'What temperature do I use?' 'Where do you keep the blender?' 'How do I keep it from sticking to the skillet?'

We are able to function in a kitchen because of familiarity – so long as it's kept simple. Just don't ask us to make a soufflé! Or gravy! Or pie crusts! This issue of familiarity can be a very serious problem in our lives as Christians. We've been around church and have a general sense of things to do or not do. We've read parts of the Bible so we have a 'feel' for what the Christian life should be. The problem is life is filled with 'soufflés'. In fact, the Christian life requires us to live in the 'cookbook' not just hunt for a recipe card on occasion.

Today's verse offers a nice parallel. If we have to walk in the dark, we would always have a light with us, even if we are familiar with the path – let alone if we are dealing with rocky, uneven or unknown terrain. It enables us to walk safely and securely – avoiding unexpected obstacles. Familiarity with the Christian life is no substitute for having an intimate, thorough knowledge and understanding of God's Word. Life is filled with 'darkness' even in the middle of the day, where decisions have to be made right then. God's Word within us provides the 'light' to guide our steps no matter how difficult or unfamiliar the terrain.

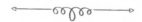

The example of our neighbor Zach

James 1:27 Religion that God our Father accepts as pure and faultless is this: to look after orphans and widows in their distress and to keep oneself from being polluted by the world.

Zach & Neva and their two daughters lived two houses over from us when I was a boy growing up. They were friends of my parents and were like close relatives to us. Our families celebrated birthdays together and just enjoyed one another. When I was a high school senior, Zach helped me get a really good part-time job. They were great neighbors. They were members of an evangelical church.

From my earliest memories, they were always Zach and Neva - never Mr. and Mrs. McPherson or 'Uncle Zach and Aunt Neva' – just Zach and Neva. While Zach had a regular job, he was also a handyman. He was one of those blessed individuals who knew how to fix or repair all kinds of things. I remember admiring his work area in his basement. He had all kinds of tools and invariably he was always working on a project.

Of all the memories I have of Zach, one stands out far above all the rest. It's not just one incident, but it's a whole bunch of them that are wonderfully similar. Zach was always working on a number of houses in our neighborhood. I would see him at these houses painting, repairing things, putting up or taking down storm windows. It was a normal sight that I grew up with.

I finally got old enough as a child to wonder about it and so I asked my folks why Zach was frequently working at these houses. You can guess the answer. These houses were the homes of older widows or people who needed help. Zach was there for them – year after year. He never talked about it – he just did it. Whenever I read this verse in James about looking after orphans and widows, I think of Zach.

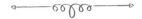

The incredible opportunity we all have!

*Daniel 10:11a He said to me, "Daniel, you are a man treasured [by God]. -
Holman Christian Standard*

How would we be described by our spouses, children, friends or co-workers, if they were asked what kind of people we are; and they answered with brutal honesty? Their answers would say a lot about who we are; what we do; how we do it; what are we like to be around; how honest are we; how thoughtful; how 'other' oriented; do we brighten their days – and so on. (Sounds like a candid eulogy, doesn't it?)

How would God describe us? This gets to the heart of the issue. He loved us while we were sinners and showed that love by sending Jesus, through whom we have the opportunity to become His children. But now that we are family, we need to recognize not only the responsibility we have, **but the opportunity!**

We want our children and loved ones to become people of quality. It's not a matter of us loving or not loving them – it's a matter of the lives they lead. We experience great joy and pleasure as we see them grow and mature in Godliness. The same holds true with God. How we grow – or not grow – in Godliness, is critically important to Him. It impacts how He views and interacts with us. (Don't be thinking judgment here – but think as a loving parent.)

I rejoice that He has given us Daniel as an example of what will happen in lives that are totally given over to Him. Consider how Scripture describes God's view of Daniel:

- you are a man treasured [by God]. – Holman Christian Standard

- for you are very precious to God – New Living Translation

- for you are greatly beloved. – Amplified

- you who are highly esteemed, – NIV

Think of it!! We have the opportunity to become men and women that God would describe as He did Daniel: treasured, very precious, greatly beloved, highly esteemed. By walking in His word, the Holy Spirit produces the character and likeness of Christ in every area of our lives. This is the result of truly loving God. We don't pursue it for recognition – but for the wonder of pleasing and blessing Him.

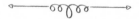

Don Schmidt

Sailing in Bermuda: An important lesson learned

Hebrews 5:14 But solid food is for the mature—for those whose senses have been trained to distinguish between good and evil.

Although I grew up in a small port city on the Lake Michigan, I never got to experience sailing until I earned a sales trip to Bermuda. One of the events for the participants was a sailboat race. There were three big sailboats and a course laid out for the race that involved sailing in all directions – with and against the wind. A staggered start was used with the slowest boat going first and the fastest last. Donna and I were on the middle sailboat.

What a wonderful adventure. We passed the first sailboat and managed to keep ahead of the fastest one that was methodically gaining on us. We were still leading when we had one more buoy to sail around and then it would be a sprint for the finish line. The other sailboat was closing and the strong cross-wind was a real challenge.

I was standing next to our captain as we rounded the final buoy. He commented that he thought the other sailboat would pass us and win the race, but then he let out a whoop, and yelled, "We're going to win!" He explained that the other captain misread the wind and made a wrong move. This resulted in his sails collapsing and a loss of momentum. It took him several minutes to regain his speed but by then we were nearing the finish line.

That captain lost because he misread the wind. Our verse today speaks of acquiring a similar skill – that of distinguishing between good and evil. Sometimes telling the difference is easy, like sailing with the wind at your back. But other times, it can be much more difficult – thus the imperative of having our senses trained. Being able to distinguish good from evil is an absolutely essential skill that every believer must practice and develop. We need it every day and cannot afford to misread the 'wind'.

Here is the Amplified version of this verse which makes it even clearer how important this skill is: *"But solid food is for full-grown men, for those whose senses and mental faculties are trained by practice to discriminate and distinguish between what is morally good and noble and what is evil and contrary either to divine or human law."*

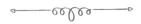

Recognizing when fear is a doorway and not a barrier

Hebrews 13:6 So we say with confidence, "The Lord is my helper; I will not be afraid. What can man do to me?"

Years ago when our oldest sons were young, we went to Six Flags over Georgia. Although I'm the one in our family who had a fear of heights and was allergic to roller coasters, it was my fate to accompany the boys on a couple of rides that I would never have chosen.

I have such a vivid memory of standing in line for this super rollercoaster, dreading every minute of it, while all the children and other adults around me are so excited they can hardly stand it. Then there was the parachute drop! Again it was my fate to accompany Jamie on it. While in line I was timing things so I knew just how long it would take to ascend and drop.

Our turn came and we sat on the tiny board that passed for a seat. It felt like it was about 4" wide and that I was going to slide off even though we were belted in. Then, instead of hitting the button to send us up, the guy forgot and turned to the second parachute – prolonging my agony. He finally turned, saw his mistake - and hit the button As we ascended, seemingly forever, I kept telling myself I would live through this. By the time we got to the top, the board underneath me felt like it was 2" wide.

Needless to say, I lived. I can laugh now, but fear is a reality of life. Life is filled with opportunities that seem to have fear associated with them. While sometimes it can be healthy, and keep us safe, often it is a barrier that we must overcome to accomplish what we need or want to do. Rather than viewing fear as a negative and being repulsed by it, see it as a sign of an opportunity to grow.

Sometimes fear will still be a companion – like with me when I fly. But with God as our helper we can keep fear in its place and thrive in the opportunities that come - whether they be cold calling, speaking in a meeting or going on a mission trip to Afghanistan. It's important that we see that often fear is not a barrier - but a doorway. With God's help, we can walk through it.

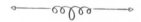

Loving insight into my behavior

Romans 2:4b ...not realizing that God's kindness leads you toward repentance?

Have you ever had a friend or someone in your life that believed in you and was for you, no matter what? Have you ever been that person for someone you know? The relationship is so strong and motivation so right that difficult things can be communicated because the trust is there.

Many years ago when we were involved in ministry, we moved back to an area we had lived in before. When we arrived we heard very negative things about two individuals we knew – Bill and Erik. Bill had been a very good friend and Erik was more of an acquaintance. Erik was a newer Christian and bit more radical. He had also been the recipient of some good things that I thought (at that time) should have come to me.

Although I am forgiven, I am still humbled by my very different responses to these two brothers. I was so troubled by what I heard that I met with Bill at our center late one night. I shared with him what I had become aware of and reaffirmed my love for him and our friendship. I let him know that I would help him in anyway that I could. We shared, wept and prayed with each other.

With Erik, the troubling things I heard fit with my perception of him. I simply wrote him off. Sometime later after we had moved away, the Lord confronted me with the question of why my responses to these two brothers were so different. As I pondered the question, the answer became so embarrassingly obvious: I loved Bill and didn't love Erik!

When the Lord showed me this, it wasn't like a trip to the woodshed or the Principal's office. It was like a treasured friend taking me aside and sitting down with me for a talk. Although painful to hear, the relationship enabled me to hear and receive the truth about myself. Instead of experiencing rejection, my Lord had His arm around my shoulders – affirming me.

Because of God's kindness, I was lovingly being offered insight into my own misbehavior so that I might repent and learn. Isn't that one of the most marvelous realities of our life with Him? He will regularly show us where we need to change – and enable us to change - so that our lives will be a continuous, ongoing transformation into the image of Christ. May we all see that this is our daily way of life with Him and recognize His kindness.

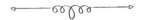

Suppose you are asked "Why?"

Part 1 of 3: *2 Corinthians 3:2 You yourselves are our letter, written on our hearts, known and read by everybody.*

Picture yourself on a jet that has just taken off for a long flight. You begin a conversation with the person next to you and discover that he is searching the various religions to find the right one. His background is not Christianity but he has been reading the Bible as part of his search. He is filled with questions and begins to ask you them.

Why are you a Christian? If you had to identify one or two aspects of your life as a Christian that were the most important to you, what would they be? How does your daily life reflect your Christian faith?

What would your answers be to him? Would you be experiencing excitement at the opportunity to share your faith? Or would your experience be tempered by awareness that other 'stuff' has diminished the vibrancy your relationship with Christ in your life? If your daily life of thoughts and actions were written out what would they reveal to him about you and your faith? What would they reveal to those around you?

Today's Scripture presents the reality that our lives are being read by those around us. Their lives are being read by us. That is simply the reality of life. It is not an issue of being judgmental, it's a matter of people being cognizant of the encounters they have.

Is faith reflected in the story, or letter, of our lives? Do our lives consistently reflect more of our Lord than the worldliness of our culture? The Holy Spirit is leading each of us to make Jesus the true love of our life. Hopefully, each chapter of our lives will reflect us coming closer to achieving this goal.

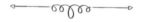

An incredible, unforgettable experience!

Part 2 of 3: *1 Corinthians 3:6 I planted the seed, Apollos watered it,*
but God made it grow.

Yesterday I asked you to picture yourself on a jet that has just taken off for a long flight. The person next to you is not a Christian and is searching the various religions to find the right one. He has been reading the Bible as part of his search and is filled with questions and begins to ask you them.

This specific scenario happened to me and a young friend named Andy several summers ago. We were in Europe and were on the first leg of our trip home. The young man next to me was raised a Muslim but had concluded that it was not the answer. In his search, he had narrowed it down to Judaism and Christianity. He had been particularly struck by the concept of 'loving one another'.

The more we talked the more apparent it became just how thorough his search had been. He was aware of the price he would pay with his family but determined to find the truth. He had been waiting for over a year to make this trip to come to school in America. The Lord timed the flight so that we would have the blessing of being with him on this leg of his trip. How I thought of this verse as we experienced the joy of responding to his questions and sharing our faith with him.

Shortly before the end of the flight, Andy told me that the young man had said to him, "It was no accident that I sat down with you two!" What a marvelous opportunity this was to be a part of God's plan to bring someone to Himself. We had been given the opportunity to water the seeds others had planted. In the subsequent months, I wondered if this young man had completed his search. You can imagine my joy and gratitude to the Lord when I received the following email at Christmas of that year:

"Merry Christmas Don,

I guess you don't remember me. Well, we met in plane when we were travelling from Ukraine to Amsterdam this July.

Let me share something with you what god has done to me, it may surprise you. If you remember me then you will remember that I was on a spiritual journey. And I was not able to find god's way or light. I was living in darkness. And when we met, I was on the point where I knew that God's way was in Judaism or Christianity. Well, on the night of 14th Oct, when I was talking to a pastor I found a light. I was literally crying afterwards. I found Jesus. I tell you after that night, I have lived every moment as a complete life. I am thankful to him that he could come to a sinner like me.

Well, I just wanted to share my experience with you.

I wish you a Merry Christmas and a very Happy New Year."

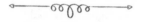

Meeting Jesus is just the beginning!

Part 3 of 3: 1 Peter 1:8 Though you have not seen him, you love him; and even though you do not see him now, you believe in him and are filled with an inexpressible and glorious joy,

This morning I am still overflowing with joy over the wonder and thrill of what Jesus does – and has done – in our lives. Yesterday's devotional seemed to just trigger an eruption of that joy. It recounted how God used my friend Andy and me in His plan of drawing this young Muslim man to Jesus. The experience of that flight was priceless, but then to receive the email of him finding Jesus! It just tapped into the wellspring of gratitude and joy that I have for my own experience of finding Jesus.

I'm sitting here writing this, grinning and basking in the inexpressible and glorious joy that Peter writes of in today's verse. The joy for this young man and the joy for my own encounter with Jesus are still just engulfing me. And those salvation experiences are just the beginning!

Becoming a follower of Jesus is not a one-experience life! If our testimony is simply recounting what God did in our lives years ago, we are missing the mother lode. Yes, my encounter with Him 50 years ago was astounding. It's like the rock of Gibraltar in my life – it is huge! But that was simply the transforming invitation to 'come in'. It's like the Lord saying, "If you thought that was good, that is merely the foretaste!"

We belong to Him, and as His family we get to experience the treasure of His Word, His ways, His love, His protection, His presence, His provision…. It just goes on and on. He also surprises us, delights us, disciplines us, prunes us, tests us, comforts us, confronts us, encourages us…. Best of all, we get to experience Him.

Hopefully, this triggers joy within you and the refreshing that comes from remembering the wonder of our God. But if it doesn't, hopefully it will spark your active pursuit of Him. His plan for all of us is for our lives to be filled with an inexpressible and glorious joy because we belong to Him.

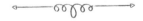

A very important learned skill

Proverbs 3:5, 6 Trust in the LORD with all your heart, and do not rely on your own understanding; ⁶think about Him in all your ways, and He will guide you on the right paths. Holman Christian Standard

Have you ever considered the idea that 'trusting the Lord' is a learned skill? The more we do it, the better we can become at it. Trusting the Lord comes through making daily choices as to where will we place our confidence. It frequently involves outward decision making, such as tithing or giving when finances are tight. We might be faced with situations that appear to require a 'small' inappropriate compromise in order to prevent a larger negative – like loss of a job, or a sale or a relationship.

Doing the right thing is important, but trusting in the Lord offers so much more. Think of the verse where we are commanded not to be anxious over anything (Phil 4:6). We can do the right thing while being beside ourselves with anxiety and concern. The children of Israel could have chosen to enter the land in spite of the giants and the negative report of the 10 spies. They were frightened but they could have still obeyed the Lord.

A most vital component in this process is the relationship we have with the Lord. The closer our walk is with Him, the greater is our freedom from anxiety and worry in difficult situations. Consider the following situations and what you are likely to experience internally in each of them:

1. You are lost, driving in a city you've never been in; you are in an unsavory area and your cell phone is not working; you have an important appointment to keep – if only you can find it.

2. Same as #1 but your cell phone begins working; so you call your friend you're meeting with - and get his voice mail.

3. Same as # 1 but you ask someone for directions and they sound a bit confused as they give them to you.

4. Same as #1 but you remember you have a GPS. You plug it in; enter the address of the appointment; push the go button and you immediately know how to get there and how long it will take.

The point isn't to go out and buy a GPS - but to recognize how different our state of being can be in different situations. The more we learn to trust in the Lord, the more we are able to have the peaceful heart response of situation #4 while in situations like #1.

Don Schmidt

Make trusting God our 'normal'

1 Chronicles 5:20 They were helped in fighting them, and God handed the Hagrites and all their allies over to them, because they cried out to him during the battle. He answered their prayers, because they trusted in him.

Today's verse presents trusting in the Lord in a way that is probably more common to most Christians. In the midst of a crisis, we call on the Lord. The Reubenites, the Gadites and the half-tribe of Manasseh were in a battle and in the midst of it they cried out to the Lord. God answered their prayers, because they trusted in Him. The Amplified Bible describes this trust as 'they relied on, clung to, and trusted in Him'.

This event is such a wonderful example of God's "normality" – His people are in situation; they pray and trust Him and He answers their prayers. The goal is to make this 'our normality' – but with the recognition that it applies to every area of our lives. We must avoid at all cost life-habits that in reality say, 'When all else fails, trust God.' Or, a more positive way of saying this negative is, 'God helps those who help themselves.'

Here is where our relationship with the Lord becomes so vital. Walking in His ways is a primary way of learning to trust Him. His ways bring blessing and when we walk in them we experience Him more and more. We learn that God can't be unfaithful or unloving or uncaring. He is always there. It becomes a given in our hearts and minds that God is intimately involved in our situations because that is the way He is. No matter what happens, He is there with us and for us.

We can experientially learn the reality that Shadrach, Meshach and Abednego expressed to the king when confronted with being thrown into a blazing furnace. They declared to him that their God was able to rescue them and they believed He would …but even if He didn't…. Their trust and confidence was in Him!

Our confidence and trust in Jesus is not predicated on the outcome – it becomes experientially a given in our lives. No matter what – He is true and we stand securely in that knowledge and relationship. It is not just a theological truth we affirm – it is the reality that we experience with Him.

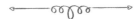

We 'get to'!

Joshua 23:11 So be very diligent to love the LORD your God for your own well-being. Holman Christian Standard

One of the things so precious to me is what I typically experience during the worship portion of our Sunday service. It is a mix of wonder, gratitude, amazement and heartfelt love that Yahweh – our God – is my father and has made me His own. I am one of His sons! He is not distant – nor is He aloof. He is my loving father.

Our four sons, John, Jamie, Andrew and Michael, will hug and kiss me when we see each other. They will do this anywhere in front of anyone. And our hugs are not perfunctory or just a little embrace, a little squeeze. Our hugs are experiences in themselves! We will embrace and hold each other tightly and just ooze with love and affection and joy in each other. We then look at each other and smile. My sons love me – and I love them. (I am in tears sitting here just thinking of my sons and the blessing they are to me).

This is what I experience with our Lord! At times I want to pinch myself because it is so unbelievable. This is what He wants for all of us! But this isn't the end of it. He gives us a way to respond so that we can experience the joy of giving back to Him. We love Him in return. Yes, we are commanded to love Him. But when we understand how He loves us, our loving response isn't a 'have to' but a 'get to'. WE GET TO LOVE HIM IN RETURN!

But it gets even more amazing! The more that our lives express genuine love for Him, the more He enables us to experience His limitless love for us! There is so much of Him that we will not experience if we don't. In reality, He's given us the keys to a storehouse of treasure that He wants us to have - if only we choose to use them.

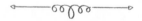

The wonder of faith

2 Corinthians 5:7 We live by faith, not by sight.

Isn't it amazing how different life can appear when seen through the eyes of faith? I look back over my life and see so many situations where things happened that I struggled with at the time. But later events would prove that those experiences were in fact blessings not curses. In fact, some of the greatest experiences I have ever had came about because of earlier disappointments where I was prevented from doing what I wanted to do.

In the midst of defeat, despair and disappointment comes hope because of faith. In the midst of opportunity, blessing and prosperity comes gratitude and acknowledgment of His blessing because of faith. When we read the Bible we see so many examples of people experiencing life – its ups and downs. Some respond well – others don't. The constant is that God is at work in and around them. The Lord wants us to understand that He does the same things with us.

He wants us to 'see' Him in everything. This is not due to eyes of sight, but of eyes of faith. I find that when everything starts going wrong, I immediately know that God is somewhere in the middle of it, and begin to look for Him. An initial negative reaction is replaced by the realization that God is there; we are not alone and things are not at all be what they seem.

Faith leads to prayer and seeking Him to provide wisdom and understanding. Faith causes us to use His word as our guide in how to respond whatever the situation. Faith affirms our desire to trust the Lord and glorify Him in any way that we can. Faith is not static - it is like a muscle that can be exercised. The more we use it, the stronger it becomes. Faith is the antidote to defeat. Without it, we cannot please God.

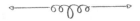

The purpose of prophets

*Hebrews 12:1-2a In the past God spoke to our forefathers through
the prophets at many times and in various ways,
²but in these last days he has spoken to us by his Son,...*

If someone were to ask you what the primary purpose of prophets in the Old Testament was, what would your answer be? Looking at this verse, you might say they were raised up to speak what God wanted said. That's true but that's not getting to the heart of it.

Think of who they were speaking to; what they were saying; and why it was being said. The prophets were speaking to the Israelites – the descendants of Abraham, Isaac and Jacob. They were typically telling them to repent, come back to God and obey His commands. The reason these things were being said was two-fold: 1) They were God's people and 2) They were not walking in His ways.

But there is so much more to it than that. <u>God loved them and wanted them to love Him in return</u>. He wanted His people to be blessed not cursed. The fact that they were the children of Abraham was important, but the crux of the issue was how they lived their lives. Did they walk in His ways?

Now we have Jesus. He offers the opportunity, through faith in Him, to become God's people to all mankind – not just the children of Israel. He provides the Holy Spirit to those who believe in Him so that they can walk in His ways and be His people. We need to understand that this is so much more than what we do on Sunday mornings. Our involvement with a local body of believers is merely the tip of the iceberg. It is the other 90% of our lives where we communicate our love – or lack of love – to our God!

<u>We must grasp the fact that God's desire now is the same as it was then. He wants His people to love Him – to walk in His ways – to reflect His glory. He wants the world to see His reflection in His people.</u> In the Old Testament they were not born again. They still had to contend with their sinful natures. But we are new creatures in Christ Jesus. We have such an advantage over them. While we still struggle with temptations and sin, we don't have our old nature as a deck stacked against us. Let us re-commit ourselves to saying Yes to His Spirit and His word as they call us to live lives worthy of our God.

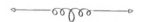

Two sources of divine revelations:
Creation and Christians

Romans 1:20 and Ephesians 2:10

These two verses have an extraordinary relationship with each other. At face value they both refer to something God has made – His workmanship. In the Greek, the word is ποιημα (poiema) and in the New Testament it only appears in these two verses. But the critical fact is that in one of these, we Christians play an absolutely critical role in what the world perceives as real.

Romans 1:20 *For since the creation of the world God's invisible qualities—his eternal power and divine nature—have been clearly seen, being understood <u>from what has been made</u>, so that men are without excuse.*

Ephesians 2:10 *For we are <u>God's workmanship</u>, created in Christ Jesus to do good works, which God prepared in advance for us to do.*

The first verse in Romans 1:20 speaks about how God is (and always has been) revealed to mankind through nature – His creation. He declares that it alone is sufficient to reveal His existence. Psalm 19:1-4a speaks so eloquently of this truth:

> *¹The heavens declare the glory of God; the skies proclaim the work of his hands.*
> *²Day after day they pour forth speech; night after night they display knowledge.*
> *³There is no speech or language where their voice is not heard. ⁴Their voice goes out*
> *into all the earth, their words to the ends of the world.*

The second verse in Ephesians 2:10 speaks about how we Christians – His people – are his workmanship created in Christ Jesus to do good works. We have written how God wants His people to love Him – to walk in His ways – to reflect His glory. His intent and equipping of us is so that the world will see Jesus when they see us.

Jesus came to enable us to do just that. Further, Ephesians 3:10 states that

> *"His intent was that now, through the church, the manifold wisdom of God should be made known to the rulers and authorities in the heavenly realms,"*

Putting these two verses (Rom 1:20 & Eph 2:10) together reveals a stunningly important reality: **God has made us both to be critically important revelations. Creation is a general revelation that God exists. We Christians are to be a specific revelation that Jesus Christ is Lord!**

What do communities see when they look at the Christians in their midst? Do they see Jesus or do they see something not at all reflective of Him. How we, who claim to be Christians, choose to live determines whether the picture we reveal is one of Jesus – or one that undermines the power of Gospel because our lives don't reveal Him.

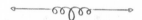

What do you delight in?

Proverbs 11:20 The LORD detests men of perverse heart but he delights in those whose ways are blameless.

What things come to mind when you consider the idea of being delighted with something? They might involve people, food, travel, hobbies, special moments – but whatever they are, they are special. They are things that give extreme pleasure, satisfaction or joy.

The first thought in my mind this morning when I think of being delighted with something is playing with my grandchildren and seeing them laugh. I delight in my wife, Donna; in beautiful sunsets; seeing flocks of Canada geese; being with our children; walks on the ocean shore; being with good friends; seeing the Ohio State Buckeyes football team win; talking about the Lord with young men and women.

You might delight in a quiet time with a good book or sitting in front of a fire place on a winter evening with a good cup of coffee. There is delight in helping others; in doing a job well; in persevering and overcoming a difficult obstacle; in worshipping the Lord and experiencing His presence.

There are so many things that can bring us delight – but shift your thinking from what brings you delight, to the sensation of delight itself. Think of the pleasure, the joy, the warm feelings – the satisfaction – the sensation of not wanting the moment to end.

'Delight' is far beyond being merely satisfied or pleased with something. It is truly something special. This is what God experiences in us when our ways are blameless. Think of it! - We are able to bring our God delight - extreme pleasure - by living our lives the way He wants us to. May we delight in delighting Him.

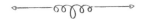

Dealing with anxiety

Philippians 4:6 Do not be anxious about anything, but in everything, by prayer and petition, with thanksgiving, present your requests to God.

Whether it is one task or situation or a slew of them, it is not unusual to find ourselves being confronted with anxiety. Our situation can be so daunting we feel like the disciples in the boat in the midst of the storm: we're overwhelmed and Jesus is asleep. Their focus was on the storm, the wind and the waves – rather than upon the fact that He was with them. Then when they did cry out to Jesus, they were frantic. How often do we do the same?

From reading today's verse, it's pretty clear that God knows about our tendency to become anxious. From finances, to illness, to family issues, to jobs – our lives are ripe with opportunities for us to choose the wrong way to go when the 'storm' of anxiety comes. But it's important that we recognize that His prescription isn't intended to be a 'fire alarm' - pull in case of fire – although it can still work that way.

It prescribes a way of life and the establishment of a relationship that will enable us to live in peace while in the midst of stormy situations. We are to live the verse day by day. Think of a college student who doesn't really study all term and then crams like crazy for the final, versus the student who has faithfully studies day by day throughout the term. Both might do well on the final, but one has chosen wisely and the other hasn't.

Each day, the Lord wants us to be looking to Him. He cares about us, the situations we face and He wants us to become confident of that. Praying and presenting our requests to Him daily with thanksgiving is His wisdom for us. Doing this develops a protective barrier for us and is an antidote to becoming bogged down with anxiety. Through these actions He also enables us to become so much more aware of His working in our lives. Our confidence in Him becomes strong resulting in appreciation and gratitude. Thankfulness becomes the reality of our lives.

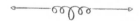

He will cause your thoughts...

Proverbs 16:3 Commit to the LORD whatever you do, and your plans will succeed. (NIV) - (Amplified Bible): <u>Roll your works upon the Lord</u> **[commit and trust them wholly to Him; He will cause your thoughts to become agreeable to His will, and]** <u>so shall your plans be established and succeed.</u>

There's the story of the two guys in a boat way out in the ocean. The one says, "Man – look at all the water!" The other replies, 'Yeah – and to think that's just the top of it!" Words have meaning – and those meanings usually involve a whole lot more than we might think. It's amazing how life changing words in Scripture can be when we understand the depth of meaning that they have.

When I first read this verse in other versions of the Bible it seemed like a simple, straightforward recipe for success. In order to succeed, all we have to do is commit what we're doing to the Lord. That seemed pretty simple to do. But what exactly does it mean to commit something to the Lord? What about all the times when our plans are unclear or we're questioning what God wants us to do? And doesn't God's idea of success sometimes differ from what we think?

When I first read this verse in the Amplified Bible it seemed to jump off the page. I saw what was involved in committing my way to the Lord! But more than that, the verse describes how God would respond and impact our thoughts, our plans and their development! The understanding that *"He will cause your thoughts to become agreeable to His will"* is priceless to the committed believer.

We want to do His will. We want our plans to conform to His plans for us. We want every decision we make – from the big ones to the little ones that fill our day - to be consistent with a Christ-centered life. This verse contains the promise and blueprint of how it can happen.

By embracing this process, the Lord will grow our confidence in Him. We will see the quality of our decisions and lives improve. The more we commit our way to Him; the more we allow Him to transform our thoughts and plans – the more we will experience the 'God-results' that He has for us. <u>('God results' = God's idea of success)</u>

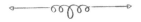

Donna's divine appointment

Proverbs 16:3 Roll your works upon the Lord [commit and trust them wholly to Him; He will cause your thoughts to become agreeable to His will, and] so shall your plans be established and succeed. Amplified

Yesterday I wrote about this verse and how God will cause our thoughts to become agreeable to His will when we commit what we do to the Lord. One of the wonderful things that God does with this is put us into 'divine appointments'. I was reading in my journal from 2006 about how God did exactly this with my wife Donna.

It was Sunday June 24 and we were living in Colorado Springs. On this particular day Donna had a 'bee in her bonnet' about going to look at a new subdivision of 24 homes in a nearby suburb. Upon arriving there she recognized the salesperson as Jill – someone she had worked with at a different subdivision when Donna had a job as a temp employee. They talked and Donna wound up sharing the events in her life since they had worked together – particularly focusing on her termination the previous August of her job as a sales coordinator with a wonderful new home builder.

Donna shared how much she loved her job - and how she cried all the way home after being told they had to let her go (due to the downturn in the real estate market). But she recognized that she had two choices 1) blame God and react negatively, or 2) recognize that God was closing one door but others would be opened. She shared with Jill how she chose to look to God, making the right faith response.

The very next day, Jill was let go by her employer. She just could not get over the fact that Donna had been there less than 24 hours earlier talking to her about that exact experience! Jill had never had anything like that happen before. They both were so blessed by this Divine Appointment.

It is important to recognize that it became a Divine Appointment because of what was shared. If Donna hadn't shared her experience, the opportunity would have been a missed. But by doing so, Jill was able to experience the Lord's love and concern – plus through Donna, He showed her the way to go and an example to follow.

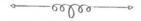

The wonder of gratitude and where it can lead us

Colossians 3:15 Let the peace of Christ rule in your hearts, since as members of one body you were called to peace. And be thankful.

Whenever I go outside I love to hear the soft song of a Mourning Dove. It is something that has always been special to me. I am thrilled that these special birds have been common wherever we've lived. During our last year in Colorado Springs we had the blessing of a pair of these doves nesting on the top of our trellis below our deck. We were able to daily see them and watch the whole process from building their nest to raising their young.

When I see or hear Mourning Doves I stop, enjoy their beauty, think of my Lord Jesus, and am filled with gratitude for Him and the blessings He has given me. My enjoyment of these birds triggers this process that leads me to a quiet, rich reservoir of gratitude for my God.

I love bouquets of fresh flowers. One of my favorites is blue hydrangeas. The blue color is rich and deep and they are so beautiful. At Williamson Christian College where I worked there is a large bush of them. I tried to keep a vase of these flowers on the front desk where everyone could be blessed by their beauty during the day. The wonderful thing is that these flowers trigger the same process within me that the Mourning Doves do. I go from seeing and enjoying their beauty to savoring the richness of my love relationship with God.

I believe this is a process that we all can and should experience repeatedly each day. We are surrounded by beauty, whether in flowers, birds, nature or the people around us. We need to ask the Lord open our eyes to see and enjoy it. It is then simply a matter of His Holy Spirit creating the links within us that go from seeing beauty to enjoying the peaceful place of gratitude for Him. The neat thing is that pretty soon we start seeing beauty everywhere and it all leads us to Him.

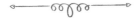

The impact we can have

Colossians 4:5 Be wise in the way you act toward outsiders;
make the most of every opportunity.

This morning I've been thinking about the amazement I still have over my experience of becoming a child of God 50 years ago. The encounter I had on that day where Jesus became my Lord and Savior was so beyond imagining – so radically life changing, that I am still in awe of it.

The thing about it that struck me this morning is that I didn't see it coming. I wasn't aware that I was seeking God or that I was 'lost'. The only reason I went to the retreat was to honor my parents. There was nothing going on at college, the camp was nearby and I knew it was important to them for me to go.

The message of the evangelist was unlike anything I had ever heard. I had never heard anyone talk about Jesus like they had met and knew Him. As I listened, I was struck by the thought that he described Jesus in a way that, if He were real, it was what He would be like. I had no idea that I was about to meet Him too! It's like I was a ripe fruit ready to pick and just didn't know it.

The question this morning is how many people that we interact with are in a place similar to where I was? They are going to having a life-changing experience with the Lord but might not even have an idea that they are searching? God is simply working in their lives to prepare them for that moment. We need to understand the impact our lives have in that process. If our lives are Christ-centered it will be positive; if not, we have missed an opportunity – or worse, created an obstacle to be overcome.

Jesus said we are salt and light. Our very lives are to reveal Him and His love to others. All of our encounters and interactions in life are opportunities. When we live our lives wisely we are going to be a significant influence for Christ in the lives of people around us. God will use His richness in our lives to draw others to Himself – and sometimes we get to be there when it happens!

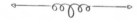

Eureka moments: doorways to repentance

Psalm 139:23, 24 Search me, O God, and know my heart; test me and know my anxious thoughts. ²⁴See if there is any offensive way in me, and lead me in the way everlasting.

Eureka! I don't know how much this word is used today. Possibly most people think of a brand of vacuum cleaner when they hear it. Historically this was an exclamation attributed to Archimedes that he made to express his triumph of discovering an important process involving gold. It was a shout made by gold miners when they discovered gold. It became a general term used to describe the discovery moment when something being looked for was found, or a difficult problem was solved.

Teachers talked about students having 'Eureka moments' in their studies – those wonderful times when the 'light goes on' and something that has been elusive is finally understood. Think of the times when reading the Bible, the Lord opens our eyes and we see something we haven't seen before. A verse or a truth just comes alive and it's like discovering gold.

Sometimes these 'Eureka moments' occur when the Lord opens our eyes to see behaviors and attitudes in our lives that are negative and hurtful, both to us and to others, and we just haven't 'seen' them. It's like our grasp of the obvious has been turned off. We're clueless to the red warning light flashing on the dashboard before us.

On the one hand, my life has too many of these embarrassing moments where Jesus has opened my eyes to see and understand such things in my life. But on the other hand, they are unspeakable treasures because they are answers to the prayer of this verse. They are 'Eureka moments' because they are priceless 'doorways' to repentance. They are intended to lead us to times of forgiveness and transformation – not condemnation! They enable us to become more like Jesus.

The problem of 'Why?'

Psalm 139:23, 24 Search me, O God, and know my heart; test me
and know my anxious thoughts. ²⁴ See if there is any offensive way
in me, and lead me in the way everlasting.

Scripture plays a critical role in our lives in helping us respond to the conviction of the Holy Spirit. It forms the framework upon which we can evaluate whether something within us is right or wrong - whether a behavior is offensive or wicked (KJV).

A major problem that we have with the more subtle sins is that we don't see or recognize them. We can be blind to them and their deadly work. It's like our grasp of the obvious has been turned off. We're clueless to the red warning light flashing on the dashboard before us.

We might be blind due to the hardness of our hearts, or the blindness may stem from certain behaviors being well established habits. Praise God when He opens our eyes to see behaviors and attitudes in our lives that are negative and hurtful, both to us and to others.

There is a 3 letter word that can be a source of much pain and even sin. It is the source of a most negative life habit that afflicts us all. It is the word 'why'. Our response to this word profoundly affects our communications, thoughts, attitudes, behavior and relationships. Unfortunately, once we start contemplating it, our response almost always leads us to sin and we're not even aware of it.

Consider the following situations:

- A friend walks by you and doesn't speak to you

- Your spouse forgets something important

- Someone doesn't smile at you

- Someone is curt with you

In each of these and a myriad of other circumstances our natural (fleshly) tendency is to immediately think of the question, "Why did they do/say that?" "Why" wants to know the motivation that precipitated the action we question. "Why" wants to know what the reason is so we can judge whether or not we think it's valid. Should we be offended or hurt? Maybe they aren't a true friend after all, and so on...

The problem is that judging motives is forbidden by Scripture. It is something we are to avoid like the plague. Romans 14:10a raises the question, *"You, then, why do you judge your brother?"* Instead of looking to judge, a more redemptive practice would be to use such behaviors as triggers for prayer. Instead of indulging our own insecurities, we need to focus our trust upon the Lord. Allow perceived negative behaviors to roll off us like water off a duck's back.

Instead of "Why did they do that to me?" perhaps our response could be, "O Lord Jesus, they must be struggling today. Please show them your grace and mercy." Instead of taking affront, we should respond with grace.

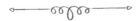

A memory from the Mill

Psalm 34:8a Taste and see that the LORD is good;

We lived in Colorado Springs from 2005 – 2009. During that time it was our privilege to be a part of a marvelous Friday night gathering there called "the Mill". Up to 1,000 college age and 20-somethings gathered each Friday night for over two hours of worship and teaching.

The pastor of theMill at that time was Aaron Stern. The Lord so gifted him in communicating to this age group. One of the more memorable times was when Aaron spoke on this verse. After some preliminary comments, he brought out a box of Krispy Kreme glazed donuts.

Aaron proceeded to talk about the company that made these donuts. He went on for some time talking about how successful they were; how they were growing; how many stores they had; just on and on. He then opened the box of donuts and began describing what they looked like. How many there were in the box; what the smell was like. Then he lifted a donut out to examine it and for everyone to see it.

He finally looked at everyone, grinned and said how it wasn't enough to know about Krispy Kreme and the donuts they made. He had to sample one – so he did. Aaron proceeded to slowly take one bite after another – oohing and ahhing as he savored each bite. He just ate the donut and said it was so good he had to eat another. So he ate another continuing the sound effects of just super-enjoying what he tasted. As you can imagine, the crowd was going nuts while he was doing this.

This all led him to the point that it wasn't enough to know about God – we have to experience Him. We have to taste him and see just how good He is. In 1 Peter 2:1-3 Peter is giving them instructions in light of the fact that, *"...now that you have tasted that the Lord is good."* When we walk in His ways our daily lives will be filled with 'tasting' Him and being consumed with His goodness.

PS – At the end of Aaron's message he announced that out in the foyer there were Krispy Kreme donuts for everyone to taste and enjoy.

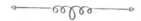

Lucy and the Magician's book

Matthew 7:1 Do not judge, or you too will be judged.

Judging others can be a bit like having termites in the house – the problem is there for a lengthy time before we become aware of it. Then we have to discover how extensive the problem is and deal with it. A powerful example of judging wrongly comes from CS Lewis' book, The Voyage of the Dawn Treader.

In a house on an island, Lucy discovers a Magician's book that offers her all kinds of opportunities – not all of which are appropriate. She speaks the words of a spell that will enable her to know what her friends thought of her. As she's looking at the pictures in the book, she is aware that she is seeing and hearing two classmates, Anne and Marjorie, speaking about her on a train back in England. The conversation does not go as she expects.

Anne asks Marjorie if she is going to continue spending so much time with Lucy; she asserts that the last term (at school) Marjorie was crazy about Lucy. Marjorie replies that she wasn't crazy about Lucy, saying, "I've got more sense than that. Not a bad little kid in her way. But I was getting pretty tired of her before the end of the term."

Lucy explodes with indignation calling Marjorie a "Two-faced little beast." She then realizes that she's talking to a picture in the Magician's book, but still is distressed by this perceived betrayal by her friends, particularly Marjorie. Lucy had really befriended Marjorie, but she now wonders if her other friends are the same.

A few minutes later, Lucy sees Aslan in the room with her – He had been there all the time. He speaks to her about eavesdropping on her two friends and how she had misjudged Marjorie. Aslan tells her, "(Marjorie) is weak, but she loves you. She was afraid of the older girl and said what she does not mean."

We are too prone to snap-judgments, and thinking we know why someone did something. Doing so is sin and has such significant consequences – spiritual and otherwise. Instead of judging, we must release things to the Lord and look to Him. I thank God for how He has used this scene to warn and keep me from making the mistake of judging others. Pray that He will do likewise for you.

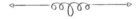

Dad, since when does the sun rise in the west?

Joshua 24:15a But if serving the LORD seems undesirable to you, then choose for yourselves this day whom you will serve,

In 1996 my two oldest sons and I went on a mission trip to Romania with a small group led by a close friend from Seattle. We flew into Munich, picked up our van and spent the first night in Europe at the YWAM castle in Hurlach, an hour west of there.

The next morning we left early to beat rush hour in Munich. We had to drive south from Hurlach and pick up the highway going east toward Munich and then on to Hungary where we would spend the night. We got on the highway and after about 15 minutes, John, my oldest son asked an important question: "Dad – since when does the sun rise in the west?"

We had inadvertently taken the wrong ramp and were headed for France – not Munich and Hungary! Thank God that it wasn't a rainy morning and that my sons noticed this major discrepancy. The dawn and the sun coming up on a clear morning are kind of hard to miss.

We need to recognize that life is filled with opportunities to take mistaken directions in terms of the attributes that characterize our lives. The wrong choices become easier to make when we are distracted from following the Lord and become preoccupied with other things. Instead of choosing righteousness, we make choices that are more appealing to our fleshly nature.

We get careless and wind up going the wrong way without being aware of it. Such decisions frequently made become life habits and contradict or undermine our faith: situation ethics, shading the truth, the ends justify the means, a little promiscuity, cutting corners, let someone else do it, no one will know, getting even – hey everybody does it. If you're reading the Bible and are sensitive to the Holy Spirit, you hear echoing within you, "Don't go that direction!"

Unfortunately, hearing these course corrections doesn't mean listening and obeying them. Worse, our spiritual eyesight becomes dull and we don't see the warning signs around us – (i.e., the sun rising in the west!) We become comfortable with our Christianity being something we put on like a T-shirt. Outward appearance might seem okay but inwardly we become filled with rot and decay. Look at our society – about 75% consider themselves Christian, but you sure wouldn't know it by looking at our culture.

We must recognize that our choices are the true reflection of whether we have chosen to serve the Lord. It's not what we say. It's not what we think we believe. It's not what we do on Sunday mornings. The consequences of our choices are immense. "Choose for yourselves this day...."

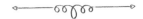

Focusing on Him

Nehemiah 8:10 Nehemiah said, "Go and enjoy choice food and sweet drinks, and send some to those who have nothing prepared. This day is sacred to our Lord. Do not grieve, <u>for the joy of the LORD is your strength</u>."

I was recently struggling with something and my wife Donna was able to greatly encourage me and get my focus back on the Lord – where it belongs. By focusing on Him, I was able to tap into His marvelous reservoir of joy and wonder that is so transforming. This is such an important lesson for us.

We may be in the midst of grief, difficulty, disappointment or despair – like the children of Israel were who received this word from Nehemiah. But it's amazing what God can do within us while we are in the midst of such things! When we tune in to Him, He shares His joy with us that provides us with such strength. We recognize who He is for us and that is dominant over whatever difficulties we have.

Think of the scene in The Lion, The Witch and The Wardrobe when Aslan arrives at the witch's castle and starts breathing upon all the creatures who have been turned to stone by the witch. We see these stone creatures being transformed and coming back to life. We see the vibrant colors of life replacing the drab, lifeless gray color of stone. That is what God's joy can and will do within us.

I found this wonderful quote from CH Spurgeon, a great man of God who lived in the 1800s. It vividly describes what is involved within us as we focus upon Him, with His joy becoming ours:

> "All these attributes of my God are mine: his power, my protection; his wisdom, my guidance; his faithfulness, my foundation; his grace, my salvation." He is a God who cannot lie, faithful and true to his promise; he is all love, and at the same time infinitely just, supremely holy. Why, the contemplation of God to one who knows that this God is his God for ever and ever, is enough to make the eyes overflow with tears, because of the deep, mysterious, unutterable bliss which fills the heart."

If the joy of the Lord is elusive to you, don't give up. It is there for you to find – and when you find it, you find Him!

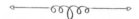

Two sides of the same coin: creature and child

Psalm 29:2 Ascribe to the LORD the glory due his name; worship the LORD in the splendor of his holiness.

Our God is wonderful all the time. But having said that, He does some of the most special things in our lives to bless us and communicate that we are His. In a worship service I experienced something wonderful yet difficult to put into words. As we were singing the Revelation Song, I was caught up in the absolute wonder and majesty of who God is: Holy, holy, holy is the Lord God Almighty…With all creation I sing Praise to the King of Kings.

Then in the midst of this glorious worship of our King, He did something that I didn't expect. I don't know how to describe it, but He provoked the joy-filled realization within me that I was His son who brought Him pleasure. One minute I was part of creation worshipping and adoring Him – the next I was a son basking in His pleasure. The only thing I can think of to describe what happened was – it was like He winked at me!

Over the years I've seen the President do that. In gatherings he would see someone dear to him and would make eye contact and wink with a hint of a smile. In the midst of all the seriousness, he subtly acknowledged the relationship and brought pleasure and blessing to the recipient. We've probably all experienced something like that with a loved one.

The wonder of belonging - we are not our own, we are His! Jesus isn't an add-on to our lives; He becomes the very core of our being. Seven days a week we are His and He is ours. While duty and responsibility play a roll in our lives, there is so much more. We get to live for Him basking in the warmth of our relationship with Him.

The Lord is the God of the universe, but He is also our Father. We are family. When we love Him we bring Him pleasure. As we worshipped, I moved back and forth between awestruck creature and beloved son - enjoying and being enjoyed by His Lord. It's like they were the two sides of the same coin. What a marvelous combination! May we respond to Him with lives that increasingly reflect a true and vibrant love for our God.

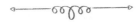

Do we view God through a 'referee / fairness' model?

2 Corinthians 5:7 We live by faith, not by sight.

Have you ever noticed how common mistakes are? Fortunately we don't have video replay in our daily lives where family and friends can relive our blunders. It's bad enough listening to our kids hilariously remembering them. But the sporting world provides some wrenching examples of errors by referees / umpires, and usually there is video replay that everyone has to live with – for better or worse. While no one expects perfection, you just hope mistakes are inconsequential. Unfortunately, some errors that come to mind were anything but.

Some years ago a Detroit Tiger pitcher was deprived of a perfect game by an umpire's mistake. With two outs in the bottom of the ninth inning, the umpire mistakenly called a runner safe at first when replays clearly showed he was out – the last out! Afterward, the umpire was devastated to see the video replay of his mistake that deprived the pitcher of a rare perfect game. Yes, umpires make mistakes, but this one involved the final out of a perfect game.

Most sports use technology or video replay to some degree to ensure against significant refereeing mistakes. Soccer does not. In a World Cup game, on the same day, Germany and Argentina advanced in games marred by refereeing errors. The whole world saw that England scored against Germany to tie the game up before the half at 2-2. Unfortunately the referee and his linesman missed it! Germany went on to win 4-1. That evening Argentina beat Mexico 3-1, but Argentina's first goal should have been disallowed because it was scored by a player clearly offside. Note: The 2018 World Cup was the first time video review (VAR) was used.

Such mistakes really offend our sense of fairness – particularly when video replay confirms the error! If only the mistakes could have been corrected, the results might have been different. If only the baseball Commissioner had overturned the umpire's call… If only video replay had been used in World Cup games… If only God had….

Our response in difficult situations reveals what we really believe about God – who we think He is. Is He our rock, our refuge, our comforter, our sustainer, our enabler, our inspiration, etc…. Or is He a referee who occasionally gets it wrong – who allows things that aren't fair? Do we get upset because something happens that is 'against our understanding of the rules' and we complain and question and argue: "He should have caught that!"

We need to understand that walking by 'sight' leads us on the path to the 'referee / fairness' model that results in victims and blown calls. Walking by 'faith' leads us to the reality of who God is and how incredibly secure we are in Him – no matter what our circumstances look like. Remember, God never has an "Oops!"

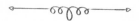

Responding when we get upset

2 Corinthians 5:7 We live by faith, not by sight.

There are times when things happen where we respond by becoming angry and upset. I remember a time when my response of distress, disappointment and frustration over a situation in sports that surprised me with its intensity. Fortunately I recognized that I had to get over it.

How did I do it? First, I realized my own embarrassment at the intense reaction I was experiencing over something that was really a non-issue in my life. That led to thinking of real situations of betrayal in the Bible: the Garden of Eden, Joseph and his brothers, David and Uriah, the people of Israel and God, Judas and Jesus.

Then my thoughts went to a Bing Crosby song: Count Your Blessings (Instead of sheep). That might sound awfully simple, but it got me thinking of the true blessings in my life: the Lord, family, friends, job, health, etc… Dealing with a sports situation just isn't in the same world as illness and family tragedies.

Then I thought of the song, It is Well with My Soul. The writer, a Christian and friend of DL Moody, lost a son to scarlet fever, most of his fortune in a Chicago fire, and then his four daughters in a collision of two ships at sea. Only his wife survived the sinking of their ship. This man penned the Words while sailing to join his wife in Wales when the captain informed him they were over the spot where the ship with his family sank.

I'm grateful that the Lord didn't just tell me to, "Get over it!" But the Holy Spirit led me in a process where all the 'junk' going on in me was replaced by a wonderful sense of gratitude for the Lord. The intensity of the negative was gone, replaced by the intensity of the love shared with my Lord. I never cease to be amazed at God's kindness and mercy.

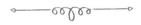

An insight into learning His will

Colossians 1:9 For this reason, since the day we heard about you, we have not stopped praying for you and asking God to fill you with the knowledge of his will through all spiritual wisdom and understanding.

Back in the 1990s many of us were involved in Promise Keepers – a wonderful move of God among men. In 1996 PK held a large conference for pastors in Atlanta and most of the pastors of the church we were attending in Akron, OH were able to attend. While there, they were exposed to the marvelous study Experiencing God by Dr. Henry Blackaby.

In January 1997 we kicked off a church-wide 13-week study of Experiencing God. Before the study, there were about 15 weekly home groups, during the study the number of home groups expanded to over 50. It was truly an extraordinary experience for the entire church.

One of the most important lessons from Experiencing God is incorporated in today's verse – and that is the importance of being filled with the knowledge of God's will. We each have a tendency to focus on, "What is God's will for me?" – a much more subjective and self-centered approach. Unfortunately, this can lead to a lifestyle that is more about us than about God. We become pre-occupied with ourselves rather than seeing the larger picture.

A priceless insight from this study is that our focus should instead be on knowing what God's will is – for all believers - and doing it. Doing God's will is like Basic Christianity 101. Through faithfully living out God's will in our daily lives, God will make clear where He has unique things for each of us. His specific will for 'me' is to flow out of a life centered on living a life pleasing to Him - being Christ-like in every situation.

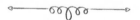

Priceless memories and seeing Him

*1 Chronicles 16:11-12 Look to the LORD and his strength;
seek his face always. Remember the wonders he has done,
his miracles, and the judgments he pronounced,*

The other day I had an unexpected surprise. It was a typically busy day with lots to do and not enough time to do it all. In the midst of this I went to get a document I needed and it wasn't where I thought it was. So I had to hunt for it.

The search took on a life of its own. I knew it was in the office but the issue was where. (Those who know me have heard of my Prego filing system -"It's in there.") While going through a stack of stuff that I hadn't looked at in quite awhile, I encountered the surprise. No it wasn't money – but in some ways it was even better. It was a stack of pictures from years ago. Needless to say, I stopped my search and sat down and looked at the pictures.

The joy I experienced in savoring each one. Our sons growing up, dogwood trees in bloom at our home in Peninsula, grandbabies, being with friends, trips to Brazil… Some of the pictures were more special than others because of the memories and good times they linked to. They were like a doorway into a gallery of memories – of treasured experiences that had not been thought of for too long.

One common theme running through so many of the pictures was the goodness of God to Donna and me. Yes there have been difficult times, stressful situations and all the other stuff of life – but through it all and overshadowing it all has been the presence and blessing of our Lord.

How good and powerful it is to remember Him and the things He's done – in our lives and throughout history. The wonderful memories develop hearts of gratitude and strengthen our faith! How good it is to recognize Him in the midst of everything. We can become so blind that we don't see the forest for the trees. He is with us, intimately involved in every aspect of our lives. We are never alone. We need to recognize just how important it is to regularly set aside time to remember what He's done and treasure the memories we have of Him.

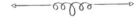

A priceless learning moment

James 1:19 My dear brothers, take note of this: Everyone should be quick to listen, slow to speak and slow to become angry,

In the mid-seventies I got to attend Wheaton Grad School. It was one of the richest times in my life. One of the more embarrassing and revealing memories I have of that time was in a counseling class I took. On that particular day the instructor had us bring our spouses with us to class, so my wife Donna was there with me.

We were all seated in a large circle and discussing some subject. At one point I became engaged in a dialogue with another male student on the other side of the circle. It was a lively discussion as we disagreed with each other on whatever the subject was.

All of a sudden, the instructor who was sitting in the circle listening to all this, broke into this 'dialogue' the two of us were having. She looked at me and asked, "Are you angry?" I looked at her and said, "What?" She pressed her point and asked, "Are you experiencing anger right now?" I replied, "Of course not. We're just having a lively discussion."

At that point the whole class just exploded with laughter. One of the guys in the class that had become a friend of mine shouted out to me, "You're so angry, steam is coming out of your ears!" I had no idea. I sat there, dumbfounded, trying to grasp the reality of the situation. How could I be so angry and not know it?

What a blessing that experience turned out to be! I became aware of a major 'blind-spot' in my life and it involved something – anger – that can be so destructive. Needless to say this set off a process of discovery for me. Fortunately, I wanted to change which meant that I had to learn to recognize when I was becoming angry and stop it from occurring.

Praise God for family, friends and co-workers who were willing to be a part of my repenting process. Think of the value of being asked, "Do you know you're becoming angry?" when you don't want to be angry. The Holy Spirit used their valuable input to help me change.

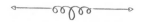

The importance of becoming a lover of the truth

John 8:31, 32 To the Jews who had believed him, Jesus said, "If you hold to my teaching, you are really my disciples. ³² Then you will know the truth, and the truth will set you free."

One of the more important teachings that I heard years ago that has impacted me greatly involved these verses. It had to do with becoming and staying free. Simply put, in order to become and stay free we each must become a 'Lover of the truth'.

Yesterday I wrote of the blessing of family, friends and co-workers who were willing to be a part of my repenting process in dealing with my anger. This was something I asked them to do. But how do we respond when such input hurts or comes in an inappropriate manner or from someone we don't like?

Suppose you're in an interaction that becomes a bit unpleasant. As you walk away, a close friend discreetly says to you, "You could have been more kind in your response." Versus, being told by a participant, "Boy, were you a jerk in that meeting!" and then he walks off.

Criticism or 'descriptive observations of our behavior' are more palatable to us if they're offered in a kind manner. Even so, they can still be difficult to receive. A concerned spouse says, 'You're angry." Your response, "NO I'M NOT!!!!"

When such information is offered in anger, or sarcasm, by someone we don't have a relationship with, or particularly by someone we don't like, we tend to react defensively. The tendency is to reject the message because we reject the messenger! Whatever truth might be in the criticism/observation offered us we tend to reject out-of-hand because of who offered it or the way in which it was given. We choose to react rather than respond – and it is a choice!

At times God will specifically use unpleasant people with negative deliveries to present us with an important truth about ourselves. It's a test – and life is filled with them. Will we look past the messenger and how the message is presented to find and embrace the truth He has for us? The more we become lovers of the truth, the freer we become. We choose to respond rather than react. Lord Jesus, help us all become lovers of the truth!

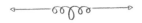

The canopy of honor

Proverbs 15:33 "The fear of the LORD *teaches a man wisdom, and humility comes before honor." Isaiah 66:2b "This is the one I esteem: he who is humble and contrite in spirit, and trembles at my word."*

Another of my favorite movies is Fiddler on the Roof. It is a musical about the life of a family in the small Jewish village of Anatevka, Russia Set in 1905 it tells the story of Tevye, his wife, Golde, and their five daughters and how they cope with the difficult realities under Tsarist Russia. It is filled with wonderful music and many moving scenes.

Among the most moving for me are the wedding scenes for their oldest daughter, Tzeitel. She fell in love with Motel, the young tailor and her father, against tradition, agreed to let her marry him. In the Jewish ceremony, the couple stands underneath a wedding canopy. The scene struck me as being very special – particularly the canopy.

This scene of the canopy came to mind when I was studying these verses. Humility comes before honor. God esteems the one who is humble and contrite in spirit and trembles at His word. Honor is not something we can give ourselves. It is given to those whose lives merit it. It is something that is bestowed – and will remain as long as the life is consistent with God's requirements.

Here is where the picture of a canopy is such a blessing. Think of the honor and esteem that come from God as a canopy that is lowered down over us when our lives meet God's requirements for it. It will abide with us and over us as long as we are faithful. The only control we have over it is to live lives that God considers worthy of it. In John 12:26b Jesus says, *"My Father will honor the one who serves me."*

The wedding scene also includes the very special and moving song, "Sunrise, Sunset" sung by the family. Towards the end of it, Perchik & Hodel, wanting to be married too, sing the line, 'Is there a canopy in store for me?' Let us think of the canopy not in terms of a wedding, but in terms of living such a life that God bestows His canopy of honor over each one of us.

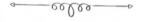

An illustration of quarry stones

Acts 4:11 This [Jesus] is The stone despised by you builders,
who has become the cornerstone.

Do you ever stop to think about the really special things that God has done in your life? If you had to, could you identify the most meaningful experiences that you've had with Him – the ones that just stand out above the rest? Maybe you've written about them in a journal or in some way recorded them because they are so special. If not, you need to.

Donna and I have a significant number of such experiences with the Lord like that. They are encounters with God and His power and love that are so important in our faith. Miracles, amazing answered prayers, supernatural provision and exquisite encounters with Him – they are more than treasure. They are part of our foundation in Him. They are part of the rock we are built on. The Lord has given us an illustration that really reveals the role these special experiences with Him play in our lives.

We had an old house in Peninsula, OH where we raised our boys. Nearby was a swimming hole that used to be a stone quarry. The foundation of our house was not built upon bricks or cement blocks. At its core, the foundation was made up of quarry stone. Some of these stones were massive: six feet long, two to three feet wide and two feet tall. It was rock solid!

The Lord let us see that these special experiences that we've had with Him are like quarry stones. They are massive and strong and are in the foundation of our faith embedded next to Jesus, the chief corner stone. They represent God's interventions in our lives that cannot be denied. The reality is we couldn't deny them and Him even if we wanted to. Because of Jesus, they make an unshakable foundation for our faith.

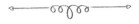

Unfortunately we can forget

Joshua 4:20-24 ²⁰And Joshua set up at Gilgal the twelve stones they had taken out of the Jordan. ²¹He said to the Israelites, "In the future when your descendants ask their fathers, 'What do these stones mean?' ²²tell them, 'Israel crossed the Jordan on dry ground.' ²³For the LORD your God dried up the Jordan before you until you had crossed over. The LORD your God did to the Jordan just what he had done to the Red Sea when he dried it up before us until we had crossed over. ²⁴He did this so that all the peoples of the earth might know that the hand of the LORD is powerful and so that you might always fear the LORD your God."

Yesterday we talked about remembering the wonderful things that God has done in our lives – the extraordinary things that stand out over the years. I likened those events to quarry stones – massive and strong experiences that form a rock-solid foundation for our faith with Jesus the chief cornerstone.

Today's verses underscore just how important it is to remember the wondrous things that our God does. The children of Israel were to stack these 12 stones as a memorial, so they would never forget what the Lord had done. Through His people, the Lord wanted the people of the earth to know that the hand of the Lord was powerful.

The thing that is so amazing to me is that after Joshua and that whole generation died, *"another generation grew up, who knew neither the Lord nor what He had done for Israel."* Judges 2:10 Unfortunately, mankind has a problem with forgetfulness.

This really struck me when I was reading in one of my journals from years earlier. I came upon a time with the Lord that was so significant and so special, that I wrote in my journal, "I will never forget this!" Unfortunately, I had forgotten it – and wondered how many other things have I forgotten..

We need to share these experiences particularly with our family. They affirm the greatness of our God and cultivate hearts of gratitude within us. They also build the understanding in all of us that they are but a foretaste of the many experiences that the Lord has for us. The best is yet to come. Not just in eternity, but here and now. God wants to show Himself strong amongst His people – so that the world will know!

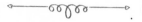

Tokens of kindness from the Lord

Psalm 62:8 Trust in him at all times, O people;
pour out your hearts to him, for God is our refuge.

Have you ever noticed how refreshing some little things can be? Like a gentle breeze on a warm summer's day when you're working outside? When you're going through some difficulties and a friend calls to encourage you simply because you were on their heart. Reading a Scripture, a testimony or about a Biblical truth that speaks precisely to your situation.

Some of these things are what I refer to as 'tokens of kindness' from the Lord. It is so wonderful when the Lord gives them to us. A few summers ago we were really busy with a lot going on. Added to it was the word from our landlord that we needed to move before our lease expired September 30. She was planning to move back into the house we were in.

One night in late July when we went to bed, we were really feeling it and Donna said we need to pray – so we did. In the midst of the 'stormy stuff' going on we prayed to our Lord, acknowledging that we were looking to Him and trusting Him to lead and guide us through everything.

The next morning I woke up really early and was working around the house. I picked up a book that I hadn't looked at for a long time, not even remembering what was in it, and just opened it. I didn't even look at the front cover. It turned out to be filled with two page true stories of His Mysterious Ways – Miracles of Prayer by Guideposts.

The random story I turned to and the two that followed all described situations where He provided supernatural presence and guidance to people in need. One was a blind woman and her guide-dog out in a snow storm with an angel walking with them. The other two dealt with people driving through dense fog and a snow storm and making it due to following the lights of vehicles that turned out not to be there!

These three stories all spoke precisely to God being with us and guiding us – just as we had prayed hours earlier. He might not have manifested His provision supernaturally as He did in the stories, but He didn't have to. They reaffirmed the importance of our focus and trust in Him. What a timely token of kindness!

We weren't in danger of giving up or anything. It was simply our Lord giving us some loving encouragement that lifted our spirits – like a drink of cool water when you're thirsty. It's amazing the sustaining power such experiences can have!

We still got to walk through the situations we were in. But we did so with a renewed joy simply because we had been reminded of and refreshed by His wonderful love for us. Pray that our 'eyes' will see Him more and more as He works in our lives.

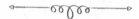

Threats? - or - Opportunities?

Matthew 5:38-42 *[38] "You have heard that it was said, 'Eye for eye, and tooth for tooth.' [39] But I tell you, Do not resist an evil person. If someone strikes you on the right cheek, turn to him the other also. [40] And if someone wants to sue you and take your tunic, let him have your cloak as well. [41] If someone forces you to go one mile, go with him two miles. [42] Give to the one who asks you, and do not turn away from the one who wants to borrow from you.*

I woke up this morning thinking about going the second mile. When I looked up the verse I was stuck by its context and by how unlike our typical thinking it is. This is a whole different mindset – a different world view. It is seeing and responding to things so differently.

An old classic movie comes to mind that illustrates how radically different things can be seen and how things sometime aren't what they seem. That movie is the Wizard of Oz. It begins and ends as a black and white movie. I remember as a boy seeing it and being so stunned when Dorothy wakes up in Oz and everything is in full 'living' color. The richness of the color versus the paucity of the black and white – they don't change the story line, just what we're seeing. Then there is the ogre-like Wizard who is so authoritarian on the screen, but in reality is a little old man behind the curtain. Here, what is perceived is very different from its true reality.

I would suggest that the situations described in these verses are like the Wizard up on the screen – their reality is very different than how we tend to perceive them. We typically respond to them as threats (like the ogre on the screen), rather than as opportunities. Our viewpoint is one of self and cultural orientation, and we react accordingly. It's like living in 'black and white'.

But Jesus wants us to perceive these as opportunities and not as threats – and we must recognize how critical our perception is to the process. It's not about us but it's all about Him. It's not about reacting but responding with faith. They are opportunities to glorify our God in how we respond – or not. Our lives are to be salt and light in the world and reflect the 'living color' of the life of Christ. What a contrast!

Jesus wants our perceptions, understanding and responses rooted in His Kingdom – not in the world. In this world we tend to react rather than respond. We look out for ourselves rather than be guided by His ways. Life is filled with opportunities for us to respond wisely, reflecting His life within us. We need to remind ourselves just how different a citizen of His Kingdom is from one of this world. The people around us will be drawn to Him by seeing us live such lives.

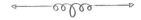

Salvation is just the beginning

Exodus 19:4-6 'You yourselves have seen what I did to Egypt, and how I carried you on eagles' wings and brought you to myself. ⁵Now if you obey me fully and keep my covenant, then out of all nations you will be my treasured possession. Although the whole earth is mine, ⁶you will be for me a kingdom of priests and a holy nation.' These are the words you are to speak to the Israelites."

About three months after the Children of Israel left Egypt, God gave Moses this message to share with them. It was a communication of His heart for them. He was giving them the opportunity to be His treasured possession – out of all the nations, He chose them! They simply had to respond by doing what He required. Unfortunately, they responded with words not with their lives.

God has always been after a people that will be truly His. He wants to shower them with His love. He simply asks that they respond with love in return. Fortunately we Christians have been born again and received His Spirit. Our new natures in Christ free us to respond without the "deck stacked against us' by our old nature. It can still be difficult, but we have such an advantage over the Israelites. It makes me pause to think of Jesus' comment, to whom much is given, much is required. (Luke 12:48)

While it is priceless to be His – to receive salvation and become one of His children – it is even more so to live the kind of lives that He has always wanted His people to live. Salvation isn't the end, it's the beginning! It enables us to pursue lives that truly reflect that we are His people. In 1 Peter 2, Peter is exhorting the believers to rid their lives of sin – to abstain from sinful desires that war against their souls. He is calling them to live lives worthy of who we are in Christ.

In 1 Peter 2:9-10, Peter writes,

"⁹But you are a chosen people, a royal priesthood, a holy nation, a people belonging to God, that you may declare the praises of him who called you out of darkness into his wonderful light. ¹⁰Once you were not a people, but now you are the people of God; once you had not received mercy, but now you have received mercy."

This stunning reality that we are His is beyond words! It is a privilege beyond measure that we have. The more we recognize and grasp that, the more we will live lives that declare us to truly be His people. His mercy, His grace, His Spirit and faith in Jesus Christ enable us to do exactly that!

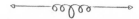

Yahweh's response to our walking in His ways

From the book of Proverbs

Yesterday I wrote about the privilege of being God's people. We Christians must live lives that declare us to truly be His people. In simple terms, the issue is not God's love for us but our love for Him. He loves us more than we can imagine. He has given us everything so that we can experience the extraordinary blessings associated with loving Him.

How we live truly affects our relationship with God. When we walk in righteousness, He responds! But I want to personalize this in an important way. Yahweh is the name our God chose for Himself*. Yahweh is the God of Abraham, Isaac and Jacob. When we talk about God, He is the one we are talking about. Here are some excerpts from Proverbs that describe the blessings he has for His people who walk in His ways:

- Yahweh is pleased with the prayer of the righteous.

- Yahweh loves those who pursue righteousness.

- Yahweh is pleased with the thoughts of the pure.

- Yahweh hears the prayers of the righteous.

- Yahweh is a shield to those whose walk is blameless.

- Yahweh guards the course of the just.

- Yahweh protects the way of His faithful ones.

- Yahweh takes the upright into His confidence.

- Yahweh blesses the home of the righteous.

- Yahweh gives grace to the humble.

- Yahweh loves those who love Him.

- Yahweh provides favor to the good man.

- Yahweh delights in the men who are truthful.

- Yahweh provides peace to the man whose ways are pleasing to Him.

- Yahweh blesses those who trust in Him.

- Yahweh provides life, prosperity and honor to those who pursue righteousness and love.

- Yahweh blesses the man who always fears Him.

- Yahweh enables men who seek Him to understand justice.

- Yahweh keeps safe those who trust in Him.

Think of it! Every one of us is capable of walking in each of these – growing stronger and more Christlike! Think of each of these as a continuum. The more we pursue our Lord, the more Christ-like we become. This is not about earning salvation but about living a faith-filled life that pleases Him – a life that declares His praises.

When we pursue living our lives as His people, His Spirit works an incredible wonder within us. Our desire is transformed from wanting to be blessed by God to wanting to bless Him. That is the result of our hearts being overwhelmed by gratitude for His goodness and love. Let it sink in, to the depth of your being - He has chosen us to be His! WOW!!!!!

*Note: A wonderful book is "Who changed God's Name" by Dr. Jim Harvey

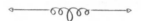

Growing in faith while dealing with delays

*Psalm 27:14 Wait for the LORD; be strong and
take heart and wait for the LORD.*

Have you noticed how God just loves to use the experience of 'waiting' in our lives? We have such a tendency to expect things to happen a whole lot sooner than they do. When we encounter delays, we typically discover that patience isn't one of our stronger suits. We want the Lord to give us patience now!

Some years ago when we were living in NE Ohio, we believe the Lord called us to move to Colorado Springs. We put our house on the market. Twenty-eight months later (January of 2005) the house still hadn't sold. To say we didn't understand the delay is a bit of an understatement! At that time we had a 10 ½ year old blond cocker spaniel name Rascal and we knew he wouldn't be making the move with us. I wish I had $10 for every time we read something or were told that we were never going to find a home for him. People just didn't want old dogs – particularly 10 ½ year old dogs.

That month we took a trip to Brazil to visit our son and his family. The kennel we had used for nearly 20 years wasn't available so we found another on the opposite side of the Akron area. When I dropped Rascal off, I told them of our need for a home for him. Upon our return we discovered that the groomer there had told her pastor about Rascal. The pastor had a 10 year old female blond cocker named Josephine and they had been to visit Rascal several times while we were in Brazil. Rascal had a new home!

Two weeks later, I was really struggling over the delay in selling our house and just not understanding what was going on. My hope had taken some severe hits by the wait. In the midst of crying out to the Lord, He answered so clearly with a thought out of the blue: "It is more difficult to find a home for a 10 ½ year old rascal of a dog than it is to sell a reasonably priced house with a great real estate firm!"

It's amazing how God used that thought to calm the storm within me. Everything was in His hands. Providing the home for Rascal was more than a kindness to us. He used it to help us trust Him and recognize that in His time everything would fall into place. The delay had to do with His timing and provided us with an opportunity to grow in faith and trust in God.

PS – The house sold 1 month later.

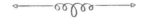

The 'skimmins' in our lives

Proverbs 17:3 The crucible for silver and the furnace for gold,
but the LORD tests the heart.

Many years ago I heard the story of an old cowboy Christian. He described God's dealings with him as gold being purified. Apparently the impurities bubble up to the top and can be skimmed off. That is how he was experiencing God's dealings. He became aware of a behavior or problem in his life as God caused it to 'bubble up'. He would repent and God would 'skim it off'. He would no sooner get rid of one than another would bubble up and it too would be 'skimmed off', Well, God was dealing with so many things in his life that he was concerned that he would be nothing but 'skimmins'.

Seeing all the 'skimmins' in our lives is not particularly pleasant. The good news is that when we see them (or have them pointed out to us –ouch!), we can – and must – choose to deal with them. Typically a great environment for this to happen is when we are overloaded with stress or situations that push us out of our comfort zone. Issues involving work, friends, faith, family, finances, etc… can all work together to create an environment of 'heat'.

Think about the crucible and furnace. It's the heat that melts the ore and causes the impurities to rise to the top. Likewise in our lives - God uses our circumstances to reveal things to us about ourselves as well as giving us opportunities to glorify him by how we respond. Frequently it's all going on at the same time. We can be doing wonderful things but in the midst of it, 'skimmins' appear.

Fortunately the Lord is in the midst of it all. He is for us! He wants our lives to become all they can be and He is committed to that process. As we are all aware, this process usually takes place in public rather than private. Others experience our 'skimmins' and we experience theirs. He expects us to be faithful in how we respond. Proverbs 17:17 says, *"A friend loves at all times, and a brother is born for adversity."* Other translations use *"to help in time of need"* or *"in difficult times "* instead of *"adversity"*.

Fortunately, forgiveness, repentance and understanding are the currency of the kingdom of God. Times of 'skimmins' are opportunities to respond righteously rather than react as the world would (such responses are 'skimmins' in themselves). That's why His grace and mercy are so abundant. They enable us to show forth His love in the practical situations of day to day living.

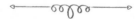

Don Schmidt

A happy and sad experience

James 1:2 Consider it pure joy, my brothers,
whenever you face trials of many kinds,

I remember a very special happy and sad experience. I talked to a man who was one of our closest friends in the early 70s. His name is Bill. We got to see him once in the last 30 years and that was 10 – 15 years ago. He's about my age. I wrote about an experience I had involving him in the May 6 devotional when I described how I loved Bill and didn't love Erik.

Another friend (Tom) from that same era that we had lost contact with tracked me down through Facebook. He gave me Bill's number and after several attempts I was able to reach him that night. When he answered the phone I recognized his voice in spite of the difficulty Bill has in speaking. You see, Bill suffered a stroke a couple years ago and now lives in an assisted living facility.

We laughed and cried together on the phone. Although he is limited physically due to the stroke, his mind is still sharp. While we were talking I could sense his struggle trying to say the things he wanted to say. Then the Lord seemed to intervene.

It was one of those times where you just sense His presence and anointing. God has dealt Bill a difficult hand, but the Lord wants him to focus on all he can still do. The fact that God had taken away his mobility and independence simply means that God had other opportunities for him. The limitations that he is experiencing are only physical. The sky is the limit spiritually.

God wants him to understand that he can pray and intercede. He can pull down strongholds and impact the heavenlies. The Lord wants him to look for issues to intercede in behalf of and God will show him results. There is still so much for him to accomplish.

Donna and I prayed for him and he prayed for us. What a blessing to hear his voice and hear his heart. After all these years, the love we have for each other is still vibrant. This whole conversation reminded us that we tend to place value on what we can do. God is more concerned with who we are. In spite of significant physical limitations, he has not been set aside. God's intention is for Bill to accomplish wonders in the Kingdom of God.

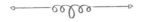

The wonder of my Blue Sections of Scripture

Psalm 9:1 I will praise you, O LORD, with all my heart;
I will tell of all your wonders.

Have you ever thought of praying Scripture? Years ago I heard a teaching on this idea and it has been a wonderful blessing. Simply put, you personalize Scripture so that the verses express what you want to say. But more than that, many are the times that I'm not sure how to pray and they give me the words and the guidance – the path to pray.

Among my favorites are the ones I've identified as "The Blue Sections". (My Bible is kind of highlighted to the hilt!) I have used a blue highlighter to mark over 30 different sections of Scripture that focus upon God and His greatness and wonder. They are not about us – they do not include requests for help or assistance. They are declarative about Him.

I frequently found myself at a loss when it came to expressing to God what was in my heart. I wanted to tell Him how wonderful and glorious He was. It occurred to me that Scripture describes Him more accurately and effectively that I can. So I searched for those Scriptures that did exactly that and marked them in blue. They run the gamut from entire Psalms to a single verse. But when I pray them, personalizing them, my heart rejoices because it is accomplishing what it desires.

For instance Psalm 19:1-4 begins "*The heavens declare the glory of God; the skies proclaim the work of his hands.*" When I pray this, I personalize it so it becomes "O Lord, the heavens declare your glory, the skies proclaim the work of your hands!" By using Scripture, my affirmations are rooted in eternal truth. I know I am expressing reality and my heart is filled with a sense of accomplishing something so important.

It takes me about 25 - 30 minutes to pray through my Blue Section verses out loud. Frequently, the experience provokes tears of joy and gratitude because it leads to such an intimate experience with God. They help me to praise the Lord with all my heart and tell Him of His wonders!

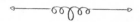

Our tendency is to avoid this like the plague

Proverbs 27:5-6a Better is open rebuke than hidden love.
⁶Wounds from a friend can be trusted,

One of my classes at Wheaton Grad School dealt with resolving conflicts. We each had to take a test that measured our view of confrontation. Among the students in the class were pastors, missionaries, teachers and workers in Christian organizations. We were all a bit surprised when we discovered that we all wanted to avoid confrontation like the plague!

'Confrontation' is one of those words like 'commands', 'obey', 'obedience', 'submission' that we seem to have an allergic reaction to instead of seeing it as vital to healthy Christian living. We tend to think of explosive, angry, unpleasant interactions that make the problems worse.

Rather, it's important to recognize that facing up to problems, issues or people is essential – and to do so in love is a requirement of Scripture. It is a multifaceted redemptive skill that we must learn. Key to confronting situations is learning how to do it, when to do it and if in fact it needs to be done.

Years ago my dad belonged to a men's Bible study. One day he commented that he was going to quit attending it – that most of the men had already quit coming. I asked him why. He said, "Wally just won't quit talking and dominates everything." I suggested that he talk to Wally and tell him about this problem he has – that his non-stop talking is driving the men away. Dad said, "I couldn't do that. None of us want to hurt Wally's feelings." The men thought it better for the Bible study to die than to confront a brother with a blind spot who probably didn't realize what he was doing.

If we are doing something wrong or something that is causing a problem, wouldn't we want to know about it? Wouldn't we want a co-worker, a friend, or a loved one to take us aside and in kindness inform us of it? If we were Wally, wouldn't we want to know before we were sitting all by ourselves?

The Golden Rule is such a simple yet profound learning tool – *"Do unto others as you would have them do unto you."* When it comes to speaking to someone about a problem (think family, kids, spouse, parents, friends), we do it in a way that we would like it done if the roles were reversed.

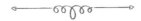

A helpful illustration

Romans 13:10 Love does no harm to its neighbor.
Therefore love is the fulfillment of the law.

Over the years I have been greatly helped by focusing on the importance of biblical love. Love always takes priority. While we are free in Christ, our freedom is always constrained by love. It is to be a guiding principle in our lives.

While Scripture gives us many 'dos and don'ts', love should not be primarily viewed that way. A helpful illustration comes from raising children Donna and I had the good fortune to receive wonderful teaching on raising children right after our marriage. One of the most essential things we learned was to focus on the principle of obedience and disobedience.

Our sons were taught to obey what we told them to do - that disobedience brought discipline. For instance, if one boy hit the other, he was not disciplined for 'hitting' his brother. He was disciplined for disobedience. We would take him aside, and say to him, "You have been told not to hit your brother. Did you obey us?" He would say no and acknowledge he had disobeyed. The discipline was never focused on the specific action the child had done. It was always focused upon the principle of disobedience.

If they broke a window by throwing a ball in the house, they weren't disciplined for breaking a window. They were disciplined for disobedience because they knew they had been told not to throw balls in the house. Lying is disobedience. Cheating is disobedience. This idea is huge. Children learn the principle rather than a big list of dos and don'ts.

Likewise, we must learn the principle of love as defined by Scripture (not by our culture). The more we understand what constitutes love, the greater is our ability to apply it in every circumstance we find ourselves in. God's Word is so essential to this process. The more we grow in love, behaving in an 'unloving' manner becomes as recognizable and inappropriate for us as disobedience is for children.

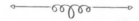

Don Schmidt

A great Grad School experience

Proverbs 22:6 Train a child in the way he should go,
and when he is old he will not turn from it.

Yesterday I used the illustration of training our children when they were little in the principle of obedience and disobedience. The focus of any discipline was upon disobedience not upon the specific action they did or didn't do.

This brought to mind a very significant experience that we had in Grad School that underscored the effectiveness of this approach. I was taking a class on Moral Development. The (secular) textbooks we were using described that children had to be 7 or 8 years old before they were developed enough to understand certain things. They contained the following illustration:

Billy is asked to help set the table for dinner. While carrying a tray of 5 glasses to the table, he trips and breaks all 5 glasses.

Nancy is told that she cannot have a cookie before dinner. But when her mother is in another room, she gets a chair to stand on to reach the cookie jar. While reaching for the cookies she bumps 1 glass, knocking it to the floor, breaking it.

Who is naughtier – Billy or Nancy?

The authors indicated that children younger than 7 or 8 would say Billy was naughtier because he broke 5 glasses while Nancy only broke 1. Their focus would be upon the number of glasses broken. The one who broke more was naughtier.

We had 2 sons at the time and they were 3 and 4 years old. The next day I read the illustration to Johnnie, the oldest, and asked him, "Who is naughtier – Billy or Nancy?" His answer was wonderful. Johnnie replied, "Only Nancy was naughty. She disobeyed. Billy wasn't naughty because it was an accident."

Needless to say I shared this experience with the class the next week.

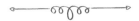

Having a heart after the Lord

Acts 13:22 After removing Saul, he made David their king. He testified concerning him: 'I have found David son of Jesse a man after my own heart; he will do everything I want him to do.'

Think of God being able to describe someone as "a man after my own heart, he will do everything I want him to do." This was the opposite of Saul. The people had wanted a king like the other nations, so God gave them Saul, who looked like a king – outwardly. Scripture describes Saul as being impressive and a head taller than the others. He would have really stood out in a crowd. Unfortunately his heart was not where it needed to be and because of the choices he made, God rejected him.

When the Lord had Samuel go to Bethlehem to anoint one of Jesse's sons as king, even Samuel was impressed with outward appearances. When he saw Eliab, Jesse's oldest son, he thought that surely this was the Lord's anointed. But the LORD said to Samuel, *"Do not consider his appearance or his height, for I have rejected him. The LORD does not look at the things man looks at. Man looks at the outward appearance, but the LORD looks at the heart." 1 Samuel 16:7*

Each one of the seven sons of Jesse with him in Bethlehem passed in front of Samuel but the Lord chose none of them. Finally Samuel asks, "Are these all the sons you have?" No, there was one more, the youngest, but he was out tending the sheep. So they sent for him and didn't sit down until he arrived. He was the one the Lord chose.

I find this event to be both motivating and encouraging. It's motivating, in that I want to more and more have a heart after the Lord like David had – that I would do whatever the Lord wants me to do. It's encouraging because even though David wasn't there, things weren't going forward until they got him.

Think of the times in our lives when opportunity called – literally. We receive a phone call or letter regarding a job, a ministry or some kind of opportunity because the Lord brought us to mind. He knows who we are and where we are. Let us sharpen our focus on becoming men and women after His own heart.

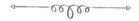

What is our response to opposition?

1 Samuel 17:37 The LORD who delivered me from the paw of the lion and the paw of the bear will deliver me from the hand of this Philistine." Saul said to David, "Go, and the LORD be with you."

A favorite story in the Bible is that of David and Goliath. Isn't it amazing that David, whom King Saul considered just a boy, was totally unafraid of this ranting giant? For forty days, Goliath, who was a warrior nine feet tall, railed against Saul and the army of Israel. Every morning and evening he would come out shout his defiance. Saul and all the Israelites were dismayed and terrified.

David arrived at the battle line with supplies and ran to greet his brothers. As he was talking with them, Goliath came out and shouted his defiance. The Israelites all ran from him in great fear. But David wasn't afraid. He considered Goliath a disgrace that must be removed from Israel. The Lord had identified David as a man after His own heart and here we see what that looks like.

Making the situation even more interesting for David was the fact that the men told him that King Saul would give great wealth to the man who killed Goliath. Here all the fighting men of Israel were terrified and David wasn't. What is a nine foot tall man compared to a bear or a lion? David also did not allow the anger of his oldest brother to deter him from ridding Israel of this warrior.

At the heart of the issue for David was the Lord. David knew and declared to King Saul that it was, *"the LORD who delivered me from the paw of the lion and the paw of the bear will deliver me from the hand of this Philistine."* He wasn't intimidated and he wasn't foolishly brash. His trust and confidence were in the Lord.

David did what the Lord wanted him to do – with boldness, firmly acknowledging that his confidence and trust were in the Lord. Goliath was slain and the Philistines were defeated. We won't face 9' giants, but we will face political correctness and those who oppose any genuine expression of faith in Jesus Christ. We will get to deal with our fears and have our confidence and trust firmly in Him. May the Holy Spirit give us the same faith and boldness – and the opportunities – to show forth His love and live to His glory in the face of opposition.

His steadfast love

*Lamentations 3:25 The LORD is good to those whose
hope is in him, to the one who seeks him;*

This morning as I was considering what I would write, my mind was filled with lots of stuff. We have a lot going on and my mind was just cluttered with details and concerns – unusually so, for early in the morning. As I was trying to focus upon the Lord, the following song began playing in my mind. Mentally, I stopped and just listened – allowing the words and music to minister to me.

> The steadfast love of the Lord never ceases
> His mercies never come to an end
> They are new every morning
> New every morning
> Great is thy faithfulness O Lord
> Great is thy faithfulness

It's a lovely song and its impact upon me was significant. I experienced a settling calm that was like the Lord saying, *"Peace - be still."* to the storm in my thoughts. I thought of how the first rays of dawn dispel the darkness - and the beauty of a sunrise. The turbulence in my mind just faded away. But it was more than just having a sense of peace in my mind so I could better do the task at hand.

It was Him. It was experiencing Him and His goodness to me. The peace was and is a blessing – but far greater is the blessing of being captivated by who He is. Think of the ten lepers who all were healed. One - a Samaritan - came back to Jesus praising God and he threw himself at Jesus' feet. The healing was wonderful but foremost, he had to express his praise to God and his thankfulness to Jesus.

May we all more deeply recognize that our hope is in the Lord. Today, may we more deliberately look to Him and seek Him in the midst of our daily life. If we do, we will experience a heightened awareness of His goodness and His presence with us. The fact that the Lord is good to those whose hope is in Him is not just a theological truth – it is an experiential reality for us to enjoy each day.

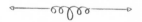

Dealing with 'wilting' around us

Proverbs 12:25 An anxious heart weighs a man down,
but a kind word cheers him up.

For a season I worked at Wal-Mart in the Garden Center. The spring and summer were really busy times and we had thousands of plants for sale. Those plants all needed to be watered each day and it typically took hours to do it.

My job was outside in what was called a corral where bricks, soils, fertilizers and more plants were kept. I would load the purchased items into a customer's vehicle. Needless to say I got a lot of exercise. Although watering the plants wasn't my responsibility, there was something that just had an affect on me that I couldn't ignore. Periodically, I would see plants that were in a full wilt because they had been missed in the watering process.

It just bothered me so to see plants dying when all they needed was water. As much as possible I would water those plants to bring them back to life. My eyes became trained to spot them. What a blessing to walk by later and see them fully revived and blooming.

Have you noticed that we have people around us that are in various stages of 'wilting'? It's not from lack of water but it is from anxiety, concerns, family crises and all manner of difficulties. Maybe it's just from being buried at work.

A kind, encouraging word can do for them what water will do for a plant. It can cheer them up; it can revitalize; it can be sunshine on a cloudy day. We're not talking about a major conversation, but a simple, sincere word of kindness that will lift someone's soul.

Take time today to notice those around you. Remember water isn't just for wilting plants. Water keeps healthy plants blooming – it prevents them from wilting. The same is true with people.

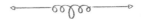

What an amazing contrast

Luke 19:10 "For the Son of Man came to seek and to save what was lost."

Don't you just love the story of Zacchaeus? Here the guy was a crook! As chief tax collector he was wealthy and had cheated all kinds of people out of their money. He was a little guy, maybe the size of Danny DeVito – and probably a bit feisty to deal with too. The people called him a sinner and that was probably the nicest name they called him.

So here Jesus comes to Jericho and Zacchaeus wanted to see who Jesus was. But due to the crowd and his short size he couldn't. And given his reputation, I imagine the people weren't exactly willing to let him through to see. So he ran ahead and climbed a sycamore tree to see him, since Jesus was coming that way. Zacchaeus didn't know it but he was about to have a 'divine encounter'.

So there he was in the tree and when Jesus got to that spot he was probably stunned to hear Jesus call him by name; telling him to come down immediately because they were going to go to his house! I can see him scrambling down, welcoming Jesus gladly. But as they walked together to his house I bet his mind was filled with questions like: WOW??!! How did he know my name? How is this happening? Why me?

Scripture doesn't provide us with what Jesus said once there, but it seems that the presence of Jesus provoked the righteous response that is typical of a heart that 'wants to be found'. In Luke 19:8 we read:

But Zacchaeus stood up and said to the Lord, "Look, Lord! Here and now I give half of my possessions to the poor, and if I have cheated anybody out of anything, I will pay back four times the amount."

What an amazing contrast to the rich young ruler? Who when Jesus told him to sell what he had and give it away and follow Him, he turned away because he was wealthy. Here Zacchaeus, in response to the presence of the Lord, freely gave half of his wealth to the poor and promised liberal restitution to all of those he cheated. Zacchaeus was lost and ready to be found – and Jesus sought him out and found him!

May we too be led by our Lord to find those who are lost and ready to be found and introduce them to Jesus.

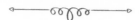

The Macedonian jailor – God came to him too!

Acts 16:9 ⁹During the night Paul had a vision of a man of Macedonia standing and begging him, "Come over to Macedonia and help us."

Isn't it incredible how an encounter with Jesus can change your life?!!! In reading about Zacchaeus I think of the jailer in Macedonia who was saved through the ministry of Paul and Silas (Acts 16). Paul had been looking to go elsewhere but he received a vision of a man of Macedonia, standing and begging him, "Come over to Macedonia and help us." So they went.

Their trip to Macedonia is such an incredible story. God sovereignly led them there and for many days they were experiencing a quiet, uneventful time of ministry. I wonder if Paul was thinking it was too quiet given God's intervention with the vision to get them there.

Then, Paul cast a spirit out of a slave-girl that enabled her to tell the future, earning a fortune for her owners. Because of their loss, her owners drug Paul and Silas into the marketplace. They were accused of creating uproar in the city and in essence became Public Enemies 1 & 2.

Of course the crowd joined in on the attack, and the magistrates ordered them to be stripped and beaten. Then after being severely flogged they were thrown in prison – in an inner cell - with feet fastened in stocks. The jailer was commanded to guard them carefully.

What did Paul and Silas do in response to such unjustified brutal treatment? At a time like that, instead of complaining or bemoaning their fate, they were praying and singing hymns to God in the middle of the night – and the other prisoners were listening.

Then a violent earthquake struck - opening the doors and loosening everyone's chains. It appears that the prisoners could have escaped, but they didn't. The jailer woke up and seeing the doors open, was about to kill himself but Paul stopped him.

The jailer must have been stunned that they all didn't escape. What happened next tells us that the jailer had been listening to Paul and Silas as well.

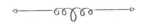

The response of Paul and Silas glorified the Lord

Acts 16:27, 28 ²⁷The jailer woke up, and when he saw the prison doors open, he drew his sword and was about to kill himself because he thought the prisoners had escaped. ²⁸But Paul shouted, "Don't harm yourself! We are all here!"

Yesterday we considered how Paul and Silas wound up in stocks in the inner jail after having been stripped, beaten and severely flogged during their brief ministry in Macedonia. Then the violent earthquake struck - opening the doors and loosening everyone's chains. The jailer woke up and seeing the doors open, he drew his sword and was about to kill himself but Paul stopped him.

"The jailer called for lights, rushed in and fell trembling before Paul and Silas. He then brought them out and asked, "Sirs, what must I do to be saved?". He knew the importance of being saved and asked them what he must do to have it happen. They replied, "Believe in the Lord Jesus, and you will be saved—you and your household." (Then they spoke the word of the Lord to him and to all the others in his house. At that hour of the night the jailer took them and washed their wounds; then immediately he and all his family were baptized. The jailer brought them into his house and set a meal before them; he was filled with joy because he had come to believe in God—he and his whole family. Acts 16:29-34

It seems that the uproar, stripping and severe flogging of Paul and Silas were simply required by the Lord in order to reach the jailer and all in his house. I treasure the picture of the two of them praying and singing hymns at midnight and all the prisoners listening just before the earthquake struck. Paul and Silas never lost sight of the Lord and what they were about!

I had an entirely new thought regarding this Macedonian experience. What if the earthquake was the given - that it was going to happen with all the prisoners escaping and the jailer killing himself? Could everything that happened to Paul and Silas be God's answer to preserve the jailer's life and bring about his salvation? Who knows? What we do know is that they glorified the Lord by how they handled themselves in a most difficult situation. Instead of a night of defeat and tragedy – it was a night of triumph and joy!

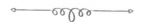

Don Schmidt

It takes more than a recipe

James 3:13 Who is wise and understanding among you? Let him show it by his good life, by deeds done in the humility that comes from wisdom.

Don't you just love a wonderful meal? The enjoyment we experience as fragrant aromas fill the air building the anticipation of the delights to come. The table is well set and the foods presented attractively. Think of tasting and savoring the first bite of each food and having "Oh my goodness is this wonderful!" moments.

Then making the meal even more wonderful is the fact that we are sharing it with family or friends. The tangible satisfaction we experience by being together and enjoying one another's company. It's easy to take that for granted, particularly when it is on a regular basis, but we are blessed by not overlooking it.

Many are the times that guests ask for the recipe of a dish Donna has made – and, many are the times when we have asked for a recipe. Everybody enjoys good meals. Good recipes + good ingredients + good preparation + timely presentation = wonderful meal. This formula is accomplished through intentionality and the development and application of learned skills. It is not accomplished on a consistent basis by accident.

The same is true of a wise and understanding life, filled with good deeds done with humility. Such a life requires focus and commitment. Focus touches on the intentionality while commitment recognizes its daily requirement – like preparing a meal to eat. It happens multiple times daily. We must also be concerned with quality. It is not enough to do good deeds – although the doing of them is important. Our faith must address the way we do them. The humility is the "seasoning" that sets them apart.

There is such satisfaction and joy to be experienced in both the living of such a life and for those who interact with it. Isn't it wonderful to be around those whose lives are described by this verse? Seek to become like them. Learn of them. Ask them for their recipe!

Focusing on Him turns darkness into light

Isaiah 42:16 I will lead the blind by ways they have not known, along unfamiliar paths I will guide them; I will turn the darkness into light before them and make the rough places smooth. These are the things I will do; I will not forsake them.

This promise to Israel is a promise from the Lord for us as well. You might have to read the verse several times to have it sink in. The Lord quickened this verse to me a number of years ago while I was in Brazil visiting my son John and his family. It was a time when I was really struggling with direction and God's plan for me. I was having difficulty understanding what was going on in my life in terms of job/ministry/direction.

The "details" of my daily life were giving me problems as I grappled with them. At the same time, I did understand that the Lord wanted me to walk in faith. My struggle was between focusing on the Lord and dealing with my circumstances that I didn't understand – back and forth.

Into this mix one morning, the Lord gave me this verse as a token of kindness. It says that there are times in our walk with the Lord when He leads us in ways we have not known, along unfamiliar paths. Our unfamiliarity translates into darkness, like finding our way on an unfamiliar hiking trail in the dark through treacherous terrain. We usually aren't aware that He is leading us because we simply find ourselves in difficult unfamiliar circumstances and have to deal with them.

But here is where the faith element comes in. He will turn the darkness into light – our anxiety and distress over where we find ourselves is replaced by the peaceful confidence that comes from Him. Think of being on that hiking trail in the dark in treacherous terrain and having a trusted guide meet you. We still have to traverse the trail but we're not alone. The presence of this guide and our justified confidence in Him results in the rough places becoming smooth.

Our problem is that we are so inclined to focus on our troubling circumstances. The Lord wants us to understand that life is filled with these situations - but He is always with us. That is reality, not just a theological promise. We might not know where we're going or the details of how things will work out, but we have our God with us. He provides the light in our darkness. He guides and strengthens us in the journey. He delivers us from fear and uncertainty. That is something to rejoice in no matter what else is going on!

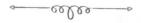

The fragrance we can have

Psalm 13:5 But I trust in your unfailing love; my heart rejoices in your salvation.

When I first met Donna 50 years ago and through the early years of our marriage she wore a wonderful perfume named Most Precious. It was the only perfume that she would ever wear and she wore it regularly. The fragrance was so special and so her. Unfortunately in the early 80s they quit making it. Then several years later, we discovered some Most Precious on eBay and were able to purchase it. It was so delightful to have the perfume again.

One of the special memories associated with having the perfume again involves our son, Andrew. He came home after we had received and opened the perfume. I had the perfume box out of sight and I asked him to close his eyes and tell me what he smelled. I then held the box near his nose and he immediately exclaimed, "That's Mom!" He was born in 1980, so his early years were a time when Donna wore Most Precious. Even though it had been many years since she had worn the fragrance, he instantly recognized it.

This idea of having a fragrance that characterizes us came to mind this morning as I was praying and worshipping with a wonderful song that we have sung at church - I Give You My Heart by Reuben Morgan of Hillsong. When singing it my thoughts went to the coming week – I want the message of this song to resonate within me daily. It is not just for Sunday – it is for every day. I want it to be the "fragrance" of my life – of our lives – each and every day. Slowly, read the words and allow them to bless you.

I Give You My Heart by Reuben Morgan

This is my desire to honor You
Lord with all my heart
I worship You
All I have within me
I give You praise
all that I adore is in You
Lord I give You my heart
I give You my soul
I live for You alone
Every breath that I take
Every moment I'm awake
Lord have Your ways in me

When you have time, I have attached a link to Hillsong singing this song at a concert. Join them in worshiping our incredible Lord. http://www.youtube.com/watch?v=1uqBxizNZJ4&feature=related

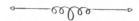

Don Schmidt

A 'wellspring' of forgiveness

Ephesians 3:32 Be kind and compassionate to one another, forgiving each other, just as in Christ God forgave you.

Have you ever ran out of water? If you've ever lived in a home that used a well, you might have had such an experience. My first encounter with running out of water was in our home in Peninsula, OH. I was in the shower covered head to toe in soap when the water ran out. Making the experience even more memorable was the well could still generate a slow drip of cold water. I got to stand there for a long time until the cold, slow drips rinsed me off.

We were told a good well had a recoupment rate of 3 - 5 gallons of water per minute. Ours was 1 – 2 quarts per minute. We learned how to adjust our water usage so we wouldn't run out (most of the time). As the well got weaker, we drilled deeper and found some improvement. We added holding tanks in the basement to increase our usable supply. Eventually, the well ran dry and we had a choice to build a cistern, like many in the village had, or we could drill in another place on our 1 acre. We chose to drill.

The individual who drilled wells asked if we wanted him to 'witch' for it. We said, "No. We'll pray for you that the Lord will guide you where to drill." The result was amazing. He not only found water, but he said this was the strongest well in town. He could measure up to 25 gallons of water per minute recoupment and this was beyond that! What a gift from the Lord!!

I would like you to consider that forgiveness – specifically, the ability to forgive – as a gift from the Lord to each of us, that has amazing similarities to the 'well / water' illustration described above. There is an abundant supply available, we simply have to live lives that tap into it. Just like water, we use forgiveness repeatedly every day. Some have 'strong wells' and are able to forgive with little effort or concern. The supply is there in abundance because of decisions they have made to conform to the teachings of our Lord.

Others have 'weaker wells or drying up wells', where they find forgiving others to be more difficult and at times they seem to 'run dry'. Instead of soap, they find themselves covered with anger, resentment and bitterness and no 'water' (read ability to forgive) to deal with it. Unfortunately, it is a whole lot easier for us to recognize when we run out of water, than it is to recognize when we run out of forgiveness.

The ramifications of unforgiveness are profound. No matter what happens to us, the Lord expects us, and requires us, to forgive one another – just as we have been forgiven. Proverbs 4:23 speaks to this in a particularly fitting way given our illustration today: *"And guard your heart for it is the well-spring of life."*

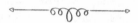

Don Schmidt

Things might not be what they seem

1 Peter 5:8 Be self-controlled and alert. Your enemy the devil prowls around like a roaring lion looking for someone to devour.

When we last flew from Denver to Colorado Springs (COS) there was a most interesting experience. It occurred as we were approaching the runway in our landing in COS. The flight from Denver was smooth – no turbulence at all. Typically, this has been a bumpy flight so I thought the smoothness was due to it being early morning when there is little wind and the air is still.

But in our approach I was looking out my window and saw something that indicated that it was really windy in COS. Just before reaching the runway, our jet passed a reservoir that was covered with white caps. There were also waves washing up on the shore.

Because the flight and approach were smooth even as the plane changed directions, I assumed there was little wind. Seeing the whitecaps and waves, surprised me because I recognized they were caused by a strong wind. Someone else might have looked at the reservoir and never associated what they were seeing with wind.

Because the flight was smooth, I incorrectly assumed no wind. This realization struck me as an important reminder. Things aren't always what they seem! We at times make casual assumptions on limited information. This can be true of us in how we view relationships, movies, programs, movements, organizations, TV shows, etc… It can also be true of our actions and attitudes. If we're not observant, we can miss situations that contradict assumptions we've made. Something that would be a warning signal – a red flag – is missed and we suffer for it simply because we don't recognize it.

Think of watching a movie that was said to be good and things start becoming explicit. Do we recognize the signs and stop the movie or change channels? If we are with a group of people and friendly conversation starts becoming gossip. Do we recognize it and direct the conversation in a redemptive way?

We might be shading the truth in what we say and the Holy Spirit convicts us to stop. Do we respond to His convicting presence and speak with integrity? How do we recognize if the company we're with is bad – particularly since bad company corrupts good character? Let us ask the Lord if there are warning signs in our lives that we have missed and enable us to recognize them whenever they occur.

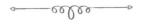

Being aware of Him

Psalm 105:3 Glory in His holy name; let the hearts
of those who seek the LORD rejoice.

Isn't it wonderful that we have a miracle working God who is intimately involved in our lives? Isn't it incredible that our God, who made the universe, wants – no, make that insists – upon a personal relationship with each of us. But He doesn't take a distant, unapproachable, sterile approach of demanding we serve Him. He woos us as a lover! His goal is for us to love Him in return. All of creation is speaking to us, drawing us to seek and to know Him.

Our God is the Holy One of Israel. He is the God of Abraham, Isaac and Jacob. He is Yahweh. He gave His son Jesus to die for us and because of that sacrifice; we have the opportunity and privilege of becoming His family. Jesus is our Lord! He is incapable of failing, or lying, or being unfaithful. He never has an 'oops'. Nothing escapes His notice. He never leaves us; He is always with us, inside of us. He wants us to be aware of Him always. The more we are aware of Him, the more we seek Him.

I remember a special trip to Colorado where I was so aware of the weather and my surroundings. The weather was perfect: temperature in the 70s, low humidity, bright sunshine, high visibility and a strong cool breeze. Enhancing this pleasure for me was the sound of the wind in the trees. It was always there. Then there was the beauty of the surroundings, the trees, the mountains and the open sky – the pleasure of the quaking aspens. After a summer of high temperatures, high humidity, warm nights, little wind and frequent cloudy skies; my senses were just alive to the change and the pleasure of it.

The Lord wants us to be aware of Him throughout each day, just as I was aware of the weather and the beauty of our surroundings in Colorado. He is always present and just as refreshing as a cool breeze on a warm day. In the midst of all we do, He gives us reminders throughout each day that invite us to be aware of Him and seek Him. These reminders can be as obvious as the sound of the wind in the trees. We simply have to notice them and embrace them. When we do they bring us pleasure. Our hearts rejoice because we are seeking Him.

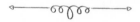

Don Schmidt

'Requirements' a part of grace and mercy

What are these devotionals really about?

Suppose we had eyes to see that some important things in our lives weren't what they seemed to be. Things that we thought were fine and good turn out to be not so good – incompatible with whom we want to be. Some areas of life are much more obvious when it comes to telling the difference – while others much more difficult.

Think about the word 'requirement'. It's a word that appropriately applies to many aspects of our lives. What is required to be a student; an employee; a husband; a wife; an employer? Different things have different requirements – that's a normal part of life.

But what happens if we misperceive what the requirements truly are of something important in our lives? We form an understanding of what 'normal' is; but that understanding in reality is really sub-normal or contrary to what it should be.

In such situations, what does it take to make us aware that something is amiss in our understanding? Often it is through encountering information involving that subject that provokes a re-evaluation of our understanding and behavior. Insights are persuasively presented that often highlight the differences between what our understanding is and what it should be.

Getting back to that word 'requirement', we often don't associate it with our Christian faith. We tend to focus more on grace and mercy – particularly with the passing of time. We often fail to recognize that our salvation experience was just the beginning of God's work in us, not the 'we have arrived' moment.

We're not talking about earning salvation; nor are we talking about legalism. We are talking about loving God and all that implies – and the implications are enormously wonderful. The net results are not culturally acceptable living patterns.

My goal isn't to hit readers in the side of the head with a 2 x 4 to get them to change. My goal is to present the glorious truth of the Gospel in such a way that readers hear the Holy Spirit speaking to them and encouraging them to respond to Him. Consider Paul's powerful instructions in Romans 12:1, 2 The Message,

So here's what I want you to do, God helping you: Take your everyday, ordinary life—your sleeping, eating, going-to-work, and walking-around life—and place it before God as an offering. Embracing what God does for you is the best thing you can do for him. Don't become so well-adjusted to your culture that you fit into it without even thinking. Instead, fix your attention on God. You'll be changed from the inside out. Readily recognize what he wants from you, and quickly respond to it. Unlike the culture around you, always dragging you down to its level of immaturity, God brings the best out of you, develops well-formed maturity in you.

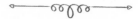

Face to face with Satan

Scripture at the end

Our son Andrew is a wonderful actor. He's also a very busy businessman. Some years ago he played the role of Satan in The Thorn, a marvelous Easter production in Colorado similar to the Passion of the Christ. In costume, makeup and mask, he was hideous. The mask had been made by professional artists and made him appear so very real!

Given his athleticism and gymnastics background, his movements made your skin crawl. He was able to give the appearance of evil incarnate. Satan's greatest moments were those from Jesus' arrest to his death on the cross. As Jesus and the cross made their way through the audience to the crucifixion site, Satan was behind him slinking, gloating and celebrating.

Andrew had prayed that the Lord would use him in this vile role of Satan however He would. Later Andrew discovered just how profoundly the Lord did use him in one young man's life. There was a high school student, who was sitting in the front row of an aisle that the procession went through.

This young man had a teacher who happened to be a Christian. A few days earlier she became aware that he was getting involved in drugs and warned him of the evil he was getting involved with – and he dismissed it. She then told him that he needed to come "face to face with Satan" in order to recognize the reality of what he was messing with.

It was this same young man, sitting in the front row, watching as Jesus, the soldiers and the cross went by. Then as Satan and the demons started to go by him, the Lord moved on Andrew to go nose-to-nose with this particular young man! So Andrew – as Satan – immediately spun, faced him nose-to-nose; and inches apart, let loose a hideous, blood-curdling scream – and then moved on. It was over in an instant, but the young man had come "face to face with Satan". This directly resulted in his repentance and salvation!!!

Many of us share a similar type of problem with that young man. We are dabbling in things we shouldn't – and we don't recognize who or what we are messing with, or the consequences of our behavior. We think we love Jesus – but we live lives that are entwined with the world and its ways. We too, need to recognize the true reality of our lives. The Apostle John puts it this way,

Don't love the world's ways. Don't love the world's goods. Love of the world squeezes out love for the Father. Practically everything that goes on in the world—wanting your own way, wanting everything for yourself, wanting to appear important—has nothing to do with the Father. It just isolates you from him. The world and all its wanting, wanting, wanting is on the way out—but whoever does what God wants is set for eternity.

1 John 2:15-17 The Message

Loving Jesus attracts trouble

*2 Timothy 3:12 Anyone who wants to live all out for Christ is in for a lot of
trouble; there's no getting around it. The Message*

Today's verse is of the prosperity likely to come to those who want to live all out for Jesus
– although it's not the kind of thing we typically think of when the subject of prosperity
comes up. This talks about trouble, and lots of it. Why on earth would godly, Christ-like
people attract trouble?

We're not talking about being obnoxious with our faith, or pushy or reflecting
unrighteous behavior of any kind. This is talking about doing it right! To put it in terms
we all can relate to, we are surrounded by people who will have an allergic reaction to our
loving Jesus. It's not due to us doing anything wrong.

Jesus spoke to the disciples about this very point:

*"If you find the godless world is hating you, remember it got its start hating me. If you
lived on the world's terms, the world would love you as one of its own. But since I picked you
to live on God's terms and no longer on the world's terms, the world is going to hate you."*
John 15:9 The Message

Live on the world's terms and it will love you. Live on God's terms and the world
will hate you!

Think about how easy it can be to get upset with those who treat Christians as though
they had the plague. Of all the ills in this world, in their minds Christianity is a curse.
(It's like Jesus is getting a little too close to them.) Yet these attitudes and these people are
to be expected – and the Lord has shown us what He expects of us, both in how we view
these situations and how we are to respond:

*"Blessed are you when people insult you, persecute you and falsely say all kinds of evil
against you because of me. [12] Rejoice and be glad, because great is your reward in heaven, for in
the same way they persecuted the prophets who were before you."* Matthew 5:11-12

When we live our lives sold out to Jesus, He prepares us for whatever we encounter.
May our responses always glorify Him.

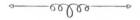

A brutally accurate description of what we are seeing

Galatians 5:22-24 But the fruit of the Spirit is love, joy, peace, patience, kindness, goodness, faithfulness, ²³gentleness and self-control. Against such things there is no law. ²⁴Those who belong to Christ Jesus have crucified the sinful nature with its passions and desires.

Question: Are we focusing more intently upon our Lord as we see the rampant lawlessness, anger and venom that are being exhibited throughout our society? We must not develop a "hold the fort" mentality in the midst of this - ("Lock the doors and hang on until Jesus comes!") As the darkness grows, the light of Christ Jesus within us must shine brighter. We are His – and are here for such a time as this!

Given Jesus' warnings about the condition of the world – particularly as we approach the end times, we shouldn't be surprised to see such behaviors becoming more and more abundant. Here is the root of the problem as identified in Galatians 5:19-21a (The Message). These are the actions of the sinful nature. :

It is obvious what kind of life develops out of trying to get your own way all the time: repetitive, loveless, cheap sex; a stinking accumulation of mental and emotional garbage; frenzied and joyless grabs for happiness; trinket gods; magic-show religion; paranoid loneliness; cutthroat competition; all-consuming-yet-never-satisfied wants; a brutal temper; an impotence to love or be loved; divided homes and divided lives; small-minded and lopsided pursuits; the vicious habit of depersonalizing everyone into a rival; uncontrolled and uncontrollable addictions; ugly parodies of community. I could go on.

That is what we as followers of Jesus have been freed from. We have a new nature and the power of the Holy Spirit to live lives that produce righteousness. Here are the "fruit of the Spirit" that must characterize our lives as described in The Message version of today's verses:

Galatians 5:22-23 *But what happens when we live God's way? He brings gifts into our lives, much the same way that fruit appears in an orchard—things like affection for others, exuberance about life, serenity. We develop a willingness to stick with things, a sense of compassion in the heart, and a conviction that a basic holiness permeates things and people. We find ourselves involved in loyal commitments, not needing to force our way in life, able to marshal and direct our energies wisely.*

No matter what happens, we have the opportunity and privilege to have our life characterized by the fruit of His Spirit. We also have the responsibility to live such lives. Lord Jesus – help us to recognize that this isn't optional for those following you!

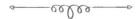

Don Schmidt

Discovering the way of love

1 Corinthians 14:1a Follow the way of love

What is the way of love? If the Lord spoke these words to you, what would your response be? "How do I find it?" "Where is it?" or "What is it?" Following the way of love is different than following a trail that simply leads somewhere. Instead of trying to find something, this is a course of action wherein we become something.

Remember the wonderful story of the man born blind who was healed by Jesus. The disciples had asked who had sinned, this man or his parents for him to be born blind. Jesus responded, *"Neither this man nor his parents sinned, <u>but this happened so that the work of God might be displayed in his life</u>."*

Jesus then spit on the ground and having made some mud with the saliva He put it the man's eyes and told him to go wash in the Pool of Siloam. The man did and was healed! Needless to say this caused quite a commotion with his family, neighbors and those who had seen him begging for years. Some of the Pharisees had a fit that this miracle was done on the Sabbath. Others of them wondered how a sinner could do such a miracle.

After the uproar and the man was thrown out by the Pharisees he had a most wonderful encounter with Jesus described in John 9:35-38,

> *35 Jesus heard that they had thrown him out, and when he found him, he said,*
> *"Do you believe in the Son of Man?"*
> *36 "Who is he, sir?" the man asked. "Tell me so that I may believe in him."*
> *37 Jesus said, "You have now seen him; in fact, he is the one speaking with yotu."*
> *38 Then the man said, "Lord, I believe," and he worshiped him.*

Ponder a moment about the spirit that characterized this man as he responded to Jesus. He not only believed – he worshipped Him. We need to realize that he was an adult who spent his entire life up to that point blind (and begging) so that the work of God might be displayed in his life. May our lifelong response to our Lord be the same as his.

It is in that spirit that we are instructed to follow the way of love - so that the work of God would be displayed in our lives. The way of love is where our lives become more and more a living display of the love of God - of the grace and goodness of our Lord. It leads to where everything we do is done in love. That is how the world knows we are truly His.

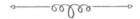

Winning when we lose

Proverbs 16:22a Understanding is a fountain of life to those who have it,

Mistakes – Errors – Goof-ups – Bad judgments – Blunders. They sure are all part of life. In sports they would be called fumbles, strikeouts, errors, interceptions, turnovers, holding, off-side, interference, wild pitches, yellow cards, red cards, etc… A very important principle applies to both categories (life and sports): when these things happen, the 'game' goes on – it doesn't stop.

Continuing the sports comparison, our error or wild pitch or yellow card might cost us the game but losses are part of sports as well. In the major league sports I recall only once has a team gone undefeated throughout the entire season and won the championship (1972 Miami Dolphins). Think about that: losing is normal – it's a fact of life.

Losing is easier to take when we do our best and our efforts are error free. Our opponent simply was better. It's harder when we believe we are the better team or the better player and we lose because of our mistakes. The issue is learning to do better – to improve – to make fewer mistakes – to learn from our mistakes. Remember the adage "practice makes perfect"? It has a much greater chance of being true if we recognize where we need to improve and practice doing it correctly.

A good memory I have is going to see our then 9-year-old granddaughter Gabi's soccer game. The game ended in a 1-1 tie. A few weeks earlier the opponent had beaten Gabi's team 5-1. On this day, Gabi's team outplayed them except for the final score. It was exciting to see how her team had improved. [Side point – I'm sitting here laughing because I just remembered the time when our oldest sons were little and playing soccer. During one of their games we happened to look at our goal and there was no goal keeper! Then we saw him behind the net picking dandelions!!!]

The Lord has given us His Spirit, Scripture, grace, mercy, forgiveness and a new life freed from the power of sin. They all are active ingredients in His provision for us to improve – become more Christ-like – live more error free lives. He enables us to put our confidence in Him and participate wholeheartedly in life – to not get side-tracked by our failings.

Thankfully Jesus enables us to see our shortcomings and learn to from them. We cannot stand around and mope about our mistakes, or when we fall short. He enables us to get over it and stay focused on Him and stay involved. Because of Him we are able to win even in life's losses.

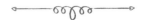

The joy of overlooking offenses

Proverbs 17:9 He who covers over an offense promotes love, but whoever repeats the matter separates close friends.

You're driving down the road in wintery weather. A truck goes by and suddenly your windshield is covered with slush and dirt. Visibility has just decreased about 99% and you can't see anything. Even with your wipers on high it just becomes a brown blur. At that moment isn't it nice to push the button and have your windshield sprayed with washer fluid? In seconds you can see again.

One of the nice things about this illustration is that in real life the consequences of not having a functional windshield washing system are immediately apparent when the need arises. For most of us, the one item that most likely could go wrong is to be out of fluid. Driving and not being able to see just don't go together.

We might not realize it but failing to overlook offenses in relationships is like driving in traffic without being able to see; accidents happen and damage occurs. Such 'mud' on the windshield of life is normal. Jesus followers have the 'spiritual fluid' and the practical ability to clear it away. We cover over the offense. We overlook it. We forgive.

We do not allow offenses to become wedges in relationships. That is exactly what the enemy of our souls wants to have happen. The Message puts today's verse this way:

Overlook an offense and bond a friendship; fasten on to a slight and—good-bye, friend!

The Amplified Bible spells out a bit more the actions involved in this:

He who covers and forgives an offense seeks love, but he who repeats or harps on a matter separates even close friends.

May we have the spiritual eyes to see the 'mud' on our windshield when offenses occur so that we will respond in a way that reflects the love we share.

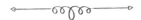

The 'flowers' of love and faithfulness

Proverbs 3:3 Let love and faithfulness never leave you; bind them around your neck, write them on the tablet of your heart.

Last night was such a beautiful evening. Donna and I sat outside and just enjoyed the perfect temperature and the cool breeze. I had earlier completed mowing the lawn so it looked great. Then there were spring flowers blooming in the gardens and the trees swaying with the breeze We just enjoyed everything and each other.

Lawns and gardens don't have red idiot lights that indicate attention is needed NOW! (They're called idiot lights because only an idiot ignores them.) Lawns and gardens simply need someone who cares and takes the time to notice - and attend them. It also helps if that person enjoys the beauty they can possess.

While well-tended lawns and gardens can become an ego thing (not good), they hopefully reflect a desire to faithfully take care of what one has – being faithful. Whether the yard and gardens are big or small, their beauty is enhanced by the tending they receive.

Isn't it interesting that left unattended, lawns and gardens have their beauty diminished? The beauty is overshadowed by the neglect of the one responsible for them. While the flowers and colors might be noted, passers-by are more struck by the neglect than they are by the beauty.

Lawn and gardens – love and faithfulness – all need regular tending. The 'flowers' of love and faithfulness are mercy, kindness and truth. What are the detractors from love and faithfulness? The 'weeds' are selfishness, hatred, hypocrisy or falsehood.

We have the opportunity to display the goodness and kindness of our God wherever we go. We have the privilege of representing Him and His character – His living Word made alive in us. The exciting thing is that our Christ-like character has a fragrance and attractiveness that draw people to Him. We get to be used each and every day as expressions of His beauty.

We're not perfect and there are always going to be 'weeds' in our lives to be tended, but they are going to be minimized in the lives of those who are truly Jesus-followers. Such lives live out the marvelous command of Jesus in Matthew 5:16,

In the same way, let your light shine before men, that they may see your good deeds and praise your Father in heaven.

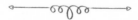

When we think we aren't making progress

Philippians 2:12b,13 …continue to work out your salvation with fear and trembling, [13]for it is God who works in you to will and to act according to his good purpose.

In high school I took a reading improvement course. It was a one semester speed reading course where we were taught to increase our reading speed (words read per minute) without losing comprehension. Part of the course was regularly viewing films that were the printed text of a story. All of the text was blurred except for a section of one line. The purpose of the films was to teach us eye movement and to grasp all of the words that appeared in the readable section of the line.

Initially, each line was divided into three segments. Rather than our eyes moving from word to word, the film forced us to absorb the words in one-third of the line at a time. The highlighted, readable section would rapidly move across each line in three jumps and so on down the page. Following the film we took a test over what we had just read to measure our comprehension. In order to stay with the fast group, we were required to maintain a 70% comprehension score on each test. Each film required us to read faster than the previous film.

Over the weeks, the films changed from showing three readable sections of each line to two sections and finally to one section. In it, the entire line was then readable and our eyes had to take in the entire line of text in one moment as the highlighted section moved down the page. I remember barely being able to keep up week after week, from the very first film until the last film at the end of the semester. It was always a strain. It never felt like I was making any progress except for the fact that I knew the word per minute reading speed was increasing.

I am so grateful that in our last class of the semester, the teacher showed us the very first film of the series we had worked through. I was amazed. This film, that 15 weeks ago seemed to move so fast that I could barely keep up with it, was now slower than molasses in winter. It was one thing to know my word per minute reading speed was much faster. It was entirely different to go back and see just how far we'd come.

Sometimes in our Christian walk we experience the strain of thinking we are not making any progress. It can seem that we are always under strain from being stretched by our circumstances and things in our lives that God is dealing with. It is important to recognize that God is at work in us – and that He is a very capable worker. Be encouraged! Let your confidence be in Him. He is making progress with us and accomplishing things in us that we might not be aware of. Ask Him to open your eyes to see what He has done.

Don Schmidt

Not just a storm but a furious squall

Mark 4:35 That day when evening came, he said to his disciples,
"Let us go over to the other side."

Have you ever noticed how sometimes it seems that everything happens at once? While such times can be filled with pleasures and wonderful experiences, that isn't usually the case. More often it seems that they are filled with stretching and demanding difficulties and problems that all demand our attention – right now! In such times we might wonder, if we see a light at the end of the tunnel, is it an oncoming freight train!

Then when our plate is as full as we think it can get, something more piles on and we feel like we're about to go under. In times like these, when the situation seems to go from bad to worse with no let up in sight, my primary reaction is to view myself as having been 'set up' by the Lord. I 'see' a great big sign in the sky above me that says, "This is a test!"

The story involved in today's verse is something similar. The disciples think they are just going across the lake to get to the other side – just like the chicken crossing the road. Little did they know what they were about to face. There was this storm awaiting them. The good news was that Jesus was with them in the boat. The bad news was that not only was he sleeping through the storm, but here is how this storm is described in Scripture: 1) furious squall, 2) waves broke over the boat, 3) the boat was being swamped, 4) there were raging waters, 4) they were in great danger!

Think about these descriptions from the gospels and remember many of these disciples had worked on the water so they could recognize their situation. It wasn't just a storm, it was a furious squall. They were not just contending with wind and waves but with raging waters and the boat was being swamped. On top of that, Scripture declares that they were in great danger. This wasn't just a storm made to sound worse through later retelling, like a fish story. They think they're going to drown and Jesus asks them, *"Where is your faith?"*

We too might feel like our circumstances are a furious squall – our boat is being swamped and we're about to go under. But the Lord is with us! Our situation didn't catch Him by surprise. Instead of feeling like we are threatened by the storm, we can rejoice in the opportunity to stand in the midst of it, with our faith focused on Him. Instead of feeling like we are overwhelmed and facing each day with dread, we can be filled with gratitude for the 'testing opportunity' He has given us. He's watching and enabling us to glorify Him in the midst of it. What an opportunity!!!

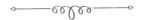

The awesome wonder of our Lord

Luke 8:24b, 25 He got up and rebuked the wind and the raging waters; the storm subsided, and all was calm. "Where is your faith?" he asked his disciples. In fear and amazement they asked one another, "Who is this? He commands even the winds and the water, and they obey him."

Fear and amazement! This was the response of the disciples to this demonstration of power and authority even though they had already seen Jesus do all manner of healing miracles and deliver many from evil spirits. We're not talking about healings that only the person who was healed would know if the pain went away. The miracles included those paralyzed, leprosy, withered hands, and demon possessed. Think of the magnitude of the miracles that would attract thousands to pursue Jesus.

They had seen these miracles first hand, yet the disciples were stunned by seeing the storm, the wind and the waves obey Him. Mark uses the word terrified to describe their response and Matthew describes them as being amazed. Somehow this was different for them. Maybe it was the magnitude of what responded. Having life come to paralyzed limbs or wholeness to a withered hand appeared small in comparison to a storm that was threatening their lives immediately becoming calm.

I think of the word <u>wonder</u>. The wonder of seeing and experiencing the miraculous power of God. Have you thought of this aspect of our God recently? Hopefully, you have experiences in your life that left you breathless and in awe of what God had done. In fact just the memory of such experiences can bring goose bumps or tears. Think of the powerful testimonies and answered prayers that you have read and heard and ponder the wonder-working power of our Lord and Savior.

If you don't have memories of such experiences, ask your Christian friends to share ones that they have or read about them. There are lots of books available that recount inspiring experiences with our God. Also, and most importantly, look to Jesus and ask Him to allow you to experience such wonder and awe. The Christian life is the most wonder-filled life that can be lived. Let us rejoice together because we get to live it.

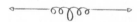

Don Schmidt

An important lesson from Andrew and his team

Hebrews 10:24 And let us consider one another to provoke
unto love and to good works: KJV

I am reminded of our son Andrew and his gymnastic team at a club in NE Ohio. There were 6 boys on the 9 year old team (Class IV) that became state champions: Andrew, Greg, Johnny, Kenny, Matt and Nick. A 50 point all-around score (6 events) is a very good score at that level and all 6 of the boys were able to score near 50 and above in competition.

This meant that their practices were something special because they all were doing so many things right. They still had fun – they were 9 year old boys – but they were seeing and experiencing commitment to excellence in every practice. They worked hard and watched one another do routines right. They helped and encouraged each other. They wanted to win as individuals but it was the team that was most important.

Today's verse talks about us provoking one another to love and good works. The NIV uses the phrase 'spur one another on'. The idea is the reverse of being jealous or depressed by seeing the efforts and accomplishments of our peers. The efforts and accomplishments of those around us can provoke similar things in us. They are meant to encourage and motivate. We can all experience excellence in the tasks we face.

When you or your friends need help with something, are there certain individuals who always seem to be there helping? This is a practical expression of loving one another – to be there when needed. It's important to have our "eyes and ears" trained to recognize the opportunities when they arise – and to use the examples of those who have helped us to spur us on to help others.

This is what we need to see in our relationships with those around us. It will encourage and challenge us. It makes us all want to try harder and support one another. It also provokes such a sense of gratitude that we get to be part of such a group. The Lord has given us such a marvelous opportunity to bless one another, our community and most of all Him. Our prayer is that we will be ever-faithful to the challenge He has placed before us.

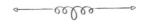

The privilege we have in Jesus

Isaiah 5:20 Woe to those who call evil good and good evil, who put darkness for light and light for darkness, who put bitter for sweet and sweet for bitter.

I read this verse and sensed that my devotional this morning was supposed to be based on it. Then an entirely different perspective of this verse came to mind and resonated with me. Instead of viewing this verse from the perspective of it being a warning, our focus today is upon the reality of what the Lord enables us as Christians, and the Church, to be.

Because of Jesus, we are able to live lives that identify good as good and evil as evil. Because of His love for us, we can put light for light and darkness for darkness. Because of the Holy Spirit we are able to put sweet for sweet and bitter for bitter. We, and the lives we lead, are God's answer for those amongst us who are searching for Him and His ways – and who often don't even know they are searching.

A few verses before this in verse 5:16 it says, *"But the LORD Almighty will be exalted by his justice, and the holy God will show Himself holy by his righteousness."* Our calling as Christians means we are to be light and salt. We are to show forth His love and live lives of righteousness that glorify our God. Amidst all the darkness and deception that our cultures and the world have, God has placed us!

This opportunity we have is expressed wonderfully by Paul: *"But thanks be to God, who always leads us in triumphal procession in Christ and through us spreads everywhere the fragrance of the knowledge of him."* 2 Corinthians 2:14 Think of it! In a world of darkness and despair He has chosen to spread His fragrance through us. Some will recoil because they are not interested in Him. But others will be attracted because they are responding to the work of His Spirit, drawing them to redemption. We get to share His fragrance with all who surround us, knowing and trusting that there are those who will respond to Him.

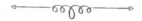

Panting for Him

Psalm 42:1 As the deer pants for streams of water,
so my soul pants for you, O God.

We had the blessing of living for twenty years in a little village in the middle of a 32,000 acre national park in NE Ohio between Akron and Cleveland. We were in a valley, surrounded by forests and fields with a river running through the middle of it. It was home to a great many white-tailed deer. We could hardly drive anywhere without seeing them particularly in the morning and evening.

After moving into our home there we soon learned that the deer considered the flowers we planted 'lunch'! Later we built a wrap-around porch on our house with hanging plants centered in the railing sections. We had to install gates on the porch because the deer would come onto it to eat the plants. Whenever we drove, we had to keep an eye out for the deer because deer accidents were so common. We had four in those years with several near misses.

One of the important side benefits of being around the deer was the way they reminded me of this verse. For years it presented a fascinating picture, but I just glossed over the part of the verse that talks of my soul panting for God. Later when the Lord began dealing with me about passion for Him I came to realize that this verse describes how He wants me to become. He wants my soul to pant and thirst after Him just like a thirsty deer pants for streams of water.

This began a great adventure for me in seeking the Lord as to how to make this happen. It's one thing to say it or claim it – it's another for it to be descriptive of what is actually occurring. One of the things that helped me in the process was the conviction that it was the Holy Spirit, at work in me, who was causing me to seek after this. Since He was the source, my hope was grounded firmly in the fact that He would enable me both to pursue and grow into this goal He had for me.

Thus began a process of daily praying for this to become me. Overall it was part of a much bigger picture of becoming passionate for God. The focus was upon seeking Him. The amazing thing is not only that God loves to play 'Hide & Seek' with us – but that He loves to be found! (When we're playing this game with our little kids or grandkids, think of the joy we have in them looking for us and finding us.)

Whenever we see deer in nature, in calendars, in pictures – even reindeer hitched to a sled. Let them all trigger thoughts of this verse and the wonderful gift that God has in it for those who seek after Him.

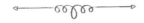

Can this really happen to us?

Isaiah 6:9-10 He said, "Go and tell this people: "Be ever hearing, but never understanding; be ever seeing, but never perceiving.' ¹⁰ Make the heart of this people calloused; make their ears dull and close their eyes. Otherwise they might see with their eyes, hear with their ears, understand with their hearts, and turn and be healed."

Suppose we are walking down the street and we see a man walking along throwing $100 bills in the air. What would our response be? Would we ignore him because we doubted that the bills are real? How about getting angry with him because he's littering? Would we stand back and criticize the people scrambling to pick up the bills as they were scattered on the street?

Now, let's tweak the situation a bit. Suppose that we happened to be in the bank in line behind this person when he received 1,000 $100 bills. We stood there and watched the money being given to him. We then followed the person out of the bank and saw him begin to walk along throwing these $100 bills, <u>which we knew were real</u>, into the air. What would our response be now? Would we be scrambling after the money with everyone else? Or would we be upset with him for littering? Sounds absurd, doesn't it – except it's not!

Today's verses are some of the most frightening verses in the Bible for they describe a condition that can happen to us and we won't likely know it. The condition they describe would cause us to be angry with the man for littering in the above illustration. The fact that the $100 bills were real would be irrelevant. We would be consumed with our perceived impropriety of it all.

Think of Jesus and the miracles that He did – particularly those done on the Sabbath. The Pharisees and religious leaders had a fit and wanted to kill Him for it. The fact that the stunning miracles were real was irrelevant to them. They were blind to the reality of what was going on in front of them! This is described in John 12:37-41:

37 Even after Jesus had done all these miraculous signs in their presence, they still would not believe in him. 38 This was to fulfill the word of Isaiah the prophet: "Lord, who has believed our message and to whom has the arm of the Lord been revealed?" 39 For this reason they could not believe, because, as Isaiah says elsewhere: 40 "He has blinded their eyes and deadened their hearts, so they can neither see with their eyes, nor understand with their hearts, nor turn—and I would heal them." 41 Isaiah said this because he saw Jesus' glory and spoke about him.

To be continued…

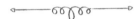

Do we see Him in the midst of our difficulties?

John 9:1-3 As he went along, he saw a man blind from birth. His disciples asked him, "Rabbi, who sinned, this man or his parents, that he was born blind?"
"Neither this man nor his parents sinned," said Jesus, "but this happened so that the work of God might be displayed in his life.

These verses begin the wonderful story of Jesus healing the man born blind. It is so fascinating because of all it reveals about the Pharisees and the difficulty they had grasping the obvious. They were confounded by the miracle, particularly because it was done on the Sabbath. But more than that is the reality that Jesus describes in these verses above.

Do we understand that this man was born blind because that was God's plan? That God wanted him blind so that His work might be displayed in his life? Think about the difficulties that he and his parents had to deal with all through his life. They weren't victims, they were experiencing God's plan for them.

The Bible is filled with difficult situations and painful experiences that God brought into people's lives in order for His plan for them to unfold. Does our understanding of God and His ways recognize that He does all manner of such things today? Specifically, that God will do such things in our lives? Sudden loss of a job, illness, accidents, birth defects, financial ruin, unexpected deaths of loved ones, good situations made difficult – the list is long.

We have a tendency to respond negatively to difficult things that occur in our lives – more likely to view them as a curse rather than as a blessing. So how are we going to respond? Will we recognize and embrace the fact that they present opportunities for us to experience God's work in our lives? Regardless how we view them, we still have to deal with the difficult circumstances in our lives. But when we see God in the midst of them, there with us and for us, it changes us. Not only is there is no problem too big or situation too difficult for us to walk through but He will transform the way we walk through them.

Faith in the Lord produces the heavenly wisdom spoken of by James in 3:17, *"But the wisdom that comes from heaven is first of all pure; then peace-loving, considerate, submissive, full of mercy and good fruit, impartial and sincere."* Think of having the inner well-being described by this verse within us as we navigate the difficult adventures that God brings or allows in our lives!

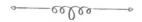

My grasp of the obvious was missing!

John 9:25b "…One thing I do know. I was blind but now I see!"

I think we all are thrilled when our grasp of the obvious is working. For some of us, it's like a visitor who only shows up once in a while or someone who leaves at a most inopportune time. Not too long ago my grasp of the obvious was long gone and I had one of the most embarrassing moments in my life. Fortunately, this event took place between me and the Lord. But now I get the blessing of sharing it with you all. (How do you do a happy face? ☺ - Wow! I didn't know this computer would give me a real one when I tried to make one!)

I briefly worked with an organization as a travelling representative and was gone every other week. Nice hotels were provided as we travelled from city to city. On a Monday I arrived at my hotel somewhere in the south and when I entered my room I discovered the ugliest bathroom I ever saw. It was big, barren with railings everywhere. I couldn't believe they would have something like this and nearly went down to the front desk to insist on a room change. (I can't tell you how embarrassing this is!)

Fortunately I just accepted it. Two days later as I was driving across the middle of nowhere, my grasp of the obvious suddenly returned. In a nano-second it struck me. As you have already likely figured out, the bathroom was designed for handicapped individuals! If I had been in a wheel chair or on crutches or simply needing assistance, this bathroom would have been exactly what I needed. What I considered 'ugly' would have been beautiful to the one needing it. (As I drove I thought of the Spaniard in Princess Bride and "humiliations galore!")

The Lord really used this experience in a powerful and serious way with me. At the time we were going through some very difficult things and there were ways of addressing the difficulties that I thought were 'ugly' and had dismissed them. It was after this experience that I recognized that what I considered ugly – wasn't ugly at all. They were appropriate and a blessing to assist us in our adventure. We needed them as much as we would need railings in a bathroom if we were in a wheel chair or on crutches.

Needless to say this has been a humbling experience. It has made me much more careful about drawing conclusions about what I think I see and what I think I perceive. It is too easy to miss the obvious sometimes. I thank God that while driving across the middle of nowhere, the Holy Spirit made this blind man to see!

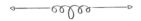

What message are we communicating?

Philippians 1:27a Whatever happens, conduct yourselves in a manner worthy of the gospel of Christ.

Have you ever thought about the fact that so much of our lives we are representing someone or something? At work we represent our employer. If we give good service or do quality work it reflects positively upon our employer. The Zenith company had the slogan, "The quality goes in before the name goes on."

If we need repair work done on our car we typically ask around to find a shop that does quality work at a fair price. Positive and negative reputations spread. Some time ago when I got a new modem/router, my research uncovered comments about how difficult it was to deal with some companies' technical help people who were described as impatient and rude.

When in Tennessee we were at Publix grocery store and the young man who bagged our groceries proceeded to take them to our car without asking if we needed him to. He was cheerful, and being the parents of four sons, we were blessed by his attitude. When we got in the car, I mentioned it to Donna and she said Publix was known for that!

What do the waiters and waitresses think on Sunday when they are serving Christians after church? If they had to rank the desirability of the various groups they wait on, would Christians be at the top? If not, why not? In Colorado Springs we were part of a Friday night service involving a large diverse group of college students & 20-somethings. This very topic was addressed several years ago because word had gotten back regarding the less than attractive behavior of the attendees when they descended on local establishments after the service. Unfortunately, they were fitting in with a general negative perception of Christians that these workers held. The good news is that repentance can result in changed perceptions in those we interact with.

Think of our relationships with family, friends and neighbors. We have so many opportunities to demonstrate the quality of life that comes from loving Jesus. Even if people don't associate kind and thoughtful behavior with the gospel, that is what they should experience when they interact with us. It is our privilege and responsibility to live lives worthy of our faith.

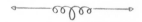

My critical experience at a large bakery

1 John 2:16 For everything in the world—the cravings of sinful man, the lust of his eyes and the boasting of what he has and does—comes not from the Father but from the world.

Years ago when our first two sons were little I took a job at a large bakery in Michigan. The ministry we were involved in was struggling and I needed to have a paying job. I discovered on my first night at work why there was a high turnover rate for this position. In fact it was not unusual for men to quit during their very first night. There were several of us racking bread. We each stood at the end of a line of rollers where the loaves of bread came. After going through a slicer and bagger machine, they came to each of us like a never-ending line rolling along. I think they came at a rate of about 50 a minute.

For eight hours we would stand in one spot and slide the bags of bread on to trays that could hold 10 loaves apiece. Then we would slide the trays filled with bread into big racks on wheels. If any of us fell behind there was emergency shut off button we could push to stop the bread coming down our line but that meant we got yelled at. But at least that was better than the loaves going off the end of the rollers onto the floor at our feet.

One night while working I got to thinking about our sons (who were 1 & 2). I thought of them in elementary school and the teacher asking students what their daddies did for work. The students one by one answered, "My daddy is a teacher. Banker. Doctor. Lawyer. Engineer…." Then it was my son's turn and he said, "My daddy racks bread at Schafer's Bakery." I was mortified. Here I had a college degree and was racking bread!

Immediately, the Lord took me to task for my prideful attitude. My mind was filled with questions that did not originate with me and each I knew I had to answer. Is the work you are doing necessary? – "Yes". Is it dishonest or sinful? – "No". Is it enabling you to pay your bills and provide for your family? – "Yes". Is it honorable labor? – "Yes". Are you grateful for this job? – "Yes".

Instead of focusing on prideful comparison of jobs, the Lord wanted me to recognize the honor in work – and the importance of providing for myself and for my family. It is a real snare to look down on jobs as being "beneath" us because the attitude will easily translate over onto those who are doing the jobs. What a blessing it is to be able to work!

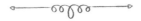

Mowing the lawn on a hot humid day

1 John 1:9 If we confess our sins, he is faithful and just and will forgive us our sins and purify us from all unrighteousness.

When we moved to Franklin, TN it was a reintroduction for me to high humidity and the effect it has in combination with high heat. I've lived with it for most of my life but for the previous five summers we lived in Colorado Springs where there was heat but little humidity. In Franklin the effects of high humidity were most noted when I mowed our lawn with a push mower on hot, steamy days. Our lawn had a slope to it so I would also get to push the mower up hill. Needless to say, I would be drenched when done.

After my mowing adventure it was so marvelous and refreshing to step into a cool shower and experience the cleansing and refreshing it would bring. An important part of the experience was putting on clean clothes afterward. It would be inconceivable to put the wet mowing clothes back on – they went into the laundry.

We can all relate to the above experiences; both the effects of working in the heat and humidity, and of the cool shower and clean clothes afterward. They present a practical picture of sin, repentance and forgiveness. Best of all is the absolutely unfailing promise of our Lord to always – yes always – fulfill this promise in our lives.

Being human, we sin. The Holy Spirit convicts us. And as a pastor friend of ours likes to say, "The Holy Spirit is not incompetent at convicting of sins." We confess our sins and he forgives us. This is where the illustration of work, heat, humidity, a shower and clean clothes come in so importantly. (I find it so helpful to have practical, daily events remind me of His love and care for me.) Spiritually He cleanses us from the sins like a cool shower would do for us. There is a cleansing and refreshing that occurs. The repentance in our lives is discarding the 'mowing clothes' and putting on clean garments. We change our behavior.

His forgiveness never grows old. It's like His compassion and His faithfulness; they never fail and are new every morning because of His great love for us. He delights in forgiving us. He knows these are things we will need every day of our lives. Blessed are His sons and daughters who recognize this and pursue Him. As Lamentations 3:25 says, *"The LORD is good to those whose hope is in him, to the one who seeks him;"*

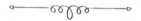

The Leper Part 1

Mark 1:40-42 A man with leprosy came to him and begged him on his knees,
"If you are willing, you can make me clean." [41] Filled with compassion, Jesus
reached out his hand and touched the man. "I am willing," he said. "Be clean!"
[42] Immediately the leprosy left him and he was cured.

Consider for the next few minutes that you are this man. Assume that you were a farmer with a wife and a daughter - that your home was filled with laughter and love. One day it becomes clear that something is radically wrong. You cut yourself and don't even feel it. You and your wife realize that it is leprosy and that you must leave, never to be with them or see them again. Imagine the pain of saying goodbye. This disease makes you unclean and an outcast, forever separated from family and friends.

Some years pass and you hear about this amazing man from Galilee named Jesus. You hear the stories of people thronging to him because of the miracles he is doing – and not just a few. But he's healing all who come to him! No one has ever had this kind of power to make the blind see and the cripples to walk. Imagine the glimmer of hope that would begin to stir within you when you first heard of the miracles. The thought through your mind that maybe – just maybe – this Jesus could and would heal you!

You finally decide that you are going to find him and see if that which was unthinkable could possibly happen. People are going to react negatively because you, an unclean and untouchable leper, are going to have to get through the mob surrounding him. But the glimmer of hope is now a beacon drawing you to this man named Jesus. You have nothing to lose.

Upon finding him, you experience something that all the stories of miracles and wonders had not prepared you for. After kneeling before him and begging him, "If you are willing, you can make me clean." - you look into his eyes and see them filled with compassion! Compassion for you! He is not telling you to get away, but instead is reaching out to you! He touches you!!! And as he does, he says, "I am willing," and "Be clean!"

And then it happens! The leprosy is gone and you are whole! Think of the smile you see on Jesus' face and the joy in his eyes as he watches your transformation. Think of experiencing that moment and try to imagine the wonder and glory and power and jubilation of that moment exploding within you! Your entire world has just been radically changed!

To be continued…

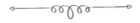

The Leper Part 2

*Mark 1:40-42 Continue to imagine that you are this man – whom we have
assumed is a farmer, a husband and father. You had to leave everything because of
your leprosy. The pain of separation, and the pain of life's hopes and dreams being
dashed had become a given in your life – until that day Jesus healed you.*

Although Jesus warned you not to tell anyone and to show yourself to the priest, your
excitement and joy caused you to tell everyone about this amazing miracle. On your knees
you begged him, "If you are willing, you can make me clean." He responded, "I am willing.
– Be clean!" How can you ever forget the compassion in his eyes! And his touch – the very
fact that he touched you, an unclean leper! No one had touched you in such a long time.

Now you are approaching your home, grateful for the bath you took and the clean
clothes you now have on. Your wife and daughter do not know yet of this miracle – but
they are about to find out. Approaching your home you experience the joy of walking
across your fields. When you are near the door to your home, your young daughter comes
out but she doesn't see you. You stand there a moment watching her – how she's grown.
And then you call her name – your voice cracking with emotion. She turns and you see
the stunned look on her face. That is quickly replaced with a smile and a squeal of joy
you will never forget as she runs to you and leaps into your arms. Never, in your wildest
dreams did you think this could ever happen again.

After holding her close, you tell her to go get her mother, your wife, but she's not
to tell her that you are there. In a moment, she comes out of the door pulling your wife
who was busy working inside. Your wife is fussing with her, wondering why she had to
come out. Then your daughter slowly lifts her arm and points in your direction. Your wife
turns and sees you standing there – smiling. You have never seen her look so stunned and
so speechless. You can no longer hold back the tears. As you open your arms, she runs to
you and is enfolded in your embrace.

For the longest time you just stand there holding each other and then your daughter comes to join the hug. Finally, the questions burst forth from their lips. They want to know what happened. How can you be healed of your leprosy? You take them inside, sit down and take a breath. Looking into their faces you begin, "There is this man named Jesus…"

Note: Max Lucado has a wonderful story of the leper Jesus touched. We have had the joy of seeing our son Andrew act out the above story in performances where the audiences wept because the story came so alive.

Note: The movie "Risen" is one of the very best! It is told from the perspective of the Romans, specifically the Roman Tribune who is assigned the task of finding the body of Jesus. One of the very last scenes after the resurrection is Jesus in Galilee rescuing, embracing and healing a highly deformed leper – who we then see become a fully healed man. I don't recall ever seeing a scene to compare to it; that so reveals the leper's deformity – and such a loving response by our Savior!

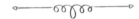

Spiritual red and white stones

Proverbs 4:6a Do not forsake wisdom, and she will protect you;

In the summer of 2007 I got to spend a month in Afghanistan. Among other things, the organization I was with had medical centers and community centers out in the rural areas – in places we would describe as the middle of nowhere. We were visiting these locations and sometimes would ride for hours to get there on these incredibly bumpy paths that were loosely called roads.

A major goal was to bring medical care to areas that had never had any. Afghanistan had the highest maternal and infant mortality rates of any county. One medical center served 57 villages and many villagers would walk for hours to get there. In the preceding 6 months, there had been 50 babies born there with all mothers and babies surviving! As we were driving to get to this particular center, I noticed that in various places along side the road there were small stones every few yards that had a brush-stroke of paint on them. There were sections of the road where the paint was red and other sections where the paint was white.

When we got to the medical center I asked Dan, the organization's leader what was the meaning of the painted rocks that we encountered in different places along side the road. His answer got my attention. Afghanistan had experienced years and years of war. Many areas were minefields where these explosive devices had been planted. The white stones indicated fields that the military had 'swept', meaning they had been cleared of the mines. The red stones indicated fields that had not been swept free of mines. To walk in those areas marked by the red stones would likely result in serious injury or death. No matter where we were going it's amazing how easy it was to notice any red rocks and avoid those areas.

God's Word and His wisdom will do the very same thing for us in our daily life. He tells us what to avoid and where it is safe to go. The more we listen and walk with Him the easier it is for us to spot danger areas where he has 'red rocks' in plain view warning us not to go there. In fact His Spirit within us will even point them out to us if we are missing the obvious. His wisdom will protect us and keep us safe but we must listen to it and not forsake it.

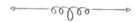

The road less traveled

Isaiah 26:3 *You will keep in perfect peace him whose mind is steadfast, because he trusts in you.*

This morning I woke up thinking about this peace that God will provide and the last stanza of Robert Frost's poem, The Road Not Taken. Reading the entire poem it would seem that the name of the poem might have been more fitting to be The Road Less Traveled because as he writes, that has made all the difference. Although the author might not have meant it this way, I have always related it to choosing to follow Christ:

> I shall be telling this with a sigh
> Somewhere ages and ages hence:
> Two roads diverged in a wood, and I--
> I took the one less traveled by,
> And that has made all the difference.

In Matthew 7:14 Jesus says, *"But small is the gate and narrow is the road that leads to life, and only a few find it."* This is the Biblical "Road Less Traveled". While great is the blessing by simply not taking the other road (that leads to destruction), there is more to it than that. It involves who we are and who we become as we take this road leading to life.

Colin Harbinson, a friend of ours, has a statement that focuses on this and my wife loves to quote him: "We are human beings – not human doings." This really gets at the heart of today's verse. The Lord will keep in perfect peace him who is steadfast, because he trusts in the Lord. Being steadfast and trusting in the Lord are the keys. The Amplified Bible helps us by 'amplifying' the meaning of these words in Isaiah:

> *"You will guard him and keep him in perfect and constant peace whose mind [both its inclination and its character] is stayed on You, because he commits himself to You, leans on You, and hopes confidently in You."*

These are the attributes of the Road Less Traveled that the Lord wants to develop within us. These are things we learn and grow in. It is so much more than a list of 'dos and don'ts'. Remember that it is not only the destination that is a prize, but it is the journey that makes the difference. It's as we walk along the road (with Him) that we experience the life-giving, life-transforming relationship with our Lord.

Life is filled with difficulties and uncertainties, but His peace is not subject to them. Likewise, neither are we. His plan and provision are for us to walk in His peace no matter what turbulence is going on around us. By focusing on Him, He transforms us so that today's verse becomes the reality of our lives.

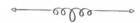

Who we are supposed to be!

Luke 4:18-19 "The Spirit of the Lord is on me, because he has anointed me to preach good news to the poor. He has sent me to proclaim freedom for the prisoners and recovery of sight for the blind, to release the oppressed, ¹⁹to proclaim the year of the Lord's favor."

What kind of people do you like to be around? When you're having difficulty or need help, who do you call on? Or better still, are there people you know that will see your need and offer to help without being asked? Isn't it wonderful to have friends who encourage us and we don't have to watch our backs around them. They are kind, considerate and thoughtful.

The past couple of days a friend and I were talking about the incredible good news that the Gospel is. Then this morning I was reading this in Luke about Jesus and was impressed with how this verse also provides a marvelous picture of the Gospel that our words, lives and relationships are to proclaim.

This proclamation of our words, lives and relationships is supposed to be – and must be – good news to the poor; freedom for those in bondage; enabling those who are blind to see again and the oppressed to be released. We are to be living examples of God's favor. That doesn't equate with financial or material prosperity, but with lives and relationships that glorify our Lord.

The words we speak aren't primarily the 4 spiritual laws or just a 'verbal presentation of the gospel'. But our words speak of kindness, encouragement, integrity and honor. We mean what we say and our words do not reflect anger. We don't gossip and say unkind things. Think of having a reputation where if someone was told you had said or done something negative, it wouldn't be believed. The response would be, "He or she doesn't do that."

God's intention is for us as Christians to live such lives. He wants everything about us to be consistent with and reflective of the Gospel. That is good news because Godliness is attractive. People will be drawn to Him because they know us. This includes both Christians and non-Christians. Remember, our lives are to be all about Him. What an incredible privilege we have!

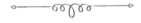

Is telling the truth optional?

Proverbs 12:22 The Lord detests lying lips, but he delights
in men who are truthful.

Is in okay sometimes to not tell the truth or to deliberately mislead? Are 'white lies' appropriate sometimes? Are there ever situations where avoiding hurting someone's feelings should take priority over telling the truth? Are 'half-truths' okay? What qualifies as dishonesty?

Have you ever done something like this? You're running late for an appointment – say 20 minutes late because you got busy and forgot the time. En route to the appointment there is a traffic accident that delays you 2 minutes. Upon arriving at your appointment, you apologize for being late and inform them you were delayed by an accident on the highway. The impression you want to give is that your tardiness is due to something beyond your control – a highway accident - versus your own negligence.

Think of being asked the question, "What were you doing?" Suppose you were playing or reading stuff on the internet instead of working; or watching an inappropriate movie; or visiting inappropriate websites; or looking at inappropriate magazines. How truthful will our answer be? This brings up and entirely different subject of "What is inappropriate?" which we will look at later.

Our God is a loving God. But He also informs us of His view of actions and behaviors. Today's verse is rather unambiguous to say the least. On the one hand He detests those who lie and delights in those who tell the truth. Note that it isn't just the lies that He detests – it's the one telling them! Conversely, He delights not only in truth but in the one telling the truth.

Here is today's verse in the Amplified version, *"Lying lips are extremely disgusting and hateful to the Lord, but they who deal faithfully are His delight."* The point isn't to bring condemnation, but to bring God's Word into play in an important area of our lives. The world thinks nothing of lying. The world would answer the questions in the opening paragraph with a resounding "Yes!" Unfortunately, far too much of the world is roosting in the lives of Christians.

While it is unpleasant to ponder the idea that God might detest some things we are doing, it is redemptive if we turn to Him and ask for His help to change. We are commanded to please Him. A more redemptive view is that we "Get to please Him!" What a blessing it is, when His word and His Spirit show us areas in our lives where we fall short. He enables us to repent and change – to replace our unrighteous actions with righteous ones. He doesn't leave us to ourselves, but is committed to enabling us to live lives that bring Him delight.

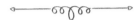

True good and evil are not culturally determined

Hebrews 5:14 But solid food is for the mature, who by constant use have trained themselves to distinguish good from evil.

In Colorado Springs it sure is easy to know which way is west – and from that all the other directions are clear. This is because the Front Range and Pike's Peak are directly to the west of the city. When facing the mountains, north is to the right, south is to the left and east is behind you. Wouldn't it be wonderful if it were that easy to tell good from evil – or right from wrong?

How do we know what is good and what is evil? What is our basis for identifying such things? Years ago I remember reading about an art forger who commented that one of the highlights of his 'career' was having art critics in Europe declare his forgery the original, and the original work of art the forgery. Apparently, his forgeries were common enough that the critics got used to them.

We have this problem that the world has its own idea about what is good and evil. Sometimes it seems that the biggest evil to the world is Christians making any kind of judgment that something is evil or wrong. Isaiah addressed this problem (that we must contend with daily) when he wrote:

Woe to those who call evil good and good evil, who put darkness for light and light for darkness, who put bitter for sweet and sweet for bitter. Isaiah 5:20

Some things are so blatantly evil that they are like a Pike's Peak – so big you can't miss them. But that isn't the general way the enemy of our soul attacks us. He tries to blur the lines and induce Christians to walk in pathways that lead to temptation – that present unrighteousness in attractive packaging. We become familiar with pathways that have his 'forgeries' presented as the norms of 'good' behavior. His goal is to have us reach a point where we affirm the forgeries and reject the 'original'. God forbid we should call his redefined 'acceptable' behavior sin!

If we insist on accurately identifying evil as evil and good as good, the enemy of our souls will try to move us to becoming overtly judgmental of others. That can produce a prideful blindness that is repugnant to God. Remember the Pharisees were so concerned with sin they missed Jesus.

God's Word is our standard. It identifies that 'good and evil' applies to behaviors, thoughts, attitudes – every area of our lives. He wants us to walk in righteousness and it is imperative that we learn to do it the right way. We must recognize that it requires focus, intentionality and training to do this His way!

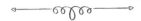

Who we get to be in Christ

Galatians 5:16 So I say, live by the Spirit, and you will not gratify the desires of the sinful nature.

Computers are a vital part of our lives. They are really wonderful when they are fast and have the software we need. One thing about computers though, is that they are also targets and require protective software: antivirus, anti-spyware, firewalls, encryption, identity protection… the list just goes on. We have spam filters, content filters and all manner of security to protect us from hackers, unwanted emails or to prevent access to sites with certain content.

Over the years Donna and I have been blessed to have friends who worked with computers. They would help and advise us in setting up our computer with the appropriate protective software. When we needed help, we knew who to call.

The focus in computers is what they can do – not that they are susceptible to all manner of negative things. There is an old saying, "An ounce of prevention is worth a pound of cure." That really applies here. Properly set up and maintained computers free the users from undue concern over vulnerabilities and enable them to focus on the things to be done.

The same principle applies to our Christian lives. As Christians, we have the Spirit of God within us. When we live by the Spirit, He enables us to overcome sinful desires we encounter. By living in Him and God's Word, 'firewalls' are erected to keep sinful desires at bay. They keep us from going to those places where dangerous temptations are located.

Recognize that 'those places' can be websites, TV programs, books, magazines, video games, etc… as well as actual physical locations like bars, clubs, stores or hangouts; being with individuals or groups that lead us astray by us becoming more receptive to the sinful desires and behaviors they manifest. When we ignore the Holy Spirit's warnings, the unacceptable can – and will – gradually become acceptable to us. Unfortunately, this problem is rampant among far too many Christians.

The Holy Spirit helps us understand and apply God's Word in unfamiliar situations where danger might be lurking. He is ever vigilant. Unlike computer software, there is absolutely nothing that can get by Him – we don't have to worry about upgrades. **He simply requires that we live by Him**.

Remember, in a computer, protective software simply enables it to do what it is designed to do. The same principle applies to us as Christians. Living by the Spirit, enables us to become the men and women of righteousness that God intends. I love 1 Peter 2:9 because it presents such a glorious picture of who we get to be in Christ:

> *But you are a chosen people, a royal priesthood, a holy nation, a people belonging to God, that you may declare the praises of him who called you out of darkness into his wonderful light.*

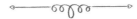

If the little Hammond organ could have talked!

1 Peter 2:9 But you are a chosen people, a royal priesthood, a holy nation, a people belonging to God, that you may declare the praises of him who called you out of darkness into his wonderful light.

Years ago one of our dearest friends named Ric was a pastor of a small church in West Virginia. A pastor friend of his came to the church for some meetings. As I recall, when the friend first arrived Ric and some of the members were showing him the church building where the meetings would be. It was then that the friend spotted the little organ.

The church happened to have a small Hammond organ that had been there for years and the people didn't think much about it. Well, Ric's friend happened to also be an amazing pianist. Right then and there he sat down at that little organ and the music that came forth was beyond anything the members of that church had ever dreamed off. They were stunned and amazed to realize that what they were hearing was coming from their 'little Hammond organ'! They had no idea that it was capable of such magnificent beauty and power. Yes, the friend was a great musician, but this was coming from their little nondescript organ.

Let me borrow from CS Lewis a bit. Suppose that little organ was alive and could talk like the animals and trees in Narnia. My guess is that it would have been as stunned as those listening. I can just see this talking organ incredulously asking Ric's friend when he finished, "How did you do that?!!!" It had no idea what it was capable of until played by a master. From that day forward, its whole world changed.

Today's verse is not to intimidate but to inspire. It is to thrill us with the glorious beauty of who we are and get to be. Because of Jesus and our response in faith to Him, we are "…[God's] own purchased, special people,…".

Just as this little organ was the source of stunningly beautiful music when played by a master, so are we. God wants each of us to understand that He is the 'master musician' in our lives. He desires, *"…that you may set forth the wonderful deeds and display the virtues and perfections of Him Who called you out of darkness into His marvelous light."* Amplified

It is absolutely amazing what He can accomplish in and through us when we commit ourselves to Him. We must understand who we are and what our destiny is from His perspective, not ours. We are not to be content with mediocrity. Because of Him, we are capable of excellence – and He is holding us accountable for it.

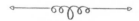

Replacing mediocrity with excellence

Hebrew 11:6 But without faith it is impossible to please and be satisfactory to Him. For whoever would come near to God must [necessarily] believe that God exists and that He is the rewarder of those who earnestly and diligently seek Him [out]. Amplified

As a student growing up, I was always content with 'B's. There was a national test we took each year in school that indicated that I was capable of better than that but I was set in my ways. In college the same continued – I was doing okay but just wanted to get through my courses. Then in my junior year I became a Christian. Studies took a back seat to prayer meetings, Bible studies, witnessing, conferences and other Christian activities. My grades sank and I ended up on academic probation.

At the end of my junior year I went to Colombia on a short-term mission trip. There the Lord gave me a 'major' revelation that He wasn't glorified if I flunk out of school. I needed to get my degree if for no other reason than to honor my parents and the sacrifices they had made in my behalf. Needless to say, I repented and went on to graduate

Several years later the Lord made it clear that I was to pursue graduate school. (PTL I had my BS degree!) I pursued going to Wheaton. As part of the application process I had to take something called a Graduate Record Exam (GRE). It is like the SAT or ACT for college graduates. I got a GRE study book and seriously prepared for the exam. Fortunately I did well and was accepted by the Grad School.

When meeting with my advisor for the first time, he noted that my GRE score was high and exclaimed, "You are capable of excellence! I'm expecting 'A's out of you!" This led to one of the most life-changing communications to me from the Lord. I did not hear an audible voice but He could not have communicated more clearly to me.

The message I received from Him was this: "As long as you think you are only capable of mediocrity you will be content with mediocrity. You are capable of excellence and I am holding you accountable for excellence!" Needless to say, I responded. For the first time in my life I got 'A's!

Unfortunately, so many Christians have unknowingly accepted the lie of mediocrity in our relationship with Jesus. We are content with so much less than He wants us to have. We read about wonderful things in the Bible or the moving testimonies of others but don't think we can experience a relationship with God like that. The message that God gave me regarding my studies applies to all of us in our relationship with Him. Every Christian is capable of experiencing excellence in their Christian life – and He is holding us accountable for it. He expects us to respond with faith to His word and His Spirit and seriously pursue Him. When we do, we experience the rewards of diligently seeking Him.

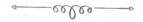

Right process produces right results

Romans 14:8 If we live, we live to the Lord; and if we die, we die to the Lord. So, whether we live or die, we belong to the Lord.

Upon entering Wheaton Grad School I was aware that I had the potential to do really well. Mediocrity was no longer acceptable but I was also aware that I had never been a great student – my study habits had to change. It's one thing to think about becoming a good student. It's another to actually become one. The Lord didn't leave me to my own devices – He gave me a life changing idea and the motivation to implement it.

I needed to hold myself accountable for how much time I actually studied outside of class. This resulted in the creation of my 'Accountability Book'. I tracked down to five minute blocks of time how much I actually studied, and I was ruthless with myself. I remember going to the library to study for the morning. My thoughts were I would study for four hours from 8:00 until 12:00. The reality was a bit different. After taking time out for getting coffee in the union, talking with friends, checking my mail, going to chapel, etc… instead of four hours of study, it was 1 hour and 40 minutes!

The lesson of the Accountability Book was if I put in the time to genuinely study, I got 'A's. This led to the realization that my focus wasn't to be on getting 'A's but upon the 'process' of studying – mastery of what I needed to learn. This led to the liberating realization that right process produces right results.

Inherent in this is recognizing that we have a lot to learn and the importance of always being teachable. Whether it's learning a job, learning to be a spouse or a parent – or learning to do these roles better – we have invaluable resources to help us achieve quality. First and foremost is our Lord who is intimately involved in our lives. He will show us where we need to improve. In addition, we have Scriptures, books, mentor/coaches, pastoral teams, Christian friends, bosses, co-workers, etc… as valuable resources.

We must recognize that being a good parent, a good spouse, good worker, etc… is consistent with (and required by) our faith. He enables us to recognize our shortcomings and become better at these things than we currently are. Never be too proud to ask for help. Our Lord wants quality in all of the roles we find ourselves in. He doesn't separate the sacred and the secular.

Our life in Christ transforms us so that we are able to glorify Him and must glorify Him with ever-improving quality in everything we do. This is what living to the Lord is all about. Beginning today, wherever we find ourselves, Jesus has a redemptive path that will enable us to do just that.

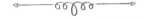

How do we do in life's 'taste test'?

Ephesians 4:1 As a prisoner for the Lord, then, I urge you to live a life worthy of the calling you have received.

What constitutes a life worthy of our calling as a Christian? What does such a life look like? Is it a given that someone who accepts Jesus as their Lord will live such a life? Is the life to be lived a progressive thing – that it becomes more consistent with Scripture with the passing of time?

There are sinful behaviors we are set free from the moment we are born again. Other things He deals with over time. I'm reminded of stories of the coal miners in the great Welsh revival a century ago. These men and women had their lives radically transformed. Drunkenness, stealing, cursing and other offences grew less. It is told that the miner's pit ponies became a problem. The ponies were so used to being cursed and sworn at that they just didn't understand when orders were given in kind, clean words!

The question then becomes what happens in our lives as the months and years and decades roll by? Although the transformation in the miners' lives was miraculous, it was akin to the Israelites leaving Egypt. They were set free in order to become the people God wanted them to become.

Living a life worthy of our calling involves who we are and what we do. It involves having a heart desire to love and please God. It entails being vigilant regarding our character, our thoughts, our intentions, motivations, attitudes and how we communicate with others. These are the things that the Holy Spirit will continually address, help us maintain and transform over our lifetime. They profoundly impact the quality of what we do and why we do it.

That desired quality is well illustrated by the experience of looking for good fruit in a market where the vendor will allow you to sample the fruit. There is appearance, ripeness, texture and flavor. It's not a matter of the fruit just looking good and feeling right to the touch. It must pass the taste test. What a joy it is to bite into eye-appealing fruit that is ripe and sweet to the taste. It's like 'a party in your mouth' - to quote a dear friend of ours. That is the experience we and others around us will have as we walk worthy of our Lord and His calling upon our lives.

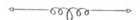

We 'get to' versus we 'have to'

Ephesians 5:1-2 Be imitators of God, therefore, as dearly loved children and live a life of love, just as Christ loved us and gave himself up for us as a fragrant offering and sacrifice to God.

I woke up this morning with thoughts of how we, through necessity or preference, engage others to address certain things we have to deal with. Think of repairing your car, changing the oil or tires, repairing appliances in your home, having someone take care of your lawn, paint or repair your house, take care of pets, plow our driveways in the winter. So many products come with service contracts where we can purchase 'insurance' that will deal with any problems we encounter with the product. All we have to do is pick up the phone and call the repairman.

We simply have to recognize that an issue or problem exists and contact the appropriate person to address it. It is then 'out of our hands' so to speak. We also have the option of ignoring such things – particularly if it is inconvenient to deal with them in terms of priorities of finances, i.e., the warning light on the dash is white not red.

Today's verse engages us in a very different way. It calls upon us to imitate God and to live a life of love. What does it mean to imitate God? What exactly does living a life of love look like? If we think we know, how do we know that our understanding is correct? We are the ones who have to live the life of love. It is not something we can delegate to someone else or ignore. But if we think of it as a 'have to do it' we've really missed the boat. We get to do it. We must want to do it.

Think of it this way. If you are a husband or wife, you don't delegate someone else to love your spouse – you get to do it. You want to do it - and if we're wise, we are always looking for ways to do it better. This means we are also noting the behaviors and attitudes in our lives that are inconsistent with love. There is no higher priority for Christians than living a life of love. Our Lord loves us and we get to love Him and others in return – what incredible privileges!

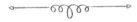

This happened to me

Philemon 22 And one thing more: Prepare a guest room for me, because I hope to be restored to you in answer to your prayers.

This verse reminds me of dear friends and a memorable answer to prayer. Shortly after we were married, we were living in Lansing, Michigan. We were going through the normal struggles that many new ministries go through. God blessed us with an older couple, John and Sue, who were wonderful friends to us and were an inspiration to many. They opened their home and lives to so many young men and women to help them grow in the Lord.

Fasting and prayer were vital to John and Sue and a part of their daily lives. They viewed them as essential elements in seeking the Lord and being empowered to be the man and woman God wanted them to be. We were often amazed at how God spoke to them and used them to bless others. They were loving, kind and selfless.

The Lord spoke to them about establishing a foundation and pouring everything they owned into it where they could minister to people in need of help or encouragement. They purchased a big old house and 50 acres and it became the center of their work and a place of prayer. It was a home where they could have people stay with them for various periods of time to minister and help them.

There came a time when I was struggling with the work we were attempting to do. While praying the Lord put on my heart to call John and Sue and ask if I could come and spend a few days there with them to seek the Lord. When I did they encouraged me to come. It was a blessing to be there – spending time in the word and prayer and gleaning wisdom from John and Sue.

While there I was reading Philemon and the Lord really quickened this verse to me – so much so that I mentioned it to John and Sue at breakfast. They grinned and informed me that the Lord had spoken to them a couple of weeks earlier that I was to come and spend some time with them there. They had the guest room prepared for me and were confident that through their prayers I would come. I am still blessed by memories of this simple yet profound example of God answering prayer and His using Christians to express His love.

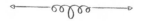

What does the 'Cross' represent to you?

Romans 6:6 For we know that our old self was crucified with him so that the body of sin might be done away with, that we should no longer be slaves to sin—

Recently we enjoyed the beauty of a full moon. I never cease to enjoy seeing one particularly when it first comes up over the horizon. But the full moon never fails to tap into a much richer vein of thought within me. For years when I've seen it, I've thought of my son John and his wife Fabi and their family in Brazil and the work they were doing. Even though they are now here, I still think of them.

One of the most common symbols of Christianity is the cross. Does seeing one make you think of church like golden arches makes one think of McDonald's? Have you given thought to what exactly the cross represents? Or just what do you think of when you see one? Is it merely a symbol that over time has come to represent Christianity?

A rainbow is God's sign to Noah – and to us – that He will never flood the earth again. It is a symbol representing a promise. But the cross represents so much more. A vital key to understanding this is the difference between 'sins' and 'sin'. God made provision for the forgiveness of sins in both the Old and New Testaments. Forgiveness always involved the shedding of blood. In the Old Testament there was the blood of lambs and goats that had to be redone every year. In the New Testament we have the shed blood of Jesus once and for all to provide for the forgiveness of sins.

But the power of sin was and is another thing entirely. Prior to Jesus, the sins of God's people could be forgiven but there was still the power of sin working in them. God's plan in Jesus was to deal with this wretched power of sin that was the result of Adams' fall. The cross represents His love gift through Jesus by which the power of sin was broken.

Through Jesus' death on the cross and resurrection we are able to be born-again – to become new creatures in Christ Jesus – freed from the old sin nature – no longer slaves to sin – able to become children of God! This is what faith in Jesus brings us – a life that is radically changed! May we rejoice in this whenever we see a cross.

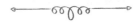

Our loving Father

Isaiah 41:13 For I am the LORD, your God, who takes hold of your right hand and says to you, Do not fear; I will help you.

When we're frightened and concerned it's a wonderful blessing to be comforted. Sometimes we are the comforter – and sometimes the comforted. And sometimes we are both at the same time. I'm laughing as I think of that scene in the movie While You Were Sleeping where Lucy and the brother are trying to walk across the icy sidewalk. They are hanging onto one another for dear life.

I think of children who are frightened and the amazing comfort they can derive from holding a parent's hand. The power is far beyond holding a hand – it is rooted in relationship with who the hand belongs to. It communicates that I am with someone I love and trust. I am not alone. It also communicates that someone is there to help.

There are times when we receive frightening news and we squeeze the hand of the one we are with. It is a way of releasing the anxiety of the moment and receiving strength from the one with us. The fact that we are adults doesn't diminish the power of the peace and encouragement that can be communicated through the touch – the hand that is held.

Our God is our Father who loves us. When Jesus taught the disciples to pray he began, *"Our Father…"*. Think of the Prodigal's father and the joy he had in the return of his son. Our Father is not is not a distant, aloof, icy individual. He is One who cares deeply for us. He enables us to experience the reality of His loving presence with us.

In Romans 8:15 Paul makes it clearer in case we lacking in our grasp of who our God is to us,

> *"15For [the Spirit which] you have now received [is] not a spirit of slavery to put you once more in bondage to fear, but you have received the Spirit of adoption [the Spirit producing sonship] in [the bliss of] which we cry, Abba (Father)! Father!" Amplified*

I know that my wife Donna had a less than positive relationship with her dad. But years ago at a conference, she had an encounter with the Lord where He communicated His Father love to her. He redefined her entire understanding of what a father's love was about. He will do the same for us if we seek Him. Remember that our loving Father is with us – and in times of need, He holds our hand and says, "Do not fear; I will help you."

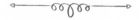

An essential reality in our lives

Revelation 3:19 Those whom I love I rebuke and discipline.
So be earnest, and repent.

Do you remember times when you were growing up when you wanted to do something and were told "No" by your parents? Did you receive it well or did you respond somewhat negatively – like "You don't love me!"? If a child is caught doing something wrong and is disciplined for it, there is a natural tendency to respond negatively unless s/he is trained not to.

How well do we respond in adulthood to such input from our spouse, employer, boss, mentor, neighbor, friend, etc...? When our two oldest sons were little (about 4 and 5) we were visiting dear friends who were like parents to Donna and me. After being with them for a couple days, they sat us down and asked us, "Do you realize your sons argue with you every time you tell them to do or not to do something?"

While it wasn't pleasant to hear, we received their counsel because 1) it was true, 2) they loved us, 3) we wanted to be godly parents, and 4) we wanted to "train our children up in the way they should go". The couple went on to instruct us how to change and bring about the changes in the boys. We had an opportunity to repent and become better parents. We embraced the process.

When I look at today's verse, I see three 'pieces'. We all have a tendency to respond or react to the second and third 'pieces' of it, glossing over the first:

- Those whom I love

- Rebuke and discipline

- Be earnest and repent

We don't like to be rebuked, disciplined, corrected or confronted – whether directly or subtly. We also have a tendency to see repentance as more of a 'big ticket item' rather than as an essential reality in our daily lives. But let's focus on the first piece of this. Notice how the Amplified version expands the context of this verse in terms of God's love for us:

"Those whom I [dearly and tenderly] love, I tell their faults and convict and convince and reprove and chasten [I discipline and instruct them]. So be enthusiastic and in earnest and burning with zeal and repent [changing your mind and attitude]."

This isn't something dry and cold – it is a love gift from the One who loves us more than anyone else. He tells us where we need to change, how to change and He enables us to change. The entire process is the way of life that is absolutely essential to our growth and godliness. Without it we would never be transformed into the image of Jesus. We embrace our God when we embrace it.

To be continued…

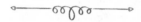

Importance of 'paradigm shifts'

Hebrews 12:5-6 [5] And you have forgotten that word of encouragement that addresses you as sons: "My son, do not make light of the Lord's discipline, and do not lose heart when he rebukes you, [6] because the Lord disciplines those he loves, and he punishes everyone he accepts as a son."

Continued from yesterday:

I would like you to consider some things that have resulted in 'paradigm shifts'. The introduction of these things was so profound that they radically changed our thinking and behavior: automobiles, airplanes, television, computers, internet, cell phones, ipods… The list could go on. Many of us have had most of these things all our lives. Some of us are old enough to remember their initial impact. Regardless, it is easy to see how society was radically changed by each of these inventions.

Paradigm shifts often come into play with our beliefs. Think of an atheist having an encounter with God. His whole world is turned right side up. Years ago we had a pastor friend who didn't believe that miracles could happen today – until one of his church members was miraculously healed. He had to come to grips with the fact that his view of Scripture and God needed to be adjusted.

Today's verses use such words as 'disciplines', 'rebukes' and 'punishes'. While we recognize that God disciplines, we appear to have an aversion to recognizing that these other two words are biblical and apply to us. We have a paradigm view of God that carves these realities out. Do we believe that 'rebuke' and 'punish' are incompatible with a loving God?

If this is our view – our paradigm – it must change because it is as wrong as viewing the world as flat. God's discipline, rebukes and punishment are all reflective of His love for us. Read today's verse in the Amplified version to get better insight how all of these things are saturated with God's love for us:

"[5] My son, do not think lightly or scorn to submit to the correction and discipline of the Lord, nor lose courage and give up and faint when you are reproved or corrected by Him; [6] For the Lord corrects and disciplines everyone whom He loves, and He punishes, even scourges, every son whom He accepts and welcomes to His heart and cherishes."

This is a process to recognize and embrace. Once we see and understand, we experience a paradigm shift - we respond with gratitude instead of resistance or resentment. We recognize this as evidence of our Lord welcoming us to His heart.

The primary purpose of prayer is not 'to get'

Nahum 1:7 The LORD is good, a refuge in times of trouble.
He cares for those who trust in him,

Intentionality is one of my favorite words/concepts because it describes something that is required of us in so many areas of our lives. I don't think I've ever purchased a lottery ticket but a good point is illustrated by the story of the man praying for God to have him win the lottery. The Lord said to him, "You have to buy a lottery ticket first." (To this some might reply, "Lord you could cause me to find a winning ticket on the ground.")

Have you thought about the question, "How do I demonstrate to the Lord that I trust Him?" Trusting God is supposed to be a way of life for Christians, but how do we know that we're actually doing it? Is trusting God one of those things where we can just take it for granted that we're doing it – only to discover that we're not? Is this something we have to be intentional about?

We heard a powerful message that was one in a series on what the good news of the gospel really is. The focus was upon having a life that tastes the goodness and power of God and that demonstrates dependence upon the Lord. The primary way this is done is through prayer. And prayer is something that defines who we are – much more that it being a weapon to be pulled out in times of need.

Prayer expresses our dependence, our helplessness and trust in our Lord. It is a continuation of our acknowledgement of our need for God that we experienced when we were born again. It is a daily acknowledgement and recognition that we need Him in all the areas of our lives – not just those where we feel needy.

The primary purpose of prayer is not to 'get'. It is the life-blood of our relationship with Him. He wants us to have times set aside for Him AND times throughout the day where we talk with Him in the midst of all we are doing.

While He encourages us to make our needs known to Him, He wants us to develop an ever-richer relationship with Him. The amazing thing is the reality of how many of our 'needs' disappear because they are dealt with by our thriving relationship with Him. It is not a problem to forget to ask about our needs when we are caught up in His presence in our times of prayer.

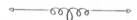

Responding to life's daily tests

*Psalm 20:7 Some trust in chariots and some in horses, but we
trust in the name of the LORD our God.*

Have you ever noticed how easy tests are where you know all the answers to the questions? It's the stuff we don't know or forget that gives us problems. If you are being prepared for an important test of some sort or an inspection by a mentor/coach, do you want s/he to focus on what you know? Or, would you prefer that they look for weaknesses that need to be strengthened?

One of the important lessons that I've learned through reading the Bible is that God has a real penchant for putting His people into situations that will test them. What are they going to do? How will they respond? Sometimes they murmur and complain. Sometimes they seek Him. There are times when they cry out to Him because of the threats they are facing, but other times when they don't.

Today's verse speaks to our God calling us to trust in Him rather than the things of strength surrounding us. He wants to create within us an inclination to trust Him that is like a compass needle always pointing north. No matter what circumstances we face – however trivial or momentous – we will always turn ourselves to the Lord. We must not become careless about this. The Bible contains many warnings about not trusting the Lord, but a powerful one is found in Isaiah 31:1.

"Woe to those who go down to Egypt for help, who rely on horses, who trust in the multitude of their chariots and in the great strength of their horsemen, but do not look to the Holy One of Israel, or seek help from the LORD."

The issue is looking to the Lord first and often. We inquire of Him as David did. He might direct us to seek help from a source, but it's important that such direction comes through prayer and commitment to Him. He uses all kinds of resources in our behalf, but He wants our trust to be first and foremost in Him. Our daily prayer life will go a long way towards keeping this from becoming perfunctory. He intends that our trust be rooted in a genuine, rich relationship with Him.

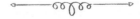

What might your testing look like?

Deuteronomy 8:2 Remember how the LORD your God led you all the way in the wilderness these forty years, to humble and test you in order to know what was in your heart, whether or not you would keep his commands.

Suppose the Lord spoke to you in a dream and let you know that the next day you were going to be tested by Him, but He didn't go into the particulars of what it would entail. When you got up in the morning you were excited and a bit nervous because you wanted to pass the testing.

Spend a moment and think about what kind of things the Lord might do to test you. Might it involve work – dealing with what you do and how well you do it? Would it involve relationships? Would it involve the possibility of a promotion, where it would be an interview or performance evaluation regarding how well you know your job. Would the testing involve big things or small things? How do we tell the difference between big things and small things?

Suppose when you got to work, your boss told you that he needed you to prepare an important presentation for that afternoon that could result in major new business for the company. This unexpected opportunity would involve you working with a bunch of people throughout the day to put it together. A lot to do; with little time to do it; with a major opportunity as the potential outcome – what a test!

Most of the day was an adventure interacting with co-workers to obtain what was needed. They all seemed to have more than enough to do on top of helping you. The presentation was completed, delivered to your boss and the big opportunity was won.

But at the end of the day, you discovered that winning the opportunity wasn't the test the Lord was referring to. Your boss was pleased with the end result, but the Lord had been looking at something else. His test involved all of the human interactions that you had in preparing the presentation. Given the importance of the project, did you fall into a more abrasive style where 'the ends justify the means' mentality kicked in – in order to get the job done? Did you assume fences could be mended later?

Or, were your attitudes, words and actions consistent with your faith? In difficult human interactions were grace and kindness there. Would your co-workers be grateful for the way you performed your task? We have a real tendency to focus on the 'destination'. The Lord is vitally concerned with how we get there. In His eyes, the process is the goal.

Don Schmidt

In a very difficult situation, God spoke to me!

Proverbs 2:6 For the LORD gives wisdom; from his mouth
come knowledge and understanding.

Years ago I was an assistant pastor and was going through an exceedingly difficult and painful situation with some members of the high school youth group and their families. In addition, there was also an amazing mini-revival going on with other high school students at the same time and I was in the middle of it all.

I was loved by some and hated by others. I had never experienced anything like it in my few years of ministry. The pain and stress of the situation was compounded by the fact that I just didn't understand why such negative things were happening – and they were happening! Fortunately, the senior pastor was very supportive of me.

This situation went on for months with no end in sight. Early one morning I was walking around the sanctuary, carrying the names of all the young people, and crying out to God for help. I finally knelt down, weeping as I cried to the Lord, because I just didn't understand what was going on. At that time, the Lord spoke to me – not audibly – but unquestionably! He simply spoke the name of a book and the chapter number in the Bible, one I hadn't read yet.

I immediately opened to the chapter and read it. I was stunned – it explained everything! – specifically!! – down to the details of painful things that had been done to me!!! It gave me understanding of what was going on and the 'why'! It explained why He had brought us there and what we were to accomplish. Importantly, it also expressed His expectations of me to respond to it all in a godly manner.

It was not information and understanding that I could use against anyone. It was meant to help me. We still had to walk through the painful circumstances, but the Lord had given us understanding and encouragement. It was like the Lord put outriggers on BOTH sides of our canoe as we were going through turbulent white water to keep us upright and stable through the worst of it.

The fact that He had intervened and answered my cry was and is beyond priceless. An incredible peace settled within Donna and me because we now understood what was going on, but more importantly, God had spoken to us. This was a supernatural intervention of God into my life that would be part of the bedrock of my faith for the rest of my life!

We were at that church for another 15 months before leaving for grad school. Before we left and in the months following, every one of those 'problem' high school students apologized to me for what they had done and the pain they had caused us. To this day my Bible has a highlighted copy of that Bible chapter that the Lord spoke to me taped inside the back page. It's like in the Old Testament when the Lord told Israel to erect a memorial to remind them of the wonder God had performed. It's an ever present reminder that God always hears our cries and is our source for wisdom, knowledge and understanding.

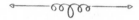

Becoming enlightened

*Proverbs 2:1-6 My son, **if you** accept my words and store up my commands within you, ²turning your ear to wisdom and applying your heart to understanding— ³indeed, **if you** call out for insight and cry aloud for understanding, ⁴and **if you** look for it as for silver and search for it as for hidden treasure, ⁵**then** you will understand the fear of the LORD and find the knowledge of God. ⁶For the LORD gives wisdom; from his mouth come knowledge and understanding.*

Yesterday I focused on verse 6 and the supernatural way that God spoke to me many years ago. We were in such a difficult to understand situation and God responded to my crying out to Him for understanding. It is so good to know that there are times in our lives where God will respond in such a way. Such experiences become part of our storehouse of treasures of our faith.

But we need to understand that God wants to respond to us daily in terms of input into our lives. In these verses He repeatedly says "IF": If you accept..., if you call out..., if you look... IF we obey His instructions it results in a wonderful THEN... He will impact and mold our thinking and thought processes, giving us insight and enlightened perspectives. He will guide us to apply His word appropriately. The supernatural is possible and He does it when we need it but He wants us to live our lives focused on seeking and trusting Him. This is where our lives, by our actions and attitudes, demonstrate to Him, to ourselves and to the cloud of witnesses (both flesh and spiritual) that surround us, that we recognize our dependency upon Him.

Consider the simple instructions in these verses:

- accept (His) words
- store up (His) commands within you,
- turn your ear to wisdom
- apply your heart to understanding
- call out for insight
- cry aloud for understanding,
- look for it as for silver
- search for it as for hidden treasure,

THEN...He wants us to have wisdom, understanding and knowledge that are derived from Him; that are enlightened and enriched by His Spirit and the life only He can give. He wants us to understand that our lives require this. Think of what a guide dog or a walking stick mean to a blind person. These instructions are a primary means of dealing with our own spiritual blindness and becoming enlightened. They enable us to become what He wants us to be and particularly to love Him. Miraculous stories are wonderful, but He wants us to experience and demonstrate the blessing and wonder of Him with us, instructing us and helping us day by day.

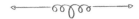

Responding to "Why?" redemptively

Psalm 9:10 Those who know your name trust in you, for you, LORD, have never forsaken those who seek you.

"Why?" This is a question that many of us frequently have. Sometimes there are ready answers, i.e., "Why did I do poorly on that test?" Answer: I didn't study. Question: "Why is my spouse upset with me?" Answer: I behaved like a jerk.

Then there are the 'why' questions that are more difficult to answer. Why did I have to lose my job now? Why couldn't that accident have been avoided? Why does it seem we are always going through difficult times? Why does it seem that everyone else is being blessed and we're not? Why did I have to lose that client? - That sale? Why did we invest our savings in something that was going to collapse? Why did she have to die?

Two thoughts for us to consider: The first is our culture is preoccupied to an unhealthy degree with the question 'Why?' We want to know the why of everything. Often this question and how we respond to it lead us down a road with no outlet - leading to frustration, discouragement, anger, a sense of 'victimhood', rejection or abandonment.

The other thought is to choose to make the question 'why' an invitation from the Lord. By that I mean that whenever we are hit with a difficult 'why', we look to our Lord for wisdom, insight and understanding. Think of it as a wonderful learned reaction. If Ohio State Buckeye fans hear someone say "O-H" the immediate response is "I-O". Likewise when we think or hear "W-H-Y" our response is "J-E-S-U-S". He is our refuge and resource. He is the one we trust. Even in silence, He enables us to become secure experientially – not just in theological head knowledge – but in the reality of His trustworthiness.

For many of us, this is going to involve a significant transition process. That is why He is our comforter, counselor and guide. He lets us know we need to change; He shows us the way and enables us to learn how to walk in it. He will help us establish new God-centered habit patterns that bring life and righteousness. The more our lives reflect our dependency upon Him the freer we become.

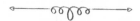

The 'skunk factor' is real!

1 John 3:3 Everyone who has this hope in him purifies himself, just as he is pure.

"Why not?" This is another question that we might frequently ask or hear asked of us. It's in response to someone questioning what another is doing or about to do. Sometimes it refers to innocuous things but at other times it is in defense of questionable or unwise actions – the nature of which we may be blind to.

How many times have we heard, in response to our 'why not?': because you have homework to do; you have to clean your room; you have to mow the lawn; it's your turn to drive the kids, it's dinner time… These are instances where we've simply forgotten or want to forget responsibilities that we have.

But there are situations where this response can be used as a defensive barrier to allow behavior that is questionable, or unwise or wrong. Consider these questions asked by someone of us – or by our conscience:

- Is s/he someone you should be hanging out with?

- Is that a program you should be watching?

- Should you be visiting that website?

- Is that something you should be doing?

- Why are you doing that?

- Why are you coming home so late?

- Should you be wearing that outfit?

- Why would you take that from your employer?

- Should you be reading that?

Last night I woke up several times and the phrase "Why not?" was center in my mind. I alternated between being asleep and awake praying for perspective and insight. Then, just before I woke up I had the clearest, shortest dream – and it startled me.

In my dream I was outside with Snuggles and she saw a little black creature with some white stripes come out the bushes and she took off to meet it. I immediately recognized it for what it was and called her to me. She immediately stopped and came back. I did not want Snuggles to be sprayed by a skunk. I then woke up. I was startled by the clarity of the dream (I hardly ever remember what I dream) and immediately connected the 'skunk factor' to "Why not?"

Think about it, assuming the animal isn't rabid – we aren't afraid of being bitten by a skunk. It's the smell we don't want anything to do with. Associate with a skunk – and you will smell like one. We recognize the 'danger' immediately upon seeing a skunk nearby and avoid it. The question for us is, "If we are honest, how many of our activities have what we could call a 'skunk factor'? They will contaminate us just as surely as a messing with a skunk would. May we pray to have our eyes opened so that we may purify ourselves of any such activities in our lives.

To be continued…

Saltiness and a hot moist towel

Matthew 5:13 "You are the salt of the earth. But if the salt loses its saltiness, how can it be made salty again? It is no longer good for anything, except to be thrown out and trampled underfoot."

Yesterday I wrote about what we allow in our lives and something I called the 'skunk factor'. A serious issue with a bit of humor applied to make a point. I received a comment from a dear friend, "Have a great skunk-free day ;-)". We must recognize that the effect of allowing inappropriate habits, behaviors, attitudes, etc... has a far greater negative impact on us than dealing with the temporary smell of a skunk.

The 'inappropriate' items I refer to include both what we do and how we do it – and what we don't do. Scripture is filled with descriptions of things to do or attributes that should characterize our lives – they reflect our 'saltiness'. Think of something as simple as saying thank you for a kindness that is done. Failure to say thank you communicates a lack of recognition or gratitude. It also might be due to an unfortunate habit of allowing a preoccupation with other details to override its expression. (Think unsaltiness.)

Saying thank you can be perfunctory – and while expressing recognition, it will be low on salt. (Think pass the salt) When sincerely done, it reflects genuine gratitude in one's heart. It communicates appreciation – rather than taking something for granted – and this quality is typically conveyed through how the thank you is expressed. (Think – oooh is this good!).

Consider this parallel illustration: On my first flight to Europe, shortly after take-off, the flight attendants passed out moist, hot hand towels to everyone. This had never happened on a domestic flight and was wonderful! I vividly remember holding that moist, hot towel against my face and running it over my hands. Such a simple thing can be so small yet so noteworthy and wonderful to experience.

Now consider these three alternatives in light of our discussion of expressing genuine gratitude: 1) Failure to say thank you = No towel – it's absence is noteworthy! 2) Saying a perfunctory thank you = A moist, cold towel – better than no towel but not what it could be. 3) Expression of a genuine, sincere thank you = A hot, moist towel – YES!

Salty lives reflect our Lord and Savior Jesus Christ. Saltiness has to do with who we are. The world is in desperate need of salty Christians!

To be continued...

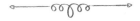

Excellence doesn't happen by accident

*Galatians 5:1 So I say, walk by the Spirit, and you will not
gratify the desires of the flesh.*

Have you noticed that everything that is considered 'excellence' requires effort and work? Music, sports, writing, college, cooking, careers, parenting, marriage, gardening, etc... it makes no difference. Excellence doesn't happen by accident. Each area of endeavor has its own requirements of things to be learned and mastered. They all have standards that identify what excellence is.

Donna, my wonderful sweetheart, makes a bread pudding to die for. The recipe came from a master chef in New Orleans that we got at a sales conference many years ago. There are 10 different ingredients in it including pecans, raisins and coconut – and a marvelous sauce to go with it. The recipe has nuances, such as the nature of the bread used, that are critical to the outcome. It is warm and moist – not dry or mushy – and the flavors are amazing. It doesn't happen by accident.

Excellent, Christian lives don't happen by accident either. We need to understand what constitutes such a life, what must be done to develop it and cultivate the desire for it to happen. The Holy Spirit is central to all of this. We must listen and respond to what He shows us. A major arena of our lives in which He will continually work with us on deals with the desires of the flesh. These are identified in many places but let's look at those identified in Galatians 5:19-21 New Living Translation

[19]When you follow the desires of your sinful nature, the results are very clear: sexual immorality, impurity, lustful pleasures, [20]Idolatry, sorcery, hostility, quarreling, jealousy, outbursts of anger, selfish ambition, dissension, division, [21]envy, drunkenness, wild parties, and other sins like these. Let me tell you again, as I have before, that anyone living that sort of life will not inherit the Kingdom of God.

These are all 'skunk factor' land and will undermine and overcome our efforts to live a Christian life. Their impact is far worse than just making us 'smell' bad. They will radically affect who we are. These are things to run from – just as you would from an approaching skunk with his tail raised. They are the antithesis of walking in the Spirit.

To be continued...

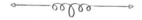

Don Schmidt

'Getting it right' is becoming like Him

Colossians 3:12 Therefore, as God's chosen people, holy and dearly loved,
clothe yourselves with compassion, kindness, humility, gentleness and patience.

We've been talking about "Why?" and "Why not?"; 'skunk factors', saltiness and excellence. All of these have addressed particulars of our lives. As Christians we all want to 'get it right'. This involves dealing with all aspects of life. But at the heart of it all is a pearl of great price – who we are in Him and who He is for us.

We are God's chosen people, but it's a whole lot more than that. We are dearly loved! He swept us off our feet. When we thought we were unlovable and lost. He found us and made us His own. When we were lonely and feeling rejected. He said, "I want you!" Do we understand that we are talking about the God of the Universe! The maker of stars and heavens and planets! He knows our names. He cares for us!

I think of little Samuel, as a child in the temple being awakened by the Lord calling his name (1 Samuel 3). The final time it says, *"The Lord came and stood there calling as at the others times, 'Samuel! Samuel!'"* Try to grasp the thought of the Lord standing by you and calling your name! I remember a chorus on this theme that has always been dear to me, "I heard the Lord call my name, listen close you'll hear the same."

Our Lord and Savior didn't just set us apart like choosing members of a team. He made us His. He made us new. He radically changed us so that we could be like Him. He desires that we show forth His love by developing and showing forth the qualities that He has expressed to us – the ones identified in today's verse: compassion, kindness, humility, gentleness and patience. Can you think of finer attributes than these?

Yes it's important to know what not to do and what to avoid – but the thrill of our hearts can be –and must be – becoming like Him. We can never repay Him for what He has done for us, but we can bring Him pleasure! He enables us to live out these very qualities that express His love and that will draw others to Him. He wants to use us to extend His family!

It's all about Him!

Philemon 4-5 Every time your name comes up in my prayers, I say, "Oh, thank you, God!" I keep hearing of the love and faith you have for the Master Jesus, which brims over to other believers. The Message

What a testimony! Think of inspiring joy and thanksgiving in others because of our love and faith in Jesus – and that faith and love overflow to those around us. Wouldn't it be wonderful if those who knew us could write such a declaration describing us?!! The issue isn't recognition but one of acknowledgement of the reality of Christ's love worked out in our lives.

Who are the Christians in our lives who really are a blessing to us and to others? Take a moment and see who comes to mind; whose lives fulfill such a description. Does the mere thought of them bring a smile to your face and a heartfelt gratitude that they are in your life?

Now think of the joy if others think of us and react with an, "Oh, thank you God!" Believe it or not, that is the destiny that the Lord has for each of us! In John 13:35 Jesus describes how disciples that are truly His will be recognized,

"This is how everyone will recognize that you are my disciples—when they see the love you have for each other."

It's not by our verbal testimony – nor by attending meetings or being part of a recognizable 'Christian' group. It is by our love for one another that all will recognize His disciples. And the quality of this love is to be the highest imaginable! In the verse preceding this Jesus describes this love: *"In the same way I loved you, you love one another."*

Instead of being overwhelmed with the thought of "How on earth do we ever do that?" our response should be closer to giddy excitement that our God enables us to love each other just as Jesus did! This is our destiny - we get to do this! And when we do, others will know that we belong to Jesus. It's all about Him.

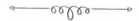

The problems with "What if….?"

Psalm 34:19 The righteous person may have many troubles, but the LORD delivers him from them all;

"What if…?" Have you ever noticed how these two words have a tendency to lead down a trail that leads to fear and anxiety? What if I lose my job? What if finances don't come through? What if something bad happens? What if I make a mistake? What if I fail? What if things don't work out?

Such thoughts when unchecked, will lead to behavior that is inconsistent with our faith. Troubles or difficulties in our lives are all opportunities to respond in faith. When we become preoccupied with 'what if', small issues that might be real can become 'giants in the land' that cause us to want to back away. To use The Wizard of Oz as an example, even legitimate concerns responded to wrongly can begin as a little old man behind the curtain that becomes the ogre on the screen that intimidates us.

Troubles seem to be a fact of life. The key becomes who or what dominates our view of such things. Do we focus on the troubles? Or do we view them as reminders to look to our Lord who delivers us from them? Typically, He doesn't simply take them away, but he enables us to be delivered from them by overcoming them. Even in those times when the troubles seem to overcome us (think about Joseph in Egypt) we have the opportunity to respond in faith and find our joy and security in Him.

God wants us to experience the joy of experiencing His presence with us, sustaining us as we contend with the troubles of life. We're never alone. This is reality not just theology. All of the difficulties or troubles we have are opportunities to walk faithfully with Him and glorify Him in how we respond. It might be stormy around us but He provides peaceful hearts to those who look to Him. Think of having a friend or co-worker come up and ask, "How can you be so calm with everything going on?" What an opportunity to talk about the reality of Jesus, evident in your life!

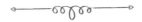

Seeing difficulties as adventures and opportunities

James 1:2, 3 Consider it pure joy, my brothers and sisters,
whenever you face trials of many kinds, ³because you know
that the testing of your faith produces perseverance.

One of my favorite characters in C. S. Lewis' Narnia Tales is Reepicheep, the talking mouse. He is gallant, fearless and a warrior. If a mouse could be a knight, then Reepicheep would be one. Nothing was too challenging. No obstacle too great. When daunting circumstances were before him, he always considered it a great adventure. He loved Aslan, the great lion and would fight anyone in Aslan's behalf.

The thing that I have appreciated most about Reepicheep is the fact that no challenge was too great. Nothing intimidated him. No matter how difficult or frightening a situation was, he considered it an adventure. The greater the risk, the greater the adventure. I have followed his example and consider life's challenges to be adventures.

The point is not to make light of serious challenges, but to view them from a perspective of overcoming faith. When the Lord allows challenging things to come into our lives, it is redemptive to step forward into the adventure rather than step back in fear. This doesn't apply just to big things, but to little things in our everyday lives.

Suppose you have an opportunity to share your faith with someone. One response is to hold back out of fear and uncertainty. The other is to view it as an adventure and to move forward; committing the results to the Lord. This dynamic occurs repeatedly in our jobs, ministry opportunities, relationships, so very many areas of our lives. Do we move forward and seize the opportunity or hold back?

Several years ago, I read one of the most moving quotes I have ever seen. It is by Teddy Roosevelt and never fails to stir me:

"It is not the critic who counts: not the man who points out how the strong man stumbles or where the doer of deeds could have done better. The credit belongs to the man who is actually in the arena… who, at the best, knows, in the end, the triumph of high achievement, and who, at the worst, if he fails, at least he fails while daring greatly, so that his place shall never be with those cold and timid souls who knew neither victory nor defeat."

"Citizenship in a Republic,"
Speech at the Sorbonne, Paris, April 23, 1910

May our focus be upon the joy we have in Jesus Christ – no matter what manner of trials we face, remembering the opportunity they give us. Our lives are about Him!

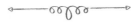

Tasting fruit and a packet of seeds!

*Hebrews 11:1 Now faith is confidence in what we hope for
and assurance about what we do not see.*

Over the years we have heard many marvelous testimonies. What a blessing it is to hear how God is working in other Christians' lives. Many times God will use these testimonies to inspire and motivate us to pursue things He has for us – to draw closer to Him. Years ago we heard a valuable illustration that helped us understand the important role that growth plays in our own faith.

When we hear testimonies of Christians who are walking in faith in a powerful and challenging way, think of it as though they are allowing us to sample their 'fruit' – the 'fruit' of their lives. Think of being in a group listening, and instead of words, the speaker is walking among us handing out tomatoes or plums or peaches – (whichever one sounds good to you). As s/he speaks, we are biting into the fruit – savoring the sweetness and richness.

The same lesson applies to reading about the saints who have gone before us. At times we are moved to tears when reading of the marvelous things they did or the difficulties they faithfully endured. 'Tasting' those precious experiences are intended to draw us closer to God. The more we taste, the more we want. **But we must remember, we are 'tasting' the 'fruit' of their faith walk with Jesus. When we leave the meeting, or lay down the book we are reading, we do not walk away with a basket of our own fruit. We walk away with a priceless packet of seeds – to grow our own; to make it ours!**

The testimonies we hear or read about are intended to produce faith within us but that process takes time and obedience. We need to recognize that trying to walk in someone else's faith can be like trying to do a downhill slalom on skis when we've only been on the beginner slopes. Typically such attempts lead to needless crashes. Allow these times to push us into the Lord; expressing our desire to grow and walk in such faith. He will lead us on His path through the 'School of the Spirit' to get us there.

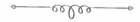

Discerning good from evil is critical

Proverbs 1:10 My son, if sinful men entice you, do not give in to them.

When I read this verse last night, I immediately thought of the character Fagan in the movie "Oliver!", based on the novel Oliver Twist by Charles Dickens. You'll recall him as someone you'd suspect of being up to no good the moment you laid eyes on him. If he suggested anything to you, you'd smell a rat.

Unfortunately, the enemy of our souls is much more subtle in many of his 'offerings'. They can have the appearance of acceptability but to the discerning eye the truth is apparent. Have you ever given thought to how you know what is evil and what is good? How do we know that we are being enticed? How do we appropriately recognize sinful men?

Think of commercials on TV and much of the programming. How do we recognize what is appropriate and what entices us to evil. Often the problem is not the product, but the content and nature of its 'packaging'. What is the advertiser (enticer) using to get us to watch the commercial and hopefully buy the product?

Fortunately, God provides the answers and the plan for us to become discerning and wise in this everyday issue. A couple of days ago I wrote about the importance of the growth process in our faith. We must recognize that this is another area we must grow in. It is significantly wrapped up in God's Word. In Hebrews 5:12-14 the writer powerfully addresses this problem:

> [12] *In fact, though by this time you ought to be teachers, you need someone to teach you the elementary truths of God's Word all over again. You need milk, not solid food!* [13] *Anyone who lives on milk, being still an infant, is not acquainted with the teaching about righteousness.* [14] *But solid food is for the mature, who by constant use have trained themselves to distinguish good from evil.*

We must become thoroughly acquainted with God's Word and its teachings on righteousness. This not only leads us to maturity in our faith, but it prepares us to intentionally and constantly train ourselves to distinguish good from evil. It doesn't happen by accident. Nor does it happen with a cursory (the opposite of thorough) knowledge and application of His word. We will miss too many things that will cause harm both to us and those we are responsible for. Even worse is how poorly our lives will present our faith and reflect upon our God if we do not embrace and live out this process.

Does this describe your heart?

Psalm 34:1-3 ¹I will extol the LORD at all times; his praise will always be on my lips. ²I will glory in the LORD; let the afflicted hear and rejoice. ³Glorify the LORD with me; let us exalt his name together.

These verses today present a wonderful 'picture' of David's heart; his reality. He had pretended to be insane in order to escape the King of Gath – after fleeing there to get away from King Saul who was trying to kill him. Sounds like a nice normal life doesn't it?

Even though David had to live with the ever-present threat of being killed for years, his reality was his heart for God. It was so rich and vibrant and full. Does this picture of his heart match a corresponding picture of our hearts – if one could be taken? When we read these verses do they describe us? Are we 'captured' by the Lord like David was? Phrase by phrase they are absolutely extraordinary!

Another picture came to mind when I was considering these verses and how they relate to us. It was a picture of a meal with the question, "What kind of meal is it?" If these verses don't describe our hearts, then we're fasting or the meal is just breadcrumbs and water. If they describe us a little, then the meal might be a piece of bologna on a piece of bread. The more they describe us, the richer the meal. Think of a dinner with our very favorite foods - where not only is the food phenomenal, but so is the setting and the loved ones we are able to enjoy it with. That is the richness the 'picture' of these verses alludes to.

I think of the rehearsal dinner for our oldest son John and Fabi that occurred in Brazil at a restaurant next to the church, one block from the ocean. The food was wonderful. It was a balmy evening with the ocean breeze blowing in the open air restaurant. I remember so clearly sitting back with tears in my eyes as I gazed at the sight of family and dear friends laughing together and enjoying a wonderful meal and one another. What a rich time!

The Lord has such richness for us in our relationship with Him if we but pursue it with Him. If these verses don't describe us, let us pray, "Lord Jesus, make these verses describe me! I want the picture of my reality with you; my heart for you to be accurately described by them." Pray it daily – for weeks, months, and years – whatever it takes. But pray it with the conviction that He will make it happen – because He will!

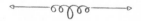

Don Schmidt

The wonderful testimony of Betsie Ten Boom

1 Thessalonians 5:15-18 Make sure that nobody pays back wrong for wrong,
but always strive to do what is good for each other and for everyone else.
¹⁶Rejoice always, ¹⁷pray continually, ¹⁸give thanks in all circumstances;
for this is God's will for you in Christ Jesus.

I am so grateful for the powerful example of Corrie ten Boom's sister Betsie and her amazing faith as revealed in Corrie's book, <u>The Hiding Place</u>. For their efforts to save Jews, they were sent to concentration camps during World War II eventually winding up at Ravensbruck where 96,000 women died. I remembered how Corrie was so frequently amazed at her sister's remarkable faith.

In the book, I found the scene that had been stirring so within me. It is when they move into the horrific dormitory in Ravensbruck. This wretched dorm that was made for 400 had 1400 crammed in with more being added weekly. Eight acrid and overflowing toilets served the entire room.

Betsie perpetually saw things so very differently than Corrie or anyone else. Her heart was moved with compassion instead of hate. She wanted to bless instead of curse. She saw positives in situations where no one else could even imagine them. Today's verses were the ones that particularly moved her on this occasion.

Their circumstances included fleas, nauseating smells, incredible overcrowding and the brutality of the guards for whom Betsie continually prayed. This combined with being prisoners in such a place of death! But Betsie continually gave thanks to God for everything about their circumstances – even the fleas!

Apparently the fleas, lice and stench kept the guards away. They had a Bible and so many women were crowded around them, it meant that so many more would get to hear about Jesus. No matter what happened, Betsie was consumed with a passionate love of her Lord.

What an example Betsie was for Corrie and for us! We face nothing compared to what they faced. But Betsie was so aware of God's love and focused on sharing it with everyone – prisoners and guards. She was grateful for so many things. She didn't get caught up in the negative. She saw evidence of God's presence, kindness and grace everywhere.

May our eyes be opened to see the wonder of our Lord in all the problems we have. May our hearts and lives be captivated by Him – rather than by the problems or difficulties we face. Betsie is such an example for us all of how rich and powerful our faith in Jesus can become.

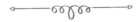

Corrie's redmeptive response to Betsie

Hebrews 10:24 And let us consider one another to
provoke unto love and to good works: KJV

I want to continue with The Hiding Place as a source of inspiration, instruction and blessing. Today I want to focus on Corrie and her responses to the provocative situations that are recorded in her book. All too often I think we relate more to her responses rather than to the responses Betsie had. Betsie always seems to have an inside track on viewing things in such a redemptive way. Corrie writes at one point after being stunned by Betsie's response to an impossible situation, "Once again I had the feeling that this sister with whom I had spent all my life belonged somehow to another order of beings."

Time and time again Corrie and Betsie were exposed to cruelty, violence and unspeakable horror. Corrie struggled with all the human responses of fear, anger, hatred, resentment and wanting to strike back. Then she would encounter Betsie's responses and find herself provoked redemptively. She struggled through the process of repentance and learning to embrace a response more consistent with her faith and the Lord she loved.

I am so blessed by Corrie. I cannot imagine facing the horrors she faced. But the thing that speaks so powerfully to me is how she continually embraced repentance after recognizing that her response was wrong. The struggles she endured weren't simple things. They were gut wrenching, but her faith and the grace of God enabled her to overcome. Her commitment to the Lord and her resolve to respond rightly shone brightly.

She rejected her sin and embraced Godliness. She went through this process time and again. Betsie continually showed her the way and Corrie followed it. What examples they are for us! Fortunately, Corrie was released from Ravensbruck due to a clerical error. All the women her age were taken to the gas chambers one week after she was released. It is not difficult at all to see God's hand in that clerical error!

We must have our eyes opened to see the shortcomings inherent in our own responses to difficult trials. Thank God for the people in our lives that He uses to help us in this regard! How fortunate we are that Jesus enables us to recognize our need, repent quickly and embrace righteousness as our way of life.

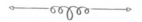

10 year old Tilly Smith and perceiving reality

John 1:45-46 ⁴⁵Philip found Nathanael and told him, "We have found the one Moses wrote about in the Law, and about whom the prophets also wrote—Jesus of Nazareth, the son of Joseph." ⁴⁶ "Nazareth! Can anything good come from there?" Nathanael asked. "Come and see," said Philip.

Have you noticed how powerfully we can be affected by our perception of things? If we perceive something to be good or positive we respond differently that if we view it negatively – particularly if it involves us. Our perception becomes our reality, which is fine and good provided that it's accurate. All too often we can find ourselves responding inappropriately because we're missing pieces of vital information that could radically change how we view something .

I am reminded of a story from the great tsunami in 2004. In many places, people on beaches in that region were fascinated by what they were seeing. The shoreline was receding accompanied by frothing bubbles. If I had been there, I can see myself standing with others discussing this curiosity that was unfolding before us – unaware that it was the precursor of something incredibly deadly.

Tilly Smith is a British girl who, at age 10, was credited with saving nearly a hundred foreign tourists at Maikhao Beach in Thailand by raising the alarm minutes before the arrival of the tsunami caused by the earthquake.

She learned about tsunamis in a geography lesson two weeks before the tsunami. She recognized the receding shoreline and frothing bubbles on the surface of the sea and alerted her parents, who warned others on the beach and the staff at the hotel on <u>Phuket</u> where they were staying. The beach was evacuated before the tsunami reached shore, and was one of the few beaches on the island with no reported casualties.

Fortunately, Tilly was believed and lives were saved. Credible information received changed something from a curiosity to a serious reality that required an immediate response. It wasn't dismissed because it came from a 10 year old girl. In today's verses, we have the well known retort of Nathanael to Philip telling him about Jesus of Nazareth: *"Nazareth! Can anything good come from there?"* When Philip ignored the retort and replied, *"Come and see,"* Nathanael followed Philip to Jesus.

Fortunately, Philip was able to let go of his perception of 'things from Nazareth' and recognized the reality of who Jesus was (and is) and became one of the twelve disciples. We too get to deal with our perceptions of who Jesus is or isn't. Either way our lives will be changed. We must question the sources and validity of our perceptions because they might be keeping us from the truth. They might keep us on the beach convinced tsunamis aren't real.

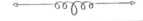

Becoming teachable: a lover of the truth

Titus 2:11-12 [11] For the grace of God has appeared that offers salvation to all people. [12] It teaches us to say "No" to ungodliness and worldly passions, and to live self-controlled, upright and godly lives in this present age,

Have you ever thought how important it is to be teachable? It's a quality that we must cultivate and protect. It's not a given that being teachable is an attribute that we will have or retain if we have had it. The more we become set in our ways, the more un-teachable we can become. Often teachable moments occur when we have to change; do things differently; do them better; to quit doing things that hinder us.

Un-teachableness has a way of diminishing our grasp of the obvious. Worse, it can be a fruit of pride – we know best! We've been there and done that. Who are you to tell me?!! We might not think these thoughts but the net result is that we don't change much anymore.

Years ago we heard a Bible teacher share a truth that has been dear to us ever since. He said, "The way to stay free is to be a lover of the truth." When we love the truth we will hear it and respond to it no matter how it comes. God sometimes sends the truth in some very unattractive packages. He might pick the person we know who annoys us the most to be the one to bring us a corrective word. We then face the problem of rejecting the truth because we reject the messenger.

Remember, repentance is a way of life for us. When we learn new things it's not unusual for it to mean we repent and embrace a better way. Jesus will show us how to be more courteous, kinder, more thoughtful, more considerate, more giving, more compassionate, etc… The Holy Spirit will also show us the things in our lives that stand in the way of these positive attributes developing into what they can and need to be.

The grace of God teaches us to say "No" to ungodliness and "Yes" to Godliness. It is a lifelong process because we give the Lord a lifetime supply of stuff to work on in our lives. Praise God for His patience and His unchanging commitment to help us become like Him. A life of godliness is the sweetest life of all.

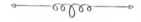

Don Schmidt

Father Chisom of The Keys of the Kingdom

Micah 6:8 He has showed you, O man, what is good. And what does the Lord
require of you but to do justly, and to love kindness and mercy, and to humble
yourself and walk humbly with your God? Amplified

My wife and I watched an old black & white movie on TCM that truly touched us deeply. This 1944 film was the second film featuring a young Gregory Peck in the leading role. His role was that of Father Francis Chisholm, an unconventional Scottish Catholic priest who struggles to establish a mission in China. His moving performance led to his first Oscar nomination.

The name of this movie is The Keys of the Kingdom and is based on the 1941 novel by A. J. Cronin. The story is so wonderful, I was hoping that it was based on a historical figure. Although it's not, the power of its message was not diminished. I found myself relating to the struggles that he faced. So many aspects of the Christian life – the joys and the hardships – are presented in this movie. Many of them are worth noting but the one that I want to focus on is one that stuck me throughout the story. I was repeatedly touched by the refreshing and vibrant humility that the character of Father Chisholm possesses.

Father Chisholm experiences many difficult challenges over the six decade span of this story. I found myself being convicted of my own pride in watching how Father Chisholm responded with humility and dependence upon God. Yes it was a movie, but I found myself repenting and being inspired to Godliness by watching the story unfold. I am embarrassed to say that I had forgotten just how moving and inspiring true humility is. "…Biblical humility is not the inverted conceit which disguises itself as lowliness." (Zondervan Pictorial Encyclopedia of the Bible, pg. 223) It is a virtue that God prizes.

I am so grateful for the book and the movie because God has used both of them to provoke me to pursue walking humbly with my God in a renewed way. Pride can be so subtle and so pervasive in our lives. Fortunately, God enables us to see our shortcomings and embrace the process whereby His Spirit will enable us to become more like Jesus.

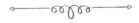

In this story, I relate to the freed slave.

John 3:16 For God so loved the world that he gave his one and only Son, that whoever believes in him shall not perish but have eternal life.

Many, many years ago a man embarked on a journey home. It required him to be on a ship for the major part of the journey. This was still during the time when slavery was common and there were slaves serving on the ship. Over the course of the voyage the man struck up a friendship with one of the slaves. As the days went by they enjoyed the times together more and more.

When they arrived in port the captain came to the slave and informed him to get his belongings because he had been purchased. When the slave discovered that he had been sold to the passenger who had become his friend he was outraged. The slave confronted his new owner and asked, "I thought we were friends! But now you have purchased me to make me your slave – to serve you! How could you do this to me?"

The man looked at the slave and said, "You misunderstand. I didn't purchase you to make you my slave. I purchased you to set you free!" Upon hearing this, the slave exclaimed, "I will serve you all the days of my life!"

I heard this story many years ago and never cease to be moved by it – maybe because I relate so to the slave. The details of my life are obviously very different from his, but I remember the struggles I was going through 50+ years ago – the loneliness, lack of direction, the inferiority complex. I always seemed to be struggling with feeling un-chosen, left out or left behind. I didn't realize it but I was a slave to these insecurities.

Only, I didn't have a voyage to get to know someone who would surprise me with freedom. For me it was totally unexpected and what He did was so much more than just physical freedom. In my stunning encounter with Jesus (October 11, 1968), my 'Matterhorn of doubt' regarding God was leveled! He made me someone entirely new!!!! I am still amazed at how utterly transformed my life was in a single moment. I so understand the slave saying he will serve his new master for the rest of his life. Even now I am overcome with emotion and gratitude thinking of what my 'new owner' did for me 50 years ago – and Jesus has never stopped doing it!!! He overwhelms me with love!

I am so grateful that I get to serve Him the rest of my life – only it is so much more than that: He enables us to love Him in return. We become friends and family – in relationship with Him every day of our lives. The more we realize the incredible wonder of what He has done for us, the more we want to love Him.

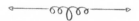

Same event – 2 opposite journal entries

Hebrews 11:6 And without faith it is impossible to please God, because anyone who comes to him must believe that he exists and that he rewards those who earnestly seek him.

This Scripture talks about faith and its importance in pleasing God, coming to Him and seeking Him. It also speaks of God rewarding those who earnestly seek Him. The Amplified Bible words the end of this verse, "…who earnestly and diligently seek Him [out]."

I have heard people discuss their view of this verse saying, "I don't need a reward for seeking Him." My response to that is – that isn't an option. Phrased another way, we do "A" and God does "B", where "B" could be anything of His choosing – but there is going to be a "B". In 1 Samuel 26:23a David declares, *"The LORD rewards everyone for their righteousness and faithfulness."* This is simply one of God's realities for us. I am reminded of the story about Henry Brooks Adams:

Henry was the grandson of President John Quincy Adams, the fourth of seven children, and began journaling at a young age. When he was 8 years old he spent a day fishing with his father – a very busy man. Henry's journal entry states: "Went fishing with my father today, the most glorious day of my life."

That day was so special that he continued to talk about it for many years. Thirty years later he looked at his father's journal entry for that day and found: "Went fishing with my son, a day wasted."

We can become so preoccupied with business and 'things' that we totally miss the truly priceless things that might be around us. We can be richly blessed if we but take the time to see and embrace them. I find that one of the marvelous 'rewards' that God offers to those who earnestly seek Him – is Himself. Though He lives within Christians, and is always with us. There are aspects of His presence that He makes available to experience that are not the norm. They are so special that they are remembered like Henry remembered the special day he got to spend with his father. They become one of the most glorious days of our lives.

To be continued…

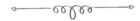

What would your response be?

1 Kings 3:5 At Gibeon the LORD appeared to Solomon during the night in a dream, and God said, "Ask for whatever you want me to give you."

Solomon's answer pleased the Lord. God said He would give him a wise and discerning heart. He also would give Solomon that which he didn't ask for – both riches and honor. In this dream God closes with this admonition for Solomon, *"And if you walk in obedience to me and keep my decrees and commands as David your father did, I will give you a long life."* 1 Kings 3:14 God was saying I will bless you with long life if you love me.

Yesterday's devotional focused on earnestly seeking God – and the fact that He will reward those that do. The same question (as in today's Scripture) was raised in terms of identifying what we would like the Lord to give us as a reward for earnestly seeking Him – if He asked.

We would probably ask for what is most on our hearts – and that could cover many things: The salvation of parents or children or friends; a better job; money to pay bills; ability to be a better husband, wife, parent or child; to love better; to be better at what we do; to love the Lord more; to be used by Him; for an opportunity of ministry; for support for our ministry; to have good devotional times with the Lord; to have a desire to read and learn Scripture; – the list just goes on. And none of these answers are wrong.

But at the end of the day, what does God really want and what is He offering? I think of John 14:21, *"Whoever has my commands and keeps them is the one who loves me. The one who loves me will be loved by my Father, and I too will love them and show myself to them."* The Amplified Bible makes this verse jump off the page:

*"The person who has My commands and keeps them is the one who [really] loves Me; **and whoever [really] loves Me will be loved by My Father, and I [too] will love him and will show (reveal, manifest) Myself to him. [I will let Myself be clearly seen by him and make Myself real to him.]"***

God wants to meet our needs and He instructs us to make them known to Him. But He wants our relationship to grow beyond seeing Him as our source and provider. He wants to be the love of our life. He wants us to want Him so much that we receive the incredible blessing of His presence which He reserves for those who love Him this way.

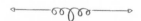

She said to me, "I trust you."

Colossians 3:5 Be wise in the way you act toward outsiders; make the most of every opportunity.

One of the great blessings of our Christian faith is the way it transforms our lives. This impacts everything from how we live at home to how we do our jobs. By living wisely, we are able to create opportunities where they might not otherwise occur. One of the more memorable sales situations I had early in my career with Blue Cross gave me an important lesson in this regard.

While calling on companies on my prospect list, I encountered a hospital that was soliciting proposals for their employee benefit program. The hospital had recently gone through major changes and was struggling to survive. They were receiving proposals from a number of agents and carriers and after meeting with their new chief executive, I was given the opportunity to quote.

Later, when I presented our proposal to this executive, she had just received another proposal that she let me see. It was clearly better than ours. I knew what flexibility I had in my proposal and informed her that we could not match it. This one competitor's offer and program were better than what we had to offer.

A bit later I received a phone call from her asking me to come by the hospital and meet with her. When we met she asked if I would be willing to review the various proposals that she had received and give her my recommendation - even though the carrier I represented was out of the running. Was this someone taking advantage of me? Or, was this a genuine request? Fortunately I recognized it as an opportunity for the long term. Every cancellation or lost sale has potential to be a future sale.

But in an important regard this was better than that. She had noted my attitude, professionalism and honesty in the times we met. She looked at me and told me, "I trust you." Can you imagine a more wonderful compliment? This was an opportunity to serve her and strengthen this relationship with a potential future client. A couple years later they became my client.

There are times when we can do the right things, regardless of our motivations. But we have a faith that enables us to 'be' the people God wants us to be. The more we walk in His ways, being wise in all our interactions, the more we are able to make the most of the opportunities He provides.

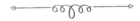

Blessed with freedom and wisdom!

Proverbs 16:22a Understanding is a fountain of life to those who have it,

About six weeks after meeting the Lord, I went up to Minneapolis for what I thought was going to be a youth retreat for high school and college age. I had just turned 21 and hitched a ride up there with 3 other Western Michigan college students in a VW Bug. I was in the back seat with a large suitcase and another large person. That was a ride to remember!

When they dropped me off, I discovered the retreat had been cancelled. The folks at the ministry center there were then wondering what to do with me. They had a Christian community / retreat center in northern Minnesota and one of the families was going up there for the weekend so they decided to take me along. It turned out to be one of the most critically important times of my entire life. I didn't know it, but I had a date with destiny.

The people at the community where we went were very kind and gracious to me. The worship and ministry times were wonderful. In my joy as a new Christian I was struggling with a serious issue that was warring within me. During one of the services, the leader called me up to the front. The Lord had divinely given him knowledge of my struggle and in a brief time of ministry my issue was dealt with and gone. My war with this issue was over and I was free!

What followed next was profoundly important. He said to me, "Don. You cannot afford dating either spiritually or financially. Seek Christian fellowship." Then he said, "I want you to pray for your wife – but don't pray, 'God, send me a wife'. I want you to pray for her like this. 'Lord Jesus, I thank you that you have the girl I am going to marry. I pray that she will come to know you – that you will protect her and bless her. Thank you that you are preparing us for one another. I acknowledge that in your time and in your way, you will bring us together. I commit her and our relationship to you.'"

So I regularly began praying in this way for the unknown girl who would be my wife. This enabled me to really release this whole arena to the Lord. Later the next spring I read an article by Billy Graham where he wrote about his children playing on a hillside. He realized that on some other hillside were the children who would one day be the spouses of his kids. So he prayed for their future spouses in the very same way. An excellent prayer for all parents!

Experiencing artistic worship

2 Corinthians 4:7 But we have this treasure in jars of clay to show that this all-surpassing power is from God and not from us.

For many years we lived in NE Ohio and attended a wonderful church named St. Luke's. The worship was particularly good and much to our blessing St. Luke's was really involved with the arts: drama, mime, dance, pageantry, painting were all part of the church-life there.

One of our favorite examples of the arts was when an artist would paint during the worship service (that typically lasted for 45 – 50 minutes). St. Luke's was blessed with a number of fine artists. On Sunday morning, if an artist's easel with a blank canvas was up front on the platform, we knew that a special blessing was coming. The artist would begin painting when the worship started.

The artist would paint what was in their heart as moved by the worship. We would sing and the artist would paint – inspiring one another. The painting would always involve some aspect of faith. The Lord used the gifting of the artist to enhance our worship and draw us closer to Him. The painting would be sufficiently done by the end of worship for everyone to be blessed by what the artist had accomplished.

Importantly it was never about the artist – it was always about the Lord. Fortunately many of the paintings have become prints that may be purchased and enjoyed. My favorite one of all is a representation of today's verse. It is painting of a beautiful blue urn riddled with cracks showing the golden glory of God filling it and shining out through all the cracks. Thankfully it is a print we own.

We have been blessed by this print for many years. It is such a wonderful reminder of the dynamic we enjoy with the Lord. He fills us with his love and glory in order that He would shine out through our lives – in spite of the vessels of clay that we are.

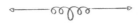

Godly jealousy: a thermometer and a thermostat

2 Corinthians 11:2 I am jealous for you with a godly jealousy. I promised you to one husband, to Christ, so that I might present you as a pure virgin to him.

Several years ago I heard a sermon where our pastor referred to a 'godly jealousy'. I was struck by the thought that those two words can't go together! Even though I knew that in the Old Testament God refers to Himself as a jealous God, somehow that didn't connect to the idea of a Christian having a godly jealousy.

Paul goes on to write in verse 3, "But I am afraid that just as Eve was deceived by the serpent's cunning, your minds may somehow be led astray from your sincere and pure devotion to Christ." The issue seems to center upon 'sincere and pure devotion'. Something that belongs to God is being given to someone or something else. Paul's godly jealousy was concerned for their well-being and particularly for their relationship with the Lord.

We tend to forget that actions have consequences. In Exodus 34:14 God declares, *"Do not worship any other god, for the LORD, whose name is Jealous, is a jealous God."* In simple terms, think of God's jealousy as both a thermometer and a thermostat. The thermometer aspect responds to what the temperature is. If our 'sincere and pure devotion' to the Lord cools – becomes less than it should be or fails to grow – the thermometer reflects this reality. The thermostat then turns the 'heater' on. By 'heater' I refer to those things that God brings about in our lives to help us repent and return to Him – to have our devotion to Him become more sincere and pure.

Haven't we all declared to the Lord that we give Him free reign to do whatever is needed to promote faithfulness and godliness in our lives? He can do anything with us – just help us to be totally committed to Him. If our spiritual ears are becoming deaf, don't we want Him to show us? If our devotion to our Lord Jesus becomes side-tracked and going the wrong way, don't we want Him to 'throw up road blocks' to get us to turn around? Anything – I repeat – anything He does or allows will be for our wellbeing!

Think of all the warnings that Jesus gave the religious leaders that they were deaf to! The reality is the same thing can happen to us. We too can be led astray from our devotion to Him. Let us heed Paul's warning and renew our commitment to be sincerely and purely devoted to our Lord.

Don Schmidt

The problem of answer driven prayer

Colossians 4:2 Devote yourself to prayer, being watchful and thankful.

I have this thing about good endings. If a movie doesn't have one, I'm not interested in watching it – and my family knows this about me. This led to one of the more embarrassing moments in my life. A few years ago I came home and Donna and our third son Andrew were watching Hamlet with Mel Gibson in the lead role. I like Mel Gibson movies and they always seem to have good endings so I sat down to watch it with them.

Some of you have already noticed the problem. I didn't know what the story line of Hamlet was. Somehow I managed to avoid Shakespeare all my life. When we got to the end of the movie I was stunned and cried out incredulously, "He dies!? He dies!?!!" To which Donna and Andrew both looked at me like I'm some kind of nut and said, "It's Hamlet. Of course he dies." With my distress overflowing, I said, "You mean you let me sit here and watch this movie knowing it had a bad ending?" Unfortunately they were laughing too hard to talk.

You might be laughing as well as you read this. But let's ask ourselves, "What is a good ending?" How do we define what that is? Good endings are nice and we all like them but a desire for good endings can become a real problem if misapplied to another area of our lives – specifically the area of prayer. When we pray for things, what is a good ending? What kind of answer or response from God do we consider to be 'good'?

The issue for us to examine is what kind of expectations and preconceived notions we have when it comes to prayer. Is our motivation for prayer, answer driven? Are we locked into a view that prayer only works if we get an answer pleasing to us? Do we become disappointed or discouraged if we don't get the answers we want? Have we responded to what we deem a 'bad answer' like I did with Hamlet?

Our prayer life is not to be answer driven. Prayer is not about getting answers – it's about our relationship with God. It's about entering further into the joy and vibrant life with Him that He has for us.

To be continued…

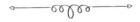

Yet I will rejoice in the Lord...

Habakkuk 3:17-19 ^{17}Though the fig tree does not bud and there are no grapes on the vines, though the olive crop fails and the fields produce no food, though there are no sheep in the pen and no cattle in the stalls, ^{18}yet I will rejoice in the LORD, I will be joyful in God my Savior. ^{19} The Sovereign LORD is my strength; he makes my feet like the feet of a deer, he enables me to tread on the heights.

Yesterday we wrote about the problem of prayer being 'good ending' driven rather than being about relationship. This can result in a view that prayer only works if we get answers pleasing to us. We might reject such a blunt assessment but we need to consider what reality is reflected in our resulting attitudes and behaviors, <u>If what we perceive to be good things don't happen</u>, do we find ourselves praying less and fighting disappointment and discouragement? Worse, do we find ourselves unintentionally rejecting God? "I prayed – He didn't answer (the way I wanted or needed Him to) – Prayer doesn't work – God isn't faithful."

Consider today's verses in a proper framework. Farmers do what they do in order to harvest. The good endings are figs, grapes and olives, crops in the fields, sheep and cattle. They would be praying AND working for these results. In an agrarian society everyone is dependent upon these 'good endings' happening. When they don't, it can mean a famine. (Imagine being unable to get food with all the grocery stores closed and empty for months on end!) It is in this framework that Habakkuk describes all the farming results as being negative. There are no crops, no animals and no food, but because of who God is, those are just details.

Habakkuk describes relationship triumphing over results!

"...yet I will rejoice in the LORD, I will be joyful in God my Savior. The Sovereign LORD is my strength; he makes my feet like the feet of a deer, he enables me to tread on the heights."

These aren't just words – they are reality! The wonderful news is that through our faith in Jesus Christ and the transforming power of the Holy Spirit, God will enable our relationship with Him to experientially reflect this reality too!

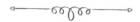

Using Scriptures for wonderful prayers

Philippians 1:9-11 ⁹And this is my prayer: that your love may abound more and more in knowledge and depth of insight, ¹⁰so that you may be able to discern what is best and may be pure and blameless for the day of Christ, ¹¹filled with the fruit of righteousness that comes through Jesus Christ—to the glory and praise of God.

In an earlier devotional I wrote about the power of praying Scripture particularly in the context of being able express to God His greatness. We can personalize the words of Scripture and they enable us to express what is in our hearts in a way that is Biblically sound. Today I would like us to look at praying Scripture for one another.

How often have we struggled in our desire to pray for people over the words to use or over the issue of "What is God's will for them?" How often do we use words that just express a general positive for someone such as, "Lord, I pray that you will bless so & so."? Within each of us is a desire for our prayers for others and ourselves to become more faith-filled and effective.

Consider today's verses which is a prayer by Paul for the Philippians. Pick someone whom you love, care about or are concerned for and personalize these verses – this prayer – for them. I am going to pick Joe, a wonderful friend and our pastor:

"Lord Jesus, I pray that Joe's love may abound more and more in knowledge and depth of insight, so that Joe may be able to discern what is best and that he may be pure and blameless for the day of Christ. I pray that Joe will be filled with the fruit of righteousness that comes through You—to the glory and praise of God."

Not only is that a wonderful and powerful prayer – we also have confidence that it is God's will for whomever we might pray it for. Let's pray these verses for ourselves:

"Lord Jesus, I pray that my love may abound more and more in knowledge and depth of insight, so that I may be able to discern what is best and that I may be pure and blameless for the day of Christ. I pray that I will be filled with the fruit of righteousness that comes through You—to the glory and praise of God."

The Bible teaches that the prayers of a righteous man are powerful and effective (James 5:16b). Praying Scripture is one tool that we have to help us become such individuals.

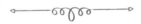

The impact of our perceptions

*Genesis 50:15 When Joseph's brothers saw that their father was dead,
they said, "What if Joseph holds a grudge against us and pays
us back for all the wrongs we did to him?"*

Have you ever considered how dependent we are upon our perception of things? Our perception of something can become our reality – whether it's accurate or not. Perceptions influence our emotions, attitudes and actions. It's also amazing how rapidly our attitude can change when our perception changes.

Think of those individuals who were upset because they were delayed and prevented from being on time for work at the World Trade Center on September 11, 2001. One moment they were distressed and the next moment they were overcome with relief that they were late. Sometimes it takes awhile for our perceptions to change in spite of what we see and know.

Joseph's brothers were unable to shake their fear that Joseph was going to pay them back for what they had done. In spite of his earlier assurances and the experiences they were having with him, they could not believe that his comments were genuine. Then we have Joseph's wonderful reply to them after they expressed their concerns once again:

[19]But Joseph said to them, "Don't be afraid. Am I in the place of God? [20]You intended to harm me, but God intended it for good to accomplish what is now being done, the saving of many lives. [21]So then, don't be afraid. I will provide for you and your children." And he reassured them and spoke kindly to them. Genesis 50:19-21

I am continually blessed by Joseph's example. So many negative things happened to him yet he never allowed them to lead him astray. He kept God at the center of his life. Given the power and position he had, he could have done his brothers great harm, but there is no indication that he was even tempted by such thoughts. Rather than allowing his negative experiences to undermine his faith, his view of everything that had happened was formed by his faith that God had always been in control.

This is our test day by day. Will our perceptions be governed by our experiences or by our faith? Do we see ourselves as potential victims of circumstances or are our perceptions faith-based and secure in the keeping power of our God? By trusting in the Lord, our faith becomes a secure 'vessel' able to withstand any assault that might come against it. This is not something we talk ourselves into – but it is the inescapable and unshakeable fact of our relationship with God.

Don Schmidt

The impact of fear on our perception of reality

Exodus 16:2-3 ²In the desert the whole community grumbled against Moses and Aaron. ³The Israelites said to them, "If only we had died by the LORD's hand in Egypt! There we sat around pots of meat and ate all the food we wanted, but you have brought us out into this desert to starve this entire assembly to death."

I find this situation, described by today's verses, to be a serious warning of how our perception of true reality can be negated by fear. Here are a people that have been slaves in Egypt all of their lives. They had been in misery, crying out to the Lord for deliverance. Then God responded! Through Moses incredible miracles were performed – that they all were able to witness - that resulted in their freedom.

Capping everything off was the Red Sea experience that had occurred just a short time earlier. When they saw the Egyptian army approaching they had this same negative response. They complained that it was better to be slaves in Egypt than to die in the desert. The understanding that God was setting them free and dealing with Pharaoh and the Egyptians was lost amidst their fears.

Then they witnessed God's stunning intervention to secure their freedom. The angel of the Lord kept the army at bay over night while Red Sea parted. They experienced walking through the parted waters and then witnessed the waters consuming the pursuing army upon Moses' command. Great was their celebration of this event.

Then three days later, when they ran out of water, they complained and witnessed the miracle of the bitter water becoming sweet. Unfortunately, this next difficult situation (of today's verses) brought about an even worse negative response. All they had witnessed was once again forgotten. They hadn't being set free. God wasn't with them. They were all victims about to die. They viewed their situation in Egypt as desirable. They even found it preferable for God to have killed them in Egypt than for them to starve to death in the desert.

If only they had recognized their true situation and responded with, "The Lord didn't set us free to kill us in the desert. Let us call upon the Lord and He will provide." The Lord provided them with test after test; giving them repeated opportunities to respond with faith rather than unbelief. We must recognize that we have the same opportunities. How are we going to respond to difficult situations we face? Do we see ourselves as potential victims of circumstances or are our perceptions faith-based and trusting in God?

To be continued…

What God really wants from His people.

Exodus 19:4 'You yourselves have seen what I did to Egypt, and how I carried you on eagles' wings and brought you to myself.

What do we think of when we consider the historical record of the Israelites' journey from Egypt to the Promised Land? There are so many things that catch our attention: Moses, the plagues, the parting of the Red Sea, miracles, manna, grumbling and complaining, the golden calf, repeated testings, God's dealing with their rebellion, the spies, Korah & Dathan – the list goes on. But what is behind it all?

Today's verse contains four words that speak volumes to us if we but have the ears to hear. These words are the explanation that God gives to Moses of what He was doing through the whole process. Specifically, He was speaking of all of the Israelites: *"... (I) brought you to myself."* Do we understand how earth shaking that statement is?

God wasn't primarily interested in having a people that would be an example to the world. He wanted a people that were in intimate relationship with Him. He wanted a people that would treasure the love He gave them and respond with love in return. At best, the Israelites that left Egypt, responded with words, not love (actions).

God provided the Israelites with repeated opportunities for them to respond in faith. Unfortunately, they repeatedly failed. One moment they could be acknowledging Him and the next they would say or do things that revealed He was totally forgotten or irrelevant. Do we understand that He deals with us the very same way? Our faith – or lack of faith – is reflected daily through our thoughts, attitudes, words and actions.

Think about God's reaching out to us. Do we see that responding to God's gift of Jesus is so much more than verbal or mental assent; or an outward veneer of behavior? How far reaching is our commitment to Christ in impacting our lives? Do we understand that this depends on our perception and understanding of what God wants from us – and becoming passionately committed to giving it to Him?

A powerful and sobering reality is revealed in Hebrews 11:16 where God is talking about His people of faith: *"... Therefore God is not ashamed to be called their God."* Look at the world around us. So many claim to be Christians but their lives are inconsistent with such a claim. Their actual lives are proclaiming that they are not followers of Jesus!

Each day, the life we live, is a living testimony of what our relationship with God is all about. What does our testimony say? Our new life in Christ Jesus enables us to demonstrate and reflect our genuine and growing love for Him. **We must understand that this is the mechanism that God uses to bring us to Himself. This is why we were born-again!**

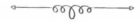

The critical nature of trusting the Lord

Proverbs 3:5 Trust in the LORD with all your heart
and lean not on your own understanding;

Years ago my mother had a powerful experience with the Lord. It involved the death of a good friend. He was a younger man with a wife and a young son. They attended the same church with Mom and Dad and had been dear friends for years. His wife had been Mom's nurse when I was born. Mom had a strong relationship with the Lord but she just couldn't understand how this young Christian man could die and this family suffers such loss.

I remember so clearly her describing the experience afterwards. She was downstairs in the basement doing laundry. She was overcome with sorrow over the death of this friend and just couldn't understand how it could happen. He and his wife were so young; life was there to be lived with his family; how could this happen?

She was standing in front of the washing machine, tears coming down her face, repeating over and over to God, "I just don't understand." Into that moment, the Lord spoke to her so suddenly and clearly, that she never doubted that it was Him. He said, 'Louise – You don't have to understand. You have to trust!"

This had an immediate and profound impact on Mom. While she still didn't understand, she turned to the Lord, and released it to Him. In Him, the edge of the pain dissipated. In Him, she found peace. In Him, she found refuge. She was no longer a tormented 'prisoner' of having to understand this death. She was able to mourn in a healthy place.

Today we remember 9/11. Our world changed when we experienced this horrific attack upon our country – and occurrences of radical Islamic terrorism have become more frequent and widespread. Ever increasing numbers of Christians are being martyred throughout the world. This is all on top of our normal life difficulties. So often we struggle with trying to understand events that happen. Today's verse is a powerful answer – not a cop-out. Proverbs 3:6 continues, *in all your ways acknowledge him, and he will direct your paths.* We must look to Him in all things.

Tragedy occurs all around us: hurricanes, tornados, flooding, earthquakes, explosions, accidents, terrorism, crimes, unexpected deaths or injuries. Life is filled with them. Usually they are things we read or hear about. But, sometimes they are near and we or our loved ones are stricken. Hopefully we have made it a way of life to trust in Him. If not, use those times to initiate a changed lifestyle of focusing on and trusting in Him. He has a way of comforting and bringing life to us when we don't understand. ***He is our source of mercy and grace to help us in our time of need.*** Hebrews 4:16

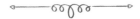

The wonder of our Father

Isaiah 6:1 ¹In the year that King Uzziah died, I saw the Lord, high and exalted, seated on a throne; and the train of his robe filled the temple.

I was caught up in the wonder that the God of the universe is our father. That is such a huge thing it's difficult to grasp. The creator of the stars knows each of us by name and made us His own. Fortunately it's only my mind that has difficulty grasping it. In my heart it's a settled issue – not because of what I have done. It is a wondrous gift from God that He gives to us when we become His children.

On the one hand we have the Glory of His magnificence. Isaiah saw the LORD Almighty and today's verses are his description. What an incredible sight it was. Earlier the children of Israel encountered God in the wilderness after departing Egypt and everyone in the camp trembled at the sight: *"¹⁸ Mount Sinai was covered with smoke, because the LORD descended on it in fire. The smoke billowed up from it like smoke from a furnace, and the whole mountain trembled violently."* Exodus 19:18

On the other, we have the reality of God being our father. While we all might come with different experiences in defining what a father is or isn't, we need to submit those to God. We are not at the mercy of unfortunate experiences with our earthly fathers. He will replace them with the reality of what true fatherhood is. He even allows us to play an important part in that process. It is something that we can grow in all the days of our lives with Him.

Jesus provides us with the key in John 14:21, 23: *"²¹Whoever has my commands and keeps them is the one who loves me. The one who loves me will be loved by my Father, and I too will love them and show myself to them."* ²³Jesus replied, "Anyone who loves me will obey my teaching. My Father will love them, and we will come to them and make our home with them."*

Our Heavenly Father's love for us is not just a theological reality. It is an experiential reality that He will manifest in our lives here and now – and for us to enjoy forever. Isn't it something to look at the heavens and know that our Father made them?

To be continued…

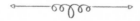

Don Schmidt

My wife's amazing experience with her Heavenly Father

Psalm 45:10-11 [10] Listen, daughter, and pay careful attention: Forget your people and your father's house. 11 Let the king be enthralled by your beauty; honor him, for he is your lord.

Today's verses are the beginning of a section of Psalm 45 (verses 10-17) that is very dear to my wife Donna and to me; to her because God used these verses so powerfully in her life; to me because God so touched the woman I love through them. It is a section where God speaks to His daughters.

Donna's father's house was painful for her both as a daughter and as a woman. Her daddy was an alcoholic. Possibly key to that was the fact that when Donna's older sister was 3 years old, she was killed when he accidentally ran over her backing his car out of the driveway. Donna's parents were married, divorced, re-married and re-divorced. He was not someone who knew how to show love.

When Donna was 19, she had a marvelous salvation experience where God gave her an amazing vision of Jesus on the cross. When she saw the blood dripping from his hands and feet she knew he died for her. Over the years her relationship with the Lord grew and she has been a blessing to so many. But there was something the Lord wanted to heal in her and that happened in a woman's conference in Canada back in the early 90s. The Lord freed Donna of the hurts and wounds that lingered still as a result of her daddy not being a loving father – not being the man God intended him to be.

The Lord wanted her to have the joy and freedom that come from a healthy, vibrant view of Him as her Father; to receive His love and affection. As part of that healing process, God spoke these verses to Donna as speaking to His daughter. I vividly remember the tearfully, joyous phone call I received from her when this happened. She was overwhelmed by the love from her Heavenly Father and with love for Him. The pain from her daddy was gone. In its place was the joy and wonder that she was a beloved daughter of the King.

God is a master at freeing us from whatever restrains us. He wants us to know and experience Him as the loving Father He is. If we have 'stuff' like Donna had, He will set us free too.

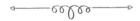

Remembering what God has done

*1 Chronicles 16:12 Remember the wonders he has done, his miracles,
and the judgments he pronounced,*

Raising 4 sons is an adventure to say the least. (We are now getting our daughters the easy way.) One of the guiding principles of our family life has been to build memories. We did things together and in such a way that the activity or experience became a lasting memory. I record special things in my journals, but Donna and I recall them and we talk about them when we are together as a family.

This is particularly important when it comes to our life with our Lord. It is too easy for special experiences with the Lord to become kind of lost in the busy-ness of life. The Lord, through Moses, warned the children of Israel many times about this,

*"Only be careful, and watch yourselves closely so that you do not forget the things
your eyes have seen or let them fade from your heart as long as you live. Teach them
to your children and to their children after them." Deuteronomy 4:9*

Such memories sustain and build our faith – and the faith of others. Our human tendency is to forget the memories, and to also forget the Lord who produced them. Yesterday's devotional about Donna's encounter with the Lord as her Father was such a memory.

When we were living in Franklin, TN, our pastor, did a series on keys to healing – in our lives, our relationships and our world. We were able to share with him about this experience where God healed the wounds in Donna due to the relationship with her earthly father. Donna became teary talking about this powerful experience with God making Himself known to her as her father. Then she made a statement about this experience that I had forgotten. She said, "This was the first time in my life where I felt like I was a daughter!"

While there is pain in what she lived through, it is so overshadowed by the wonder of who God is and what He did. He settled within her the issue that she was His daughter; and that He was her Father! This memory brought forth such a well-spring of gratitude and joy and wonder and passion. Not just for what God did – but more importantly for who He is and who He considers us to be. How good and important it is to remember the wonders and miracles He has done!

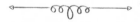

Don Schmidt

Are you weary and burdened?

Matthew 11:28-30 [28] *"Come to me, all you who are weary and burdened, and I will give you rest.* [29] *Take my yoke upon you and learn from me, for I am gentle and humble in heart, and you will find rest for your souls.* [30] *For my yoke is easy and my burden is light."*

Thanks to the trees on our property, in the heat of summer I have the opportunity to plan my work in our yard to be in the shade as the sun moves through the day. Working in the shade sure beats working in the sun when it's hot and humid – and better still is to have a breeze come up. Isn't it amazing the marvelous impact that a cool breeze can have upon us when we're working outside on a hot day?

This passage from Matthew is truly special. How encouraging it is when we're weary and burdened to hear that we can be given rest. The key is the speaker, for it is Jesus speaking and He is telling us that rest is available if we come to Him. He is our 'shade' and our 'cool breeze' as we work in the 'hot days' of our lives.

When we think of a yoke, we tend to think of oxen and work. But Jesus says to take His yoke upon us and learn from Him. When we do, we learn He is gentle and humble of heart and we find rest for our souls. Even more amazing is the discovery that His yoke is easy and His burden is light. He has a way of transforming everything – no matter what kind of circumstances we find ourselves in.

One of the difficulties we often deal with is the tendency to allow our faith to be pushed to the background by the burdens and life-struggles that we contend with every day. We get busy and overwhelmed and focus upon everything else – not fully embracing our Lord and our faith. This isn't our intention, it just happens to be the way it works out all too often for many of us. He doesn't condemn us or abandon us to our own devices. But He lovingly pursues us to hear and respond.

This promise is true whether we are Christians or not. Anyone can come to Jesus and find rest. Better than that is the life He has for all who do come to Him. If we are weary and burdened, we need to be reminded that we have the greatest resource imaginable in our Lord. We must come to Him, put Him first and spend the time learning of Him to experience the refreshing wonder He has available for us.

Right and wrong – there is an objective standard

Isaiah 7:15 He (Jesus) will eat curds and honey when he knows enough to reject the wrong and choose the right.

Right and wrong. What is right – and what is wrong? For the past few days I have been aware of this topic stirring within me. Being able to identify right from wrong is very important for us. We must recognize that it's a requirement of our faith. Who determines what right and wrong are? Is it like beauty being in the eyes of the beholder – what is wrong in one person's view might be right in another's? Further, what is the implication of identifying right from wrong? Is there something required of us?

These and a lot more questions have been swirling within me. This morning I looked up Scriptures involving this subject and found myself surprised by how many there are – and their significance. Today's verse speaks prophetically of Jesus growing up and learning to reject the wrong and choose the right. That alone makes it a critical skill for us to learn.

Given the impact of culture upon our lives, and particularly upon the church, it is far more critical than many of us might think. It is something we must all become more aware of because it is so involved in our daily lives – with a much greater frequency than we might imagine. In Exodus 23:2a the Israelites are admonished, *"Do not follow the crowd in doing wrong."* What is the basis for determining the crowd is wrong? A very important aspect of this whole process is added in Exodus 15:26, *He said, "If you listen carefully to the voice of the LORD your God and do what is right in his eyes,"* There is an objective standard as to right and wrong.

One of the disconcerting things about this subject is the fact that an individual can be convinced he is right … and be wrong. In Proverbs 12:15a it says, *"The way of a fool seems right to him,"*. But in Proverbs 14:12 it says, *"There is a way that seems right to a man, but in the end it leads to death."* We can be foolish and/or sincere and miss it. Fortunately, we have His word and the Holy Spirit to teach us. We simply have to respond and learn from Him. This is more than a subject He wants us all to master – it's a way of life.

To be continued…

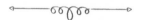

Being blind to doing wrong

Isaiah 1:16c-17a Stop doing wrong, learn to do right!

Today's verse was an exclamatory statement from the Lord to the Israelites. They were religious but their lives were not lived according to what God wanted. In fact the context of Isaiah 1 presents a picture of a people who were the antithesis of what God wanted. In describing their religious activities, God uses the following descriptive terms: no pleasure in the blood of bulls and goats and lambs, trampling my courts, meaningless offerings, detestable incense, evil assemblies and hated festivals and feasts.

It is in this context that He issues His command to *"Stop doing wrong, learn to do right!"* In the following verses where He instructs them how to live we find the well known promise of forgiveness, *"Though your sins are like scarlet, they shall be white as snow; though they are red as crimson, they shall be like wool."* The Lord takes no pleasure in the death of the wicked. Rather He is pleased when they turn from their ways and live. (Ezekiel 18:23)

Later in Isaiah 29:13a the Lord says, *"These people come near to me with their mouth and honor me with their lips, but their hearts are far from me."* The problem is a people who think they are living right, when they're not. They are living in deception – deception so serious that they do not recognize the truth when they hear it. Or if they do recognize it, they don't do anything about it.

It is imperative to actively pursue with the Holy Spirit, the application of God's Word and ways to every area of our lives as the years go by. In our culture there are many temptations that we have to deal with that have cultural approval. Among them are the following:

- Situation ethics

- There are no absolutes (except this absolute that there are no absolutes)

- If it feels good do it

- Cheating

- How we dress

- White lies

- Political correctness

- Sexually impure content of commercials, programs, internet sites, video games and movies

- Gender identity

- What we communicate and how we communicate

It's important to recognize that all wrongdoing is sin (1 John 5:17a). Fortunately, we are not left to ourselves as we pursue living godly lives. We have the great promise in 1 Corinthians 10:13, *"No temptation has seized you except what is common to man. And God is faithful; he will not let you be tempted beyond what you can bear. But when you are tempted, he will also provide a way out so that you can stand up under it."* May the Lord enable us to see and repent of the things in our lives that are not considered right by Him.

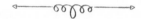

Obligations becoming opportunities
that bring blessing to Him

1 Thessalonians 4:1 As for other matters, brothers and sisters, we instructed you how to live in order to please God, as in fact you are living. Now we ask you and urge you in the Lord Jesus to do this more and more.

Suppose you're driving your spouse's car and you notice the gas gauge is nearly on empty. Even though you're rushed for time you stop and fill up the tank. You might do it simply because it needs to be done; without really thinking about it. There is nothing wrong with that. A helpful deed is done that is good in its own right.

Or while you're standing there filling the tank, you have a smile come upon your face as you think about blessing the one you love. It is an act of kindness that has its own fulfillment. It's possible that your spouse might not even notice that it was done, but that's not important. You did it to bless them.

Have you ever noticed that an obligation doesn't have to feel like something we have to do, like one more demand upon our time? It can be perceived as an opportunity, rather than one of simple duty. Much of the time we might not even notice or think about these activities – we simply do them because they're the right things to do. It is part of being responsible.

But these same obligations can also have the rich feel of opportunity. They are something to be done that brings blessing and pleasure; to the one they are being done for and to the one who does them.

The more we learn to differentiate right things from wrong things, the more aware we become of our opportunities (rather than obligations) to do the right and avoid the wrong. (Sometimes the wrong thing is simply not doing the right thing we see needs to be done – James 4:17) While this can take on the feel of duty, doing the right thing is positive in its own right – and such an opportunity if we have the eyes to see it. In every one of these situations we can recognize that we have the opportunity to do something pleasing to God. We get to experience the joy of blessing Him.

Making wise choices and living righteously are pleasing to Him and enriching to us. They communicate our love to Him (and to those around us) in a way that is genuine and biblical. Words are important, but they don't compare to actions done with our motivation centered in Him. The Holy Spirit will transform us as we pursue these opportunities that enable us to live lives that please Him more and more.

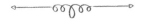

Passion for the Lord

John 12:3 Then Mary took about a pint of pure nard, an expensive perfume; she poured it on Jesus' feet and wiped his feet with her hair. And the house was filled with the fragrance of the perfume

I've read a number of really good books including Jack Deere's book entitled, Surprised by the Power of the Spirit. It's a wonderful book that concludes with focusing on passion for the Lord and then its relationship to power. It is so important that we recognize that passion for God is absolutely essential to our life with God; it along with obedience.

This passion cannot be just a sense of longing or affection for the Lord. It must be a life changing condition of our heart that brings about those actions that characterize individuals who truly are passionately in love with Him. We must want to be such men and women!

There are Psalms and numerous songs that we sing in worship that describe attributes and actions that reflect passion for Him. Do these describe us? Our prayer should be for the Lord to transform us so that those words reflect our true condition more and more. We want to be genuine Godly men and women. The issue is not to be able to rejoice in our Godliness but to rejoice that He enables us to passionately love Him. Let each of us wholeheartedly desire:

- To thirst for the Lord as a deer thirst for streams of water

- A heart that yearns within me for Him;

- To earnestly seek Him;

- My soul to thirst for Him;

- To think of Him through the watches of the night;

- For Him to be my joy and my delight;

- For my soul to yearn and even faint for His courts;

- For my heart and soul to cry out for Him;

- To be a doorkeeper in His courts;

- To sing for joy on my bed because of Him;

- My heart to yearn to gaze upon the beauty of the Lord and to seek Him in his temple.

This passionate love for Jesus becomes our heart's motivation. I believe that is what motivated Mary to anoint Jesus. She was consumed with passionate love for Him and her heart responded to the inspiration of His Spirit and she just gave herself to anointing Him. The focus was Him. Her actions were genuine and selfless.

Later she probably experienced real joy that she had been able to do this for Jesus, but at the time she was motivated purely by the Holy Spirit and her heart of love for Him. May we be continually transformed so that more and more of the things we do are motivated by such love for our Lord.

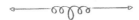

The importance of salt and light

2 Timothy 3:5a having a form of godliness but denying its power.

Consider these questions: 1) Is the Church a victim of the degenerating culture that surrounds it? Or 2) Is it the other way around – is the surrounding culture reflective of the Church having a form of godliness but denying its power? Jesus taught that we are the salt and light of the world. Salt and light prevent decay and darkness.

The context of today's verse is Paul's warning to Timothy of the godlessness of the last days. Some of that godlessness is inevitable but to what extent is it reflective of 'unsalty' Christians – or Christians who too often turn off their 'light'? A major issue we have to deal with is selective obedience (or selective disobedience). This results in having a form of godliness but denying its power.

The power of the gospel of Jesus Christ is beyond anything we can imagine. But how we choose to respond to His gospel is critical. Let's look at the older brother in the well known parable in Luke 15 of the lost son. Upon the younger brother's return and seeing the response of his father:

28 "The older brother became angry and refused to go in. So his father went out and pleaded with him. 29 But he answered his father, 'Look! All these years I've been slaving for you and never disobeyed your orders. Yet you never gave me even a young goat so I could celebrate with my friends. 30 But when this son of yours who has squandered your property with prostitutes comes home, you kill the fattened calf for him!' 31 "'My son,' the father said, 'you are always with me, and everything I have is yours. 32 But we had to celebrate and be glad, because this brother of yours was dead and is alive again; he was lost and is found.'"

The older son has been 'obedient' for years, everything the father has is his and he has always been with his father but his negative response could not be more different from that of his father. Who are his bitterness and accusations focused upon? He's more upset at his father than he is with his brother. Over the years, outwardly everything might have looked fine, but inwardly the older brother was so far from where he should or could be. The brother's return and his father's response revealed the reality of where he was.

The point of this is that the same thing can happen to us. We can look good on the outside – having a form of godliness; but inwardly we can miss so much because we selectively respond to Gods' word – resulting in a denial of its power. Unfortunately we can be blind to this reality occurring in our lives.

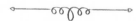

The opportunities 'testing' brings

James 1:13 When tempted, no one should say, 'God is tempting me.' For God cannot be tempted by evil, nor does he tempt anyone;

In the Lord's prayer there is the passage, "…and lead us not into temptation". I heard a Bible teacher many years ago paraphrase this in a very helpful way, "Lord, let there not be anything in my heart that would cause you to put me to the test." God does not tempt anyone with evil but He does provide testing situations that will bring things into the light that need to be exposed and dealt with.

In the story of the prodigal son, the return of the younger brother afforded the older brother just such an 'opportunity'. The older brother reacted to his father's positive response to the return of his younger brother. His negative reaction revealed much that was going on in his heart that both he and his father might not have been aware of. Even though he was apparently doing things 'right' on the outside, his heart contained much that was not 'right'.

We might not realize it but this is a primary way that God deals with us. He allows circumstances to come into our lives that reveal what is going on within us. Frequently these circumstances involve unpleasant or difficult things. We might respond rightly – or in the event we don't, He makes us aware of what is within us and gives us the gift of an opportunity to repent!

Sometimes this happens where only He and we are aware of what needs to be repented of. Other times it happens with more people involved. In either situation, we have a choice to make. Are we going to recognize our need for repentance or are we going to ignore what the Holy Spirit is showing us about ourselves? This process plays such an important role in His transforming us into the image of Jesus.

Hopefully, when such things happen in our lives and we respond wrongly, we will recognize our sin and repent. Further it is important to cultivate a heart of gratitude for such workings of the Holy Spirit. If He didn't allow us to see our sin, we would never change. Think of it this way. He allows us to see where the 'termites' are in our dwelling. And who wouldn't want to get rid of the termites?

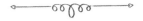

What happened to the apostles?

Acts 5:40b-41 They called the apostles in and had them flogged. Then they ordered them not to speak in the name of Jesus, and let them go. ⁴¹ The apostles left the Sanhedrin, rejoicing because they had been counted worthy of suffering disgrace for the Name.

A book that really moved me was The Heavenly Man – the story of Brother Yun. I had the privilege of hearing him speak a few years ago at a conference focused on Afghanistan. He is a leader in the Back to Jerusalem movement involving Chinese Christians.

His personal story involves a great deal of suffering for the gospel of Christ. But he counts that suffering as joy because of the privilege of being a Christian and serving Jesus. His focus was not on himself but upon the Lord and fulfilling the opportunities that the Lord gave him.

In recounting what has transpired in the church in China, he presents an accounting of what happened to the apostles and some key early Christians. It was good to be reminded that nearly all of them were destined to be martyrs.

They loved and served our Lord Jesus and that <u>righteous road</u> they walked led to an end that not many of us would sign up for. I wonder if our tendency would be to view such a fate as being due to our failure to really follow the Lord – rather than it being the culmination of following Him. Needless to say, I was, and am, greatly humbled and moved by the recounting of their destinies.

There are some variances in the historical records we have but here is one accounting of those who have gone before us:

- John – exiled to Patmos

- Stephen – stoned to death by an angry mob

- Matthew – stabbed to death by an angry mob in Persia

- Mark – died as two horses pulled his legs apart

- Doctor Luke – was cruelly hanged

- Peter – crucified on a cross

- Philip – crucified on a cross

- Simon – crucified on a cross

- Bartholomew – skinned alive by heathen

- Thomas – died in India as five horses pulled his body apart

- James (Apostle) – beheaded by Herod

- (Little) James – cut in half by a sharp saw

- James (brother of Jesus) – stoned to death

- Judas – tied to a pillar and shot with arrows

- Matthias – beheaded in Jerusalem

- Andrew – crucified on a cross (like an X – became known as St Andrew's cross)

- Paul – a martyr under Emperor Nero

May our hearts be so consumed with love from and for our Lord that we too will joyously follow Him wherever He leads. There is a world out there that needs to know Him.

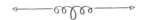

Memories of Afghanistan

Acts 4:12 Salvation is found in no one else, for there is no other name under heaven given to mankind by which we must be saved.

I have referenced my trip to Afghanistan some years ago as part of a Christian NGO (Non-Governmental Organization) in a number of devotionals. It was truly a wonderful, eye-opening trip. I treasure the memories of the Afghan Christians and Christian workers I encountered on that trip. Seeing first hand, the deadly cultural reality faced by Afghans who become Christian there was a stunning reality for me.

The leader of our NGO and I would take prayer walks in the mornings after our arrival. During those initial walks, he first assured me that I wasn't doing anything wrong. Then, speaking of the gospel, he went on to instruct me that I must always be aware of the fact that, "Here in this Muslim culture – the wrong word at the wrong time could get someone killed." Wisdom and an awareness of who was hearing what was being said were absolutely required.

Totally new to me was coming to grips with a common reality that men and women who had accepted Christ were then unable to share that with their Muslim spouse or family. How could an Afghan who had genuinely been changed by Christ be silent? The answer was the knowledge that in their Muslim culture, the extended family would likely kill the believing spouse when they learned of their Christian faith. This wasn't – and isn't – 'urban legend' but a reality that happened to people they knew first hand and had worked with.

This also kept many Afghan Christians from becoming part of an underground church – or any Christian gathering for that fact. They didn't know whom they could trust and who might be there for the hidden purpose of identifying them. The exposure could result in their death. Recognizing this ever-present threat shielded me from the temptation to become judgmental and question the reality of their faith. My western background had never encountered anything like this.

It appears that world-wide upwards of 100,000 Christians are martyred each year. Those are all brothers and sisters in Christ who lost their lives simply because they believed in Jesus. The difficulties we face pale in comparison to the dangers many Christians around the world face – and that isn't even addressing the poverty of their societies compared to the wealth we have in the west.

Thank God for the many Christian workers who are going to the nations to share the 'true wealth' of the Gospel of Christ. Praise God for the untold number of conversions throughout the world due to God giving dreams and visions of Jesus – sometimes to entire villages. Millions of Muslims worldwide are becoming Christians each year. They respond to the love of God and the Good News of the Gospel just like we did! May our hearts be moved to prayer and compassion for these believers – our brothers and sisters. May their joy be overflowing as they grow in the wonder of our Lord.

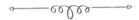

Coming to grips with our perceived reality

The Scripture is at the end of the devotional

Our lives are filled with things we do that typically produce results. Sometimes the results are good – sometimes not so good. It helps to have a clear idea of what the result is supposed to be and what must be done to produce it. If we want to take a trip we identify where we are going; when; for how long; and how are we going to get there. If we're going to Miami and wind up in Duluth somebody goofed up.

If we are in sales, we had better sell. If we're in auto repair, the cars we work on must be fixed when we're done. But what happens when we become casual or are misinformed as to results we should be having? What if we think we're doing things right and we're not? Is it possible to become so mistaken as to the nature of what we are doing that we can walk comfortably in that delusion?

I remember when one of my sons got his family a video game system called Wii (pronounced wee) for Christmas a number of years ago. This system allowed you to play an immense number of games. It had a sports component that included games such as bowling, tennis, golf and wave-boarding where your physical motions with the control in your hands and your body movements determined how well you did. Now suppose we had Wii and became really good at these various 'sports' on this game system. We would likely have shared our excitement with friends who also have such games. This could have led to us discussing how we are improving at golf or tennis or bowling.

Picture people so caught up in these video sports that they considered their performance as the real thing. Wii golf became golf. Wii tennis became tennis. Wii bowling became bowling. Then, what happens when they meet someone who doesn't know about Wii, who invites them to play golf? Our Wii player is then surprised when s/he is taken to a golf course instead of a game room. What does the Wii player say when confronted with the real McCoy? Do they respond, "This is not the way we play the game."?

Is it possible to become so comfortable with the artificial that we are unaware of what the real McCoy looks like? Can we become so mistaken that we completely (and sincerely) distort reality? Consider the Lord's admonition to the Laodiceans:

[15]I know your deeds, that you are neither cold nor hot. I wish you were either one or the other! [16]So, because you are lukewarm—neither hot nor cold—I am about to spit you out of my mouth. [17]You say, 'I am rich; I have acquired wealth and do not need a thing.' But you do not realize that you are wretched, pitiful, poor, blind and naked. Revelation 3:15-17

To be continued...

What is being a Christian?

The Scripture is at the end of the devotional

One of the sights that we periodically see is young people at the front of stores in their uniforms raising funds for their season. There are different uniforms for baseball, track, football, soccer, cheerleading, basketball and the list goes on. One thing they all have in common is that it's pretty easy to recognize that they all involve sports – even though we might not recognize which one.

While the uniform indicates sports, it is how they play the game that counts. Games have rules and require learned skills. Typically they also have officials, umpires, referees or judges to assure that rules are observed. Sports involve teamwork, practice and include features that measure how well something is being accomplished: getting the ball in the basket, scoring runs, completing passes, keeping the ball within the lines.

In our culture today it is easy to fall into the trap of treating Christianity somewhat like a sport, but without the officials or referees. Certain outward behaviors and acknowledgement of certain things indicate we are Christians; they are our 'uniform'. The differences between the things we believe, place us in different 'teams' of Christians. Unfortunately, this 'sport' of Christianity has lots of players modifying or ignoring the 'rules'. In spite of sincerity, we can succumb to the temptation of creating our own definition of how the sport is played.

But what constitutes being a Christian? Is it as simple as acknowledging that Jesus is Lord, confessing we are a sinner and adopting certain behaviors (like putting on a uniform)? Mentally, most of us would say there's a lot more to it than that. But what is the actual testimony of our lives, thoughts, attitudes and actions. What does God say about it?

Yesterday we concluded with the Lord's admonition to the Church of Laodicea. They thought they were rich but in reality they were "wretched, pitiful, poor, blind and naked." They were lukewarm – neither cold nor hot. The Lord also speaks to the Church of Ephesus. They are commended for doing many things right, but then the Lord says this,

" 4'But I have this against you, that you have left your first love. 5'Therefore remember from where you have fallen, and repent and do the deeds you did at first; or else I am coming to you and will remove your lampstand out of its place-- unless you repent." Revelation 2:4-5

These admonitions are serious! They raise questions that we must consider: What are lives really like that have Jesus as their genuine first love? Do our lives reflect such love? What is our basis for knowing? And how do we respond if our lives don't reflect such love?

To be continued...

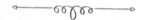

Don Schmidt

The appropriate response to His loving us

2 Kings 2:19 Then the men of the city said to Elisha, "Behold now,
the situation of this city is pleasant, as my lord sees; but the water is
bad and the land is unfruitful."

This Scripture has always fascinated me. The men communicate to Elisha that their city is a pleasant situation – with a very significant 'but'. There are a few little problems: the water is bad, the land won't bear crops and the animals can't reproduce. But it is a pleasant situation! It looks good from a distance – just don't ask too many questions.

Fortunately for that city, Elisha receives a miracle from the Lord for them. He asks them to bring him a new bowl and to put salt in it. He then goes to the spring and throws the salt in it saying, *"This is what the LORD says: 'I have healed this water. Never again will it cause death or make the land unproductive.'"* No more death from the water. The situation became a whole lot more pleasant.

Many of today's Christians seem to have a lot in common with the men of that city. They consider their Christianity to be 'a pleasant situation', but there are a whole lot of problems that don't seem to go away. Unfortunately they don't recognize that the source of these problems is their very lives and the way they live them.

It's like Christianity looks good from afar, just don't get too close and ask too many personal questions. Putting it in the context of today's verse, it's like they were hoping that becoming a Christian was the equivalent of having 'salt' thrown in their spring. The natural results would be wholesomeness and productivity.

We are made new when we are born again and God so remarkably transforms our very lives. But here is where we have a choice as to the road we take. One road leads to a lifestyle of adding Jesus to the stuff we've been doing. Sort of, God threw 'salt' in our lives; we're grateful; and we go about our business. Our lives might produce 'fruit' but much of it is unrighteous fruit that has a lot of sourness and bitterness in it – similar to the culture around us.

The other road is where the Lord says to us, "I have a way and I want you to walk in it – along with Me." He has given us His word and His Spirit to enable us to learn His ways and walk in them with Him. This road leads to passion for the Lord and the fruit is His righteousness in every area of our lives. It doesn't mean we won't have problems, but faith and godliness will characterize us. They will also characterize our dealing with those problems. It is a faith-process requiring our continual commitment and adherence to His word. People will see Jesus when they see us. It's called loving God, and is the only appropriate response to His loving us.

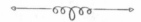

Sincere love

Romans 12:9 Love must be sincere. Hate what is evil; cling to what is good.

In the coming days, these devotionals are going to involve the marvelous verses of Romans 12:9-21. There is such richness contained in these 13 verses. Each sentence and phrase contains treasure to dig for – to pursue and discover the richness they hold. They are guiding principles and qualities that we must have in our lives in order to be the men and women that God has chosen and destined us to be.

Imagine for a moment someone you love speaking these verses to you; carefully and lovingly, not rushing through them as a list, but focusing upon each thought. They present a picture of who we are to be. They identify the attributes that must characterize our very being. We get to discover what they each mean and partner with the Holy Spirit to work them out fully in our lives.

Today's verse raises all manner of questions:

- What exactly is this love that must be sincere? Is it feelings? Is it actions? How do we know that what we think is Godly love, really is? Does God's Word define it for us?

- What exactly does it mean for that love, whatever it is, to be sincere?

- What is evil? Are God and the world (our culture) on the same page when it comes to identifying evil? Where do we look to find out? Might we consider something okay that God considers evil? What does it mean to hate evil?

- What exactly is 'good'? Who defines what is good? How does one cling to what is good?

The point that I'm getting at is that we must be careful not to use worldly wisdom in determining the answers. Here are two other versions of today's verse to give us some additional insight – and also raise some more questions:

"Love from the center of who you are; don't fake it. Run for dear life from evil; hold on for dear life to good." The Message

"[Let your] love be sincere (a real thing); hate what is evil [loathe all ungodliness, turn in horror from wickedness], but hold fast to that which is good." Amplified

Do we 'run' for dear life from evil? Do we 'loathe all ungodliness, turn in horror from wickedness'? How do we do these things in a way that honors God; in a way that attracts people to God rather than repelling them from us? Jesus spent a lot of his time with sinners. He demonstrated that there is a way to hate sin and love the sinners.

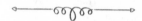

The joy of glorifying God with our lives

Romans 12:10 Be devoted to one another in brotherly love.
Honor one another above yourselves.

Being devoted to something is pretty normal in our society. People are devoted to families, sports teams, hobbies, TV, Facebook, Twitter, etc… Today's verse points us in an important direction. The Lord expects us to be devoted to one another in brotherly love. This is something we do as part of Jesus' command for Christians to love one another. In John 14:34, 35 Jesus declares, *"A new command I give you: Love one another. As I have loved you, so you must love one another. ³⁵By this everyone will know that you are my disciples, if you love one another."*

Isn't it wonderful to be loved? Isn't it a blessing to have friends who are caring and devoted? Think ossssf the richness of relationships we have with those who live out this verse. Think of individuals that you know who exemplify this truth. Their lives engender appreciation and gratitude within us. We are to be the same kind of people. We have the opportunity for others to experience the devotion and love flowing through our lives. We get to be blessed by being a blessing to them.

One of my favorite verses is Matthew 5:16, *"In the same way, let your light shine before others, that they may see your good deeds and glorify your Father in heaven."* When we are genuinely devoted to one another in brotherly love, the result is our Father in heaven being glorified. What a thrilling thought that others will glorify God simply by seeing us live the lives He wants us to live. Not only that, but loving one another is a primary evidence that we are Jesus' disciples.

When I read of honoring one another I think of humility. What a refreshing quality that is! The Message presents another thought on humility, *'Be good friends who love deeply; practice playing second fiddle.'* We get to honor and defer to others. Bless them. Take the lesser seat – not grudgingly, but joyfully. Be other-oriented rather than self-centered. One of the great blessings of this process is the heartfelt gratitude we develop. The more we become what God intends us to be, the more gratitude we have for His kindness and grace.

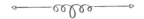

Be aglow and burning with the Spirit

Romans 12:11 Never be lacking in zeal, but keep your
spiritual fervor, serving the Lord.

This morning when I was asking the Lord about today's verse, I was reminded of some friends of ours. Their home is in the north where the winters are long and cold – like below zero. They heat it with a wood burning stove. Having a bonfire in the fireplace once a week, while nice, just doesn't do it. They have a wood supply and habit patterns that include tending that stove so it produces heat around the clock; day after day.

If they want the house to be a comfortable temperature, they maintain the stove and all it involves. Their physical bodies are constantly aware of how well they are doing or not doing. When the temperature in the house is comfortable, their 'bodies' are 'quiet'. But let the temperature drop in the house (somebody forgot to put wood in the stove) and their bodies start 'communicating'! Can't you just imagine being busy and all of a sudden your 'body' speaks up saying, "Excuse me! We are shivering and turning blue. Put some wood on the fire!!" Ignore it some more and it says, "The pipes are going to freeze to say nothing about us!"

At this point we look at the goose bumps on our skin; notice that we are rubbing our hands trying to warm them up; the 'rice-buddy' around our neck isn't keeping us warm – so we go tend the fire. Again, we don't build a bonfire, we just add wood to the stove to produce the needed warmth. A fact of life is that our bodies are very difficult to ignore; they can get our attention.

In a similar manner, we must learn to pay attention to our spiritual condition. It, along with the Holy Spirit, will communicate that our 'fire' is getting low. Unfortunately, it is much easier to ignore our spirit – and the Holy Spirit – than it is a shivering physical body. Today's verse in The Message reads, *"Don't burn out; keep yourselves fueled and aflame. Be alert servants of the Master."* We must train ourselves to tend to this because it is far more important than physical warmth. Tending this 'fire' is a daily thing – not something done once or twice a week.

We cannot be the people we must be – that He wants us to be - if we don't. The Amplified Bible states the phrase in a wonderful way, *"…be aglow and burning with the Spirit…"*

Don Schmidt

We are the frame, He is the picture

Romans 12:12 Be joyful in hope, patient in affliction, faithful in prayer.

These verses of Romans 12 that we are looking at are really wonderful. Each phrase is like a delightful desert that is so rich and full of flavor that we savor each bite! Earlier we wrote about the difficulty so many Christians have with the whole subject of obedience to commands. Just the word 'command' can cause a negative reaction. We've seen in 1 John 5:3 that loving God is defined, by God, as obeying His commands. But when we think of commands, do we realize that these verses are some of the commands He's talking about?

All too often people think of commands as the 'thou shalt not…' kind of thing – dos and don'ts that somehow are like having to eat vegetables we don't like. We allow ourselves to be deceived into the notion that His commands are intended to keep us from enjoying life. Even worse is when we just don't think about it – life is just too full and busy with other more important things.

But God's truth is just the opposite of all that. It is the source of our greatest blessing. He gives us hope and enables us to be joyful in it. Life is filled with affliction and He enables us to develop patience (one of the fruit of the Spirit) in the midst of it. He teaches us to pray and through spending time with Him we want to pray more. On top of all that we learn that these concrete actions have an ever greater reality to them. They are specific expressions of our love for Him. We love our Lord by being joyful in hope. We love our Lord by being patient in affliction. We love our Lord by being faithful in prayer. And, each of these actions are things that we can grow in – meaning that the more we grow, the more we love God.

Just about everyone is in the middle of something. We are all going through difficulties of one kind or another. There are those around us who need to hear about the power of prayer and see that they too can have joy and hope and patience in the midst of all they're going through. God will provide us with the opportunities to share our faith as we live out these qualities each and every day. God wants to use us to show them Himself. We get to be the frame and He is the picture.

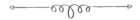

The importance of being 'other' oriented

Romans 12:13 Share with the Lord's people who are in need. Practice hospitality.

In the spring of 2010 when the greater Nashville area experienced severe flooding, the churches played a huge role in bringing relief and assistance to those who were victims of the flood. Some areas received as much as 26 inches of rain in 36 hours. The motivation of the churches wasn't to receive recognition; it was a spontaneous response to the obvious crisis that descended upon this region.

While applicable to major disasters, today's verse particularly speaks to the needs we Christians have in our daily lives. It speaks to us about the importance of being aware of the needs in the lives of Christians around us and helping to meet them. Widows, the unemployed, the sick, those in financial distress, family crises, accidents, the hungry, – the list of needs goes on. The Lord wants to use us to meet the needs of one another. This is another powerful attribute that must characterize who we are

A few days ago we began looking at the verses starting with Romans 12:9. They contain a list of righteous attributes that identify God's people. In order for the church to be what God intends it to be, these attributes must characterize it. That means they must characterize us!

> *⁹Love must be sincere. Hate what is evil; cling to what is good.*
> *¹⁰Be devoted to one another in love. Honor one another above yourselves.*
> *¹¹Never be lacking in zeal, but keep your spiritual fervor, serving the Lord.*
> *¹²Be joyful in hope, patient in affliction, faithful in prayer.*
> *¹³Share with the Lord's people who are in need. Practice hospitality.*

I have underlined the phrases that form a consistent thread running through these verses. They are all other-oriented – and all positive in nature. They reflect Christians loving one another in practical, useful ways. They reflect the body of Christ living out a lifestyle that is most attractive; a lifestyle of salt and light. Such lives will cause people to become thirsty for God.

Unfortunately we allow our lives to become self-oriented. We allow the busyness of life to deprive us of rich opportunities to bless and be blessed – to see and become aware of needs in other Christians' lives, and to help meet them. Instead of extending hospitality to others, we assume they prefer a motel – thus missing the blessings hospitality bestows. The more we do it, the better and richer it becomes. May our lives richly reflect these wonderful attributes that glorify our Lord.

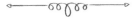

How must we respond to persecution?

Romans 12:14 Bless those who persecute you; bless and do not curse.

What does it mean to be persecuted? Can we think of a time or times where we believe we have been persecuted? Do those experiences, if we had them, seem more like they fall in the categories of insult or disrespect? Or, do they fall into the category of physical threat or intimidation? Were our lives at risk? Do we view persecution to be more of a general category where Christians as a group are 'persecuted' by being discriminated against? Might the Supreme Court decision in 1963 banning organized prayer in public schools be an example of such 'persecution'?

When it comes to persecution, here in the West, it is a different world than that which many Christians deal with particularly in the Middle East, parts of Africa or the Far East. I think it is accurate to say we would prefer to be prohibited from publically reading or displaying our Bible than to be arrested for having one. Likewise, we would rather be ridiculed for our faith than to be imprisoned and tortured.

Think of being forced to choose between Jesus and a son or daughter or spouse. If you chose Jesus, the likelihood is that you will never see your family member again in this life. This is happening today and has been happening for decades in other parts of the world.

Persecution runs the gamut from being picked on or discriminated against to martyrdom. The amazing thing is that our response to those who do the persecuting is to be the same – we are to bless them. Hating them or cursing them isn't an option. Not even cursing under our breath. This means that annoyance, anger, disgust and other 'fleshly' responses are off limits too.

I cannot help but think of two different Scriptures that speak to this topic. Jesus' statement in Matthew 10:22 *"You will be hated by everyone because of me, but the one who stands firm to the end will be saved."* Then there is the wonderful attitude expressed by the Apostles in Acts 5:41 *"The apostles left the Sanhedrin, rejoicing because they had been counted worthy of suffering disgrace for the Name."*

We must learn to bless those who persecute us. We must learn to be the expressions of the Kingdom of God that He wants us to be in the face of opposition. Our goal must be to do it His way – bless and not curse!

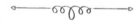

"I just helped him cry."

Romans 12:15 Rejoice with those who rejoice; mourn with those who mourn.

The Amplified Bible adds a bit of understanding to this verse, *"Rejoice with those who rejoice [sharing others' joy], and weep with those who weep [sharing others' grief]."* Author and lecturer Leo Buscaglia once talked about a contest he was asked to judge. The purpose of the contest was to find the most caring child.

The winner was a four-year-old child, whose next door neighbor was an elderly gentleman, who had recently lost his wife. Upon seeing the man cry, the little boy went into the old gentleman's yard, climbed onto his lap, and just sat there. When his mother asked him what he had said to the neighbor, the little boy just said, "Nothing, I just helped him cry."

I can sure relate to that little boy. There are times when friends or co-workers are suffering a loss or are in a very painful situation and I just want to be near them – and 'help them cry'. Unfortunately, we can become paralyzed because we don't know what to say. This can lead to saying or doing nothing out of fear of being embarrassed or causing more hurt. The Lord wants us to move forward, not hold back. It's helpful to recognize the value in quiet presence.

Often it's not what we say, but the thoughtfulness of being there – our presence, a gentle touch, a compassionate smile. Sometimes a simple phone call to friends who are in mourning can mean a great deal. We briefly tell them we love them; are praying for them and just wanted them to know we cared. If ever there was a time when, "It's the thought that counts," applied, it's in times of mourning.

The other side of the coin is rejoicing with those who are rejoicing. One of the wonderful attributes we can develop is that of having vicarious pleasure when wonderful things happen to people we care about. This is the opposite of jealousy. Dear friends of ours had their home on the market and it just sold. At the same time they found a wonderful home that they are buying. What a time to rejoice with them! Part of the rejoicing will mean we get to help them move. That is part of our rejoicing with them!

Hopefully we are making a priority of building lasting relationships. It's so important that we are close enough to those around us so we know what is going on. Friends – particularly Christian friends – are so wonderful to have when it comes to sharing the highs and lows of life. That's what friends are for – we get to be there for each other.

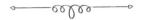

The joy of living out this verse!

Romans 12:16 Get along with each other; don't be stuck-up. Make friends with nobodies; don't be the great somebody. The Message

Have you noticed that Jesus could relate well to anyone? Tax collectors, sinners, prostitutes, Samaritans, – everyone that the Pharisees had an attitude about. What an example Jesus is for us. The Pharisees, on the other hand, appear to be a strong example for us on how <u>not</u> to relate to others. They put people into categories and were consumed with pride and arrogance. Their blindness to this condition caused them to miss the miracle-working Messiah who was right in front of them.

Unfortunately, there are cultural tendencies that we live with that encourage us to look down upon people that are members of various groups. This can lead us to be proud or arrogant about groups we might belong to. If we have experienced such condescension or discrimination, we know firsthand how refreshing it is to have relationships where this negative baggage is not present; where we are treated as people of worth. Living out today's verse is imperative for us, in all the circumstances of our lives: church, work, daily interactions, family and friends.

At Williamson College, the Christian college where I worked, we experienced the blessing of having an incredible mix of students from about 18 different countries. We had home grown Americans, immigrants and foreign students. Although the majority of their students were Christian, there were any number of other religions represented including Hindu, Islam and Buddhist. We had the honor of serving them all – helping and enabling them to pursue their education.

The college and curriculum were Christ-centered and the students all understood that. What an opportunity that was for us to live out our faith! Our faith was reflected in how we as staff got along with and served one another. It was revealed in the quality of relationships that faculty and staff and students had with each other. Students were not required to become Christian to attend, but they knew they were going to be exposed to the Christian faith; both in terms of teaching and in the overall experience they had there. The qualities reflected in these verses of Romans 12:9-21 (that we have been looking at) are required of us, in order for the Christian faith we demonstrate to be the real thing!

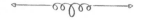

The Holy Spirit becomes our 'instrument panel'

*Romans 12:17 Do not repay anyone evil for evil. Be careful to do
what is right in the eyes of everyone.*

Back during the depression my father worked in a bank. One of his memories was that the tellers at the bank he worked at were not trained to spot counterfeits by looking at examples of counterfeit currency. The focus was upon learning what the genuine bills looked like. They became so familiar with the real that when they were flipping through the bills, a variant would stand out no matter how small or subtle the difference was.

Taking a look at today's verse, consider evil and wrong (the opposite of right) as counterfeits. We can spend our time focusing on what not to do, but that raises the question of how do we know whether an action or attitude is evil or wrong. It makes a whole lot more sense to focus on learning what is right.

What is the right way to respond when evil is done to us or those we love? How do we determine what is right when in the midst of turbulent circumstances? Let's consider another illustration that we can relate to. Why do pilots get trained and licensed to fly on instruments? The reality of flying is that all manner of weather is encountered. We've all heard the stories of pilots in flight simulators who fly them 'into the ground' because they lose their bearings. Their instincts are telling them they're doing fine, but the instruments indicate they are headed for disaster. Pilots must trust their instruments when they are flying in adverse conditions.

These two illustrations present a unique picture for us. God's Word is the ultimate and absolute source of defining what is right. It contains the principles and instructions that provide the basis for recognizing what is right in every situation. The Holy Spirit in essence becomes our 'instrument panel'. He communicates to us the insights and understandings needed to safely navigate every situation – no matter how difficult or confusing.

We learn His voice. He brings to mind appropriate understandings of God's Word that apply to the situations at hand. We learn to trust Him, not our instincts, public opinion or what seems right. We look to Him. It doesn't mean we won't make mistakes, but by doing this we become increasingly aware of our dependence upon God. The more we look to Him and live out His ways, the more right choices we will make.

Righteousness and peace kiss each other

*Romans 12:18 If it is possible, as far as it depends on you,
live at peace with everyone.*

When I read this verse I think of the many wonderful things the Bible has to say about peace, and peacemakers. I think of Jesus - He is the Prince of Peace. In the midst of turbulence and strife we can be filled with peace because we have learned to trust in Him. In Isaiah 26: 3 it says, *"You will keep in perfect peace those whose minds are steadfast, because they trust in you."*

Have you noticed that we can share the peace we have with others? It's like the widow's pot of oil in the Old Testament – there is a never ending supply. We must understand the powerful impact God wants us to have in the lives of those around us, particularly when they are upset and stressed out. The words we speak, and the manner in which the Spirit leads us to do it can have such a redemptive impact.

In Proverbs 25:11 it says, *"A word aptly spoken is like apples of gold in settings of silver."* Our faith and trust in the Lord make us immune to their lack of peace – their nervousness and anxiety. In fact our destiny is to be peacemakers. Remember in the Sermon on the Mount that Jesus said, *"Blessed are the peacemakers, for they will be called children of God."* Matthew 5:9

The more we walk in God's ways – meaning bringing our lives into conformity with His word – the more we love Him. The more we love Him, the greater the blessing we will be to all around us. When we are faithful to Him, we won't rise to provocation or insist on having our way. We acknowledge when we are wrong and others are right. We apologize and ask for forgiveness.

We are other oriented. Instead of contributing to the anxiety and unrest, making bad situations worse, He will use us to defuse the unrest and turn the situations in a redemptive direction. He will use our righteous responses (meaning doing things His way) to positively impact the situations we find ourselves in.

The themes our lives are to involve love, faithfulness, righteousness and peace. These qualities are so evident in the verses of Romans 12:9-21 that we have been looking at. It's like peace is the fruit or guest that comes when the other three are present. Psalm 85:10 presents such a beautiful picture of what God does in us when we love Him: *"Love and faithfulness meet together; righteousness and peace kiss each other."*

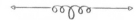

The priceless key of forgiveness

Romans 12:19 Do not take revenge, my dear friends, but leave room for God's wrath, for it is written: "It is mine to avenge; I will repay," says the Lord.

Have you ever noted the perverse delight we experience when we are able to get even with someone who's done us wrong? And have you noticed how we can be preoccupied or even consumed by negative thoughts of someone who's wronged us when they seem to get away with it? I call that negative meditation. I think it's accurate to say that none of this is redemptive.

Getting even! Tit-for-tat! Giving them what they deserve! In some cultures of the world such thoughts and values lead to the shedding of blood and the taking of lives. Some of our Christian brothers and sisters face this each day because they have rejected the faith of their culture and became Christian. Our problem isn't that we want to kill someone, but it's more in the idea of successfully "doing unto them as they did to us" – but in an appropriate way.

The fruit of such thoughts and actions are deadly and forbidden. Today's verse tells us don't insist on getting even; that's not for you to do. "I'll do the judging," says God. "I'll take care of it." This is like the Lord saying to us, "Don't play in the minefield!" Jesus taught us, *"Do to others whatever you would like them to do to you. This is the essence of all that is taught in the law and the prophets."* Matthew 7:12 This truth applies – always. It means we act and respond to all circumstances and provocations in a way consistent with God's Word. But in the heat of a moment or in the stinging aftermath of being hurt how do we get there?

I find that the priceless key for me is forgiveness. It is the escape hatch from this path of revenge and getting even. Forgiveness is a decision of our will and is not dependent upon our feelings. It is like cracking open an egg. Once done, it's done! We cannot undo it. Then we seek the Lord's help in dealing with our anger, bitterness, frustration, etc... Think of Jesus forgiving from the cross. Think of Stephen forgiving while he is being stoned to death. Think of glorifying God when we are negatively treated. Remember that Jesus taught us to, *"Bless them that curse you, and pray for them which despitefully use you."* Luke 6:38. When unrighteousness happens to us, let our prayer be for God to grant repentance and mercy to the one doing it.

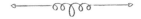

Opportunities with those who are unkind or nasty

Romans 12:20 On the contrary: "If your enemy is hungry, feed him;
if he is thirsty, give him something to drink. In doing this, you will
heap burning coals on his head."

There are probably people in our lives that we wouldn't mind seeing burning coals heaped on their head. But the overall context of this verse really speaks to our attitudes and actions toward those who wouldn't make our friends list. Paul has been writing about being a people whose love is sincere. This includes blessing those who persecute us; to bless and not curse; and not repaying anyone evil for evil

This is the Kingdom of God way of life – just the opposite of how our old natures want to respond. The Message states this verse this way, *"Our Scriptures tell us that if you see your enemy hungry, go buy that person lunch, or if he's thirsty, get him a drink. Your generosity will surprise him with goodness."*

Jesus takes it even further. He tells us to, *"…love our enemies, do good to those who hate you, pray for those who mistreat you."* He asks what credit is it to us if we only love those who love us; if we only do good to those who do good to us; if we only lend to those from whom we expect repayment? Our heavenly Father is kind to the ungrateful and wicked and He expects us to be merciful just as He is. (Luke 6:27-36)

There are two examples given in Exodus 23:4-5 that flesh out this reality in a practical, helpful way. *"If you come across your enemy's ox or donkey wandering off, be sure to return it. 5 If you see the donkey of someone who hates you fallen down under its load, do not leave it there; be sure you help them with it."* Think of it this way. If we're driving down the road and see someone who is nasty to us with a flat tire and in need of help, we stop and help them. Or if they are taken ill and we have the opportunity to help with meals or assist them in some way, we do it.

But let's add a twist. We must be careful not to assume that our kindness will produce an immediate change in them. That is for the Lord to do. How do we respond if the person we help then continues to be nasty - and then we encounter him needing help on the road again? Do we drive by and say, "You deserve it! I'm not going to help you!" Or do we stop again, because we have forgiven them and this is another opportunity from the Lord to bless them (and us)? Maybe an angel did in the tire because he knew we were coming and wanted to see what we would do.

Don Schmidt

How do you recognize....

Romans 12:21 Do not be overcome by evil, but overcome evil with good.

This verse really underscores the importance of the Scriptures and the critical role they play in our lives. Their absence is debilitating while their presence is empowering. By absence, I mean that we have a casual approach to the Scriptures and the role they play in our lives. By 'presence' I mean that we embrace the Scriptures; learn them and apply them. They develop the framework through which we view life. They are the basis for us defining what is good and evil.

How do we resist being overcome by evil if we don't recognize the evil that surrounds us? While much evil is obvious, there is much that is not. Likewise we must learn to recognize good. The problem is twofold: the society around us at times is clueless as to good and evil; and the Church is greatly affected by the fact that our culture has so infiltrated the church. This results in the problem that Isaiah identified in 5:20 where he pronounces a warning:

Woe to those who call evil good and good evil, who put darkness for light and light for darkness, who put bitter for sweet and sweet for bitter.

We must recognize that this is going on all around us now and the Scriptures enable us to address it. In Hebrews 5:13-14 we see the reality of this problem and the vital role God's Word has:

13Anyone who lives on milk, being still an infant, is not acquainted with the teaching about righteousness. 14But solid food is for the mature, who by constant use have trained themselves to distinguish good from evil.

The Lord wants our lives to glorify Him. We are able to do that by living lives that are not overcome by evil, rather we overcome evil with good.

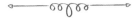

The lives disciples are called to live

Matthew 28:19-20 "Therefore go and make disciples of all nations, baptizing them in the name of the Father and of the Son and of the Holy Spirit, ²⁰and teaching them to obey everything I have commanded you. And surely I am with you always, to the very end of the age."

The 'Great Commission' struck me as a fitting capstone to the last three weeks of these devotionals. It speaks of making disciples and what they are to be taught; what kind of people we are to become as disciples of Christ. Over this period of time we have been looking at the treasure contained in Romans 12:9-21. As we noted at the start, these verses contain guiding principles and qualities that we must have in our lives in order to be the men and women that God has chosen and destined us to be. They identify what a Christian should be like.

Here is the list contained in the verses of Romans 12:9-21

- Love must be sincere

- Hate what is evil

- Cling to what is good

- Be devoted to one another in love

- Honor one another above yourselves

- Never be lacking in zeal

- Keep your spiritual fervor

- Serve the Lord.

- Be joyful in hope

- Be patient in affliction

- Be faithful in prayer.

- Share with the Lord's people who are in need

- Practice hospitality

- Bless those who persecute you

- Bless and do not curse

- Rejoice with those who rejoice

- Mourn with those who mourn
- Live in harmony with one another
- Do not be proud
- Be willing to associate with people of low position
- Do not be conceited
- Do not repay anyone evil for evil
- Be careful to do what is right in the eyes of everyone
- If it is possible, live at peace with everyone
- Do not take revenge
- Leave room for God's wrath
- If your enemy is hungry, feed him
- If he is thirsty, give him something to drink
- Do not be overcome by evil
- Overcome evil with good

What a beautiful list of attributes that should characterize each of us! The more we look like these – the less we look like the world. Do we recognize that the items in this list are in reality Jesus' commands to all who would be His disciples? It is by doing these things (i.e., obeying His commands) that we love God and demonstrate the reality of our friendship with Him.

My birthday in Jesus

1 John 3:1a How great is the love the Father has lavished on us, that we should be called children of God! And that is what we are!

Today is my birthday in Jesus. October 11, 1968 was the day my world was forever changed. Prior to that day, it never entered my mind that anyone could have a tangible, loving relationship with God; a relationship that went both ways. He loves to express His love to us and we get to express our love to Him.

A relationship with Jesus is not just a theological reality – it is a whole new world. Being born-again means we become His son or daughter but there is so much more to it than that. It means that we become restored to a place where we can live our lives with Him and for Him. It becomes our starting place.

Think of it! We get to walk with Him. We get to love Him. We get to please Him. We get to experience His affection. Likewise each day He is with us. He loves us. He blesses us. He guides us. He disciplines us as sons and daughters. We are His!

Our relationship with God is so incredibly practical. He deals with who we are – transforming us into the image of Jesus. He gives us the desire and helps us learn the things we need to learn – the doing part. The more we become like Him, the better able we are to glorify Him in our daily lives. A man or woman with a life characterized by the love of Christ and the fruit of the Spirit is in a much better place to become a Godly husband or wife; a father or mother; friend; neighbor; son or daughter….

As I write this, I am overwhelmed with gratitude. It is like an artesian spring within me. It just never ends. No matter how difficult things might become from time to time, it is there. What a treasure He gives us. When I met Him, 50 years ago, I wondered how such an incredible experience could last a lifetime. It never occurred to me that it could or would get even better!

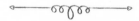

Choosing to be an overcomer not a victim

2 Corinthians 12:10 That is why, for Christ's sake, I delight in weaknesses, in insults, in hardships, in persecutions, in difficulties. For when I am weak, then I am strong.

While in Brazil we all went to a farm with friends for a few days. It was about 2 hours west of Recife, up in some mountains. These friends and their farm have been like an oasis for John and Fabi and we were greatly blessed to be there with them. One of the interesting highlights of our time there was a little brown Labrador puppy. There had been seven puppies born but unfortunately the mother only had six well-formed teats for nursing. This little guy was odd man out – the runt of the litter.

By the time we got there, three of the puppies had already gone to new homes. This little puppy was ½ the size of each of the other three puppies still there. He also bore the scars of being the target of their rough play. Fortunately he was receiving extra milk, food and care to help him grow. He was sweet, playful, and the chosen recipient of our granddaughters' affection.

If the puppy could think about it, I wonder if he would have thought of himself as a victim or a survivor / overcomer. He had been dealt a hand in life that put him at a real disadvantage – circumstances to deal with that were totally beyond his control. Our granddaughter Becca considered him a 'survivor' (that was her term). He was not going to let his size or 'misfortune' hinder him.

While thinking about this puppy's situation a number of Biblical characters came to mind:

- Gideon - *"Pardon me, my lord,"* Gideon replied, *"but how can I save Israel? My clan is the weakest in Manasseh, and I am the least in my family."* Judges 6:15

- Joseph - *"Here comes that dreamer!" they said to each other.* Genesis 37:19

- Moses - *Moses said to the LORD, "Pardon your servant, Lord. I have never been eloquent, neither in the past nor since you have spoken to your servant. I am slow of speech and tongue." ... Moses said, "Pardon your servant, Lord. Please send someone else."* Exodus 4:10, 13

- David - *So he asked Jesse, "Are these all the sons you have?" "There is still the youngest," Jesse answered. "He is tending the sheep." Samuel said, "Send for him; we will not sit down until he arrives."* 1 Samuel 16:11

It is so important to remember that we are not victims – no matter what lot in life we are dealt. We are survivors / overcomers because of the God we serve. Where we are weak, we look to the Lord and He makes us strong. Our focus is Jesus. There is nothing He cannot redeem.

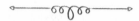

How wonderful it is!

James 2:23 And the Scripture was fulfilled that says, "Abraham believed God, and it was credited to him as righteousness," and he was called God's friend.

This morning I woke up with a thought running through my mind and it was also an experience while it was happening. The thought was, 'How wonderful it is to be loved by God!' I was experiencing pleasure and joy while I was thinking it. While it is a fact that God loves us all, it is a particular delight to experience His affection; to experience the wonder of relationship with Him.

Think of the joy we have with those who love us and those we love. Our lives are richer because of them. I remember the week one of our dearest friends from Seattle was with us. Paulette and her husband Jon have been dear friends since we met in Chicago in 1978. When they moved back to Seattle, the miles could never diminish the relationship. We are so grateful for all the times we have been together over the years. A highlight was when we went to Romania for the wedding of their daughter in 2003.

We joke that when Paulette and Donna get together it borders on illegal – they have such fun and enjoyment. They are kindred spirits. When they are together, they do everything together – work, play, shop, cook, dance, clean, read and laugh. They have a riot watching a movie together! The relationship is rich and filled with special and precious memories. What a joy it is to see the joy they share.

Part of the wonder of our relationship with Jesus is that He wants us to become His friends – to experience all the wonder of what that means. Donna and Paulette enjoy each other. It is a deep, vibrant living relationship. They have been through good times and hard times together. The friendship deepens because they pursue it. That is what God offers us with Him. His mercy and grace are doorways into His presence. There are so many things that He does, while they are blessings in themselves, they are invitations to a deeper relationship with Him. Let us pursue our friendship with Him. He even tells us how to do that!

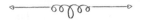

The precious gift of testing!

Proverbs 17:3 The crucible for silver and the furnace for gold,
but the Lord tests the heart.

Where are we? Where are we going? And, how do we get there? Isn't God good to use testing to show us! Has the thought crossed your mind that testing is vital to our destiny and is a priceless blessing? It's a good thing that it is, because there's a limitless supply of testing for each of us!

No matter what situations we find ourselves in, God is in the midst of them working in our lives; revealing who we are and where we are in our walk with Him. Testing highlights our strengths and weaknesses; it shows how far we've come and how far we have to go. It's like a spiritual GPS – it lets us know where we are. Fortunately, the Holy Spirit and God's Word, are the components that give understanding to the 'where we are' piece, but more importantly they are also the components that let us know where we are supposed to be going and how to get there.

Think about that. This process applies to every area and aspect of our lives: our thoughts, habits, idiosyncrasies, mannerisms, attitudes, interactions, etc... God wants to transform every area of our lives to be like Jesus. This applies to absolutely everything about us – without any exceptions. And God uses all circumstances for testing, not just the difficult times.

How do we respond when things are going well? How do we respond to praise and success? Do we have a tendency to become less dependent upon the Lord in such times? Do we walk in humility and grace; or do we become proud of what 'we' have accomplished?

When things become difficult, do we blame or question God? Do we become anxious and stressed out? Do our lives demonstrate that we are genuinely trusting God? Are we kind and considerate no matter what happens?

Fortunately, God works with us in everything. No matter where we find ourselves with regard to any aspect of our lives, He has a redemptive path for us. Do we need to repent – or are we affirmed because we responded righteously to the situation? If we responded well, could we have done better? Do we then glorify Him by properly responding to what the 'testing' has shown us about ourselves?

It's so important that we remember that we are not our own. We belong to Him and He wants us to be demonstrations of His love and grace. Just as the crucible and furnace are used to purify silver and gold, God uses the testing to purity us – so that we might glorify Him.

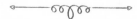

Do we desire recognition?

Matthew 6:1 "Be careful not to do your 'acts of righteousness' before men, to be seen by them. If you do, you will have no reward from your Father in heaven.

President Reagan had this wonderful plaque on his desk: "There is no limit to what a man can do or where he can go if he doesn't mind who gets the credit." The receiving of credit is a very important part of our culture. It's like earning grades in school. We grow up expecting our efforts to be recognized. Early in my sales career I experienced the disappointment of not being recognized. The top salesperson was publically recognized each month, except they forgot to do it the first month I finished on top.

One aspect of this is the negative response most of us have when credit is given to someone where it isn't deserved, i.e., someone has been cheating and then getting recognized for excelling. Or in the workplace, to see someone recognized when someone else was primarily responsible. What do we do if we are the ones who receive credit for that which is done by someone else? Do we speak up and re-direct the credit where it belongs?

More importantly, are the good things we do linked to a desire to receive recognition? Are we at peace with knowing that the Lord knows what we do? Jesus warns us here of the problem of doing the right things we are supposed to do, but with an eye to receiving credit for them – to be seen by men. The issue to me isn't the idea that we lose the reward from our Heavenly Father, but the fact that our motivation is tainted by this desire to have our efforts seen. It is bad for us and displeasing to Him.

The Lord wants our motivations to be centered in the joy of pleasing Him. Living our lives in accord with Scripture and the leading of the Holy Spirit brings the joy of knowing that every action is an expression of our love for God. Instead of the need to 'be seen by men', we live our lives to bring glory and praise to our God. Matthew 5:16 speaks powerfully to this, "In the same way, let your light shine before others, that they may see your good deeds and glorify your Father in heaven." That is the motivation that we want to fill our hearts!

Buffeted by the storms around us

Proverbs 9:10b and knowledge of the Holy One is understanding

Why is this happening? Why did that happen? How could that happen? I don't understand! How often are these expressions in our minds, on our lips and evidence of a storm raging within us? They reflect a cry for understanding – and given our culture, we have developed an inordinate requirement to have understanding. Something has happened or is happening that we don't understand. Frequently, it involves significant difficulties or tragedies that occur.

Currently we have a world filled with a growing amount of strife, wars and disasters. The earthquake and tsunamis that have hit Japan and Southeast Asia; the killing and rebellion that is going on throughout the Middle East and North Africa; Christians and their churches being targeted for extermination; terrorism striking throughout the world – to name a few.

These are on top of the day to day difficulties of losing jobs, unexpected tragedies and dealing with things that the enemy of our souls is so quick to strike us with the question, "How could a god of love allow that?" We find ourselves buffeted by the storms raging around us and the inner difficulties that stem from our inability to understand it, let alone explain it.

This is where knowledge of our God is so critical. The more we know of Him, the more readily we experience the shelter and source of strength that He is to us. The more we know Him, the more embedded within us is the response to turn to Him like a compass pointing 'North'.

The way we increase our knowledge of Him is by walking in His ways. The more we do, the greater is our desire and opportunity to learn of Him and know Him. Because of His Spirit working within us, our knowledge and understanding of Him go through a marvelous transformation as our eyes see more and more of the Glory of who He is and what we have in Him. He gives us peace in the midst of the storms. Jesus referred to this as having our house built upon the Rock!

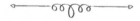

Getting rid of the 'flatness' in our lives

Psalm 95:1-3 Come, let us sing for joy to the LORD; let us shout aloud to the Rock of our salvation. ² Let us come before him with thanksgiving and extol him with music and song. ³ For the LORD is the great God, the great King above all gods.

What reality do these verses have in our lives right now? Do they describe a vibrant inner excitement regarding the relationship we have with our God? Or, are they words that we acknowledge as true, but they are just that – words? Is there a 'flatness' in our experience of reading them that is more like a soda that has been opened and the fizz is gone?

Think of eating a meal where no seasonings have been used in the preparation of the food. The food is bland to the taste, and while still nourishing, the enjoyment of it is not there. With each bite we are thinking that it is not what it could be – or should be. Our lives can become like that.

Are our days 'flat' as well? Are we so caught up in busy-ness that we don't savor or even see the wonder of the blessings we have in our lives. Think of the special ones that you work with or are friends with. Is there closeness with family members? I try to talk to my sons each week. What joy there is in hearing their voices!

Every day I get to see my Donna. I get to hear her voice; see her smile; and feel her touch. Just to be near her is beyond words. The blessing I receive when these devotionals touch those reading them. The thrill never diminishes. Yet all of these things pale in comparison to the daily wonder available to us in the relationship we have with our God. He has given us the Scriptures to reveal Him and to lead us to Him – to daily guide our steps. Finding Jesus is just the start of the adventure!

We get to serve Him with all our heart. He will enable us to weep for joy and gratitude because of His love for us. He draws us to learn to seek His face. He teaches us to love Him with all our heart. We can get so caught up in other things that we lose sight of the fact that loving and worshipping Him is the pinnacle! Out of that will flow everything else. Our hearts will be tender, our spirits will be responsive to Him and our lives will be an obedient walk with Him. Our lives will be filled with the vibrant excitement that comes from knowing Him.

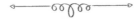

Psalm 23 and attributes of a loving family

Psalm 95:6-7 Come, let us bow down in worship, let us kneel before the LORD our Maker; ⁷ for he is our God and we are the people of his pasture, the flock under his care. Today, if only you would hear his voice,

Isn't it amazing that the God of the Universe considers us His people? Savor the reality that because of Jesus, we belong to Him. When I read these verses, I am so aware of the love and warmth that is in them. This is not talking about a sterile relationship where we are given the edict to 'Bow down!' or 'Worship!' like a dog being told to 'Sit' or 'Heel'. This is family. There is love, purpose, relationship, awe, community, growth, protection, provision, learning, ... It is the Lotto of life and we are winners!!

Think of all the positive attributes that a loving family has and they are here. Reading these verses my mind moves to the 23ʳᵈ Psalm – The Lord is my Shepherd. The attributes spoken in that Psalm describe the reality of being the people of His pasture, the flock under His care.

Recently I received one of those forwarded emails from my brother that included such a wonderful description of Psalm 23. The unkown author wrote the summary description of each phrase. This really brings home what God provides us with:

The Lord is my Shepherd —— that's a Relationship!

I shall not want —— that's Supply!

He maketh me to lie down in green pastures —-that's Rest!

He leadeth me beside the still waters ——that's Refreshment!

He restoreth my soul — that's Healing!

He leadeth me in the paths of righteousness — that's Guidance!

For His name's sake —— that's Purpose!

Yea, though I walk through the valley of the shadow of death –that's Testing!

I will fear no evil —— that's Protection!

For Thou art with me —— that's Faithfulness!

Thy rod and Thy staff comfort me ——that's Discipline!

Thou preparest a table before me in the presence of mine enemies —
that's Hope!

Thou annointest my head with oil ——that's Consecration!

My cup runneth over —— that's Abundance!

Surely goodness and mercy shall follow me all the days of my life —
that's Blessing!
And I will dwell in the house of the Lord —— that's Security!
Forever —— that's Eternity!

Most of all they reflect His love for us. Let me phrase it this way: God so loved the world that He gave us Himself in Jesus to enable us to become His people – His family – His flock – the joyful and grateful recipients of His affection. Praise God that He also gave us the Scriptures, which are His voice telling us how to return the love He has so lavished upon us.

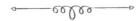

He turned aside to look...

Acts 7:30 "After forty years had passed, an angel appeared to Moses in the flames of a burning bush in the desert near Mount Sinai."

Moses was 40 years old when he fled Egypt to Midian after killing the Egyptian. He was sitting by the well when Jethro's 7 daughters came with their sheep. They had problems with some other shepherds but Moses came to their rescue. Moses later married one of Jethro's daughters and spent another 40 years tending Jethro's flock. And now as he was leading his flock out in the far side of the desert near Horeb, the mountain of God, he encountered the bush that was on fire but did not burn up.

Moses was 80 years old when this happened. Over the years I wonder if Moses ever thought about what might have been. What if he hadn't impulsively killed the Egyptian who had been beating an Israelite? What might he have accomplished with his life? He probably thought that now he would just have a family, tend Jethro's sheep and die in the desert. But God had other plans for this 'young' man.

Moses sees the bush on fire and is intrigued that it isn't burning up. So he decides to go over and see this strange sight. One of the most fascinating and stimulating verses to me in the Bible is involved in this event. It is Exodus 3:4, *"When the LORD saw that he turned aside to look, God called to him from the midst of the bush..."*

Think about it – what might have happened – or not happened – if Moses hadn't turned aside to look. God did something powerful to capture Moses' attention. He inserted this powerful event into the normal daily course of Moses' life – but then Moses had to respond to it – he had to turn aside.

One way of thinking of this event in terms of how it impacts us today, is the expression, "Opportunity knocks." Do we have ears to hear its sound? Do we have eyes to see the 'faith' opportunities that God provides that typically aren't directly in front of us, but they're 'off to the side'. When we see them with the eyes of faith, we are intrigued and we turn aside to see.

Such opportunities might be easily missed and we might have to interrupt our plans to respond. But when we 'turn aside' we encounter God-given opportunities to be used by Him to accomplish things He has planned for us. Afterward, it is not unusual to be thrilled with what happened and to have this thought running through our minds, 'We could have missed this if we hadn't turned aside!'

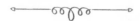

Don Schmidt

The opportunity of hospitality

1 Peter 4:9, 10 Offer hospitality to one another without grumbling. Each one should use whatever gift he has received to serve others, faithfully administering God's grace in its various forms.

There is an old story that has a powerful message about opportunities. An Arab was traveling through the desert at night to escape the daytime heat, guided by the stars. Crossing a deep dry riverbed he heard a voice call out in the night. It said, "Dismount and gather up stones from the bed of the river and go on your way. In the morning you will be both glad and sad."

He did what he was told and gathered up a handful of small stones from the riverbed, and mounting his camel, he continued on his way. At first light he opened the pouch in which he had put the stones and discovered that they were priceless jewels. At first he was ecstatic and then he was sad. He was grateful for what he had gathered but sad that he had not gathered more.

An opportunity had come to him and he had responded by filling one pouch. He could have ignored the voice; or he could have filled several pouches with stones. The blessing he received – or missed – was based on the choice he made. We encounter opportunities all the time. The question is do we have the eyes to see them and the motivation to respond if we do? We can be so caught up in our busyness that we don't recognize or even consider them. All too often, opportunities can appear to us as burdens – a pocketful of stones.

Today's verses describe a way of life that is rich both in blessings and rewards; being a blessing to others and receiving the rewards of administering God's grace. These aren't 'stones' to encumber us, but jewels to enrich us. Offering hospitality and serving others are pathways to building relationships, establishing community and expressing the love of God to one another. They are also marvelous blessings to the recipients. The wonderful thing is that our Lord opens our eyes to see the treasure that these things are while we are doing them. Pray that we will all respond faithfully to the opportunities He sends us each day.

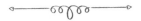

Recognizing reality even in convoluted circumstances

Isaiah 7:14,15 Therefore the Lord himself will give you a sign: The virgin will be with child and will give birth to a son, and will call him Immanuel. [15] He will eat curds and honey when he knows enough to reject the wrong and choose the right.

How do we know what is right or wrong? What is good and what is evil? What is our basis for identifying such things? Such determinations don't happen by accident or just come about naturally. They require us to learn Scripture and learn to respond to the working of the Holy Spirit within us. We become enabled to recognize and discern the truth no matter how convoluted the circumstances.

The world has its own idea about what is good and evil or what is right and wrong. Are there circumstances that make it appropriate to lie? How about situational ethics? Sometimes it seems that the biggest evil to the world is Christians making any kind of judgment that something is evil or wrong. We can become so accustomed to the world's lies that we adopt behaviors that declare the Truth to be the forgery. Isaiah addressed this problem when he wrote:

Woe to those who call evil good and good evil, who put darkness for light and light for darkness, who put bitter for sweet and sweet for bitter. Isaiah 5:20

Some things are so blatantly evil that you can't miss them. But that isn't the general way the enemy of our soul attacks us. He tries to blur the lines and induce Christians to walk in pathways that lead to temptation – that present unrighteousness in attractive packaging. Just think of much of the commercial advertising and TV programming we are exposed to. We become familiar with pathways that have his 'forgeries' presented as the norms of 'good' behavior. His goal is to have us reach a point where we affirm the forgeries and reject the 'original'. Or where we succumb to societal pressures and tolerate his redefined 'acceptable' behaviors in our lives.

If we persist in the path of accurately identifying evil as evil and good as good, the enemy of our souls will try to move us to becoming overtly judgmental of others. That can produce a prideful blindness that is repugnant to God. Remember the Pharisees were so concerned with sin they missed Jesus. But doing this the right way is our destiny and is included in learning to reject the wrong and choose the right. God is our enabler.

The Scriptures are our standard. They identify that 'good and evil' apply to behaviors, thoughts, attitudes – every area of our lives. God wants us to walk in righteousness and it is imperative that we learn from Scripture what it is and isn't, and His requirement to do it the right way. We must recognize that with the Holy Spirit we can accurately reject the wrong and choose the right but it requires focus, intentionality and learning. He expects no less of us.

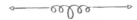

An amazing gift: the ability to forgive

The Scripture is at the end of the devotional

A few years ago I had the joy of watching part of our granddaughter's soccer game. Other than the fact that it was 37 degrees, breezy and raining – it was a great time. I did my grandfatherly duty by taking her younger sister to our van and sat with her in it with the heater on for 10 minutes during the game when her toes got too cold.

Fortunately I had on hiking shoes that are warm, lightweight and waterproof. I was dressed warmly, with a winter hat, gloves and coat and of course my favorite big golf umbrella. While it was still cold and wet out, and my face was getting the brunt of it – I was prepared for it. The 'gear' that I had protected me from the elements.

Does this scenario bring back memories to you? It sure does to me! Times when at outside events the weatherman couldn't have gotten it more wrong – or we failed to take note of updated forecasts and we didn't have the 'gear' we needed to protect ourselves. Whatever, we became wet, cold and miserable. Of course if it was a sporting event and out team won it made it a bit better!

This morning when I got up, the Lord brought to mind one of the greatest gifts that He has given us. It is an absolutely vital component of our spiritual 'gear' that provides incredible protection regardless of the 'inclement' spiritual situations we encounter. Better still, this gift can become such a part of our lives that it automatically kicks in whenever we need it. What is this gift?

It's the ability to forgive! No matter what we encounter; no matter what kind of hurt, disappointment, offense or insult – our ability and practice to immediately forgive provides a priceless protection to our lives. It frees us to respond righteously to whatever circumstances we find ourselves in.

Unforgiveness has been described as putting arsenic in your own body with the intent to get even with someone else. It's imperative that we recognize just how vital forgiveness is to our spiritual well-being. It keeps us dry, warm and healthy no matter what kind of inclement spiritual storms we encounter. Let us renew our commitment to this truth Jesus taught us that describes how we are to live – Luke 11:4:

"And forgive us our sins, for we ourselves also forgive everyone who is indebted to us [who has offended us or done us wrong]. And bring us not into temptation but rescue us from evil." Amplified

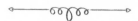

We are the 'coffee shop'

Romans 15:13 May the God of hope fill you with all joy and peace as you trust in him, so that you may overflow with hope by the power of the Holy Spirit.

Imagine going into a coffee shop to have a cup of coffee and being told that they were all out of coffee. – not just a particular flavor we wanted – but out of coffee. That would be strange if it happened once but suppose it happened again and it wasn't because they were so popular that they sold out. We'd suspect they wouldn't be in business long. Coffee shops are supposed to have coffee.

Now imagine going into a coffee shop and ordering coffee and they serve you but the coffee doesn't taste good. We try different choices they have, but they all were unpleasant. Again, we'd think it strange and wonder how they were going to stay in business. We wouldn't go back.

With these examples in mind, let's consider today's verse. There is such beauty contained in it. It talks of God's people trusting in Him and being filled with joy and peace and hope. These are qualities that people long for and are very apparent when they're present. From one perspective, we as Christians have the blessing and excitement of recognizing that this is the life God has for us. These are qualities that He wants us to have. But there is another side to this coin.

These are qualities that He expects us to develop in Him. They are required of us and not optional. We are the 'coffee shop' and theses qualities are the 'coffee'. The world and those around us might not realize that they are asking for 'coffee' when they encounter us, but God has placed within them a hunger for this 'coffee' - real joy, real peace and real hope. They want someone or something they can truly trust in.

We are surrounded by people in all stages of coming to know our God. If these qualities are absent in us, or if they are 'sour', important opportunities are missed and negative perceptions result. But, when people are able to 'taste' these qualities in our lives, they are attracted to Him even though they might not know it (think salt making someone thirsty). They want more. God uses us to bring people to Himself.

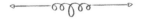

The wonder of our God

Psalm17:7a ...the wonder of Your love....

Let's think about some things that produce a sense of wonder within us. In the spring I am so blessed by seeing everything begin to bloom after the winter season. The redbuds and dogwood trees never cease to strike me with their beauty and color. I love seeing the woods take on the hint of green with the coming of the first leaves.

One cannot escape a sense of wonder at the mountains. Their size, beauty and majesty are awe inspiring. One of my favorite memories is of salmon fishing with my dear friend Jon out in Seattle. We were in the boat fishing before dawn on a clear morning. In the midst of the darkness, we beheld the sight of the first rays of dawn reflecting off the snow capped peak of Mt Rainier. It was absolutely breathtaking and its wonder caused us to sit and behold the dawning of the morning light.

The ocean and the seashore are particularly special to Donna and me. One of the great joys of my life is to walk along the seashore listening to the surf – enjoying the sights, sounds and smells. We both love to be in a hammock, on an ocean-front cottage porch, listening to the sounds and feeling the breeze as we read or simply rest.

It's not just that these things are pleasant or enjoyable – but there is a sense of wonder within us that is present even just thinking about them. And as great as all these things are, they pale in comparison to the wonder we experience over the love of our God for us. It is a tangible sensation within us that produces such joy.

The wonder of our God is far beyond the simple fact that He made the things that bless us so. He has shown us – and repeatedly shows us – His great love for us. That is the stunner! The God who made everything – the entire universe – loves us and makes Himself known to us! Through Jesus, we are His family and dear to Him. He enables us to experience the exquisite pleasure of Him becoming dear to us each and every day of our lives. Oh, the wonder of it all!

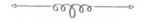

Don Schmidt

The Pet-factor

Galatians 5:22, 23 But the fruit of the Spirit is love, joy, peace, patience, kindness, goodness, faithfulness, ²³gentleness and self-control. Against such things there is no law.

Have you ever considered the thought that we Christians should always be the best friends that anyone could possibly have? We should be the best spouses; the best family members; the best workers; the best bosses; the best neighbors; the best strangers.

Taking this one step further, is the thought that anything less than that is missing our destiny of who God intends us as Christians to be. Paul, in writing to the Corinthians describes the reality of what are lives are and are to be, "You show that you are a letter from Christ, the result of our ministry, written not with ink but with the Spirit of the living God, not on tablets of stone but on tablets of human hearts."

Our lives, like letters, are read by all the people we encounter, only the messages we communicate are far beyond just words. Think of how differently we respond to encountering a neighbor's pet that is always friendly versus encountering one that is grumpy or one that can be friendly but will also snap at you. With the second one, we stay away; with the third one our guard is up. We don't want to be snapped at.

Applying the 'pet-factor' to our lives, ask the question, "What are we like?" Are we grumpy? Do we have a tendency to 'snap' unpredictably? Do we have a tendency to be undependable or worse, to be jerks? Or are we consistently someone that people enjoy being around because we reflect the qualities of our faith identified in today's Scripture? If asked to describe us (in an anonymous and candid survey) there wouldn't be a 'but' in their description.

It's critical that we recognize that our lives are about so much more than us. We are an intimate part of God's plan to reach and transform the world. How we lead our daily lives has a profound impact on what our lives communicate. <u>Our destiny, corporately and individually, is to be a love letter from Jesus Christ to those around us.</u> So what are they reading when they encounter us?

Think 'burning bush', the fire that doesn't consume

1 Corinthians 8:3 But the man who loves God is known by God.

When I read this verse I think of Moses and the burning bush. The bush was on fire but it didn't burn up. It caught Moses' attention and in the midst of shepherding his sheep, he turned aside to see this strange sight. Once God saw that he had turned aside to look, He called to Moses from within the bush.

Moses responded and encountered God in a stunning way. It strikes me that in today's verse, *'the man who loves God'* is the bush and *'is known by God'* is the burning part – the fire that doesn't consume. This verse is there, like a bush on fire, that doesn't burn up, with God waiting to see who will be attracted and turn aside.

There are other verses that have this same feature – this same element of mystery and attraction. They are there - waiting – to see if they will cause us to 'turn aside'. James 4:8a says, *"Come near to God and he will come near to you."* Stop and think about that. God is everywhere. He's omnipresent. As Christians He lives within us. So what is He talking about when He says if we come near to Him, He will come near to us? Could He be talking about something more intimate?

Then in John 14: 21b Jesus says, *"The one who loves me will be loved by my Father, and I too will love him and show myself to him."* This verse is explosive! The one who loves Jesus will be loved by His Father! But, doesn't God already love us? Isn't that why He sent Jesus? Is it possible that somehow, when it comes to the love of God, there is a whole lot more we can experience?

The Amplified Bible states the last clause of John 14:21 this way, *"...and I [too] will love him and will show (reveal, manifest) Myself to him. [I will let Myself be clearly seen by him and make Myself real to him.]"* WOW!!! This shouts that there is unspeakable treasure waiting for those who love God! Not in terms of things, but in terms of relationship and intimacy with our Lord God. All of this is there waiting for the ones who love Him.

These experiences are reserved for those who truly pursue loving God. It's almost like God saying that when we first come to Him, as marvelous as our experiences might be, it's only the 'tip of the iceberg'. There is so much more of Him that only the ones who love Him will get to experience. The choice is ours.

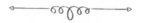

Becoming a nation in a day

Isaiah 66:8 Who has ever heard of such things? Who has ever seen things like this? Can a country be born in a day or a nation be brought forth in a moment?

Monday May 14 2018 was the 70th anniversary of Israel becoming a nation again – in a single day, just as the prophet foretold. What an amazing thing! It's even more stunning when we consider that the descendants of Abraham, Isaac and Jacob had been a people without a homeland since Bible times.

God had promised this land to the descendants of Abraham, Isaac and Jacob forever: *"The whole land of Canaan, where you now reside as a foreigner, I will give as an everlasting possession to you and your descendants after you; and I will be their God."* Genesis 17:8 I remember back in the early 70s seeing a marvelous movie titled His Land; put out by Billy Graham. Golda Meir, the then Prime Minister of Israel said she had never seen her land look so beautiful.

While I don't begin to understand everything God is doing today with Israel, there is no doubt whatsoever in my mind that He is the one who brought them back; that the current Israel is at the center of what He is doing in the Middle East. Unfortunately, Israel is surrounded by those who want to see her destroyed. To listen to the World's media and her enemies in the Middle East and around the world, one could easily conclude that the world would be better off if only Israel were gone.

We must remember that the Jewish people are the people of the Patriarchs, the Prophets and our Lord Jesus. They are the people of the Bible and it behooves us to pray for them. In Psalm 22:6 we are instructed to *"Pray for the peace of Jerusalem: May those who love you be secure."*

We must pray that God will protect Israel and bring them to Himself. Pray that He will undermine and thwart the plans of Israel's enemies to do her harm. Pray that those who have come to know their Messiah in Israel will have grace and favor to share this wonderful truth with their fellow citizens. Israel belongs to the Lord and we want to see them come to recognize that Jesus (Yeshua) is their Messiah.

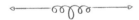

Hiking provides a helpful illustration

James 1:2 Consider it pure joy, my brothers and sisters,
whenever you face trials of many kinds,

The house we lived in Tennessee backed up to a school yard that had a ½ mile walking path. I would typically walk it at a very brisk pace. In one corner the path has a slight incline in it. Walking at a leisurely pace it might not be noticed, but at the rate I was going it was noticeable.

There are other places to walk that go across hilly terrain that are a bit more taxing. At the far end of the spectrum are paths or trails in the mountains that are very rigorous. In Colorado a very popular trail is the Pike's Peak Incline – a railroad tie stairway up the mountain. A friend of ours, has taken groups to Nepal to climb to the Mt. Everest Base Camp that is at about 17,590 feet. It takes about 2 weeks to hike there and back. It's not only a rigorous climb but because of the height, there is altitude sickness to contend with.

When considering today's verse, using the illustrations of hiking, many of us only think of it in terms of big or rigorous trials – like encountering mountains. We tend to perceive it as being instructed to have joy when we encounter mountains to climb – not the little hills or inclines. But that severely limits this verse and our accountability to this command.

Again, thinking in terms of hiking terrain, the 'trials of many kinds' in today's verse applies to everything from 'a slight incline' to going to the Base Camp'. No matter how small the 'incline or hill' we are to have joy.

Maybe the word 'trial' throws us. Consider some words used in other translations instead of the word trials: temptations; tests; challenges; troubles. Think of all the 'little' things that occur everyday we encounter and we have to deal with. The little 'tests'; the little 'troubles'; the many temptations to respond in situations unrighteously – these are the heart of this verse. These are the places where our joy is to be evident. Do we respond with joy – or with annoyance, frustration or anger? These are the places that prepare us for the 'big' trials.

In looking at other versions of today's verse, two in particular really stood our. Please consider these as you go through your day:

- *Consider it a sheer gift, friends, when tests and challenges come at you from all sides.* The Message

- *Dear brothers and sisters, when troubles come your way, consider it an opportunity for great joy.* New Living Translation

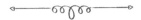

Opportunities calling us out of our comfort zone

Matthew 14:28 "Lord, if it's you," Peter replied,
"tell me to come to you on the water."

Have you ever dreamed of what it would be like to be in the boat with the disciples when Jesus walked on the water? How would we have responded to seeing Him? Remember it was a very windy night and the disciples were struggling to survive let alone get across the lake. In the midst of it, they saw a figure walking on the water that was about to pass them by and were terrified. They thought it was a ghost. But then Jesus spoke to them saying, *"Take courage! It is I. Don't be afraid."*

Even then they weren't sure it was Jesus as indicated by Peter's response, *"Lord if it's you…"* Isn't it amazing that Jesus chose a stormy night – and not a calm one for this encounter. (Note: God does the same thing with us.) Imagine Peter's excitement when he heard (above the sound of the wind and waves) the Lord say "Come".

I wonder what went through Peter's mind. Did he simply want to be with Jesus? Or was it more, "I'd sure like to do that!" Whatever, Peter didn't allow the risk involved to stop him. Picture him trying to hang on to a bouncing boat as he got his legs over the side and then began to walk. Peter experienced an incredible wonder - before he began to sink. Remember the water wasn't flat or calm but was wind-swept waves. Peter did walk on the water and came toward Jesus.

Then his focus shifted from Jesus and the wonder of what he was doing, to the adverse conditions around him. Although he did succumb to fear and begin to sink, Jesus was right there to rescue him. Peter experienced the miraculous because he responded to the opportunity that Jesus gave him. He didn't allow fear to keep him in the security of the boat.

God uses the same principle in His dealings with us. In the midst of our often difficult circumstances, He will give us opportunities to respond to Him. We have to have 'eyes' to see the opportunities and the willingness to respond. In spite of the safety of the 'boat' - our lifestyle and circumstances that we are comfortable with - will we overcome our fear and the risk involved to respond to the Lord bidding us to come? It's amazing the wonders He has for us to experience if only we will respond to Him.

Note: One of my favorite authors is John Ortberg. He has a wonderful book on this very subject that I highly recommend titled, <u>If You Want to Walk on Water You've Got to Get Out of the Boat.</u>

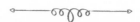

      Don Schmidt

The blessings available in testing

Matthew 6:13a "And lead us not into temptation,..."

Years ago I heard a Bible teacher give a very illuminating paraphrase of this verse: "Lord, let there not be anything in my heart that would cause you to put me to the test." We know from Scripture that God doesn't tempt anyone. (James 1:13) But God will allow situations to arise that will reveal what is within us.

I think of King Hezekiah in 2 Chronicles 32:31 – *"But when envoys were sent by the rulers of Babylon to ask him about the miraculous sign that had occurred in the land, God left him to test him and to know everything that was in his heart."* The same Bible teacher explained that the way God leaves us is to withdraw our conscious awareness of His presence. We think we're alone, but we're not.

God uses these experiences in our lives for our benefit – not as 'Gotcha!' moments. They are God's gifts to us that allow us to show ourselves strong in His behalf; or to have faults within us revealed that we then can deal with. If we have 'termites' or are building our 'house' upon sand rather than rock (Matthew 7:24-27), isn't it critical that we find out and repent?!

Sometimes the situations we encounter reveal our unbelief or lack of faith. When we see our deficiencies, they are not putdowns - but are revelations that enable us to change for the better. The Holy Spirit is working within us to conform us to the image of Christ in every area of our lives. The opportunity to repent is such a gift from God!

God wants and expects excellence from us in every area of our lives. If we think we are only capable of mediocrity, we will be content with mediocrity. But with the Holy Spirit we are not only capable of excellence; we are held accountable for it as well. Not in a judgmental way, but as recipients of the greatest gifts ever given: the new birth and the Holy Spirit. This news isn't meant to intimidate us but exhilarate us!

God is working incessantly within us to enable us to become a glory to Him. He is the Master Craftsman. When people see us (the work of His hands), His intent is for them to recognize His craftsmanship. They will see Him in us; and experience Him when interacting with us! We are an intimate part of the process so let's embrace it with the passion it deserves.

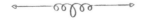

Missing the obvious - big-time!

Luke 6:37 "Do not judge, and you will not be judged. Do not condemn, and you will not be condemned. Forgive, and you will be forgiven."

A few weeks ago I wrote about my adventures with my 'difficult to start' weed whacker. I wrote about it in the context of recognizing the many trials we face on a daily basis and responding appropriately in a faith-filled manner.

Well - I had a new adventure with this delightful little contraption and am still laughing over it as I write. The machine works fine once it is running. The problem is getting it started and today I set the record for futility!

I was thinking of my earlier devotional as I got it out after mowing the lawn. I confess that when I earlier wrote of having to pull the starter cord about 100 times, it was a bit of an exaggeration. Today I was thinking about how it would start faster than ever. I pushed the priming bubble and started pulling. Because I thought it would start quickly, I was counting my pulls.

Well, nothing was working! 6, 12...30...48...60...72...78 pulls plus adjustment - not a hint of response. In the midst of this, I'm praying; asking the Lord for wisdom; asking Him to 'heal' the machine. I'm kneeling next to it in the heat, sweating from mowing the lawn, my arm was ready to drop and I'm laughing at this goofy machine and the difficulty I'm having getting it going. All the while talking to the Lord, trying to understand what is going on.

Then I saw it! - and could hardly believe it. It was right in front of me. If the Lord had chosen to speak audibly to me, He would have said something like, "Son - You have to turn it on first." Well, I turned the switch on and in 3 pulls it started!

In my elation (and feeling a bit dumber than dirt for missing the off/on switch) I thought this is my next devotional. The lesson in this just jumped out at me. First things must come first. Similar to "If...then" propositions. If this happens - then that can happen. God gives us all manner of instructions that must be obeyed in order to produce Godly results. How often do we skip something that needs to be done first and then wonder why the results of subsequent actions are less than desirable?

Think of forgiving, apologizing, acknowledging we've made a mistake, asking for forgiveness...to name a few. These are all actions that are critical to relationships and our growth. Failure to do these things when incidents happen radically affects the outcomes and the quality of our relationships. It's like trying to start a weed whacker without turning the switch on!

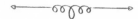

The example of my boss, Mike

*Nehemiah 1:5 Then I said: "O LORD, God of heaven, the great
and awesome God, who keeps his covenant of love with those
who love him and obey his commands,"*

There is a scene in the movie Fantasia called Night on Bald Mountain. It is a scene where the mountain top becomes the god of evil; one of Disney's most powerful and terrifying villains. In the middle of the night he unfolds his wings and the whole mountain top becomes this evil being. He terrorizes his minions and is frightening to behold. But the coming of the dawn, forces him to withdraw and conceal himself once again.

I find this representation to be the antithesis of our 'great and awesome God'. Yes we read in Exodus 19 where God came down on Mt. Sinai with thunder, lightning, billowing smoke and the whole mountain trembled violently. And I truly believe that the fear of the Lord includes elements of this Mt. Sinai reality. But Nehemiah's prayer in addressing the LORD, refers to his covenant of love with those who love him and obey his commands. Daniel addresses the LORD in the very same way in his prayer (Daniel 9:4).

While we must come to grips with the serious reality of our God, our focus is upon the amazing love relationship that He has established with us. We are not minions, but sons and daughters. He does not terrorize us, but He is totally for us and works in us to be totally for Him. We are able to daily experience His love for us and express our love to Him.

The experiences I had with my last boss at Medical Mutual provide a really helpful perspective in understanding my daily relationship with God. I remember Mike's first meeting with our unit in Cleveland. He was very pleasant, but he let it be known that if something was of unethical or illegal or even close to it, he didn't want us even thinking of doing such things. He went on to describe the working relationship that he wanted us to have – which was wonderful.

He was a joy to work with and for; but he was no one to mess with. The more I got to know him the more thrilled I was. He cared about what we thought - and more than that he cared about us. Mike was a wonderful Christian man. Importantly, he lived his faith in all his actions and attitudes with us at work. He was a picture of integrity and doing the right thing.

I worked with and for Mike for the next 3½ years. Never, in all my years of working had I worked for a more wonderful, caring, competent person. He was there for us whenever we needed him. The practical outcome of this was both functional and relational. I was able to excel in doing my job – it was both my opportunity and responsibility. I also relished the relationship with my superior (boss) and how it was able to thrive as I responded consistently with his (appropriate) expectations. He relished my success.

Day by day, our Heavenly Father wants us to experience the joyful reality that comes with being His child **and** living our lives for Him. We get to experience and live out His covenant of love in all the situations we find ourselves in. It's easy to understand why He cares so about what we do: our actions have such impact on our relationship with Him – and that's what He treasures most of all. It is a covenant of love.

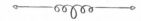

Is telling the truth optional?

Acts 5:8-9 Peter asked her, "Tell me, is this the price you and Ananias got for the land?" "Yes," she said, "that is the price."⁹ Peter said to her, "How could you agree to test the Spirit of the Lord? Look! The feet of the men who buried your husband are at the door, and they will carry you out also."

Picture this situation: A little kid has been told to stay out of the cookies. He comes into the room and his mother asks him, "Did you get into the cookies?" With jam and crumbs all over his mouth, he says, "No I didn't." It is both funny and serious. Funny, in that the little kid doesn't realize the truth is evident on his face; and serious in that he knows he did something wrong and is trying to cover it up.

Unfortunately, if the lying isn't dealt with, it will lead to him learning to wipe the jam and crumbs off his mouth before he leaves the cookies. It becomes 'easier' to hide his lying. As he grows older the questions become more serious: Where are you going? Where have you been? Have you done your homework? Did you cheat? Where did this come from? What time did you get home? Are you doing drugs? Were you drinking? What websites are you visiting? – and the list goes on.

The news these days seems to be filled with situations where people are found out to be lying. It's almost as though telling the truth is something foreign. People do things they know they shouldn't and then lie to cover it up. It becomes a way of life. Where it really hurts is when individuals who have proclaimed their faith in Christ are found guilty of it.

Ananias and his wife Sapphira sold property to give the proceeds to the church. But instead of giving all the proceeds, they withheld some and represented their gift as being the entire amount. It cost both of them their lives! They died when confronted by the truth. Scripture says that "great fear seized the whole church and all who heard about these events."

Suppose at any time, in any situation, someone we know or someone in authority might ask us a similarly pointed question regarding actions we have taken or words we have said. Further suppose that a false answer on our part could cost us our lives. Is there anything in our lives that comes to mind that must be dealt with? Lies and untruth cannot be a part of our lives. If they are, repent; seek the Lord and get help from mature believers. Remember, God's view of such things hasn't changed from the days of Ananias and Sapphira. We must be lovers of the truth!

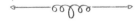

What comprises our 'Heavenly GPS'?

Isaiah 7:15 He will eat curds and honey when he knows enough to reject the wrong and choose the right.

I grew up in southwest Michigan. I remember hearing my older hunting friends talking about the compass problems they encountered in parts of the Upper Peninsula due to the presence of iron ore. The ore can cause the magnetic needle of a compass to spin crazily or to point the opposite to where it should. That's not good to be in the middle of the boondocks, relying on your compass for directions and to have it go haywire.

Other things can help when our compass can't identify true north. If the sky is clear and the sun is setting or rising, general directions can be figured out. But how do we determine direction in the middle of the day, with clouds, rain or fog; or finding ourselves in the middle of deep woods (and we don't have a GPS)?

There are a number of major scandals that are unfolding in the news right now where it seems a whole lot of people got 'lost in the woods' due to malfunctioning moral compasses – assuming they had them. I wonder how many of those involved are Christians – or 'church goers'?

Maybe their jobs were threatened if they didn't 'go along'. Maybe more significant threats were involved – or maybe none at all! Maybe their moral compasses were so inadequate that they didn't recognize that 'wrong' was being substituted for 'right'. Or they simply accepted the perceived reality that they didn't have a choice, but to go along.

It's not an issue of being judgmental but one of learning what could happen to us when we find ourselves in similarly tempted. How do we know right from wrong? How well will we do in the 'fog and rain' of similar circumstances that might threaten us? Will our moral compass be immune to the cultural 'iron ore' around us, that will try to misdirect us? Will we choose the right? Or if we choose the wrong, will we justify our actions because of the consequences of not going along?

In any circumstances we as Christians find ourselves in, we have a 'Heavenly GPS' to guide us. It not only tells us where we are (a compass can't do that); it also tells us where to go; but we must be attentive! The assets of our Heavenly GPS include: 1) We are new creatures in Christ Jesus, freed from the tendency to sin, 2) We have the Holy Spirit within us, 3) We have the Scriptures, 4) We have God's grace to enable us, and 5) The faith in God to trust and believe.

These resources enable us to choose righteously no matter what we face. The Holy Spirit is with us, to guide our decision making process as we go step by step through any trial. He enables us to choose the right - no matter what the cost. The choice is simply ours. Choosing the wrong must never be perceived as a tenable option. Our goal is to live for Christ and to always honor Him.

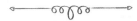

Imagine the excitement!

Scripture is at the end

Imagine living 2000 years ago in the Middle East in the land of Judea; specifically in a region called Galilee. There are no hospitals, no pharmacies, no vaccinations, no antibiotics and very little medical care of any kind. Injuries and illnesses that today are no big deal were life changing or deadly back then.

Our neighborhoods and families would likely have individuals who were crippled or sick with conditions that greatly affected their daily lives and the lives of those around them. Chances are that some of us would be among those with such conditions, with no hope of them ever improving.

Into this mix comes word of a Nazarene carpenter named Jesus who is doing unbelievable things. He's going around doing miracles! Cripples are being made whole, deaf are now able to hear, the blind are receiving their sight, the sick are no longer sick, lepers are being healed, demon-possessed are set free and there are even cases where the dead are brought back to life! On top of that - we have seen individuals whom we know personally who experienced miraculous healings and restorations through this Jesus!.

Yes he is teaching about God, but teachers have always been a part of Jewish life. Although people say he is teaching like no one they've ever heard. No one has ever done what he is doing – and it's not just isolated cases here or there. He is healing everyone who comes to him!!!! Multitudes are flocking to him.

Can we imagine the excitement? Do we think that we'd be sitting around, discussing whether we were going to go see this Jesus - or not? Rather, doesn't it seem likely that we would be beyond excited; doing everything we could to gather all our sick and crippled family and friends - helping them to get to him? Jesus was so much more that a 'great teacher' – there has never been anyone like him. Here is Matthew's description of the above scenario that we have been imagining together (4:23-24):

23 Jesus went throughout Galilee, teaching in their synagogues, preaching the good news of the kingdom, and healing every disease and sickness among the people. 24 News about him spread all over Syria, and people brought to him all who were ill with various diseases, those suffering severe pain, the demon-possessed, those having seizures, and the paralyzed, and he healed them.

He was AND IS the Christ – the Son of the living God! He is our Savior and Lord!

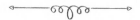

Do your 'checks' bounce?

James 1:22 Do not merely listen to the word, and so deceive yourselves.
Do what it says.

Year ago, back when I was surviving as an insurance salesman, I made a significant sale to a small business twice – at least I thought I had. I remember how excited I was because at the time it was my biggest sale – which meant it was also my biggest commission. You can imagine my disappointment when their payment check bounced! I went back to see them again. They apologized; gave me another check and it bounced too. I never did complete a sale with them.

Prior to that as a salesman I would say I knew I had a sale when they gave me a check. That saying was forever changed in my mind to I knew I had a sale when the check cleared. The check was a promise of something real. It is the money in the bank that gave value to the check. If there isn't adequate money in the bank, the check bounces.

One of the problems that has always confronted Christians is having their lives back up what they say when they verbalize the Gospel. Words are a whole lot easier to express than the Godly lives that give the words credibility. There's an old expression that describes this "Talking the talk and walking the walk". There is such power when the testimony of following Jesus is backed up by lives that reflect His glory.

Putting this in the context of my sales experience, the Godly reality of our lives is the money in the bank that gives value to the check – the testimony we give about Jesus and our faith. If we have inadequate reality of Him in our lives – the check bounces. This isn't about walking in perfection but about there being ample evidence of us being a Godly work in progress.

Being a doer of the Word affects everything in our lives – our thoughts, attitudes, words, actions, responses, beliefs – our hopes, our fears – everything. This impacts what we say; how we say it and how we are perceived. There is such joy and confidence that come with being a doer of the Word – having lives that truly give witness to the Lord we serve. Remember, <u>this is something we get to do</u>!

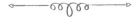

How to respond when these happen to you?

Psalm 9:1, 2 I will praise you, O LORD, with all my heart; I will tell of all your wonders. ²I will be glad and rejoice in you; I will sing praise to your name, O Most High.

Think of what you experience if you are overwhelmed with tasks to do and some of your friends show up unexpectedly because they've come to help you get it all done. Think of what you experience if your vehicle is broken down in the middle of nowhere – and you have no cell phone – and someone pulls up and is able to fix your car and sends you on your way.

Suppose you are in ministry, 'living on faith' and you have no money or food – and someone arrives with groceries because the Lord put you on their heart. Suppose everything in your life seems to be going wrong and you can't figure out what is going on. And in the midst of it, God gives you understanding of it all.

Suppose you are struggling with disappointment and discouragement and a friend calls to encourage you because you were on their heart and they were concerned. And, when they pray for you, their prayer precisely addresses the things you're struggling with.

In all of these experiences we would experience gratitude and joy – relief and exhilaration. We would likely find ourselves deeply moved as well – possibly overcome with the wonder of our God and His goodness to us.

Now take all of the positive responses to the situations above and imagine God using them to create a 'spiritual' artesian spring within us – a never-ending source of wonder and gratitude for Him. When I read these verses, their reality – a vibrant, passionate description of the wonder of our God – is there within me; enveloping me.

No matter what we are going through, He wants our bedrock reality to be centered in the passionate wonder and gratitude for who He is. That is what He has created within me – and He will do it for you.

PS – All of the situations written above have happened to Donna and me.

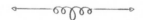

Remembering the positives

Exodus 20:12 "Honor your father and your mother, so that you may live long in the land the LORD your God is giving you."

If my parents were still alive they would be approaching their 90th anniversary. Oscar Schmidt and Louise Diamond were married just before the start of her senior year in high school. She was 17 years old. My father promised her father that she would graduate from high school, which she did. They were married 63 years when my father went to be with Jesus. Mom joined him about 10 years later.

They weren't perfect people and had their share of faults. But they also had many important qualities. One of the difficulties in life is our tendency to focus on the negatives in relationships rather than the positives. But love overlooks the faults and the failings. It's not that they aren't dealt with; it's just that they can become overblown in our minds and we lose sight of the treasure that is there.

Although my dad and I argued all the time when together, when we were apart (my going to college) we seemed to get along much better. Then he had a powerful experience with the Lord at a prayer retreat in Michigan in the fall of 1967. It really transformed my dad. A year later they invited me to join them at this same retreat. I really didn't want to go, but nothing was going on at college and it came down to not wanting to disappoint them because I knew my coming was important to them. It was there that I encountered the Lord in a way beyond anything I could imagine!

As their faith grew, Mom's friends nicknamed her Andrew, because she was forever telling someone about Jesus. She and Dad made quite a pair. They became prayer warriors (intercessors). I'm sure it was through their prayers that my brother (Richard), sister (Judy) and I received many blessings.

All of us are somebody's kids – and most of us are parents. Take some time over the next few days to focus on the positives in your relationships with your parents and your children. Look past the negatives and hard places. Allow the Lord to increase your appreciation for the positives that are there and to have wisdom in how to pray so that the relationships will be strengthened. Appreciate those you have while they are still here.

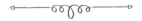

What are we building?

Isaiah 31:1 Woe to those who go down to Egypt for help, who rely on horses, who trust in the multitude of their chariots and in the great strength of their horsemen, but do not look to the Holy One of Israel, or seek help from the LORD.

Once upon a time there were 3 little pigs. One built his home out of straw. The second built his home out of sticks, while the third built his out of bricks. The wolf comes upon each of the pigs in their homes with the result that straw and sticks are no match for his "huffing and puffing". Their houses get blown down and they suffer the consequences. But the wolf was no match for the third little pig with the brick home. Not only did it withstand his "huffing and puffing", but this little pig outwits the wolf resulting in the end of the wolf. He also wasn't shaking with fear at the wolf at the door. He actively countered whatever the wolf tried.

Right now there is a whole lot of "huffing and puffing" going on all around us. So many things seem to be taking on a threatening nature. How are we responding to it? Is our 'house' beginning to shake and come apart? Do we find ourselves awake at night consumed with fear – because of the 'wolf' at the door? Where do we turn for help and assurance? Where do we place our trust?

The Israelites were tempted to go down to Egypt for help because they had horses and chariots and horsemen for hire - in spite of God's warning not to. With the threat of enemy armies approaching, it seemed reasonable to want something that can be seen versus trusting what isn't seen. But it's where do we place our faith? It's tempting to succumb to the worldly wisdom that faith is nice but we need something that we can get our hands on. If we're going to be in a 'war', we need an army; we need to be able to defend ourselves.

Fortunately, God is calling us, if we only have ears to hear and eyes to see. We are to look to Him, the Holy One of Israel, to seek help from the LORD. Even if we've built our lives out of 'straw' or 'sticks', it is never too late to turn to Him. He not only will be there for us, He will likely lead us to those who have built their lives with 'bricks' so that we might learn of His ways from them. He will use them to help us to stand securely in the circumstances we face. God loves to overcome the 'wolves' in our lives when we truly turn to Him.

Tomorrow we will talk about the relationship of the bricks and the Rock.

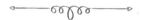

Don Schmidt

Building with bricks upon the rock

Matthew 7:24 "Therefore everyone who hears these words of mine and puts them into practice is like a wise man who built his house on the rock."

In my NIV Bible, the heading for this portion of Scripture is "The Wise and Foolish Builders". How we respond to the words of Jesus determines the foundation of the house we build. It's a major league choice that we have because the alternatives are rock or sand. The structures built upon rock survive the storms and floods while those built upon sand don't.

Yesterday I used the Three Little Pigs children's story as an illustration of foolish choices and misplaced trust. The first two little pigs were more interested in playing than working and took the shortcuts that enabled them to play. They didn't consider the consequences of their decisions until it was too late. In terms of today's Scripture, they were the foolish builders. Their homes built of straw or sticks are the equivalent of building them upon the sand.

The third little pig built correctly. He was the wise builder and his home of bricks is the equivalent of building upon a rock foundation. It not only withstands the storm and wind (huffing and puffing), but it withstands the floods as well. When the foundation of a house goes – the house goes with it. The issue is to be able to withstand whatever comes.

Such a simple story yet it's significance is profound: doing things the right way leads to good results, while doing them the wrong way leads to catastrophic results. The obvious question then is how do we determine what the right way is? Or more accurately, what are the right ways?

Every area of life is affected: how we live, work, raise our children, relate to others, treat our spouse, respond to our parents – to authority, to responsibility – it goes on and on. There are so many 'voices' saying, "This is the way." – and so many of them lead to building upon sand – houses of straw or sticks.

How do we recognize the wise from the foolish? Jesus makes it clear that the answer is hearing His words AND putting them into practice. His words aren't suggestions where we can pick and choose. Nor do we have the option of not becoming familiar with what they are. Our lives are to embrace them. We are to become so a part of them that they are engraved upon our lives. Let us set our hearts upon becoming wise builders so that every area of our lives will glorify our Lord.

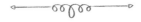

The lesson of a Southern Magnolia tree

Psalm 119:130 The unfolding of your words gives light; it gives understanding to the simple.

An interesting insight occurred to me recently. It connects the Old Testament to Southern Magnolia trees. In this insight, the attributes of the tree are reflective of the view that a person has of the Old Testament. I realize that many of you might not be aware of what a Southern Magnolia looks like, but we'll get to that.

If the Old Testament is something that we don't read much, except for some of the Psalms or Proverbs, than the tree that is reflected by our actions is very small with few flowers on it – if any. We have a misperception of what it is and what the Lord has there for us. But here is where the other side of the coin comes in to play. What is the true reality of what Southern Magnolia are?

I thought they were at most trees that could grow to 20'-25' high and I had never seen one loaded with flowers. I still remember how stunned I was to see how big these trees can be and to see them in full bloom! They can grow to 80'– 90' tall. In the spring and early summer they are covered with huge flowers that can be over a foot in diameter. The beauty of these flowers is amazing and their fragrance is so special. I never cease to be amazed by seeing the buds grow and turn white and then open into such spectacular flowers. The Old Testament and what God has there for us is even more stunning!

The Old Testament is not a small flowerless tree. It is a very large tree, filled with flowers that are open and buds that are about to be. The Lord is beckoning us to come and look for them. It is a treasure to be studied just as the New Testament is. Once we recognize what the Lord has for us there, we spend more time in it – and our perception and appreciation for it grows.

The insights that the Lord gives us are like the flowers that open on the Southern Magnolia. We can be reading a passage of Scripture and the Lord just unfolds an amazing truth or insight to us, just like the Magnolia blossom opening. I think of time-lapse photography that shows in seconds what might take hours or days to happen. We are captured by the beauty and blessing of what we are seeing.

I was so blessed when we lived in Tennessee because these trees were everywhere. Thinking of them, I am reminded of all the treasure the Lord has in the Old Testament that He wants to bless us with. Every time we see things in His Word, it is just another magnificent, fragrant flower opening up on this magnificent 'tree'.

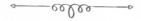

Don Schmidt

Which image comes to mind when you think of Him?

Mark 14:61-62 But Jesus remained silent and gave no answer. Again the high priest asked him, "Are you the Messiah, the Son of the Blessed One?" ⁶² "I am," said Jesus. "And you will see the Son of Man sitting at the right hand of the Mighty One and coming on the clouds of heaven."

When we think of Jesus, what images come to mind? Depending upon the time of year we might think of the baby of Bethlehem or Jesus upon the Cross. Possibly we think of Jesus upon a mountain side teaching multitudes or Jesus as the Good Shepherd with a flock of sheep.

We might think of Him driving out the money changers in the temple; walking upon the water; entering Jerusalem to the cheers of the crowd; or at the Last Supper with His disciples. There are many different images that we have of Him from Scripture. All of them are rich in meaning and present wonderful aspects of our Lord.

This morning I was struck by the image of Jesus as He describes Himself to the high priest. He is the Messiah, the Son of the Blessed One. When He told the high priest that they would see Him as the Son of Man sitting at the right hand of the Mighty One and coming on the clouds of heaven, they would have recognized His description as it appears in Daniel 6:13-14,

"In my vision at night I looked, and there before me was one like a son of man, coming with the clouds of heaven. He approached the Ancient of Days and was led into his presence. ¹⁴ He was given authority, glory and sovereign power; all peoples, nations and men of every language worshiped him. His dominion is an everlasting dominion that will not pass away, and his kingdom is one that will never be destroyed."

John describes Jesus as he encountered Him in Revelation 1:12-16

"I turned around to see the voice that was speaking to me. And when I turned I saw seven golden lampstands, ¹³ and among the lampstands was someone "like a son of man," dressed in a robe reaching down to his feet and with a golden sash around his chest. ¹⁴ His head and hair were white like wool, as white as snow, and his eyes were like blazing fire. ¹⁵ His feet were like bronze glowing in a furnace, and his voice was like the sound of rushing waters. ¹⁶ In his right hand he held seven stars, and out of his mouth came a sharp double-edged sword. His face was like the sun shining in all its brilliance."

What a glorious picture of our Lord! He reigns on high! He is Lord of Lords and King of Kings! He is coming again! No matter what is going on around us; no matter what the enemy of our souls tries to bring against us – Jesus triumphs over all!!

Two sides of the same coin

Revelation 1:17-18 When I saw him, I fell at his feet as though dead. Then he placed his right hand on me and said: "Do not be afraid. I am the First and the Last. ¹⁸I am the Living One; I was dead, and behold I am alive for ever and ever! And I hold the keys of death and Hades.

Have we ever thought of what our response would be if the Lord took us to heaven in the Spirit as He did the Apostle John? I imagine the nature of the encounter with Jesus could take on many forms. I wonder if John ever thought about such a thing happening – and if he did, did he think that his response upon seeing Jesus would be to fall at his feet as though dead.

Of all the apostles, he is the one identified as having a special relationship with Jesus. He is repeatedly described as the 'one whom Jesus loved'. That doesn't mean that Jesus didn't love the others; it's just that John's relationship with the Lord had a special love element of closeness in it. For me, that is what makes his response in this encounter with Jesus so stirring and provocative.

We tend to think along the lines of Jesus warmly embracing someone (one of His own) who goes to heaven and encounters Him. Sort of a welcome home, like the father greeting the prodigal son. Joy and gladness just overflowing - and that might be the way it normally occurs. But here we have something very different. Does our understanding of God and the relationship that we have with Him include the aspect of what is revealed in this verse? Can we see ourselves responding to Jesus as John did?

The fear of the Lord and the love of God are two sides of the same coin. Jesus' first words to John after falling at His feet as though dead were "Do not be afraid." It's vital that we understand that although we are recipients of God's love and are His children through faith in Jesus, He is the Lord of Lords and King of Kings. In Revelation 5:11-12 John gives this glorious description:

Then I looked and heard the voice of many angels, numbering thousands upon thousands, and ten thousand times ten thousand. They encircled the throne and the living creatures and the elders. ¹²In a loud voice they sang: "Worthy is the Lamb, who was slain, to receive power and wealth and wisdom and strength and honor and glory and praise!"

This is our Savior and Lord. He is the One who died for us and rose from the dead. He is the One who loves and treasures us so; the One that we have the incredible privilege to love each and every day of our lives. May we fully embrace His ways so that our lives do just that!

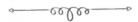

Tasks & relationships, which has priority?

1 Corinthians 14:1a Follow the way of love...

This morning I woke up thinking about one of the more important and useful concepts that I became aware of in Grad School. God has used it ever since to give me insight and help me in my daily life. It involves tasks and relationships – two things that fill our lives. Each day is filled with tasks to do and many of them involve working or interacting with people.

In a class, we grad students took a test that measured our personal orientations to tasks and to relationships. When the scores were graphed we each discovered a picture of how we functioned in such situations. At one end of the spectrum were those whose pre-eminent concern was the task. Whether big or small, it had to get done. If it meant sacrificing relationships, so be it. Relationships were irrelevant to getting the job done.

At the other end of the spectrum were those who placed pre-eminence upon relationships. No task was so important that it would warrant sacrificing relationships. When these individuals are confronted with situations where they have to choose between a task and a relationship(s), the task won't get done. They don't want to hurt anyone's feelings or create an unpleasant situation for themselves or anyone else. They back away from tasks where they perceive a risk to relationship might exist.

Then there was everyone in between where they reflected a mix of task or relationship priorities. The goal was to be in the middle where both tasks and relationships are important. Such individuals find ways to get tasks done while preserving and strengthening relationships. They don't sacrifice the task for a relationship and they don't sacrifice a relationship for the task. Both are important and vital.

This seems to be the way of love that we are called to walk in. God's Word and the leading of His Spirit enable us to find the balance that preserves relationships while getting tasks done. Sometimes they might be painful even when done wisely in love, but the way of love produces righteous fruit – both in us and in others. Think of the Golden Rule, "Do unto others as you would have them do unto you."

In all situations we want to glorify the Lord. We want our lives to accomplish His purposes and reflect His life within us. The way of love enables us to do that day by day and His Word tells us how to do just that. It's up to us to embrace it. The way of love enables us to transform situations that seem to be 'Lose-Lose' or 'Win-Lose' into Win-Win'. Tasks get done and relationships are strengthened.

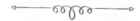

Don Schmidt

The 'gift' of food appreciation

Matthew 28:19a Therefore go and make disciples of all nations.... Acts 11:26b
The disciples were called Christians first at Antioch.

I wonder if among God's gifts, is one of food appreciation. If there is, I think I have it. Good food, prepared well is such a joy to eat. Each bite is a pleasure in itself. Have you noticed how we especially anticipate a meal where a favorite dish is being served? Then, when we take the first taste, we evaluate everything about it to see if it measures up. That might take all of a split second if it is done right. A friend of ours describes his response to one of Donna's desserts as a 'party in his mouth'!

But what if that first taste generates a 'something is amiss' response? Maybe it's something simple like salt or pepper which can be remedied right there at the table. But what if it's overcooked or undercooked; too dry or watered down; or somehow significantly different? What if it's not at all the dish we were led to believe was going to be served because the recipe has been changed – it is new and improved! Unfortunately, it sure isn't the dish we love.

Three things are at work here: 1) Recognizing that specific dishes are called for, 2) Making those dishes correctly and 3) Being able to recognize the correct dishes when tasted. A dish might qualify as food, but if it isn't a required dish or made according to the correct recipe, it's not acceptable – no matter how well meaning or sincere the cooks are.

You might be asking yourself, where is all this going? Christians are disciples of Christ. As Christians we are to be disciples - and are to make disciples. In today's illustration, disciples are made according to very specific recipes found in God's cookbook (Bible). Disciples are NOT simply things that fall into the general category of food. Contrary to our culture, the term Christian is only correctly applied when it refers disciples ('dishes') made by truly Biblical recipes.

The term 'Christian' is being used less and less by many because it has become far too general. In our food illustration it now refers to anything edible – rather than the specific dishes the Bible requires. The descriptive terms 'Christ follower' and 'follower of Jesus' are attempts to bring the focus once again upon the required characteristics of such a life. God requires us to not only be such people, but to work with Him to produce such people. He has the recipes and they must be followed in order to be a disciple of Christ or to make them. His recipes are the only ones that count.

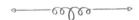

The way we enter in

*Ephesians 3:17-18 so that Christ may dwell in your hearts through faith.
And I pray that you, being rooted and established in love, ¹⁸ may have
power, together with all the saints, to grasp how wide and long
and high and deep is the love of Christ,*

The Lord of the Rings is a marvelous trilogy. In the 1st book, The Fellowship of the Ring, there is a scene where the group is trying to get into Moria. In order to continue their journey they must enter and get through this vast dwelling place of the dwarves under the Misty Mountains. But in order to get the stone doors to open, they have to figure out a subtle riddle that is inscribed on the doors, "The doors of Durin, Lord of Moria, speak friend and enter."

Gandalf spends quite a bit of time speaking every password that he can think of. Finally, Frodo comes up with the answer: *Mellon*, the elvish word for 'friend'. It was there right in front of them. Gandalf speaks "*Mellon*" and the stone doors open in the nick of time and they enter this underground world. Their reality was that they couldn't enter in until they came up with the key to open the door.

This morning I woke up thinking about Jesus. I was aware of how everything that we do is about Him. But more than that is the awareness of His love and sacrifice for me. Jesus is right in front of us. He is the way we enter in, when we through faith allow Him to enter into us. How often are we like Gandalf, trying to think of some way in when the answer is right before us? When we embrace Jesus, we experience first hand His incredible love for us.

One of my favorite stories is told of Dr. Karl Barth. He was considered by many scholars to be one of the most brilliant theologians of the 20th Century. Once when he was lecturing at Princeton Theological Seminary, a student asked him what was the greatest truth he had ever learned. Dr. Barth thought for a moment and then said: "The greatest truth that I have ever learned was at my mother's knee, 'Jesus loves me, this I know, for the Bible tells me so.'"

It sounds so simple yet it unlocks the most incredible door to love vast as the ocean. Such is the love of Christ!

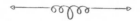

Don Schmidt

Thank God for these special companions

Romans 12:12 Be joyful in hope, patient in affliction, faithful in prayer.

Isn't it fascinating that of the six items identified in the above verse, only the one we generally perceive as negative is a given in our lives? All of the others can be companions that radically change the nature of our journey. The Lord of the Rings offers another helpful picture in this regard. Remember the Council of Elrond in The Fellowship of the Ring, when they are discussing the ring and how to destroy it? In the heaviness of that discussion, Frodo steps forward and says "I will take the ring though I do not know the way."

For this difficult journey (think affliction), Frodo knows that at least he will have Sam with him. But Elrond informs him that they will not be alone. There is to be a 'Company of the Ring', and that company will include those most important to him. Great is Frodo's joy when he finds this out because he knows and trusts most of these companions. They will make the journey so much better for they will help him find the way and he won't be alone.

Affliction is our journey. But instead of us having Gandalf, Aragorn, Gimli, Legolas, Sam, and the others accompanying us, we have the opportunity to have Joy, Hope, Patience, Faithfulness and Prayer as our companions. We are not alone in the midst of the afflictions we face. These are the 'companions' that the Lord wants us to cultivate and have because He knows how incredibly important they are to our journey.

In 1969 I went on a short-term mission trip to Colombia, S.A. I wound up losing about 20 pounds on the trip fighting off Montezuma's Revenge. Included in our adventure was a very difficult trek of several miles back through the mountainous jungle to a village. When it was time to return from the village, I was exhausted with no strength, facing miles of muddy mountain trails. Thank God that on this return trip there were donkey's to carry our backpacks and I had a staff to lean on! We still had to walk out of the jungle but my load was lighter. The Lord enabled me to do it, one step at a time – for miles!! That is an example of how these marvelous companions can impact our journey!

I particularly like Frodo's joyous reaction upon learning that Aragorn (Strider) will be with him! Aragorn is the true king. In addition to the above companions, we too have the true King with us as well. Jesus promised to never leave us or forsake us. These other companions all enable us to better experience the wonder and blessing of His presence.

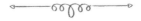

Not just the absence of the negative

Who are our companions?

Yesterday we talked about the idea of companions – not being people but instead referring to the attributes that characterize our lives. We were looking at affliction and used the example of Frodo and the Company of the Ring. The journey he volunteered to undertake to destroy the ring of power (affliction) was made so much better by the companions who began the journey with him. Instead of Gandalf, Aragorn, Sam, etc… we considered joy, hope, patience, faithfulness and prayer as the 'companions' of affliction and how powerfully they impact our lives (Romans 12:12).

This idea of referring to attributes as 'companions' has really captured me because I've never thought of it this way before. The reality of our daily lives is tht we have 'companions' and it's important that they be identified. Consider the 'companions' listed in these two verses:

> Colossians 3:5a Put to death, therefore, whatever belongs to your earthly nature:
> sexual immorality, impurity, lust, evil desires and greed, which is idolatry.

> Colossians 3:12 Therefore, as God's chosen people, holy and dearly loved, clothe
> yourselves with compassion, kindness, humility, gentleness and patience.

I am reminded of the red and white stones I encountered on my trip to Afghanistan in 2007. We visited villages far from metropolitan areas. Along side some of the roads we traveled on were sections where every few yards there were small stones that had a brush-stroke of red or white paint on them. The white stones indicated fields that the military had 'swept', meaning they had been cleared of the mines. The red stones indicated fields that had not been swept free of mines. No matter where we were going we paid attention to red stones and avoided those areas.

The Scriptures warn us that the earthly nature 'companions' of the first verse are 'red stones'; they result in serious harm and we are warned to avoid those 'fields'. Those of the second verse are 'white stones' where serious dangers have been removed.

Who are our companions? Do we surround ourselves with white stones? Or do we have a mixture of red and white stones? – meaning we have danger areas in our lives that can cause great harm both to ourselves and those around us. Jesus wants our 'fields' swept clean!

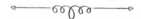

The wonderful blessing of kindness

Ephesians 4:32a Be kind and compassionate to one another,...

A special memory from several years ago: "I am sitting in my leather recliner typing with Pappy, a small Poodle, squeezed in next to me on the seat. My left arm is resting on his back as I type. It's funny, when I went to sit down, he was off to the side but when I sat down, he was already in the chair next to me. Pappy is Tom & Karen's dog. They are good friends of ours and Pappy is a good friend of Snuggles, our Pekingese."

While living in Tennessee, Donna and I so appreciated the fact that when we went out of town, Tom & Karen watched Snuggles, and when they went out of town, we got to watch Pappy. It was a twofold blessing. The blessing to us wasn't just when our pet was being watched by them. There was an equal blessing to us when we watched their pet. We know how we feel when we're the ones traveling. We didn't worry about Snuggles because she was with them. Likewise, they didn't worry about Pappy, because Pappy was with us. While it's wonderful to save the cost of a kennel, the blessing is far more than monetary. It was a very special kindness that both couples were able to experience – and one that any owner of a pet can appreciate.

Stop and think about the wonderful blessing of 'kindnesses'. Can you think of incidents in your life where similar types of kindnesses occur? I'm talking about where we experience an awareness of being blessed; where we want to say thank you to the one(s) extending the kindnesses to us. Kindnesses can be big or small. Sometimes the smallest things done at the right time can bring extraordinary blessing. They are like seasonings in our lives – making things 'taste' better.

How about where we are the ones seeing the needs of others and helping them? Jesus said, "Do unto others as you would have them do unto you." We don't 'do' to 'get' – but He was describing something that is to become a way of life for us. It is the wonder of being other-oriented. Today's verse can be viewed as a command that we have to do (which it really is) or we can view it as one of God's keys to great blessing: we get to be kind and compassionate!

An important thought to remember: kindnesses are actions – not just feelings of good will. They are things we do. It is seeing opportunities around us and responding where we are able. Remember how blessed we are when others see our need and are kind to us. Let us do likewise.

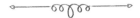

Jesus made a way for you

John 16:33 I have told you these things, so that in Me you may have [perfect]
peace and confidence. In the world you have tribulation and trials and distress
and frustration; but be of good cheer [take courage; be confident, certain,
undaunted]! For I have overcome the world. Amplified

"God will make a way where there seems to be no way. He works in ways I cannot see. He will make a way for me." These are the words of a wonderful song by Don Moen that speak to the heart of the issue for us. We are surrounded by tribulation, trials, distress and frustration – just like Jesus said. But in the midst of it all, we have reason for good cheer. Jesus has overcome the world.

The 'world' would have us believe that our only reality is to be dominated by anxiety and fear. Since so much of the negative stuff going on is beyond our control, we are tempted to succumb to the world's view that we are – or about to be - victims. The question, "What if…?" becomes a dominant theme in our thinking. The anxiety and fear provide a fertile ground for anger and resentment that will have a profound negative impact in our lives and relationships. We struggle with feeling trapped with no way out. If life was a Monopoly game, we feel like we're stuck in Jail.

Fortunately, Jesus has "Get out of Jail" cards for us! We don't have to remain mired in the world's emotional/mental responses to tribulation, trials, distress and frustration. Better still, the Lord let's us know that it's not just having those negative feeling go away, <u>He enables us to have good cheer in the midst of it all.</u>

We, as Jesus followers, are equipped to walk through everything with courage and confidence! We are not victims! Think of the 'refreshing breeze' we can be to those around us. Think of being asked, "How can you be so calm and cheerful with all this junk going on?" No matter what happens to us – the courage, confidence and joy are to be constant. We are not victims. Jesus has overcome the world and we are in Him.

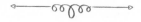

Choosing wisely!

Hebrews 1:3 The Son is the radiance of God's glory and the exact representation of his being, sustaining all things by his powerful word. After he had provided purification for sins, he sat down at the right hand of the Majesty in heaven.

I have really enjoyed some of the Indiana Jones movies. A couple of my favorite scenes are in The last Crusade when they get to the cave and encounter the old Crusader still guarding the 'Holy Grail' – believed to be the cup used by Christ at the last supper. There is only one problem – the room has a whole bunch of cups without any indication which is the right one.

Of course the wealthy, learned leader of the bad guys insists on choosing and picks out a magnificent ornate cup, in his mind worthy of the Lord. He drinks from it expecting some sort of heavenly wonder but unfortunately he chose the wrong cup. He ages a few hundred years in a few seconds and is no more, to which the old Crusader responds, "He chose poorly."

Due to the wounding of Indy's father (Sean Connery), Indy has to choose quickly among the cups. The story line attributes miraculous power to the cup – like the Ark in the Old Testament – and Indy needs to get it to his father to heal the wound that would kill him. Well, Indy learned from the bad guy's mistake and scours the table for the cup of a carpenter and chose a very humble plain wooden cup; to which the old Crusader responds, "You chose...wisely."

We find ourselves in a world filled with gods – all being represented as the true God. When we look at all of these competing gods, how do we know what He (the True One) looks like? This isn't simply an intellectual exercise – this is true reality! While He doesn't put a gun at our head or a sword at our throat forcing us to choose, the stakes couldn't be higher.

The good news is that the One True God didn't leave us to our own devices to figure out which 'cup on the table' was Him. He has made everything available for all to 'choose wisely'. He even works with us to guide us in the path that leads to finding Him. He has communicated that it's not His will that any should 'choose poorly'!

Fortunately, He has given us a vibrant, living picture of Himself. He even enables us to recognize that it is Him - we then, simply have to choose. And when we do, He confirms our wise choice by allowing us to experience the wonder of Him.

Jesus is the radiance of God's glory and the exact representation of His being! When we become His, He begins the transforming wonder whereby we become like Jesus. The more we are transformed, the more others will see Jesus when they see us – and they too will be drawn to Him.

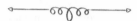

The impact of Jesus on slaves

1 Corinthians 7:22 For he who was a slave when he was called by the Lord is the Lord's freedman; similarly, he who was a free man when he was called is Christ's slave.

Consider another time and another place. Consider that we and our families are in a society where slavery is commonly practiced and it is not racially based – where anyone could find themselves in slavery, i.e., the Roman world. Finally, consider that slavery is the lot we find ourselves in – and the world we live in it is accepted as a given. There is no anti-slavery movement. We are slaves and will likely remain so for all of our lives.

Maybe our masters are cruel – maybe not. We have to live with what the reality is. Then into our lives comes the Gospel! We become born again, when called to faith in Christ Jesus. We are transformed and become freed men and women, even though we still find ourselves in slavery. Slaves yet free. They are independent of each other!

Our focus becomes sharing the love of Christ with other slaves and becoming the best slaves that we can be. Possibly, God will use us to reach our owners with the Gospel and transform them. This is not done with the purpose of being set free from slavery. It is done in joy because of the wonder of the love of Christ. We want all men and women to come to know Him.

Yes, we might hope to one day be freed from slavery, but just like Joseph, we live our lives in a way that honors our God. Our lives are so transformed we want to share the love of Christ with everyone. This sharing is far more than just words about Jesus. Our lives become filled with acts of kindness and doing the right things by God's standards. We live to please Him.

Think of slaves shivering outside in the cold and we, as Christian slaves, taking them blankets and something warm to drink. We do it not to tell them about Jesus, although that might result. We do it because it is a kindness that we would want if we were in their situation. We see needs and meet them as we are able.

The Gospel is a 'Prosperity Gospel' for all who receive it but not in the sense that we western Christians might first think of. It is not about becoming rich materially. It is about the incredible richness that we have in Christ no matter what our circumstances. We must separate the reality of the Gospel from the cultural trappings that so easily hinder us.

We must fight the tendency to view the Gospel through the lens of our culture and circumstances rather than recognizing that the Gospel enables us to live first as citizens of His Kingdom. We are able to experience His love and prosperity no matter what our situation. We are free – even if we are slaves.

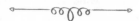

God can find 'another 2 yards' in us enabling us to change

James 1:20 For man's anger does not promote the righteousness God [wishes and requires]. Amplified

One of my all time favorite films is Chariots of Fire* - the 1981 British film that tells the fact-based story of two athletes in the 1924 Olympics. One is Eric Liddell, a devout Scottish Christian who runs for the glory of God, and the other is Harold Abrahams, an English Jew who runs to overcome prejudice.

In the film, Harold Abrahams is a gifted runner who was stunned by being beaten in a race by Liddell. He recognized the need to run faster, so he approached Sam Mussabini to become his coach. After watching Abrahams run, Mussabini said to him, "I can find you another two yards." Two yards to a sprinter can be the difference between the Gold medal and being an 'also ran'. Abraham embraced the good news that Mussabini could enable him to improve.

There were things Abraham needed to change in order to experience the excellence he was capable of – and he committed himself to do it. This is such a vital principle that we need to understand in dealing with the 'stuff' in our lives that we must continue to deal with. There are habits or remnants of habits that might not keep us from being 'good' or 'better', but they can definitely keep us from becoming the best that we can be.

Earlier I wrote of my experience at Grad School where I was totally unaware of becoming angry. In that classroom discussion I was so angry that 'steam was coming out of my ears!' Talk about being blind to the obvious! Our anger does not promote the righteousness of God (James 1:20). It is a habit that will promote unrighteousness.

Thank God the Lord made me aware of this problem and enabled me to effectively deal with anger over the years. He has done the same with many Christians. But how many of us recognize that there may still be subtle remnants of anger that pop up in our lives. Such remnants keep us from the excellence we are capable of and that God expects from us. Let us remember that no matter how much we improve, the Lord can always find another 'two yards' within us.

Both men won Gold medals in the 1924 Olympics.

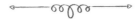

Are we frightened by our circumstances?

Psalm 27:1 Yahweh is my light and my salvation. Whom shall I fear? Yahweh is the strength of my life. Of whom shall I be afraid? World English Bible

David spent years living with the reality that men were pursuing him to kill him. King Saul wanted him dead. Even though an army besieged him, in Psalm 27:3 David wrote, *"... my heart will not fear."* Although bravery played a role in this, there is far more to it than that. At the center of his life was Yahweh, and He made all the difference. In 1 Samuel 13:14 it declares that David was *"a man after His own heart".*

This verse describes such a marvelous and practical aspect of our life in Christ. The peace and confidence that are there for us; to sustain, encourage and protect us in the midst of fear. We can get them by embracing Him. Sadly, that old saying that you can lead a horse to water but you can't make it drink can be all too true of us. Just because God has provision for us, doesn't mean we will take advantage of it.

It's probably safe to say that none of us have men and armies pursuing us to kill us. But take a look around us and we see all manner of frightening things: economic uncertainty, job losses, threats of terrorism, immorality running rampant, marriages and families falling apart, Christians being persecuted throughout the world and here in the United States as well – the list just goes on.

Those with younger children, have the concern of raising them to be true Christ-followers. We read of young Christian men and women losing their faith when they go off to college. We can succumb to the fear of thinking that 'greater is the one in the world, than the one within us' - rather than recognizing that as a lie of the enemy of our souls.

Is our focus going to be upon things that frighten and intimidate? Or is our focus and 'life-embrace' going to be upon our Lord Jesus? We cannot be casual in this or approach it half-heartedly. The enemy of our souls is using these things to pursue us, just as Saul's men pursued David. Our response must be to have our lives turn whole-heartedly to our Lord. He is our light and salvation. He is our strength.

We must learn to love Him with all our heart and soul and mind and strength. We must learn what exactly that means, and do it – embracing a lifestyle that truly reflects us being men and women after God's own heart.

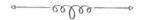

What is our 'normal'?

I Thessalonians 5:16-18 Be cheerful no matter what; pray all the time; thank God no matter what happens. This is the way God wants you who belong to Christ Jesus to live. The Message

It's been a bit frustrating, as I've grown older to lose some of my sense of smell. I particularly notice it when it comes to sweeter more subtle fragrances – like perfume on Donna or food cooking. Likewise my hearing isn't what it used to be (what an understatement) and I miss things – though in the middle of the night, it's not so bad. Praise God for hearing aids. They do wonders. When people speak softly, I can push a button and the volume increases.

I think these physical phenomena are similar to how we live each day and how we respond to what goes on around us. We have deficiencies and God wants to fix them. These verses talk about being cheerful; praying all the time and being thankful. This is how God intends us to live. This is being normal. God's plan is for these attributes to become second nature to us; they are to become who we are. Unfortunately, they can be diminished just like my sense of smell and hearing are.

The verses go further – we are to be cheerful **no matter what!** We are to be thankful **no matter what happens!** We are to pray through it all – meaning that our focus is upon the Lord. There is to be constancy in our lives that is reflective of the wonder of our God and His goodness that overrides everything – no matter what! But it's easier to be cheerful and thankful when things are going well than when they aren't.

How often do we hear of a close friend who has died; or that someone very dear to us is unexpectedly having surgery for cancer; or that a contentious situation unexpectedly arises that has to be dealt with by those close to us; – and this is all on top of the stuff we are already dealing with. This is part of life.

Fortunately, God has made gratefulness and focusing upon Him to be like an artesian spring within Donna and me – they are always there, flowing. They've become normal. The wonder and blessing of their genuineness never ceases to amaze us. We experience the joy that comes from the utter confidence that we and those we love are not helpless or alone; that we have a God who adores us! Through tears and pain, the joy and gratitude are there. All of these difficult situations just cause us to embrace Him all the more – they push us into Him. We don't have to understand – we have Him.

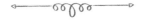

His impact on the unexpected

Psalm 23:1 The LORD is my shepherd; I lack nothing.

The unexpected is a fact of life. Think how often in our daily routine that we encounter the unexpected. Simple things: running out of paper, ink, dish detergent, the shirt you were going to wear is in the laundry, the lawn mower won't start; your appointment is delayed. Then there are those that are a little more noteworthy: traffic jams, cancelled appointments, a friend lets you down, something is forgotten by someone who shouldn't forget, the car breaks down, extra work is dumped on you in your job....

These (and many other) things when viewed from a distance don't seem to be so bad – annoying maybe – but they aren't major issues. We usually don't perceive them as tests of our faith. They don't fall into the category of losing a job, losing investments, losing a loved one, being injured in an accident, being betrayed by a friend, discovering you have a life threatening disease, etc....

But all of these things, whether big or small, have something important in common. They are all opportunities. Opportunities for what you ask? Each and every one of them gives us the opportunity to reflect the reality of our life in Christ. These opportunities are windows into our soul that give insight to those around us - and ourselves if we have eyes to see it.

Take a moment now and re-read today's verse. Now, read it again, out loud, pausing after the first phrase. This verse describes an unshakeable, bedrock reality that God intends to become ours as we walk in His ways – truly becoming a disciple of Jesus. It becomes the reality of who we are to the depth of our being. The reality of God in our lives is an unshakeable settled-ness that is reflected in our responses to everything we encounter.

The Lord is my Shepherd; I lack nothing. Although a storm may be raging around us, it's peaceful in the boat. The storm doesn't shake us. Jesus is our Shepherd and the reality of our life in Him is reflected in all of the unexpected 'opportunities' we encounter. Hopefully, that reflected reality is of someone walking in His ways.

The importance of detecting fear

Psalm 23:4b I will fear no evil, for you are with me;

Wouldn't it be handy to have a gadget that could measure or detect the fear in our lives just like a thermometer or Geiger counter? Whether we use the thermometer typically depends on how bad the symptoms are. If you have an active child and all of a sudden you find them curled up and quiet a first response might be to feel their head to see how hot it is. If it's hot, we find the thermometer. A Geiger counter is useful because it detects something we don't even know if it's there.

Unfortunately, fear can be such a normal 'companion' in our lives that we don't recognize that it's there. I have written earlier about being angry in a classroom discussion at Grad School and was oblivious to my anger – until the instructor interrupted and pointed it out. I had become so accustomed to it that it appeared normal. Unfortunately, those closest to me suffered for it. Thankfully, God's grace enables us to repent and change.

Some of the fear symptoms that occur are worry, anxiety, anger, annoyance, impatience, lying, deceiving, complaining, selfishness, rebellion, immorality, jealousy, envy, and the list could go on. These can be indicative of other problems as well, but they are part of the mob that accompanies fear. What kind of fear? Well there are lots of them, but to name a few:

Fear of failure
Fear of rejection
Fear of the unknown
Fear of what 'might' happen
Fear of what 'might not' happen

The antidote to fear and the negative behaviors associated with it is walking in God's ways. The verse preceding today's verse says, *"He guides me in paths of righteousness…"* Even when our journey takes us through the *"valley of the shadow of death, I will fear no evil, for (God) is with me."* Psalm 23:4a

If you ask, "What are the paths of righteousness?" The answer is they are the paths you walk in order to be a follower of Jesus. They are defined in Scripture. Unfortunately, the term Christian has become so broad that in the minds of many it includes all manner of behaviors that a follower of Jesus will not and must not do. These are all identified in Scripture.

The Holy Spirit and Scripture are our 'Geiger counters' to detect the fear in our lives. Likewise those who love us can help point out where we're not where we are supposed to be. Ultimately, fearlessness is rooted in God. The more we follow Jesus, the more 'fear-less' we become, because He is with us.

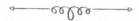

Accentuate the positive! Eliminate the negative!

John 15:5 "I am the vine; you are the branches. If a man remains in me and I in him, he will bear much fruit; apart from me you can do nothing.

Have you ever thought about how wonderful it is to do things right? To be told, "Good job!" To have people express their gratitude for what you've done or for whom you are? Boy, talk about something that puts a spring in your step!

Yes, such comments can lead to pride, but they also can lead to us experiencing a heartfelt gratitude for what God has done and is doing in our lives. Importantly, they can be such an encouragement to do more 'right' things; to be more of a 'right' person; and in the context of today's verse, to bear more fruit. Better still is the desire God gives us to learn what those 'right' things are and do them more and more.

Think of sports, hobbies, relationships, work – our goal is to do them well. The reality is that more often than not, the wrong is eliminated simply by doing the right! Being kind eliminates unkindness; being patient eliminates impatience; being thoughtful eliminates thoughtlessness; being generous eliminates stinginess; being loving eliminates being unloving; being other-oriented eliminates self-centeredness.

Then as we bear these wonderful fruits of righteousness, the Holy Spirit asks us, "How would you like to do them even better?" "How would you like to bear more fruit?" To which, we reply. "Oh yes Lord! Show me how!" And He does so, in a most affirming way.

There's an old song that Bing Crosby made famous: Accentuate the Positive. The first three lines are

> You've got to accentuate the positive / Eliminate the negative / Latch on to
> the affirmative

This is the point! Our attitude about repentance goes through a significant switch. Instead of its focus being our wrong doing, the focus becomes "Eliminating the negative" so we can "Latch on to the affirmative." It becomes a vital tool in the hands of the Holy Spirit to enable us to bear more of His righteous fruit. The more fruit we bear the more joy we have and the more we glorify our God. It's not about us. It's all about Him.

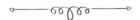

An essential component

John 15:5 "I am the vine; you are the branches. <u>If a man remains in me and I in him,</u> he will bear much fruit; apart from me you can do nothing.

Picture a large sailboat, out at sea, with sails unfurled and moving gloriously with the wind. (Hopefully imagining this doesn't make you seasick!) Wouldn't it be wonderful to be on such a ship, on such a day, with a group of dear ones? Wow – what a great time that would be! Donna and I have been able to do this very thing a couple of times and the memories we have are ones we treasure.

But take a moment to think about all of the needed 'ingredients' in this adventure. What must we have to make it happen? First we've got to have a sizable body of water for sailing on. Then we must have a sailboat big enough to handle the group of friends that are going on the adventure – and a crew to sail it.

We would like to have a beautiful day with a strong breeze. How about doing the sailing amidst a group of islands with beautiful scenes to behold – and a group of dolphin accompanying us? Of course we want to have something wonderful to eat, so why don't we make it a morning sail and we enjoy homemade coffee cake and coffee and orange juice as we sail. Can't you just picture enjoying one another, the breeze, the sea spray, the beauty and the wonder of it all!?

In considering the necessary 'ingredients', does anything seem to be missing? Not at first glance. But there is something absolutely essential that is taken for granted in the above items. Without this 'essential' the adventure doesn't happen – except that we sit on the sailboat, wherever it is, and enjoy the scenery, the food, the breeze and one another – but we don't go anywhere!

What is this essential – that is taken for granted to be there? Answer: Sails. And what is a sail? It's a piece of material extended on a mast to catch the wind and propel a boat, ship, or other vessel.

From God's perspective, walking in His ways is as much as a given for Christians as sails are for a sailboat. Just as a sailboat won't go anywhere without the sails being unfurled, Christians who don't walk in His ways won't 'go anywhere' either. This is why we are more and more hearing the term Jesus Follower. This is how we remain in Him! This is how we bear righteous fruit! Sailboats with sails = Christians who obey Scripture = the adventure is on!!

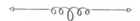

Don Schmidt

A speedboat or a sailboat?

John 3:8 "The wind blows wherever it pleases. You hear its sound, but you cannot tell where it comes from or where it is going. So it is with everyone born of the Spirit."

What is the difference between a speedboat and a sailboat? Duh – one has a motor and the other doesn't? One doesn't need sails while the other does. One needs gasoline and the other needs wind. One can move independently of the wind, the other cannot move without the wind. One is a whole lot easier to get where you're going, when you want to get there and how fast you want to get there – guess which one!

The speedboat (any boat with a motor) offers independence – it's at the whim of its 'captain'. The sailboat is dependent upon the wind. No wind – and it isn't going anywhere. A speedboat can be driven by just about anyone, even someone who's never been on water; just start the motor and off you go. Whether a child or an adult, if you can steer anything – from a kiddie car, go-kart, automobile – you can steer the speedboat. It's also easier to stop!

The sailboat is different; there's a whole lot more to learn and a lot more skill involved. But the key things are its dependency upon the wind and the ability of its 'captain' to read the wind and sail the boat where it's to go, and the route the sailboat goes to get there.

Think about it: how do you get from here to there with a headwind blowing straight at you. That means that the wind is blowing from the direction you want to go. Instead of being at your back, it's blowing in your face. The question then becomes are we sure that's where we want to (or are supposed to) go? If it is, the sailboat can do it, but it sure isn't a direct route. Kind of sounds like what we experience with the Holy Spirit sometimes doesn't it? He leads us to do something and we encounter 'headwinds' – difficulties, opposition, obstacles, etc... As I suggested in yesterday's devotional, for the Christian (Jesus Follower), a life of obedience to Scriptures, becomes the sails of our boat. Walking in His ways, becomes the skill to sail the boat – to read the wind and allow it to choose the route whatever it might be. Loving God develops the life-dependence upon Him.

That dependence is essential if our lives are to be about Jesus (sailboat)! Without it, our lives are about us (speedboat)! We must beware of the spirit of independence that is so common in our culture and in our lives. The Holy Spirit is given to us so that we may have relationship with Him and live the lives that experience, enjoy and reflect the glory of our God.

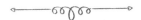

How will we respond?

Matthew 13:54, 55 Coming to his hometown, he began teaching the people in their synagogue, and they were amazed. "Where did this man get this wisdom and these miraculous powers?" they asked. 55 "Isn't this the carpenter's son? Isn't his mother's name Mary, and aren't his brothers James, Joseph, Simon and Judas?

If you saw a miracle happen, would you believe it? Or would you immediately dismiss it because 'miracles don't happen' today! What if you were the one in need of a miracle? Would you listen to those around you dismissing it – or would you set aside these opinions and see if a miracle could happen to you? Some of the people in Nazareth did respond and they experienced what God had for them.

But for the most part, the people of Nazareth and the Jewish leaders represent one of the most difficult to believe 'phenomenon' in the Bible for me to understand. They chose to adhere to opinions they have rather than respond in faith to what is going on before them. The Scriptures say the people of Nazareth were amazed at what they saw and heard, yet they responded with unbelief. They chose to hold to what their 'common sense' was telling them.

This is a significant principle that God uses and we have to adjust accordingly. It all boils down to whether we are going to respond appropriately to what He is doing. Will we respond with unbelief, listening to common sense or fear? Or will we respond in faith to what we are encountering? Will we seek Him and allow Him to guide us?

The Lord gives us opportunities to follow Him and accomplish things that He has purposed us to do. But in the midst of those things, He allows all manner of problems, difficulties and obstacles to arise. They can be fearful or overwhelming. How are we going to respond?

It might not seem fair, but we have a path to choose. We can be fearful and succumb to worldly wisdom or fear – or we can seek and trust the Lord, lifting all of the problems to Him. I think of Joshua and Caleb and the other 10 spies sent in to explore the Promised Land. There were giants there, but only the Joshua and Caleb had their focus on the Lord. They knew He would see them through. The other 10 focused on the giants – fear and 'common sense' dictated how they responded.

Don Schmidt

The things we sometimes face can lead to similar choices. We can focus on the 'giants' or we can focus on our God – unbelief versus faith. Each is an opportunity for the Lord in His greatness to enable us to overcome. The choice is ours. How will we respond to the challenging things He allows in our lives?

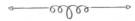

Like water off a duck's back

Proverbs 3:5 Trust in the Lord with all your heart and lean not on your own understanding...

I grew up next to Lake Michigan and there was a large marsh nearby called Grand Mere where ducks and geese were abundant. Waterfowl have always held such a fascination for me whether watching them fly in formation, land in a marsh or pond or just swim and feed. If I had gone into Wildlife as a career, it would have been as a waterfowl biologist.

One of the interesting details that I learned about waterfowl is that they have a tiny oil-secreting gland located at the base of their tail known as the *uropygial gland* or 'Preen Gland'. When a duck is preening, as we have all seen, its head and beak are spreading this oil over its feathers. This oil helps to maintain the luster of the feathers and makes the outer feathers waterproof. Without this protective barrier, a duck's feathers would become water-logged.

Water is a fact of life for waterfowl. It is not just an occasional thing that these birds encounter once in awhile. The daily preening creates and maintains this protective barrier for them. Think about all the things that happen in our lives, on a daily basis that can cause us to respond in a way harmful to ourselves and others: change, the unexpected, criticism, bad news, insults, the thoughtlessness of others, additional work to be done, disappointment, discouragement. I'm sure you can think of more.

Remember the expression, "Like water off a duck's back"? The water just rolls off – it doesn't penetrate or soak in. Now, think about all those items we just mentioned. They happen – all the time! God's plan is for us to be protected from the negative effect they can have. But we play a role in the development and maintenance of that protective 'barrier'. Our focus and trust must be upon the Lord – not the circumstances. Trusting in Him means we don't succumb to discouragement because we don't know the answers to the challenges facing us.

If our focus and trust aren't in the Lord, we likely become 'water-logged' with anxiety and fear. The 'adventures' in our lives are opportunities for us to hold steady in Him. Think of it – what the oil in the 'Preen Gland' does for a duck, faith and trust in the Lord does for a Christian. When regularly and actively applied, they provide a protective barrier enabling us to live securely and walk faithfully through the challenges that come.

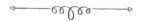

Special memories and a great truth

Numbers 6:24-26 The LORD bless you and keep you; ²⁵the LORD make his face shine upon you and be gracious to you; ²⁶the LORD turn his face toward you and give you peace.

Remember the story of the little boy who was the ring-bearer for the wedding ceremony and when he went down the aisle he growled at everyone. When asked why, he replied, "That is what a ring BEAR does!" We probably all have wonderful memories of children and the words that they hear being a bit different than the words that are spoken.

When our son Andrew was little, he was convinced the name of the movie was Raiders of the Lost Dark. No matter how Donna tried to convince him otherwise, he wouldn't budge. She finally said, "There is no DARK in the movie!" To which he replied with great exasperation, "I KNOW – IT"S **LOST**!!!!

Another event in the heritage of misheard words occurred here a number of years ago. Every night our oldest son's wife, would sing to and pray with our 2 granddaughters at bedtime. Well one night something really sweet happened. We heard about it the next morning and every time I think of it I laugh. She sang the song that consists of today's verses to the girls at bedtime.

> The Lord bless you and keep you;
> The Lord make His face to shine upon you;
> And bring you peace, And bring you peace, Forever!

So after she finished, one of the girls said to her, "Mom, why do you pray like that for me? Do I really need it?" She answered, "Of course, Honey! We all need it!" To which our granddaughter replied, "But Mommy, I really hate **PEAS**! Please don't ask for that again!"

But after the laughter, remember these thoughts about this hymn that was adapted from Numbers 6:24-26. The great evangelist D. L. Moody, in his *Notes from My Bible*, made the following statement about this benediction:

"Here is a benediction that can give all the time without being impoverished. Every heart may utter it, every letter may conclude with it, every day may begin with it, every night may be sanctified by it. Here is blessing—keeping—shining—the uplifting upon our poor life of all heaven's glad morning. It is the Lord Himself who (gives us) this bar of music from heaven's infinite anthem."

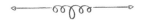

We can have 'pollutants' in our hearts

Matthew 5:8 Blessed are the pure in heart, for they will see God.

This is a verse that is so rich in promise and at the same time contains a foreboding warning that we must not ignore. As born again followers of Jesus, we can have 'pollutants' in our hearts – stuff that just shouldn't be there. Unfortunately, we tend to be far more concerned over what is in the food we eat or the water we drink.

I think of the religious leaders in the time of Jesus. Here they had Jesus, the Christ, the Son of God right in front of them and the 'pollutants' in their hearts caused them to focus on everything but the reality God had right in front of them. What were miracles, signs and wonders and the greatest teaching that mankind has ever heard compared to who Jesus was eating with; who he was talking to; who he was associating with; and whether he did something he 'shouldn't' do on the Sabbath.

The scary thing is that the same thing can happen to us. We can be so affected by the unclean stuff in our hearts, that we miss God. We can become spiritually blind and disoriented. That which should be avoided is embraced; while that which should be embraced is avoided. It results in us missing the life and blessing that God has for us – the wonder of Him working in us day by day.

We like to hear about being 'Blessed' and 'seeing God' but it is the core of being pure in heart that must command our attention. We must come to understand what that means and commit ourselves to getting there. Matthew Henry has some helpful thoughts on this verse:

"Here holiness and happiness are fully described and put together. The heart must be purified by faith, and kept for God. Create in me such a clean heart, O God. None but the pure are capable of seeing God, nor would heaven be happiness to the impure. As God cannot endure to look upon their iniquity, so they cannot look upon his purity."

A clean heart is what God desires. Let us remember Jesus' words that describe the uncleanness that can come from within – when we do not take following Jesus seriously:

"'For from within, out of men's hearts, come evil thoughts, sexual immorality, theft, murder, adultery, [22]greed, malice, deceit, lewdness, envy, slander, arrogance and folly. [23]All these evils come from inside and make a man 'unclean.'" Mark 7:21-22

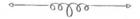

A moving scene from Ben-Hur

Galatians 6:10 Therefore, as we have opportunity, let us do good to all people, especially to those who belong to the family of believers.

This morning I was pondering this verse and while pouring myself a cup of coffee, I thought of a moving scene in the movie Ben-Hur. Judah Ben-Hur, a Jewish prince, is betrayed into slavery by a friend who is an ambitious Roman officer. While being marched with other slaves to the sea they go through Nazareth. All of the slaves are desperate for water.

The entire group is getting water from the people of Nazareth- except for Judah. The people are forbidden by the guards from giving him any water. Judah collapses to the ground in utter anguish overcome with thirst. But then, into the scene comes a young man, a carpenter, who had observed what was happening from his hut. Ignoring the guards, he comes and kneels and lifts Judah's head and gives him water to drink. I am in tears writing this, overcome with the power, tenderness and kindness exhibited in the scene.

The guard angrily yells at him to stop but the carpenter doesn't. Instead, he stands and faces the guard who then backs down, unable to withstand the power of this carpenter as they face each other. All during the encounter, you can see in Judah's face the gratitude, the wonder and bewilderment of what just happened. He knows that his life was just saved. As he later learns, he just encountered Jesus of Nazareth.

While this is a dramatic scene, the point I want to make is the value of offering someone who is thirsty a drink of water; someone who is weary, a helping hand; someone who is discouraged a word of encouragement; someone who is heartbroken, a shoulder to lean on; someone who feels overwhelmed, a friend who says you're not alone. May we recognize and respond to the many opportunities that surround us to do the good that our Lord expects of us. This is loving one another and is at the heart of following Jesus.

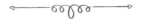

Despair to prayer to faith

Psalm 13:5, 6 But I trust in your unfailing love; my heart rejoices in your salvation. ⁶ I will sing to the LORD, for he has been good to me.

How long?? How long is it going to take me to find a job? How long will it be before you answer my prayer, Lord? How long before my spouse, or son, or daughter or friend, comes to know you? How long am I going to have to struggle with_____? (fill in the blank)

What things are going on in our lives that the above questions describe our pleas to God? Or, maybe we aren't praying but simply asking ourselves these questions in frustration. The struggles just seem to be never-ending and have led us to hopelessness and despair. We become convinced we are alone and are stuck in situations with no way out.

When reading today's faith-filled verses, we might respond, yes, but…. If you only knew…. While they declare such wonderful and important truths, we can respond thinking they are at odds with our situations. But, if we look a few verses earlier, we see that David was in the midst of serious struggles when he cried out to God with questions just like these.

Four times in verses 1 and 2 David expresses his despair in asking God "How long?"

¹How long, O LORD? Will you forget me forever? How long will you hide your face from me? ²How long must I wrestle with my thoughts and every day have sorrow in my heart? How long will my enemy triumph over me?

But then in verses 3 and 4 David's despair becomes prayer:

³Look on me and answer, O LORD my God. Give light to my eyes, or I will sleep in death; ⁴my enemy will say, "I have overcome him," and my foes will rejoice when I fall.

Praise God, David's prayer leads to his wonderful faith-filled declaration of the truth:

⁵But I trust in your unfailing love; my heart rejoices in your salvation. ⁶ I will sing to the LORD, for he has been good to me.

Despair – we cannot stop there. Prayer – is vital but is part of the way there. Faith – is where we must be, and where He will lead us.

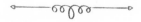

Don Schmidt

Tevye and Golde, "Do you love me?"

John 21:16a Again Jesus said, "Simon son of John, do you truly love me?"

We've written before of the movie Fiddler on the Roof. It is a musical about the life of a family in the small Jewish village of Anatevka, Russia Set in 1905 it tells the story of Tevye, his wife, Golde, and their five daughters. The repeated 'problem' that Tevye and Golde contend with is their daughters falling in love and wanting to marry.

'Tradition' – which was very important to them – held that marriages were to be arranged, by the parents and the village 'matchmaker' – NOT by the young men and women falling in love! After his oldest two daughters fall in love and receive approval to marry the ones they love, Tevye is struck by this novel idea of love being the true matchmaker. He then asks Golde this same question that's in today's verse, "Do you love me?" The ensuing song of this name is such a sweet scene. We get to watch and listen as Tevye and Golde consider this 'love' and conclude that in fact they do love one another.

Let us picture ourselves in a situation where we are alone, in a quiet enjoyable place, sitting peaceably, and thinking about our faith. Then, in the chair next to us, Jesus appears and we know it is Him. After the initial shock and thrill of sitting there with our Lord, Jesus looks at us, and with kindness in His eyes, asks, "Do you love me?" And after we likely answer, "Of course, I do." He responds by asking, "How do you know that you love me? What is the evidence of your love for me?"

Consider those questions now: Do you love Him? How do you know you love Him? What is the evidence of your love for Him? The question is not about His love for us – but our love for Him. Do we fully realize that God has defined what the evidence is of loving Him? It's not about what we think, but about the reality of what our lives demonstrate.

Our response is key to the outcome

2 Kings 5:11, 12 But Naaman went away angry and said, "I thought that he would surely come out to me and stand and call on the name of the LORD his God, wave his hand over the spot and cure me of my leprosy. ¹²Are not Abana and Pharpar, the rivers of Damascus, better than any of the waters of Israel? Couldn't I wash in them and be cleansed?" So he turned and went off in a rage.

Naaman was a valiant soldier and commander of the army of the king of Aram. He was highly regarded and viewed as a great man by the king because through him, the Lord had given victory to Aram– but Naaman was a leper.

A young girl from Israel had been taken captive and served Naaman's wife. She said to her mistress, *"If only my master would see the prophet who is in Samaria! He would cure him of his leprosy."* 2 Kings 5:3 So Naaman traveled to Israel with his horses and chariots (befitting a great man) and came to the door of Elisha's house.

Then **'the event'** happened! Elisha didn't come out, but instead, sent a messenger with word for Naaman to, *"Go, wash yourself seven times in the Jordan, and your flesh will be restored and you will be cleansed."* But Naaman exploded as expressed in today's verses and went off in a rage. In his pride, he expected to be treated with honor and respect by the prophet himself; in a manner consistent with his greatness and stature.

But it didn't happen that way. [Note: His response reminds me of how the religious leaders reacted to Jesus when he performed miracles on the Sabbath. They were so angered, they missed the Christ!] Fortunately, Naaman was an extraordinary man and he had some extraordinary servants: (continuing in 2 Kings 5)

¹³Naaman's servants went to him and said, "My father, if the prophet had told you to do some great thing, would you not have done it? How much more, then, when he tells you, 'Wash and be cleansed'!" ¹⁴So he went down and dipped himself in the Jordan seven times, as the man of God had told him, and his flesh was restored and became clean like that of a young boy.

Naaman, listened to his servants – in spite of his anger and pride – and responded in obedience, and received the miracle! If he hadn't listened – or if they hadn't spoken up – he would have returned to Aram as a leper. But he set aside his pride, responded to God's Word and received God's provision.

This lesson is HUGE for us!!! We must recognize that in our daily lives we encounter situations where if we listen, respond with humility and do what we're told, we receive the blessing. If not, we miss God's provision for us. How many times do we reject the message because we reject the messenger, or because of how it is given? May we learn from Naaman's example!

Recognizing our bad habits

Matthew 5:13 "You are the salt of the earth. But if the salt loses its saltiness, how can it be made salty again? It is no longer good for anything, except to be thrown out and trampled by men."

Do you have any bad habits? If so, how many and how bad? What if we don't know if we have any bad habits? What if we erroneously think everything is fine, when it's not? How do we know if a habit is bad or not?

One of my more embarrassing bad habits occurred early in my business career. Even worse it was brought to my attention twice! I first had a co-worker confront me and then later my boss took me aside and told me that I had body odor and it was noticeable! I remember the co-worker was one of our top sales people and he was mortified at having to tell me this but he respected me and the work I did. His discomfort at telling me was not as bad as listening to others ridiculing me.

What about being impatient? Curt? Difficult to work with? Selfish? Prone to anger? Prideful? Overly talkative? Rude? Always insisting on our own way? The list can just go on and on. Habits are involved in every area of our lives. They are the things we normally do or how we respond and they impact those around us.

Jesus tells us that Christians are to be salt and light. The question then becomes how "salty" are we. This is where our habits define us. Fortunately, one of the major things that God does in responding to prayer is to make us aware of our own shortcomings – our sins – our bad habits. Sometimes through His word and sometimes using family or friends. We then get the opportunity to respond.

When we recognize, confess and repent of these things, we are forgiven – and God is so generous with His mercy. But we must recognize that the long lasting requirement of our faith is that these habits MUST disappear from our lives. Such habits are the very nature of 'unsaltiness'. They can effectively undermine and negate any of the good that we do. Think of all the sexual impurity on TV, in magazines, in movies and on the Internet. He can free us from it – and keep us free!

Thank God that His grace and power are sufficient to enable us to walk free of any sinful behavior (bad habit). As we pray and seek Him, let us be grateful for the continuing wonder of His work in our lives. Let our hearts cry for Him to make us the salty followers of Jesus that will draw others to Him.

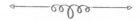

Don Schmidt

The example Ruth is for us!

Ruth 2:10-12 ¹⁰At this, she bowed down with her face to the ground. She asked him, "Why have I found such favor in your eyes that you notice me—a foreigner?"

I find such delight in reading about Ruth and the ways she responds to the difficulties and reality of her life. She has wonderful attitudes; she works hard; she loves Naomi and cares for her; by doing the right things, she is blessed by the Lord. What an example her story is for us! In spite of all the difficulty in the situation she and Naomi found themselves in, she was simply concerned with caring for Naomi and making their situation better.

The quality of Ruth's life was recognized by those around her and by Boaz who she encounters in today's verse:

¹¹Boaz replied, "I've been told all about what you have done for your mother-in-law since the death of your husband—how you left your father and mother and your homeland and came to live with a people you did not know before. ¹²May the LORD repay you for what you have done. May you be richly rewarded by the LORD, the God of Israel, under whose wings you have come to take refuge."

Her reputation preceded her and the quality of her life was apparent to those around her. Boaz's comment about her taking refuge under the wings of the LORD, the God of Israel, is a picture of God's protection. By doing the 'right things', Ruth put herself into a position to encounter God's best for her.

God led Ruth to Boaz's field, where she was safe. The timing of Boaz's arrival on this day was perfect for her. The Lord caused her to find favor with him and he became God's 'hands extended' to her, to protect her and provide for both Naomi and her. Isn't Ruth's life and Boaz's response a perfect illustration of Matthew 5:15?

> *"In the same way, let your light shine before others, that they may see your good deeds and glorify your Father in heaven."*

The simple reality of our lives is that God wants others to see Him when they observe us!

The Lord loves right attitudes. He loves the right and appropriate things that we do. He loves to provide his blessing and protection to us. He loves to guide us in the path of righteousness that He has for us. He loves to see His plan unfold in our lives. He loves it when we love Him. No matter what difficulties we find ourselves in, He is for us and with us. May our lives ever reflect these wondrous realities!

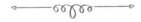

How do God's people forget?

Judges 2:10 After that whole generation had been gathered to their ancestors, another generation grew up who knew neither the LORD nor what he had done for Israel.

Today's verse describes something that I simply cannot fathom. How do a people forget they have been slaves? How do they forget Moses and Joshua and what they did? How do they forget the stories of being delivered by God in the most miraculous way – with all the plagues upon Egypt?

How do they stop telling the stories of walking through the parted Red Sea, and then seeing the Egyptian army swallowed up? How do a people stop telling the stories of the miracles in the wilderness and seeing the manifestations of their God? How does their God become irrelevant in the Promised Land?

These people served the Lord throughout the lifetime of Joshua and of the elders who outlived him and who had seen all the great things the Lord had done for Israel. (Judges 2:7) But then they did exactly what the Lord warned them might happen – they forgot the Lord who brought them out of Egypt, out of the land of slavery. (Deuteronomy 6:12) They forgot everything He did – and they forgot Him.

Let us take care that something similar doesn't happen to us. May the reality of His love in our lives and our lives lived for Him be rich and deep. Not something artificial or more talk than substance. If we 'claim it' without 'living it', may we recognize it is because we are forgetting; we are missing; we are allowing the focus of our lives to lead us astray.

We must remember the blessings that have occurred and recognize the blessings that we have. Most of all, we must be aware of the Lord and His kindness to us in everything, no matter what the circumstances look like. We are the richest people in the world if we have Jesus. May the awe and wonder of that fact be the ever growing reality of our lives!

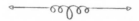

'Love letters' to Him and those around us

Hebrews 11:16 Instead, they were longing for a better country—a heavenly one. Therefore God is not ashamed to be called their God, for he has prepared a city for them.

How about we take a brief walk down memory lane? Let's think of some occasions when we were growing up when our actions resulted in our mom or dad or family being proud of us. Hopefully we all have an abundant supply of them. Maybe you didn't cheat on a test when others did. Maybe you found a wallet with money in it and returned it.

Maybe you were a good student or a good team player who played the game well and by the rules. Maybe you helped around the house or possibly helped a neighbor who needed it. Maybe you willingly did what your parents asked you to do without arguing and causing them grief.

The reality of life is that there is another side to this coin. Maybe there are things that we did that we are very glad that our parents didn't know about. We would not have wanted to experience the pain of them becoming aware of what we'd done. Maybe we have memories of things where they did find out and we have regret that is still painful. Maybe our lives were lived in this realm of the negative and when we were younger it seemed we didn't care. We were going to live our lives the way we wanted.

Think about the prodigal son who took his share of the inheritance and lived a life consistent with the pigsty where he wound up. When he came to his senses recognizing his sinful ways, he returned to his father who overwhelmed him with his loving response. Do you think that this son was glad that his father hadn't been there to see the life he lived; that his father didn't see him starving with the pigs? Although he was a son, he recognized that based on the life he lived, he was no longer worthy to be his son.

We need to understand that as Christians – claimers to be followers of Jesus – people who are genuinely born again, saved by the grace and mercy of God – that He calls us to live lives worthy of, and consistent with, our being His sons and daughters. The choices we make play a vital role in the lifelong work of the Holy Spirit wherein He transforms us into the image of Jesus.

This is not about earning anything. It's about recognizing that we have a responsibility and destiny to glorify our Lord here and now; AND that destiny requires us to make faithful choices that reflect who we are in Him. Our lives are to be living "love letters" to Him that all those around us can read.

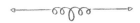

John Wesley's Covenant Prayer

*Hebrews 1:3 The Son is the radiance of God's glory and the exact representation
of his being, sustaining all things by his powerful word. After he had provided
purification for sins, he sat down at the right hand of the Majesty in heaven.*

Today I get to share with you a marvelous prayer that has really blessed me. I first encountered it in a Confirmation Service at St Luke's Anglican. John Wesley, founder of Methodism, is the author and this prayer is still a vibrant part of the church that was influenced by his ministry.

John Wesley used this prayer with all of his ministers to signify their commitment to the task of ministry. It was also used by the English Methodist churches in a service at the start of each year for "Renewing our Covenant with God".

This prayer requires a genuine humility to pray it sincerely. Let our hearts to be convicted if we are lacking in that regard. It recognizes the reality of God's claim on our lives and the attitudes our faith in Jesus Christ require of us. Jesus is the radiance of God's glory and the exact representation of His being. May we recommit ourselves to our covenant keeping God. I pray that this prayer will be a blessing to you as it has been to me.

Wesley Covenant Prayer
I am no longer my own, but yours.
Put me to what you will, rank me with whom you will;
put me to doing, put me to suffering.
Let me be employed by you or laid aside by you,
enabled for you or brought low by you.
Let me be full, let me be empty.
Let me have all things, let me have nothing.
I freely and heartily yield all things to your pleasure and disposal.
And now, O glorious and blessed God, Father, Son, and Holy Spirit,
you are mine, and I am yours. So be it.
And the covenant which I have made on earth, let it be ratified in heaven. Amen.

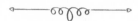

How do we or how will we respond?

John 15:18 If the world hates you, keep in mind in mind that it hated me first.

Have you ever been bullied? Have you ever been one of those people that a bully looked for and as soon as he saw you he came running to mess with you? Fortunately such things typically only happen to some of us when we're children. Plus we live in a western culture where such behavior is generally disapproved of.

But think of being in a culture where this type of behavior is a way of life and instead of the bully being an individual, it is a group, or mob or even family. Worse still consider the reality that all ages are affected by such groups – not just children – and it includes anything from beating to burning to killing. Becoming a target, results in the reality that it could cost you your life. So, what makes a person a target of such groups?

In many places in the world today, becoming a follower of Jesus Christ makes one a target of such groups, resulting in severe, often bloody persecution. Conversion to Jesus Christ requires a price that many in the West just don't realize. Fortunately Jesus is more than worth the price!

We encounter discrimination and persecution but it is more in the context Christian activities being excluded from all manner of places where they have always existed: Merry Christmas becomes Happy Holidays; Christmas vacation becomes Winter break; no prayers at graduation ceremonies; situations in the military where Chaplains are ordered not to pray in the name of Jesus.

We have had a rule of law here that has protected us. But in too many other parts of the world that law doesn't exist or is ignored. There, becoming a believer in Jesus Christ often results in disowning, disinheritance, expulsion, arrest or death. The hatred that Jesus spoke of (today's verse) is alive and well in the world.

People all over the world – today – are being tortured, beaten, enslaved, imprisoned and broken because of the truth of the Gospel of Jesus Christ. Recognizing the love of God and Jesus Christ as Lord & Savior, triggers a hateful revenge in so many places that we in the west are often clueless about. But this is what so many of our brothers and sisters in Christ are facing and experiencing.

We must remember the spiritual reality that exists in all this. Paul reminds us in Ephesians 6:12 *"For our struggle is not against flesh and blood, but against the rulers, against the authorities, against the powers of this dark world and against the spiritual forces of evil in the heavenly realms."* Fortunately, Jesus has equipped us all to face and overcome such opposition, *"because the one who is in you is greater than the one who is in the world."* 1 John 4:4b

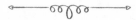

The wonder of forgiving!

Colossians 3:13 Bear with each other and forgive whatever grievances you may have against one another. Forgive as the Lord forgave you.

Do we understand that forgiving someone is a simple decision of our will? Better still is the fact that once done, once we forgive someone, it cannot be undone – no matter how upset we are or want to take it back. It's done; a fait accompli!

Think of cracking open a raw egg. It is a decision of our will and once done it can't be undone. No matter how we might want to take it back, we can't put the egg back in the shell. Remember Humpty Dumpty, the egg that sat on the wall and had a great fall? "…All the King's horses, and all the King's men - couldn't put Humpty together again."

This is beyond good news – it's great news! Unforgiveness is to be avoided like the plague. In an earlier devotional I wrote how it's been described as a person putting arsenic in their own body to hurt someone else. Unforgiveness is avoided by forgiving – particularly by making the practice of forgiving others into a daily habit pattern.

But what if we don't feel forgiving? And what about all the other 'stuff' that comes with situations where the need to forgive occurs? Stuff like anger, resentment, hurt, disappointment, frustration, desire to get even (to name a few) that readily accompany such situations. Fortunately forgiveness isn't subject to us feeling like it.

If we are out walking and have an umbrella and suddenly it starts pouring, no matter what is going on, we immediately put up the umbrella – it's second nature. It keeps us from getting wet! When hurts and disappointments come, immediately forgive – just like putting up an umbrella. It keeps unforgiveness away and allows God's grace to have unrestricted flow to enable us to handle all the 'stuff' in the situation redemptively.

Immediately forgiving others enables us to get our focus off them and our own hurt. We shift our focus to the Lord. He is the one we turn to – to help us with all of the accompanying emotions and difficulties. If we recognize that our responses our sinful, we can confess that and receive forgiveness. He, and his grace and mercy are at the center of our response.

It's amazing how readily forgiving those who hurt us enables us to pray redemptively for them. The healing process proceeds more freely. Our motivation can become one of glorifying the Lord in the situation. What a gift being able to readily forgive is!

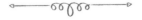

Trusting God in the midst of our trials

Proverbs 3:6 in all your ways acknowledge him, and he will direct your paths.

There have been times in our lives when we found ourselves in the midst of job hunting and house hunting. What adventures with both going on at the same time. We didn't view ourselves as victims or as being deprived. They were just times to walk through circumstances that the Lord allowed to come. Even though we struggled, we were sustained by the goodness of our Lord. By focusing upon the Lord and trusting in Him we came out fine. But I thought it would be helpful to share a bit of what we went through.

Did we encounter anxiety, fear, frustration, uncertainty and questions? Yes we did, but we didn't give in to them. Did we experience times of wondering why this had to happen? And what is the Lord doing with us? Yes we did.

Did God give us daily marching orders? No He did not. Was God quiet most of the time? Yes He was. Was it a major blessing for each of us to have the other spouse committed to the Lord and pursuing what He wants for us? Unquestionably! Did we experience times of despair and defeat? No, not at all. While it was disappointing not to get a particular job, that just meant God has something else. God provided what we needed when we needed it.

Because of the wonderful treasury that we have of experiences with God, we were able to encourage one another with many, "Remember when God did…." We reminded each other of stories of God's people in the Bible who, when faced with far greater trials, responded with faith and trusted the Lord. We also noted those stories where they didn't respond in faith and we were determined to learn from those examples.

One of the great blessings of God's goodness is by focusing on Him; He frees us from the fear of making a mistake. Being human, we're prone to make mistakes. But we just sense that by keeping the Lord at the center, we will find what He wants us to have. We trust Him that things will work out no matter what does or doesn't happen. He is looking out for us and directing us in His path. The unknown to us is not unknown to Him.

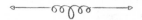

Can you picture Jesus smiling at you?

1 Peter 1:8 ⁹You never saw him, yet you love him. You still don't see him, yet you trust him—with laughter and singing. The Message

After I met Jesus years ago, I remember being told about an older prominent Christian by the name of Rufus Moseley. Apparently he had a great deal of joy and for some strange reason some church people had a problem with that. One old dour-faced Christian came up to him and sourly asked, "Do you think Jesus ever smiled?" Rufus looked at her, grinned and answered, "I don't know, but He sure fixed it so I can!"

I love to think of Jesus smiling and laughing. I'm so grateful for paintings I've seen where the artist has presented Him doing so. Then there's Johnny Cash's film Gospel Road that has such wonderful scenes of Jesus laughing and smiling with the disciples and children.

There was also a production called The Thorn that began in Colorado Springs about 20+ years ago that was very similar to The Passion of the Christ. It told the story of Jesus, and the violence done to Him was vividly represented. But this serious production also presented Jesus as a man who smiled and expressed such joy when the miracles were performed and in times with His disciples.

Think of Jesus healing crippled children and their stunned and ecstatic response. Can't you just see the incredible joy in His face as He performed these wonders? Can't you just see these children running to Jesus and jumping in His arms, squealing with delight! Think of His face and the utter joy it would express.

This is our Lord. This is the One we live with and for. The Amplified Bible presents today's verse this way:

> ⁸*Without having seen Him, you love Him; though you do not [even] now see Him, you believe in Him **and exult and thrill with inexpressible and glorious (triumphant, heavenly) joy**.*

Oh my goodness, there are times when the wonder of what we have in Jesus is so overwhelming! It just seems too good to be true. Hopefully you regularly have such moments of wonder too.

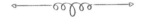

Real versus artificial

1 Peter 1:7 These have come so that your faith—of greater worth than gold, which perishes even though refined by fire—may be proved genuine and may result in praise, glory and honor when Jesus Christ is revealed.

Have you ever thought about the difference between what's real and what's artificial? Depending upon the circumstances it might be irrelevant or it might be significant. I don't think we'd want to bite into artificial fruit – we might break a tooth; but seeing a bouquet of artificial flowers is another thing. But you sure wouldn't expect to see a garden of artificial flowers. Context can make a big difference.

Personally I love bouquets of fresh cut flowers. Given my love of flowers, their beauty and fragrance, I have a couple of bouquets in the house to enjoy. But many are the times I've experienced the disappointment of being attracted to plants or bouquets only to discover they weren't real.

Do we realize that any discussion of real versus artificial takes on a whole different dimension when we talk about our lives and relationships? How do we and others present ourselves when we go somewhere? . How often do we hear of marriages breaking up and it comes as a total surprise to even close friends or family? Instead of a genuine quality relationship, the representation of the marriage was artificial.

The same problems can appear in individuals, families, friendships or working relationships. The issue isn't to broadcast our problems to the world but to recognize the importance of our lives; that as Christians – Jesus followers – they must be the real thing. There are times when we need help to get through stuff and we mustn't let pride get in the way. Beautiful gardens don't happen over night; they take work. So do quality lives and relationships.

We must take advantage of the grace, mercy, instruction and resources that God gives us; plus the enabling power of the Holy Spirit to become the genuine reality that He desires. When we do, our lives are real – not artificial – because they are the work of His of hands. He is the potter – we are the clay.

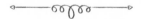

"Oh Jesus, keep me from this!"

Isaiah 29:13 The Lord says: "These people come near to me with their mouth and honor me with their lips, but their hearts are far from me. Their worship of me is made up only of rules taught by men.

One day, a number of years ago at work, I began experiencing significant chest pain. My staff wanted me to go to the hospital and get checked over. I thought I was going to be okay and refused. They insisted that I call my wife Donna. So I did and she told me just what they did – but I stubbornly insisted that I was okay.

A few minutes later my oldest son John called me in response to Donna's call to him. He had been a paramedic. I'll never forget his lovingly blunt words to me. He said, "Dad. There are two symptoms you never ignore: a pregnant lady having contractions and a guy your age with chest pain. Get to the hospital – NOW!"

So my staff took me to the hospital and over two days I went through a bunch of tests. The good news was – no heart problem. Every test came out good. But John's advice was still right on. My stubbornness and lack of grasping the obvious could have cost me my life.

Chest pains and contractions are kind of hard to be unaware of. They might be ignored for a while but as they intensify, they sure can interrupt things. Today's verse is just as serious but is much more subtle. It describes a deadly condition that we as God's people can have and yet be blind to. This verse is one I have identified on my "Oh Jesus – keep me from this!" list.

There are many descriptions in Scripture of what to avoid but there are some – and today's verse is one – that are particularly foreboding. It describes God's people as living in deception. They think they are pleasing to Him but they're not. Their words and outward actions are rendered meaningless because of their hearts.

In the New Testament (Revelation 2 & 3), think of the letters to the Churches in Laodicea and Ephesus. The Laodiceans thought they were rich, but Jesus considered them *"wretched, pitiful, poor, blind and naked"*! The Ephesians were doing many things right, but Jesus charged them with having left their first love and commanded them to repent.

Unfortunately, the same things can and do happen to His people today. May we never give our Lord lip service, with our hearts far from Him. May our hearts be truly His. May our lives be living examples of a people who are truly rich in Him. Most of all, may we learn to love Him more and more with each passing day!

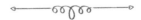

Players in the game, not spectators in the bleachers

I Chronicles 12:32 a men of Issachar, who understood the times and knew what Israel should do.

Have you ever felt clueless as to what is going on in the world around us? It seems that the media and some of our leaders are clueless to reality – at least in terms of communicating facts and truth and making sound decisions. Those erroneous communications and faulty decisions affect us all.

It's almost like a tsunami of serious events is sweeping the world right now and these events affect God's people everywhere. We have massive media and societal reactions to events with little or no concern for the truth. It seems to be about achieving desired outcomes, specifically for those creating the uproar.

We are living in the midst of this and it's imperative that we, and our leaders, respond with understanding, wisdom and righteousness. Today's verse in the Old Testament is a hidden jewel. It's easy to miss as it's included in a list of the various groups of men who came to David at Hebron to turn Saul's kingdom over to him.

The men of Issachar are described here in Scripture in a way that is such an example for us. **They understood the times and knew what Israel must do!** We need to pray for this for ourselves, our leaders, for Israel, for our military leaders and for Christians around the world. God has wisdom, insight and understanding that is available to all those who seek Him.

We have a vital role to play. We must not be clueless and resign ourselves to irrelevancy. We are born to glorify our Lord and we are at His mercy – not the mercy of the events surrounding us. No matter how helpless we might feel, we are active 'ingredients' in the hands of our Lord and Savior.

Our prayers can move mountains! Our faith-filled words and attitudes can impact those around us and influence them towards righteousness. We too can respond faithfully to the events around us and further His kingdom. Jesus, by His Spirit, will enable us to understand our times and will guide us in what to do.

<u>Let us remember – we are players in the game – not spectators in the bleachers!</u>

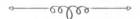

Faith and love

2 Thessalonians 1:3 We ought always to thank God for you, brothers, and rightly so, because your faith is growing more and more, and the love every one of you has for each other is increasing.

Peanut butter and jelly. Eggs and ham. Love and marriage. Prayer and fasting. Knowing to do good and doing it. Some things just go together. Some pairs we can think of don't take much or any effort to bring about a pleasant result. Others require constructive effort. Some have the element – and requirement – to grow. They aren't static.

Winning and losing. Success and failure. Pass and fail. Good and bad. These pairs go together too but are radically different than those above. They describe the results of what is done or attempted. In sporting events, winning and losing are evident if one is looking at the score. But sometimes an individual or team can lose the game but may be viewed as a success because of their growth and effort.

Think of the NCAA Basketball Tournament. Only one team gets to be champion but just qualifying for the tournament is a victory – as is progressing to the Sweet 16, the Elite Eight and to the Final Four. And it's not just an issue of effort. A fact of life is that misguided or undirected effort doesn't mean a positive result.

So many activities in our lives require instruction, practice and intentionality in order to produce desirable results. They are not passive like watching TV, or listening to the radio, or reading a book – or simply going to church or acknowledging we are Christians.

At work or in school; in sports or relationships; in family and as ones claiming the name of Jesus – results are a given. With the passage of time, any close observer will be able to assess what the results look like. We must recognize that as followers of Jesus that we bear a responsibility for the results we produce. This applies to what we do and who we are – and who we are becoming.

Two of the most critical areas of responsibility that we bear as Jesus followers are identified in today's verse: faith and love. What a wonderful assessment that Paul gives the Thessalonians! Their faith and their love for one another are growing and increasing. Godly results are being produced. May our lives be of such quality and commitment that the same assessment could be made of us.

Opportunity comes with being wrong

Proverbs 25:11, 12 The right word at the right time is like a custom-made piece of jewelry, And a wise friend's timely reprimand is like a gold ring slipped on your finger. The Message

My wife Donna has this wonderful habit. When the two of us disagree on something, she is right about 99% of the time. I'm not certain but I suspect on those rare occasions when she is mistaken, that she's just being kind and giving me an opportunity to be right.

A similar situation exists with our sons. They are right and I am wrong a whole lot more often than seems reasonable – particularly when it comes to remembering things. It's not that it happens all the time - just frequently enough for them to remind me. It typically results in smiles and laughter. The feelings I experience are similar to those I have when they share stories of goofy things I have done over the years.

I realize this sounds pretty dumb but isn't it better to discover that we are mistaken about something and accept correction than to go merrily on our way being wrong? There are situations where it's easier to accept correction like if we're going the wrong direction to get somewhere or when an event is scheduled.

But what about when our beliefs, actions or attitudes in relationships are either wrong or less than they should be? How positive (or negative) are our responses to someone informing us of that? Is this an area where we have created (through our past responses) a big NO TRESPASSING sign? Our family and friends know they go there at their own risk - sort of the only thing worse than me being wrong is you making the mistake of informing me of that fact.

It all boils down to being teachable and becoming a lover of the truth. We are to have a spirit that wants to improve and is willing to hear and receive a timely word or some corrective input. Think of how wonderful it is when something we share is graciously received. Of course it always helps if it is graciously given, but the truth is the truth no matter how it's given.

Being a lover of the truth means that we don't reject the message because 1) we reject the messenger, nor 2) the manner in which the message was given. We have our ears attuned to the Spirit and we cultivate an attitude that responds righteously to other's input. It's amazing the things we can learn about ourselves and the helpful changes we can make when we do.

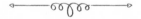

Ruth and her wonderful destiny

Ruth 1:16 But Ruth replied, "Don't urge me to leave you or to turn back from you. Where you go I will go, and where you stay I will stay. Your people will be my people and your God my God.

This is one of my favorite verses in the Bible. It speaks of such devotion, commitment and love. Ruth had lost her husband, but her mother-in-law Naomi had lost her own husband and both her sons. Naomi and her family had moved to Moab from Bethlehem ten years earlier due to the famine in the land. Both sons had married there in Moab.

Into this situation of grief and difficulty came word that the LORD had come to the aid of His people in Judah and there was food there. Naomi and the two daughter-in-laws (the other being Orpah) prepared to return to her home in Bethlehem. Once on the road, Naomi lovingly instructed the two women to return to the homes of their mothers. She believed this was best for them because her perception was that the LORD's hand had been against her.

After weeping and protestations from the young women, Orpah returned. But Ruth clung to Naomi and spoke the wonderful message of today's verse. Why did Ruth do it? Was her mother's home not desirable? Was she motivated by her love for Naomi, and therefore wanting to support her in this time of grief and change? Whatever it was, her commitment was complete because she declared, "Your people will be my people and your God my God".

Ruth wasn't aware that God was guiding her – that He was in the midst of her strong commitment to stay with Naomi. She was simply responding to the conviction in her heart that she belonged with Naomi and would not leave her no matter what it brought. In the midst of all of this, her direction was clear and she was committed to it. Little did Ruth know that her destiny required that she come to Bethlehem – and that she be there as a young woman eligible to be married. It's possible that the whole move to Moab by Naomi and her family was ultimately designed to get Ruth and bring her back to Bethlehem.

We are in the Christmas season. Bethlehem is so significant in the birth of Jesus for that is where the prophet declared that the Christ would be born (Micah 5:2; Matthew 2:1-6). Given what happens to Ruth after arriving in Bethlehem, it's apparent that she had to get there first – in order for Christ to come. Her commitment to return to Judah with Naomi enabled God's destiny for her to unfold. It required her to be there, in Bethlehem, because only there would her life became part of the genealogy of Christ, our Messiah – the son of David, the son of Abraham.

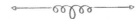

Mary's 'scandalous' pregnancy

Luke 1:34 "How will this be," Mary asked the angel, "since I am a virgin?"

We are thrilled with the birth of Jesus and the miracle of a virgin giving birth to the Christ as foretold by Isaiah. But have you considered what God had Mary and Joseph walk through to bring this about? **Who would have believed what they said** – other than Elizabeth and Zechariah?

We are all aware that Mary was pledged to be married to Joseph when the angel appeared to her and she conceived Jesus by the working of the Holy Spirit. Joseph became aware of her being pregnant and was planning to divorce her quietly. But then the angel appeared to him in a dream explaining everything so he took Mary home as his wife. But...

What did Mary say to her parents and friends when asked about the pregnancy? How likely was it that they believed her explanation? Did she tell Joseph what happened? If so, he didn't believe her prior to his dream. What did Joseph say to his friends or his relatives? Would they have believed him?

Think of the looks and comments that reflected suspicion that the baby was due to him, or worse, some other man. How likely was it that anyone believed that her pregnancy was due to God's direct intervention? On top of this, consider the thought that this "scandal" likely followed them, all the days of their lives.

Yet this was their destiny. God chose them for it – knowing that it would be hard, but that He would be with them. Mary and Joseph were chosen to raise His Son! Imagine being entrusted with Jesus!

This Christmas season, remember Joseph and Mary and the difficult path they had to walk to fulfill God's plan for them. They chose to say "yes" to God no matter what difficulties obedience entailed. They responded with faith. May we respond as well to whatever God may ask of us.

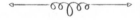

Elizabeth and Mary, chosen by God

Luke 1:45 "Blessed is she who has believed that what the Lord has said to her will be accomplished!"

Elizabeth was filled with the Holy Spirit when she declared this to Mary when Mary came to visit. Elizabeth was 6 months pregnant with John and Mary was pregnant with Jesus. What a blessing and encouragement they were to each other. Both women were chosen by God to do what appeared to be impossible – Elizabeth bearing a baby at her age and Mary a pregnant virgin. Each of them was going to bear their first child. Then there were the incredible prophecies delivered by the angel Gabriel regarding both boys and their destinies. What conversations they must have had!

The Christmas Story is truly miraculous: encounters with angels, God's supernatural intervention, skies opening and heavenly choirs singing, the Star in the East - a Savior is born! The story is amazing. But behind the scenes, God basically chose 2 couples to each bear a son and raise him. The circumstances were incredible! The task of bearing and raising children is common to nearly all.

God has a way of asking us to do ordinary things but the circumstances might be anything but ordinary. He assures us that He will provide what we need while asking for sacrifices that appear to be beyond what we have or are capable of making. Or maybe it is just responding to His Spirit in a particular situation but we are afraid to obey for various reasons.

God is going to use us to proclaim His word and accomplish many things. The more we walk in His ways and keep Him at the center of our lives, the more we will be able to experience the blessing of seeing Him accomplish His purposes through us.

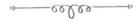

What is Christmas really about?

Isaiah 9:6-7 [6]For to us a child is born, to us a son is given, and the government will be on his shoulders. And he will be called Wonderful Counselor, Mighty God, Everlasting Father, Prince of Peace. [7]Of the greatness of his government and peace there will be no end. He will reign on David's throne and over his kingdom, establishing and upholding it with justice and righteousness from that time on and forever. The zeal of the LORD Almighty will accomplish this.

The Christmas season is a wonderful time of the year. It is so much more than lights, trees, decorations and presents; or nativity scenes, carols, families getting together and movies like White Christmas. It is a focused celebration of our Lord and Savior Jesus Christ. The more we see and recognize Him, the greater it is!

He is the one of whom Isaiah wrote in the above verses. He is the One who is called Wonderful Counselor, Mighty God, Everlasting Father and the Prince of Peace. Jesus is the One who reigns on David's throne forever. Of the greatness of his government and peace there will be no end.

The more we see Jesus the more we are overcome with the awareness that we can never thank Him adequately for what God has done for us. We were lost and separated from God but because of Jesus, we are now His. We are God's people! Peter writes of this wonderfully quoting another verse from Isaiah about this One 1 Peter 2:4-6,

[4]As you come to him, the living Stone—rejected by humans but chosen by God and precious to him— [5]you also, like living stones, are being built into a spiritual house to be a holy priesthood, offering spiritual sacrifices acceptable to God through Jesus Christ. [6] For in Scripture it says:

"See, I lay a stone in Zion, a chosen and precious cornerstone, and the one who trusts in him will never be put to shame." Isaiah 28:16

As Peter goes on to write about 'those who believe' – to whom this stone is precious, he describes what God has done and is doing with us 1 Peter 2:9-10,

⁹But you are a chosen people, a royal priesthood, a holy nation, <u>God's special</u>
<u>possession,</u> that you may declare the praises of him who called you out of darkness
into his wonderful light. ¹⁰<u>Once you were not a people, but now you are the people</u>
<u>of God; once you had not received mercy, but now you have received mercy.</u>

Because of Jesus, we are God's special possession! Because God so loved us, 'unto us a child is born, to us a son is given…' We, who were not a people are now His. We, who had not received mercy, have now received mercy. We get to spend our lives declaring His praises because He called us out of darkness into His wonderful light.

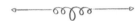

A good learning experience with a TV antenna

Psalm 28:7 Yahweh is my strength and my shield; my heart trusts in him, and I am helped. My heart leaps for joy and I will give thanks to him in song.

Recently I had some goofy experiences that provide a great illustration for us to learn from. We were watching TV where we were staying and it wasn't cable or satellite. It was simply local reception through a small antenna connected to the TV. We were close enough to Cleveland so most of the stations came in fine. But there was one station that was a 'problem child'.

The antenna would sit up on top of the TV cabinet and could receive the handful of stations fine – but not this one. When we turned to it, across the screen would appear "No Signal". Then we'd get up and move the antenna and adjust the two 'arms' on the antenna until we finally found the proper position to receive a strong signal.

This became a real adventure because sometimes, depending on the weather, that signal could be very difficult to receive. So much so, that our determination was affected by how much we wanted to watch a program or sporting event. One night, there was a program we really wanted to watch that required me to stand near the TV, holding the antenna up in order to get reception – for the whole program.

The signal was always there, but sometimes circumstances just made it more difficult to receive. Greater effort and perseverance were required of us to receive it. Also involved was how much we wanted to receive it. Now let's read today's verse again:

"Yahweh is my strength and my shield; my heart trusts in him, and I am helped. My heart leaps for joy and I will give thanks to him in song."

There are times when this reality is clear as a bell. But there are other times when we find ourselves in difficult situations where the reality of this truth becomes fuzzy and unclear. We can even find ourselves in situations where our hearts are reflecting a "No Signal" message. ("Lord, where are you?!")

It's not that this truth isn't there – it is. But by faith we have to seek after it and Him. And sometimes they can be quite elusive – but that mustn't stop us. This seeking activity is a priceless component in the process of us becoming strong in Christ. This truth and the determination to seek Him become bedrock reality in who we are.

No matter what things look like, He is our strength and shield. No matter how difficult we find our situations, our hearts can and will trust in Him. We are never left to ourselves because He helps us – no matter what. Because of Him, our hearts can and will leap for joy and we will sing thanks to Him.

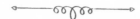

Don Schmidt

Chirping birds reminding me of Him

2 Peter 1:19 We couldn't be more sure of what we saw and heard—God's glory, God's voice. The prophetic Word was confirmed to us. You'll do well to keep focusing on it. It's the one light you have in a dark time as you wait for daybreak and the rising of the Morning Star in your hearts. The Message

I get up quite early each morning and enjoy these devotionals before the day gets going. I begin by making a fresh pot of coffee. While at the kitchen sink this morning I heard what sounded like a bird chirping convention outside. It was still dark out so I couldn't see anything but I could sure hear them. The first thought through my mind was a statement about faith that I have written in the front of my Bible.

"Faith is the bird that feels the light and sings while the dawn is still dark" Tagore. There are a couple things about this experience that really blessed me. The first was to experience something entirely normal – birds chirping when it's dark out – and my mind immediately going to a statement about faith.

The second blessing in the experience was the reminder to respond in faith even though things might seem dark – not evil, just reflecting our inability to see. Those things or situations we're praying for or waiting for God's intervention / provision haven't happened yet, but this experience refocused my mind and heart upon the faithfulness of Jesus. No matter what happens – or doesn't happen – God is faithful.

In terms of the statement above, our attitudes and actions can reflect a belief that the 'dawn' is never coming; darkness is here to stay. We become 'me' oriented, centered in disappointment rather than keeping our focus on the Lord. I love the faith response of Shadrach, Meshach and Abednego to Nebuchadnezzar, in Daniel 3:17, 18

*¹⁷ "If we are thrown into the blazing furnace, the God we serve is able to save us from it, and he will rescue us from your hand, O king. ¹⁸**But even if he does not**, we want you to know, O king, that we will not serve your gods or worship the image of gold you have set up."*

"But even if he does not…" WOW! Isn't that powerful!!! Our faith is in our God, no matter how 'dark' things might be. Our faith is not predicated upon Him rescuing us. Whatever He has for us or allows to come, our faith is in Him.

Let's also remember Paul and Silas, in Acts 16:25 in the Macedonian jail, in the middle of the night, having been beaten and flogged; they were "praying and singing hymns to God". Another WOW!!! Our focus is upon Jesus. He enables us to sing praises to Him, in the midst of darkness because He is the light of our lives.

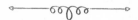

A memorable little book

1 John 2:16 Practically everything that goes on in the world—wanting your own way, wanting everything for yourself, wanting to appear important—has nothing to do with the Father. It just isolates you from him. The Message

This morning I was reminded of a wonderful little book that I read years ago – one that has had a lasting impact on my life. Its title is My Heart, Christ's Home by Robert Boyd Munger. What a treasure this is! It tells the story of a young man who invites Jesus into his life. The storyline presented in the book is one of Jesus coming to live in his house (heart) with him.

I recall in the story Jesus going through the rooms (of his heart) one by one over the passing days and dealing with the things he found there. The young man was thrilled. Remember when we met the Lord we experienced a marvelous house cleaning too. It was like Jesus had a crew that just went through and got rid of all kinds of junk. The cleansing and refreshing were amazing. But then time passes – and the things of this world seep back in.

Picture your heart having a library and Jesus going in and picking up the very books or magazines that you are embarrassed for him to see. Imagine him going into your entertainment center and out of hundreds of movies he just pulls one off the shelf and it's not one that you would want to sit down and watch with him.

I remember seeing a 'great' movie in the year following my becoming a Christian. I was home from college at the time and told my mom about it. She said she would like to see it too. Well my mom loved the Lord and to this day I can remember her repeated reactions to the little 'negatives' in that movie. I was mortified as I recognized the stuff I had missed. We got up and left in the middle of it.

I think the thing that is most painful in the book is when the young man becomes busy – too busy – to spend time with the Lord. Here Jesus is waiting for him each day, to spend time together, and the things of the young man's life just don't leave him the time to do it. As he goes rushing out the door, he has pangs of regret and the intention to make it right – but somehow the days and weeks just seem to go by. May we recognize just how easily the world can seep into our lives and isolate us from our Lord.

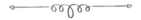

Withstanding the pressure and being evidence of Him

1 Kings 19:18 – "Yet I reserve seven thousand in Israel—all whose knees have not bowed down to Baal and all whose mouths have not kissed him."

Let's imagine ourselves as being included in those 7,000 who were faithful to God so long ago. Everywhere around us, the people have abandoned the truth of God's Word and abandoned Him. On the one hand, we would have the joy of being His people – chosen by Him. We treasure the wonders He has done. On the other, the sorrow and pain of seeing His people sinfully deny Him.

One of the challenges that we would withstand is yielding to the cultural pressure of those around us to become Baal worshippers. No matter what the cost, we would remain true to Yahweh! How would we act around those who were participating in such sin – particularly when they were friends and family? Behavior that they would think is perfectly fine is behavior that is totally unacceptable to Him.

I wrote earlier about being in a meeting with Stephen Covey where he asked everyone in the audience to point in the direction they thought was north. The theatre we were in was 'in the round' so he was surrounded by audience and hands were pointing in every direction. He then lit up an overhead projector with a compass on it where the light could shine through. The lesson? Which way is north is not subject to opinion. It is an absolute.

Do we relate to those 7,000 as we see what is going on around us in society today? The cultural perversions we see in so much of society are so distressing. Sadly much of it is in the lives of those who consider themselves Christians. God's people are called to be salt and light – the very evidence of His presence. Instead, so many 'head south' under the belief they are going 'north'.

Isaiah described so accurately what we see going on around us, *"Woe to those who call evil good and good evil, who put darkness for light and light for darkness, who put bitter for sweet and sweet for bitter."* Isaiah 5:20

Let us live lives that glorify our Lord and Savior. Let us lives lives that reflect His character and word. His Word tells us how! It's the compass that always points to the true north. Let us live lives that truly reflect goodness, light and sweetness. As we celebrate the birth of Christ and begin the new year, let those be the 'presents' that we bring to Him as we kneel before Him!

Encountering Jesus in your life

Luke 5:10b-11 Then Jesus said to Simon, "Don't be afraid; from now on you will catch men." ¹¹ So they pulled their boats up on shore, left everything and followed him.

Picture yourself a fisherman. That is your livelihood. You and your partners have just spent the entire night fishing and come up empty. You're on shore washing your nets when this new friend, a carpenter by background who is doing some amazing things comes up with a crowd around him listening to him teaching.

He sees two boats at water's edge and gets into one of them – yours – and asks you to push it out a bit. He then sits down and teaches from the boat. When he finishes speaking (to the crowd) he says to you, "Put out into deep water, and let down the nets for a catch." I wonder what goes through your mind at that moment; maybe something like, "Yea – right!"

Maybe you roll your eyes, but who he is gets the better of you - although you do let him know the facts of the situation. "Master, we've worked hard all night and haven't caught anything. But because you say so, I will let down the nets.

Maybe you're thinking that he should stick to what he knows. Even so, you go along with it. All of a sudden you and your companions catch such a large number of fish that the nets began to break. You signal your partners in the other boat to come and help, and they come and both boats are filled so full of fish that they began to sink.

To say everyone is astonished is an understatement! But this strikes you in a unique way. This is a miracle and it involved you. You're struck by your own unworthiness to be in the presence of something divine. You fall at his knees and say, "Go away from me, Lord; I am a sinful man!"

But instead of listening to you, he says something far more profound than what you've just experienced! These words come from his mouth addressed to you, "Don't be afraid; from now on you will catch men." The group of you that hear this, pull your boats up on shore, leave everything and follow him.

The marvelous thing about this story is that Jesus is inserting himself into the everyday lives and situations of his followers today – just as he did then. He will do something to get our attention – causing us to turn aside and focus upon him.

We might not understand everything that is going on but we know it's Him. Then he calls us to be fishers of men – just as he did with them by the shore. And we get to follow Jesus just as they did into the callings he has for us.

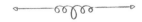

Love vast as the ocean

Hebrews 1:3 The Son is the radiance of God's glory and the exact representation of his being, sustaining all things by his powerful word. After he had provided purification for sins, he sat down at the right hand of the Majesty in heaven.

How do we ever begin to express our gratitude for what Jesus did for us? Thank God that we have wonderful music with words that speak what is overflowing in our hearts. This morning I have been so blessed worshipping with this incredible song. The words describe so wondrously what Jesus did for us.

Upon looking up the words online, I discovered that this song was a Welsh hymn. Upon reading the words it is easy to understand why it became known as "the love song of the 1904 Welsh Revival".

Between 100,000 – 150,000 people in Wales came to the Lord in this great revival. The coal mining industry was radically affected as miners came to Christ. The miner's horses even became confused when the transformed miners quit swearing and cursing at them.

Read these words and then go to the website listed below and listen to this hymn beautifully performed by Huw Priday at the CIA Cardiff during the centenary celebrations in November 2004. As the words so eloquently say, it is through Jesus that a guilty world was kissed with love.

"Here is Love vast as the Ocean"

Here is love, vast as the ocean,
Loving kindness as the flood,
When the Prince of Life, our Ransom,
Shed for us His precious blood.
Who His love will not remember?
Who can cease to sing His praise?
He can never be forgotten,
Throughout Heav'n's eternal days.

On the mount of crucifixion,
Fountains opened deep and wide;
Through the floodgates of God's mercy
Flowed a vast and gracious tide.
Grace and love, like mighty rivers,
Poured incessant from above,
And Heav'n's peace and perfect justice
Kissed a guilty world in love.

Here is the video of this hymn beautifully performed by Huw Priday at the CIA Cardiff during the centenary celebrations in November 2004. He sings in both Welsh and English.
http://www.youtube.com/watch?v=APrUPPC8bFY

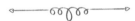

CPSIA information can be obtained
at www.ICGtesting.com
Printed in the USA
FSHW020854020620
70643FS

9 781643 981116